HOMESCHOOLING
HIGH SCHOOL

Planning Ahead
for College Admission

Revised and Updated Edition

Jeanne Gowen Dennis

Emerald Books

P.O. Box 635
Lynnwood, WA 98046

Emerald Books are distributed through YWAM Publishing. For a full list of titles, including other homeschooling resources, visit our website at www.ywampublishing.com or call 1-800-922-2143.

Homeschooling High School: Planning Ahead for College Admission
Second Edition

10 09 08 07   10 9 8 7 6 5 4 3 2

Published by Emerald Books
P.O. Box 635
Lynnwood, Washington 98046

Library of Congress Cataloging-in-Publication Data

Dennis, Jeanne Gowen.
  Homeschooling high school : planning ahead for college admission /
Jeanne Gowen Dennis.—2nd ed.
    p. cm.
Includes bibliographical references (p.   ) and index.
  ISBN 1-932096-11-6
  1. Home schooling—United States. 2. Education, Secondary—United
States. 3. Universities and colleges—United States—Admission.
I. Title.
  LC40.D46 2005
  371.04'2—dc22
                                        2003023225

ISBN 1-932096-11-6

Printed in the United States of America.

For Steve and Christine, my fellow travelers on the homeschool voyage, and for Debbie Musselman, who helped me find the courage to set sail.

Other books by Jeanne Gowen Dennis

Matt's Fantastic Electronic Compusonic

Strive to Survive series (with Sheila Seifert)
Attack!
Deadly Expedition!
Escape!
Trapped!

Q-Crew Diaries series (with Sheila Seifert)
The Clubhouse Mystery
Mystery at Crestwater Camp

Family Funstuff Bible Stories, Elementary edition (contributor)

My Time with God, Volume 2 (with Jeannette Dall)

Acknowledgments

No one writes a book of this size without the help and support of others. Homeschooling through high school was a challenge, but I truly learned the meaning of perseverance in bringing this project to completion. There were so many times when it would have been easier to quit.

I want to praise and thank my loving Creator, who is so patient with me and in whose strength I was able to finish the work. Also, this book would not have been possible without the love, understanding, and encouragement of my family. Steve, thanks for being the sounding board for my ideas, for helping me stay focused, and for reading so many drafts. Christine, thanks for your words of encouragement and for your faithfulness in praying for me. I appreciate the extra cleaning and cooking you both did.

Dad and Mom (Leo and Jeanne Gowen), thank you for your constant love, prayers, and support and for instilling in me at an early age a thirst for learning and a desire to strive for excellence in all I do. Thank you for your enthusiasm in supporting our decision to homeschool. Also, thanks to the rest of our family, my main cheering squad. I especially want to express my appreciation to my homeschooling sisters, Kathleen Breckenridge and Christine McLellan, for putting me in touch with homeschoolers in their states. To my mother-in-law, Irene Dennis: I appreciate your understanding when my time was limited. It's done! Let's do lunch! Thanks, Al, for your thoughtfulness, too.

Hundreds of college professionals also deserve to be mentioned. Dr. Richard Cornelius of Bryan College gave generously of his time and expertise and provided valuable contacts. Thank you, Dr. Cornelius, for sharing your booklist and your thirty-nine years of teaching experience. Other experts who lent their expertise for the book include Dr. Leland Ryken of Wheaton College (Illinois), Dr. Gene Edward Veith of Concordia University Wisconsin, Drs. Wayne Jones and Bob Pompi of Binghamton University (SUNY), Dr. Larry Zavodney of Cedarville University, Dr. Uwe Greife of the Colorado School of Mines, and Dr. Jack Traylor, also of Bryan College. Many thanks to the over 260 admissions directors, deans of enrollment, and other college personnel who granted interviews or responded to my survey and other questions, especially those who granted permission to quote them. I enjoyed meeting so many of you through our telephone interviews and email correspondence.

Other experts who provided information for the book include Michael Farris of Home School Legal Defense Association; school guidance counselors Judy Rodgers, Donna Poole, and Ralph Green; learning disabilities specialist Kyle Hughes; Jane Williams of Bluestocking Press; Mike Bolinsky of Science Projects; and homeschool leader Sharon Grimes. Thank you for taking the time to offer your valuable insights.

My heartfelt appreciation goes out to friends, both old and new, who also helped to make this book possible. I want to thank Darlene and Jeff Bruehl, Stuart and Tamie Goggans, and Gary and Carole Hargraves and their families for their gracious hospitality and help during my research. Thank you to Terry Hanna; Laura Foxworth; Risa, Jennifer, and Laura Killingsworth; René Hansen; Joanne Maxwell; Ashley Barnes; Peggy McKibben; the students, faculty, and staff of Bryan College; and all the other family and friends who have encouraged and prayed for me.

Many other homeschoolers kindly shared their experiences, including Debbie Musselman (my homeschooling mentor), Christie and Catherine Musselman, Beth Vellalos, Debbie Shope, Jennifer Musselman, Charlotte Revell, Cara Transtrom, Rachelle Reitz, Marty and Mark Bigger, Nadine Mullen, Nikki Riggs, Patsy and Gregg Walters, and others. Also, Rita Wise and Constance Hamilton, thank you for reviewing the draft manuscript.

I must mention fellow writers, including Bob Hostetler, Carla Williams, and Cindy Ramming, who guided me through the proposal process. Also Marianne and Doug Hering, Jeannie Harmon, Alice Scott-Ferguson, Elisabeth Hendricks, Sheila Seifert, Nancy Parker Brummet, Beverly Lewis, Mona Gansberg Hodgson, and Lin Johnson—thank you for your friendship, suggestions, and encouragement.

My undying gratitude goes to Jim Drake of YWAM Publishing for passing the manuscript along to Emerald Books. I want to thank everyone on the staff at Emerald, especially Warren Walsh for his enthusiasm, patience, and guidance; Marit Newton for her excellent editing and insightful suggestions; and Sara Mike for all the finishing touches.

For the second edition, I want to thank Dr. Wayne Jones and Jane Williams, who updated their sections, the students and graduates who allowed me to include their college essays, and Sheila Seifert, who spent a day checking websites. Special thanks go to my husband, Steve, for getting up at 4:30 for a week to help me with Appendix B and for his patience, love, and encouragement.

Contents

Foreword

by Michael Farris

As the first president of Patrick Henry College, a new college specifically reaching out to the home school community, I take considerable interest in Jeanne Gowen Dennis's new book, *Homeschooling High School: Planning Ahead for College Admission*. The number of home school families is growing, and so is the number of parents who believe that home schooling through high school is a natural extension of the success they have found at the primary level. These parents have a comprehensive view of their parenting role that includes being their child's first and foremost teacher. These parents know their children better than anyone else and are uniquely well qualified to provide oversight of their children's character development and educational progress during the key transitional years between young adulthood and adulthood.

Families who commit to home schooling during the high school years follow a legacy of success within the home school movement. Home school graduates are regularly gaining admittance to the most prestigious colleges and universities throughout the nation. In fact, many colleges are aggressively recruiting home schoolers because of their positive experiences with prior home schoolers. Home school graduates are among those who distinguish themselves on college campuses because of their academic accomplishments, leadership, and service. Home school graduates are also starting businesses and successfully taking on the challenges and rewards of a full-time commitment to their families and to a God-given calling to ministry and public service.

Some home school families, however, fall short of reaching their full potential because they question their own ability to continue along their route of success into the high school years. These families may become discouraged at the prospect of completing a high school-level curriculum and the accompanying questions from family, friends, and even governmental authorities about the reasonableness of home schooling to advanced levels of learning. For others, concerns stem from questions about how to organize and manage time commitments among older and younger children. Still others are not quite sure what colleges, universities, or future employers will want to know about their home schooling curriculum and experiences. Such concerns can be most distracting to families who are home schooling for high school while planning ahead for college admissions.

Clearly, wise counsel and realistic suggestions are needed from those who have already faced the challenges, learned from their successes and failures, and developed a strong desire to impart what they have learned to those who are coming along next. Under ideal circumstances, such mentoring would happen in the context of an "apprenticeship." Scripture affirms the soundness of this approach by admonishing that "as iron sharpens iron, so one man sharpens another" and "the older women are to teach the younger." There are rich rewards for home school parents who are active within their own local support group—learning from others and coming alongside newcomers.

Not every home school family with children entering the high school years will have the opportunity to directly interact with someone like Jeanne Gowen Dennis, who, in addition to home schooling her own daughter through high school, has researched and compiled the results of a survey of college admissions directors. This is why her book will prove so valuable. Mrs. Dennis approaches home schooling for high school as serious, goal-oriented preparation for a successful college experience. Her focus is practical and her tone is appropriate. Completing a college education is a time-consuming and expensive undertaking. Her book includes suggestions for building on the strengths and minimizing the potential weaknesses of your home high school. Among critical topics covered are moral and spiritual foundations, balancing autonomy and accountability, and practical "how-to-do-it" reviews of record keeping and evaluations.

It is a pleasure and encouragement to see the growing number of available resources being produced by veteran home schoolers who wish to reinvest themselves into the lives of younger home schoolers. Jeanne Gowen Dennis's book is certainly among these resources. I heartily recommend it to those wishing to know what she has learned about home schooling the high schooler and planning ahead for college admissions.

Mike Farris has been named one of the one hundred most significant "Faces of the Century" in education by Education Week, *American education's newspaper of record. He is the founder and president of Patrick Henry College and chairman and general counsel of the Home School Legal Defense Association. Mr. Farris has authored many books and articles on home schooling, including,* The Future of Home Schooling *(Regnery Publishing),* The Home Schooling Father, *and* A Sacred Foundation: The Importance of Strength in Your Home Schooling Marriage *(both by Loyal Publishing). Mr. Farris and his wife, Vickie, reside in Virginia and have home schooled their ten children. Their oldest daughter, Christy, graduated with honors from Cedarville University.*

Planning Ahead for College Admission

Welcome to the completely updated and revised *Homeschooling High School.* When this book was first published, the National Home Education Research Institute reported that approximately 1.23 million American children were being taught at home.[1] That number has grown. For the 2001–2002 school year, the National Home Education Network estimated that approximately 1.7 to 2 million American students in grades K through 12 (about 3 to 4 percent) were homeschooled,[2] with an estimated growth rate of 7 to 15 percent per year.[3] At least a quarter of a million of those students were high schoolers. Even though the numbers continue to grow, many homeschooling parents and students do not feel confident about their ability to plan a strong high-school program, prepare for college,[4] and complete the college application process. This book is designed to provide the tools homeschoolers need to do an excellent job in all three areas.

If you have reservations about making the commitment to homeschool through high school, this book will help you make an informed decision for your family. Included here are tips for planning a college preparatory course of study, assigning grades, building leadership skills, preparing for college entrance examinations, applying for scholarships, searching for the "perfect" college, keeping records, writing transcripts, and more. This book also contains the results of an exclusive national survey of over 250 college admissions directors about their experiences with homeschoolers. Many of these professionals have kindly offered their insights for this book. Their comments about homeschoolers present a balanced perspective, incorporating both the strengths and weaknesses they have observed and their suggestions for building on the strengths and minimizing the weaknesses. When you read the survey results (discussed in chapter 8), you will discover that most colleges are eager to welcome well-prepared homeschool graduates.

If you are familiar with the first edition of *Homeschooling High School,* you will notice many changes in this second edition. The science and language arts sections of chapter 5 have been improved and expanded, and the guidance counseling information in chapter 6 has been updated. In Appendix B you will find many exciting new resources. All of the entries have been brought up-to-date. The new Appendix E provides examples of college admissions and scholarship essays. Over half of the colleges that provided information for Appendix A reviewed and updated their entries. At the same time, I gave them the opportunity to participate in a new survey about scholarship availability and GED/certified diploma requirements for homeschooled applicants. The results can be found in chapter 8. Please note that where I report homeschooler/college statistics, they refer to the original survey unless noted otherwise. Although you will find many changes throughout the book, most titles, positions, and institutions of college personnel have been left as they were at the time of the original interviews, even though some people have moved on to other positions and institutions.

I wrote *Homeschooling High School* to encourage homeschoolers not to give up when they reach the high school level and to help those who are considering homeschooling for the first time to understand what is involved. Having educated my daughter at home for over eight years and through high school, and having taught many other homeschooled students, I am well aware of the concerns of homeschoolers. Also, I have gained a better understanding of colleges' needs through my two surveys of admissions directors.

This publication is for all homeschoolers, regardless of beliefs, and most of the information I present will be applicable to all. However, I also address the particular concerns of those who share my Christian faith. Therefore, Christians will find information specifically for them throughout the book.

Home high schooling is a challenge and a tremendous responsibility. Even the best home educators have periodic doubts that their children's education will be strong enough and complete enough for them to compete with traditional high schoolers. That is why *Homeschooling High School* is also designed to equip you. By utilizing this book, a good curriculum, and some of the hundreds of homeschool resources available to you, you should be able to provide an excellent and thorough education for your teens at home. However, I believe you will discover that the greatest dividends of home high schooling are your children's increasing development in both character and maturity and the cultivation of closer family relationships.

The teen years can be some of the most enjoyable times you spend with your homeschooled children because home high school provides the opportunity for parents and students to relate to one another on a new level. As teens mature and shoulder more responsibilities, the parent-child relationship matures as well. Older teens, while still remaining under your authority, can become more like close friends. The homeschooling situation is, I believe, what allows this dynamic to occur because of an atmosphere of mutual love and respect. It seems that traditional students and their parents seldom reach this level of friendship before college or even later.

Home high schooling is different from teaching younger grades in several ways. First of all, it counts for college. High schoolers also tend to take more responsibility for their own education and for planning their time than younger students do. During the high school years, students often work, do voluntary community or church service, and participate in team sports, orchestras, and choirs, leaving less time for field trips and visiting with homeschool friends. High school is a more serious, goal-oriented time, but it can comprise some of the most rewarding years of a homeschool student's education. It is a time for students to discover where they fit in the great scheme of life, a time to try to "put it all together" and become adults.

High school was a rich and fulfilling continuation of homeschooling for us. We were sorry to see it end, but it ended in success. Our daughter excelled academically in college, becoming an active and respected member of her campus community. She graduated *summa cum laude* from Bryan College and married a wonderful young man who also was homeschooled through high school. They plan to carry on the homeschooling tradition with their children. Most importantly, our daughter strives to live by the values we taught her at home. Perhaps homeschooling can do the same for your children.

At the first workshop I gave on homeschooling through high school, I met a mother who was about to give up on homeschooling. She told me that the workshop, and eventually this book, helped her decide to continue teaching her daughter through high school. She did persevere, and her daughter has now graduated from college. Knowing that my work has made a difference in the lives of even one family makes all my labor worthwhile. I hope it will encourage you to finish the race, as well.

---

1. Ray, Brian, Ph.D. *Home Education Across the United States: Family Characteristics, Student Achievement, and Longitudinal Traits*, 1997, Brian D. Ray and Home School Legal Defense Association.

2. The terms *home school* and *homeschool*, as well as their derivatives, are used interchangeably in published materials. For quotations in this book, I have left the authors' original spelling. In all other cases, I have used the combined forms.

3. Figures are from the National Center for Home Education at http://nche.hslda.org/research/faq.asp#1 and were extrapolated from Dr. Brian Ray's estimates for the 2000–2001 school year. Dr. Ray is president of the National Home Education Research Institute.

4. The word *college* will be used in this book to mean either a college or a university.

Chapter 1

Is Home High Schooling for You?

I wouldn't give up home schooling the high school years for anything in the world.

Michael Farris

Is high school at home the right choice for your family? Before you can answer that question, you will need to understand what it takes to homeschool through high school. You must proceed with your eyes open to the realities—the advantages, the disadvantages, the possible consequences, and most of all, the priceless rewards that await you. For when the going gets rough, as it almost always does, you will need the commitment to press on to the finish line. Perhaps you are already homeschooling and are unsure whether to continue through high school. Maybe you are considering homeschooling for the first time. In either case, it is important that you know what to expect.

As with almost any endeavor, teaching high school at home has both advantages and disadvantages. Most homeschoolers believe that the advantages far outweigh the disadvantages because of the ability to alleviate problems and fill any gaps in a student's education. Nothing offered in traditional schools can replace the unique benefits homeschooling has to offer.

Advantages of Home High Schooling

Why should you consider teaching your high school student? If you are already a home educator, your original reasons for homeschooling during younger grades are still valid in high school. In fact, the high school years might be the most crucial time to educate your children because they are the final years of preparation for adulthood.

Philosophical Freedom

Teaching your children at home has numerous benefits. The most valuable is probably the freedom you have to direct your children's learning. Because you are in control of the education your students receive, you can insist that school subjects are taught from your worldview, or at least you can make sure that your worldview is accurately represented.

In addition, your children at home are free from the peer dependence and undesirable influences found in traditional schools. Students will not be carrying drugs and weapons in your school, and your students will not have to contend with daily sexual pressure and personal criticism.

Homeschool veteran Marty Bigger does not think her children missed anything important by being homeschooled through high school. "There are some negatives they missed, but that's what I wanted them to miss," she says. "It's so unreal to spend all your time at a desk eight hours a day, or whatever. That's not real life. You have to work and interact with all ages, not just your age."

There is freedom of religion in the homeschool that is not found in the public schools. Every homeschool course is a potential forum for discussion and application of your faith to life and learning. The Bible admonishes parents to teach God's commandments to their children and "talk about them when you sit at home and when you walk along the road, when you lie down and when you get up" (Deuteronomy 6:4–8). Homeschoolers have ample time to do this.

Academic Excellence

Academic excellence is another advantage of homeschooling. As both teacher and parent, you can closely monitor your students' progress. You can encourage excellence and ensure that your students leave high school with the skills necessary to succeed in college and life. Parents seldom monitor their children's progress in traditional schools as carefully as they do in homeschools, simply because homeschool teachers continually have close contact with their students and are ultimately responsible for the results.

Since homeschooling is a tutoring type of learning environment, your students receive daily feedback and personal attention. They also have more motivation to direct their own education. These factors usually result in higher academic achievement.

"Our homeschooled applicants are extremely well prepared academically," says Mike Williams of Harding University. "Their academic preparation typically is self-directed and initiated, which builds strong research skills. Since many of them work at their own pace, many will go far beyond a traditional curriculum."

Typically home school students demonstrate a bit more independence in their learning. They have learned to be responsible for their educational development, an excellent quality to possess given the importance of lifelong learning in contemporary society.

David Ormsbee, Dean of Enrollment, Cedarville University

For those subjects you do not teach or your student does not study independently, you have the opportunity to select the kind of teachers you want to influence your students. For our daughter, Christine, we chose outside instructors with high moral and academic standards and enthusiasm for their subjects. Because we are Christians, most of the instructors we chose were Christians as well. Experts in various subjects can teach your students in a classroom, internship, apprenticeship, or online setting. Apprenticeships are especially popular among homeschoolers for gaining valuable training and work experience.

Self-Motivation

To a large extent, homeschool students are self-motivated and self-taught, even when parents direct the education. As they mature, children often develop strong interests in one or two specific areas. Whereas traditional school schedules generally do not allow enough time to accommodate individual interests, homeschooling does. The high-school years are the ideal time for students to hone their talents or to delve into intriguing subjects.

Homeschoolers repeatedly prove that students who have been taught *how* to learn can teach themselves almost anything with the right materials. For example, homeschooler Catherine Musselman wanted to study oceanography, so she asked Scripps Oceanographic Institution to recommend an oceanography textbook. They suggested a college-level book. Undaunted, this ambitious eighth grader ordered it and completed the course. Her sister Christie had an interest in medicine during tenth grade. She found someone to lend her the voluminous, unabridged *Gray's Anatomy* and read it in her spare time.

Catherine and Christie are not exceptions among home-schooled students. It is not uncommon for homeschoolers to enroll in college courses or to finish high school several years ahead of their peers. The children in the famous Swann family typically completed their master's degrees by correspondence at age sixteen.[2]

Although home high schooling is a full-time commitment for most parents (usually mothers) who do it, some parents who wish to homeschool cannot devote full time to teaching their children. Dr. Arthur Robinson developed a self-teaching program for his six children so that they could continue home-schooling after their mother died. The plan was ideal for him as a single parent, and he now sells his program to other home-schoolers who are interested in a self-teaching curriculum. (See Appendix B for this and other options.)

Self-taught courses are a good idea. They build self-discipline, independence, and self-confidence. However, when parents are available to teach, I think it is better for them to teach some courses, or at least to discuss lesson topics with students on a regular basis. Much of the value in home education is the inter-action students have with mature adults, especially parents who love them and care about their education. When you depend solely on a self-taught curriculum, others—the curriculum writers—are educating your students instead of you, and that partially defeats the purpose of homeschooling, no matter how wonderful the resources.

Practical Advantages

If you have homeschooled before, you have no doubt experienced the convenience of being able to use the library and other community resources, such as museums and galleries, when they are less crowded. As homeschoolers you are free to adjust your school schedule to allow for family vacations, illnesses, and educational travel. This scheduling flexibility also allows students to accept part-time jobs during the day when other students are not available to work.

With careful scheduling, your students may be able to complete high school early, finish high school with more credits than required, or get a head start on college. If students want to participate in some local high school classes or activities, this involvement is an option if the school allows it. However, classes at a local community college or four-year college might be more beneficial, especially if students can earn dual credit. It is common for homeschool students to complete college courses locally or by correspondence while still in high school. Often they earn enough credits to enter college as sophomores or juniors.

Home High Schooling
Advantages

- *Your worldview is taught.*
- *Your faith is welcome in the class-room.*
- *You can ensure excellence in your children's education.*
- *Your students receive daily personal attention and a strong foundation to build upon.*
- *Local experts that you select can be enlisted to help teach.*
- *In-depth study is possible.*
- *You can use community facilities when they are less crowded.*
- *Your students can work part-time during the day.*
- *Your schedule has flexibility.*
- *Your students are not exposed to negative peer influences.*
- *Your students may be able to participate in school activities.*
- *Your students may take college courses at home for credit.*
- *Family unity is enhanced.*
- *Students develop self-discipline, maturity, and social skills.*
- *Colleges want homeschoolers because they are strong students.*

Disadvantages

- *Resources and equipment are less available than in public schools.*
- *Science, sports, and arts activities are harder to provide.*
- *Parents have to be teachers and guidance counselors.*
- *Parents or students are responsible for all subjects at all levels.*
- *Students may be exposed to just one teaching style.*
- *Potential social problems exist.*

Family Benefits

Some would not consider it an advantage having their family together all hours of the day and night. The strain of the turbulent teen years wreaks havoc on many families. Relationships between parents and their teenage children may deteriorate, and siblings often grow apart. My sister and I, for example, were best friends growing up, but we became virtual strangers during high school. We were too busy with our own friends, activities, and homework to have time for each other or the rest of our family. A similar scenario was repeated with our younger brother and sister. Again and again I have watched loving sibling relationships strained during junior high and high school by peer relationships, stress, or apathy.

Homeschoolers generally escape these problems, and family unity has become a hallmark of homeschool life. Apparently, daily togetherness develops understanding that helps most families escape serious relational problems. Homeschool teens generally enjoy spending time with younger siblings, and they actually converse with their parents and other adults, unlike the seeming majority of their traditionally schooled peers. During home high school, the parent/child relationship is enhanced because the lines of communication remain open. These students do not have to prove their worth constantly, because they know they are loved. Homeschooling has helped to destroy the myth of quality time. It is the large *quantity* of time parents give and the devotion they show to their growing children that I believe is the chief reason for the success of homeschooling.

> *Homeschooled students often exhibit a sense of "responsibility" for their own education that other students do not have.*
>
> Buck James, Dean of Enrollment Services, Palm Beach Atlantic College

Marty Bigger's children are in their twenties. She says, "We're still very, very close, and we always have been. I think that's due to homeschooling. We were always there for [our children], so they're always there for us."

Homeschoolers are not perfect, though. They periodically struggle just like everyone else, especially if they are teens who have become peer dependent through unbridled participation in church and social activities.

College Interest

Colleges are also discovering the unique qualities that often result from homeschooling. Because of the high level of maturity, self-discipline, and academic preparation home-educated students have demonstrated, many colleges actively recruit them.

Disadvantages of High School at Home

Before making your final decision about homeschooling, you should be aware of some drawbacks to teaching your high schoolers.

Academic and Practical Disadvantages

Obviously, public and private schools have resources, activities, and equipment that homeschool families usually cannot afford. Most schools have modern computers, science labs, competitive sports, debate teams, real theatres, complete orchestras and marching bands, and numerous clubs. These group activities offer students the opportunity to learn cooperation and to develop leadership skills. Schools also may participate in state and national competitions that may not be open to homeschoolers. Groups and competitions not only have intrinsic value but also enhance college applications. Homeschool support groups can provide some similar opportunities, but traditional high schools generally have better resources and more activities to choose from.

One disadvantage of homeschooling is that parents are forced to wear many hats. In traditional high schools, the history teacher does not have to add algebra, English, foreign languages, science, Bible, and art to his or her teaching schedule. Homeschoolers not only have to teach (or provide teachers for) all their students' subjects but also have to teach continuing classes like math at each progressive level. For students who primarily teach themselves, parents need to grade work, keep records, and ensure that students cover the subjects thoroughly enough to earn credit. Obviously, home high schooling requires enormous commitment on the part of both parents and students.

Another potential disadvantage of home high schooling stems from the fact that parents are often their students' only teachers. Unless they take outside classes or learn from videos of other teachers, these students may miss the benefits of being exposed to a variety of teachers and teaching styles. Nothing is more inspirational to students than teachers who are passionate about their disciplines and who challenge pupils to achieve their highest potential. Granted, teachers of that caliber are not the norm, but they can be found at every level of education from kindergarten through graduate school.

Administrative Difficulties

Homeschool parents also have to act as guidance counselors. Not only is this more difficult for parents, but also this creates problems for college admissions departments. With limited information, admissions committees have to choose candidates with the best potential for success on their campuses. Comparing students from a wide spectrum of schools is already difficult because student populations and grading systems vary. Homeschool applicants further complicate the process because their grades may not demonstrate how they compare with other students. Also, human nature being what it is, colleges cannot be sure that parents have graded their children objectively.

"They *all* have high GPAs," says Jeff Palm, Associate Director of Admission at Hawaii Pacific University. "That's why it's hard to make a determination. We need something that's standardized."

Some colleges are satisfied with parent-prepared transcripts, student portfolios, and/or interviews. Other colleges, such as the Colorado School of Mines, verify homeschoolers' high GPAs with SAT or ACT scores. "For homeschooled students, because so little weight can be given to the transcript in terms of what the GPA means or how the student has competed among a group of peers, a lot more weight is given to standardized test scores, either the SAT or ACT. So if test scores are strong, we judge the transcript to be strong. If test scores are weak, we judge the transcript to be weak. That's about the only way we've found to objectively evaluate homeschooled students," says Bill Young, Director of Admissions.

Rodney Miller, Dean of Records and Registrar at Covenant College, concurs. "The Admissions Committee and other scholarship committees view a home school GPA as helpful, but we place greater weight on the standardized test scores. A student with a 4.0 GPA is questioned if he has a 720 SAT total. A student with a 4.0 and a 1300 SAT total has confirmed [his] academic preparation."

Limited Freedom

Your state's laws or the requirements of the college your student will eventually attend might limit your choice of methods for homeschooling during high school. Many colleges prefer grades that have been documented by a reputable outside organization. If grades and high school graduation have not been certified, some colleges require that homeschool students earn a GED, which is a high school equivalency certificate obtained by passing an examination. Also, if your child will be applying for federal financial aid, proof of graduation or an acceptable score on an ability-to-benefit test may be required unless your homeschool meets certain criteria. (See chapter 6.) College admissions and financial aid officers can help you determine your high school options.

Because the requirements of colleges vary, it is important to begin the college search process early so that you will be prepared with any documentation you need. The table of college home-school requirements in Appendix A details the information requested from homeschoolers by most of the over 260 colleges that participated in my survey. The information was correct at the time of publication. However, you should check with individual colleges to find out whether their home-school policies have changed.

Possible Extra Requirements

Homeschoolers sometimes complain that colleges discriminate by imposing stricter admissions standards on them than on other applicants. Many colleges do require certified diplomas, GEDs, or extra testing for homeschoolers. This is in spite of the fact that home-educated students have generally proven themselves to be academically prepared for college through their standardized-test scores and subsequent success in college. (On the average, homeschoolers tend to score as high as or higher than public school students on national tests, which was verified by Ray[3] and my own survey of colleges.)

In some cases of extra requirements, prejudice may play a factor. However, such policies are prompted more often by either lack of exposure to homeschoolers or caution based on prior experience. At some colleges, homeschoolers actually caused the imposition of stricter standards through inadequate academic preparation or uncooperative attitudes. For example, one school told me that it has had to tighten its policies because a few of its homeschooled students were not prepared for college-level study. All homeschoolers should strive to complete a quality education that meets or exceeds the standards of the public schools. If every homeschooler did that, colleges would have no valid reason to require extra testing for the majority of homeschool applicants who have received an excellent education.

If your students choose to apply to institutions that have additional requirements for home-schoolers, they will have to play by the colleges' rules for the time being. They can strive to change the rules, but schools have the right to set their own entrance requirements. State colleges and universities often have these rules imposed on them by other state officials or legislatures, so any changes would have to be made at that level.

> *I have noticed that many of the home-schooled students who have applied, been accepted, or enrolled had difficulty in social situations and in interpersonal communication and relationship-building.*
>
> Suellen Ofe, Vice President for Enrollment Management, Huntingdon College

Potential Social Problems

Every homeschooler has been asked the question at least fifty times. Say it with me now. "What about socialization?" In general, socialization is not a problem for homeschoolers, most of whom are active in their communities and churches and get along well with all ages. However, some homeschooled students have been too sheltered and do not know how to interact with people outside their family circle. If your students are introverts, you really should find ways to help them reach out and interact with others. They will not be happy in college or in life if they do not conquer their fears. Help them find talents to share, sports to play, or needs to fill. Try not to force them too far beyond their comfort level all at once. Make it a gradual but steady process. Eventually they will surprise even themselves.

Do not let potential disadvantages discourage you from homeschooling your teens. As you weigh the pros and cons of homeschooling your children through high school, consider how you might alleviate some of the difficulties by enlisting the help of others.

Minimizing the Drawbacks: Enlisting Outside Help

I assume, and it has been my observation, that the majority of homeschooling parents aspire to excellence in their teaching. Certainly Christian homeschoolers striving to honor God should be satisfied with nothing less than their best efforts. Sometimes your best is not sufficient, however, and you need to enlist outside help. After all, it is impossible for parents (even homeschoolers) to be experts at everything. Traditional students have access to many teachers, so they usually have more course options available. There are several ways you can increase the opportunities in your homeschool. Some options will provide students with important exposure to classes taught in lecture and discussion formats similar to the ones they will experience in college.

Homeschool Group Classes

Many homeschoolers take courses from teachers with various areas of expertise through co-ops or classes offered by individuals. Group classes give homeschool students opportunities to learn from teachers with different teaching styles, to practice taking notes during lectures, and to participate in academic discussions with their peers. By taking advantage of local experts, co-ops, and special classes, our daughter learned from a Ph.D. candidate in immunology, a Ph.D. in entomology (her dad), two people with master's degrees in English, and professionals in several other occupations. Many of these were homeschool parents.

Even if co-ops and outside classes are impossible to arrange in your area, you can still provide similar opportunities for your children. For example, your students can develop note-taking skills during sermons, meetings, radio discussions, or television documentaries. By discussing literature, politics, and other topics of interest with family, friends, and especially other adults, your students will receive the same benefits they would have from participating in classroom discussions.

Classes in Traditional Schools

In some states, it is possible to enroll your student part-time in the local public high school. For some families, this is an acceptable option; for others it defeats the purpose of educating their children at home. Often students participate only in sports, physical education, or music. Some also opt to take lab sciences. Another more expensive option is part-time enrollment in a local Christian, parochial, or private school.

Local umbrella schools, which oversee the home education of students, offer a desirable option for many families. Often the students enrolled in umbrella schools meet for some classes. The role of an umbrella school might include maintaining records, verifying grades, determining curriculum, providing support for the teacher, issuing transcripts and diplomas, and holding a graduation ceremony. Umbrella schools may or may not be accredited.

Correspondence Study

Correspondence study is another popular option with homeschoolers. Correspondence schools provide most of the same services as umbrella schools and often grade student work. Many colleges like the accountability that correspondence study and umbrella schools offer. If the school is accredited, there is less chance that your student will be required to take the GED exam.

Whether you decide to tackle high school yourself or to enroll with an umbrella or correspondence school might depend on the type of documentation a college requires. That is why it is so important to at least have a general idea of your students' college preferences as early as eighth or ninth grade. It is particularly important if your student has a specialized interest, such as veterinary medicine, aviation, or engineering.

Our daughter began her college search late, so it was not until near the end of her junior year that she realized she might have to earn a GED, depending on the college she chose. She did not want a GED for reasons I will explain later, so she enrolled in Summit Christian Academy, an accredited correspondence school that accepted her as a senior after placement testing. When we enrolled Christine, we gave up autonomy and the chance to study some exciting courses we had planned. We were especially disappointed to have to forego our study of worldviews. However, her college offers a biblical worldview class, which she completed during her first semester. As it turned out, the choice to finish her studies by correspondence was a good one.

Some of our homeschooling friends living overseas also opted for correspondence study because it was important to them that their children graduate from an accredited high school. They were concerned about their children's being eligible for acceptance to any college of their choice. They used Cambridge Academy, which was willing to transfer in some college courses and experience in music and sports for high school credit.

Obviously, correspondence study is not for all students. As mentioned earlier, many colleges will accept homeschooled students who have only parent-prepared transcripts, but others will not unless students have passed the GED exam. Some colleges require other verification, such as SAT II exams. Check with individual colleges about their requirements.

Learning Options

- *Classes taught by parents*
- *Self-taught courses*
- *Homeschool co-ops*
- *Group classes offered by local experts*
- *Homeschool classes at local colleges*
- *Video classes*
- *Audio classes*
- *Internet classes*
- *College classes*
- *Correspondence courses*
- *Umbrella school group classes*
- *Part-time enrollment in local public or private school*
- *Classes offered by churches, community organizations, or government entities*
- *Professional seminars, workshops, and conferences*

Computer Learning

With the proliferation of computer technology, it is possible for students to supplement their education, or even complete it, by taking courses over the Internet. Internet high schools have sprung up, and many colleges offer accredited courses online. I have listed some of these institutions in Appendix B. However, because of the volatile nature of Internet sites, the information may have changed by the time you read this. Homeschool magazines and websites should have current information.

College Classes and Credit by Examination

It is possible that colleges and community colleges in your area have offerings for homeschoolers. For example, Biola University offers academic classes, a musical theatre group, and supplemental tutoring in academic courses to homeschoolers who live near La Mirada, California. Our local community college also conducts homeschool classes in several high school subjects.

Students may earn dual high school and college credit through part-time enrollment in college or community college. This is often a good option for homeschoolers looking for classes in lab sciences, higher math, and fine arts, especially during their junior and senior years. Successful completion of these classes also helps to verify your students' readiness for college-level work. Courses may or may not transfer to the college your student finally attends.

Students also may earn college credits during high school through testing. There are two primary types of tests, both offered by the College Board: the Advanced Placement (AP) and College

Level Examination Program (CLEP) tests. (See chapter 6 for more information about joint enrollment and credit by examination.)

Other Opportunities

Do not overlook community and government organizations for educational opportunities. Investigate classes offered through local churches, the Red Cross, 4-H, parks and recreation centers, utility companies, Civil Air Patrol, your state cooperative extension service, private companies, and others. Also consider professional workshops, seminars, and conferences in areas of your students' interests. These can be expensive, but the education and contacts can pay off in the long run. For example, Christine attended two professional writers' conferences as part of a course I called Writing for Publication. She was already a published writer when she attended, but she benefited from the excellent teaching, made new friends, and landed more writing assignments.

Other adults are not the only ones who can provide classes outside of parents' areas of expertise. Homeschool students with advanced skills in such areas as piano, quilting, art, writing, calculus, rocketry, geology, or history can instruct their siblings or earn extra money by teaching others.

Does Your Family Have What It Takes?

Obviously, there are many ways to solve potential problems if you choose to homeschool your high schoolers. But how can you be sure that homeschooling at this level—or homeschooling at all, if you have never done it—is the right choice for you and your family?

What kind of family is successful at homeschooling? The most important quality seems to be commitment, but there are other factors that work together to help homeschooling families thrive, such as parents' reasons for teaching and their children's attitudes about learning at home.

As homeschool parents, there's so much more that you can do—travel opportunities to learn about history. And even in your own community— if you're doing an economics course you can go out and talk to bankers and financiers....

Jeff Palm, Associate
Director of Admission,
Hawaii Pacific University

Your Involvement: More Important Than Your Credentials

Someone recently asked me how homeschool teachers without any college training could possibly teach their students high school courses. Perhaps you are worried that your own education is inadequate for teaching high school. Michael Farris, Chairman of the Home School Legal Defense Association and President of Patrick Henry College, writes that hard work and parental involvement are the *only* two keys to educational success. Brian Ray's home education study supports that statement. Dr. Ray found that even among parents who did not finish high school, "a parent's education background has no substantive effect on their [sic] children's home school academic performance."[4] The homeschool students in this study averaged between the 80th and 90th percentiles in nationally standardized tests, regardless of their parents' level of education. Race was also not a factor in the performance of these home-schooled students, although it was a factor among public school students.[5]

The majority of homeschooling mothers I have met either did not attend college or attended for only one or two years. Yet these same women are producing National Merit Scholars, honor students, and other exemplary students. The strength of homeschooling is not in the formal education of homeschool teachers. Rather it is in their commitment to the excellence of their children's education. Most homeschool parents expect and require their children to work hard, and they are willing to forego life's luxuries to provide the best curriculum available. Most of all, they are willing to give of their time.

Your Reasons for Homeschooling

Before you make a final decision about home high schooling, you need to decide why you are considering it. I have already listed several excellent reasons for teaching your own children. If you think you can do a better job than the schools, you probably can, although you might need to make use of some outside resources. If your students have unusual interests or special needs, home-schooling might be your answer. If you want to pass on your faith and improve family relationships, homeschooling is ideal.

However, if you want to homeschool simply because a friend does it, or because you think it will be more convenient, or because your children want to avoid studying, then send them to school. The title "homeschooler" is not a glorified name for "dropout." Homeschoolers are dedicated teachers and students who care about quality education. Homeschooling requires incredible commitment, and those who persevere know that it is worth the cost.

Your Teens' Attitudes About Homeschooling

Talk with your teens before removing them from public or private school. If they are enthusiastic about homeschooling, it will be easy to work together on your plans for their high school education. Sometimes parents feel that they must homeschool their children, even though their teens are against it. Forcing them to homeschool may not be the best idea, although a few years ago one homeschooling magazine featured a letter from a grateful teen whose parents had done just that. You know your children best. Do what you believe will benefit them the most.

Your Teens' Social Concerns

Marty Bigger has seen parents take their children out of school and then find their children obsessed with going back to be with their friends. She said that once children get into the school mold, you have to prepare them well for homeschooling by changing their whole way of thinking because, for many students, high school is like a big social club. Bigger's daughter Rachelle was in school off and on as she grew up.

"She'd always say when she came back home the next year, 'Well, that was fun because I got to be with my friends, but now I'm going to learn something.'"

Young people need to understand that homeschooling is not equivalent to living as a hermit. Homeschoolers actually report having more time for friends and other outside activities. Studying at home gives students the opportunity to concentrate on their studies without the distractions of those schoolmates who have little interest in learning. They can go at their own pace and spend more time on the subjects and extracurricular activities that interest them. For students and parents who are committed to doing it well, homeschooling offers the best of both worlds.

The Rewards

The beauty of homeschooling is that you can do what works best for your family. You have flexibility and control over the curriculum, your students are allowed to develop their potential in a nonthreatening environment (although homeschool parents have been known to threaten reluctant students), and you can enjoy being together. As you will see from the college survey results in chapter 8, homeschooling can provide many academic and character-development benefits, as well.

If you are a Christian, keep in mind that it is extremely important to seek God's will in all decisions related to your children's education. If you feel that God wants you to homeschool your teens, you should do it. He never asks you to do something without giving you the power to accomplish it. If you are still unsure, pray about it and follow your heart. God will guide you. Trust Him. After all, He knows what your children's futures hold, and our Father _really_ knows best.

Perhaps you still need more information before making the commitment to homeschool through high school. The next chapter provides a blueprint for you to follow for successful home high schooling.

> _I will instruct you and teach you in the way you should go;_
> _I will counsel you and watch over you._
>
> Psalm 32:8 NIV

1. Brian Ray, Ph.D., _Home Education Across the United States: Family Characteristics, Student Achievement, and Longitudinal Traits,_ National Home Education Research Institute and Home School Legal Defense Association, 1997.
2. See Alexandra Swann's book _No Regrets: How Home Schooling Earned Me a Master's Degree at Age Sixteen_, Cygnet Press, 1989.
3. Ray, _Home Education._
4. Ibid.
5. Ibid.

Education Estates

"College-Bound" Model, Front Elevation

Moral and Spiritual Foundation

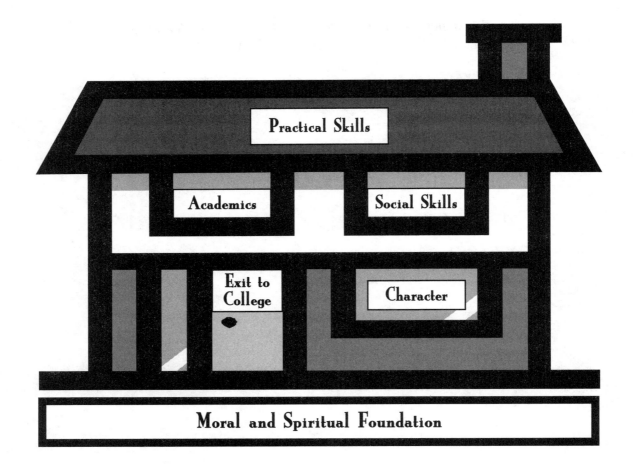

Offered by Parent Builders, Incorporated
A division of Homeschool Engineers & Constructors

Chapter 2

Blueprint for Success

Why is our ultra-sophisticated intellectual establishment increasingly unable to perform the basic social task of education, and why are these little Christian schools—and, sometimes even more dramatically, homeschoolers—having such success?[1]

Gene Edward Veith

Preparing a student for college can be compared to constructing a house. Before building, you need a blueprint and a plan of action. Your homeschooling blueprint should include a strong foundation and sturdy construction with plenty of space for growth. You have several decisions to make before beginning. On what foundation will you build? What are the best materials to use for your particular student? Should you build alone, hire a contractor, solicit the help of family and friends, or use a combination of these options?

The Foundation

Just as any building needs a firm foundation, so home high schoolers should have a secure moral and spiritual foundation and a basic philosophy of life to compare with new philosophical ideas they will encounter in their studies.

Worldview

Worldview is a popular term used to describe a person's life philosophy. People's worldviews develop through the influences of family, religious affiliation, culture, and education. No one approaches life without a worldview of some kind.

What is your worldview? If you are not sure, ask yourself what influences the way you think and the way you interpret both current and historical events. What makes you who you are? In what ways have you grown and changed, and what has caused these changes? How do your beliefs and ideas differ from those around you and from those of different cultures and times?

Do you want your children to share your worldview? High school is the perfect time to help them define and develop their personal philosophies. Some of your ideas and beliefs will already be ingrained in them, since example is a strong teacher, but the teens and early twenties are impressionable years when peers and professors can profoundly influence your students.

As much as parents want their children to share their beliefs, students also need to understand the life philosophies of others. At least four programs are available to teach students about worldviews. In his book *Understanding the Times* and its related high school course, David A. Noble deals with three current popular worldviews that he terms biblical Christian, Marxist/Leninist, and secular humanist. He examines theology, philosophy, ethics, biology, psychology, sociology, law, politics, economics, and history through each of these worldviews. David Quine offers *Worldviews of the Western World* and *Where Our Thinking Begins* through the Cornerstone Curriculum Project. Quine teaches a biblical worldview through the "windows" of music, art, philosophy, science, and government. Much of his program is based on the works of the late Dr. Francis Schaeffer.

Two resident programs that teach worldview to high school students are Summit Ministries and Worldview Academy. Summit offers its summer leadership seminars to older high schoolers and college students both in Manitou Springs, Colorado, and at Bryan College in Dayton, Tennessee. The Worldview Academy offers both weekend training sessions (sponsored by local churches) and worldview camps for ages thirteen and up. (See Appendix B for contact information for all of these programs.) For adults Summit offers worldview training through its Understanding the Times Conference in Colorado Springs.

The most important focus you should have is on your [children's] heart, not their head, for if their heart belongs to God and their parents, you have trained them in a way they will not depart from. If they are strong-willed and rebellious, you will have heartache.

Sharon Grimes,
homeschool leader

Faith

In keeping with their worldviews, all persons—whether religious or not—put their faith in something or someone. Some believe in science, education, or government. Others feel that they can depend only on themselves. However, for most of us, faith means religious faith, deeply seated beliefs that define who we are, why we are here, and how we should live. For Christians faith includes a vibrant, personal relationship with the living God through His Son Jesus Christ. Religious faith used to be a respected part of American culture. However, that situation has changed in the past fifty years. College students today often face challenges and even hostility toward their beliefs.

Various reports indicate that alarming numbers of Christian young people lose their faith in college—in Christian colleges as well as in secular ones. One study[2] estimates that about one-third of Christian college students abandon their beliefs. Explanations offered for this troubling phenomenon include the effects of peer pressure, the influence of humanistic and atheistic professors, and the teaching of the theory of evolution as fact.

Gene Edward Veith is a best-selling author and dean of the School of Arts and Sciences at Concordia University Wisconsin. His comments in a recent speech offer another possible explanation:

Sometimes students are so closed-minded, so adamantly opposed to opening their minds to anything outside their narrow little prejudices. Tragically, they use their faith as a way to insulate themselves from learning. And—as I know from bitter experience— this drives professors crazy. In response, professors often try to challenge their students' parochial mindset, including their religious beliefs, trying to do anything to shock their minds open. Sometimes, professors see the faith as an obstacle to learning, and consciously or unconsciously undermine Christian orthodoxy in the name of intellectual growth.

The irony is that students who use Christianity as an excuse for closed-mindedness, and professors who accept that excuse, and so begin criticizing biblical orthodoxy, are both missing the point. I would argue that it is precisely the biblical worldview that opens the mind.[3]

As home educators, you should help your students learn to approach all learning with intellectual honesty. Your goal here is to prepare your students to be educated, not indoctrinated, in college. Whatever your beliefs, you should help your students learn to think clearly and to consider opposing viewpoints honestly before they are faced with the amiably autocratic environment of a college classroom.

If you are a Christian and you want to help your students "own" their faith—to make it unshakable—give them a solid grounding in Scripture and allow them to explore and consider other worldviews, ideas, and philosophies while they are still under your guidance. Students should learn how to discern the meaning and motivation behind whatever they see, read, and hear. With this training, they will have a firm foundation on which to stand. Without this preparation, they will have difficulty thinking clearly in college classrooms filled with gullible students and captivating professors.

All homeschoolers should do a thorough study of the evidence for both creation and evolution. Students need to realize that it takes faith to believe in evolution, just as it does to believe in creation, because neither one can be proven. Teenagers want the whole truth, and you have the responsibility to be honest with them.

Perhaps you believe in evolution but not the Bible. Intellectual honesty demands that you consider all reasonable evidence, and there is valid scientific evidence for creation. If you want your students to be well educated, you should expose them to this evidence and help them to evaluate it fairly.

If you are Christian, consider carefully how you approach the subject of origins. Do you accept evolution, or certain aspects of evolution, as fact and also teach your children that the Bible is the true and infallible Word of God? Have you been able to reconcile the two? Even variations of evolutionary theory that acknowledge God as director of the process filter what the Bible teaches through mankind's wisdom—a wisdom that is constantly changing. (Outdated science books are proof of rapid changes in scientific thinking.) If you are among Christians who believe in literal, six-day biblical creation, you should make sure that your college-bound students also understand the theory of evolution. A blind loyalty to Scripture can be shaken easily in the classroom; an educated knowledge of the Bible can stand up to mankind's mutable science and philosophy.

Morals

Good morals are foundational for the college-bound homeschooler. However, morality depends on the conviction that there are absolute standards of behavior. Unfortunately, absolute standards are unpopular today and have been replaced with relativism, which claims that there are no absolutes. Relativism allows people to make their own rules based on personal desires and needs. This results in anarchy and increased crime, promiscuity, and suicide rates. Socrates condemned this type of thinking centuries ago when he wrote, "A system of morality which is based on relative emotional values is a mere illusion, a thoroughly vulgar conception which has nothing sound in it and nothing true."[4]

Relativistic teaching also hampers education. Some educators actually teach that there are no absolutes, even in mathematics. Two plus three may equal five, but then again maybe not. No wonder American students test so far below those in most other developed nations!

Do you recall the question that opens this chapter? Veith answers it this way:

I would argue that Christians are winning the education war because the biblical worldview provides a basis for education, whereas today's postmodernist worldviews do not. If truth is relative, or unknowable, or only a cultural construction, as contemporary scholars are saying, there is not going to be very much to teach. If there can be no objective standards, there can be no essential difference between excellence and mediocrity....[5]

Moral relativism runs rampant in America today, where the boundary between right and wrong is as flimsy as a wall of gelatin. On many campuses, the wall is nonexistent and students "go wild" once they are freed from the constraints of living at home. College campuses are communities of citizens with varying backgrounds, beliefs, and lifestyles. Students who enter these communities will both affect and be affected by their fellow citizens, for better or worse. The power of peers and other adults to influence the behavior of your students depends on their moral habits, convictions, and maturity. Students with strong moral character become leaders on their campuses; weak ones follow the crowd.

Moral choices do not depend on personal preference and private decision but on right reason and, I would add, divine order.

Basil Hume (b. 1923),
British cardinal, Archbishop of
Westminster. *Times* (London, 16
March 1990)

Before your students finish high school, try to find out how well they can stand up to moral pressure by giving them increasing amounts of independence and responsibility. The Bible warns us that the companion of fools suffers harm (Proverbs 13:20) and that bad companions will corrupt good morals (1 Corinthians 15:33). Helping your young adults to choose their friends wisely during high school will prepare them to do the same once they are on their own.

If you establish a firm moral and spiritual foundation, the rest of the building process should proceed more smoothly.

Building on the Foundation

After the foundation is established, it is time to build the framework of the house. The framework in home high schooling is your plan for helping your students develop into competent and responsible adults who are ready for college, career, or marriage. For college preparation, it includes academic courses, extracurricular activities, volunteer work, and possibly paid work. Like homebuilders, you as home educators have a job that requires diligence, commitment, ingenuity, and diverse skills. You will have to help your students decide on the best educational plan based on their learning styles, talents, preferences, and potential. At the same time you must ensure that the plan fits in with the rest of your family's needs.

Building contractors hire specialists like framers, electricians, and plumbers. You may decide to proceed alone, as many homeschoolers do. However, sometimes the demands of family life require the homeschooling "builder" to contract for outside help. If you and your students feel weak or inadequate in certain areas, do not hesitate to call in reinforcements. You may realize in the planning stages that you will require assistance, or you may discover it later, as veteran homeschooler Debbie Musselman did.

"I tried to teach Catherine trigonometry," Musselman says, "but by the end of chapter 3, Catherine was explaining more to me than I was explaining to her. So I hired a tutor. It was great. I was so relieved to be out from under it.... If you get stuck, there are plenty of other people who can help."

When the framing of a house is complete, plumbing and electrical systems are added to integrate all parts into a functional whole. The rooms in our house—character, academics, social skills, and practical skills—also need to be connected. In fact, sometimes they are inseparable. For instance, students who run their own businesses practice all the skills at once. Students who study nutrition combine practical skills with academics. As you develop your plan, consider ways to integrate the different areas, but for now, let us consider each "room" individually.

Character

Character is the main living area of our imaginary model house, influencing all actions and relationships. As such, it should receive high priority in college preparation. Young adults with a strong moral and spiritual foundation usually develop the strength of character necessary to make them good college students and exemplary citizens. Do not neglect character development in your high school training. The best academics and the most impressive list of extracurricular activities will not make up for the lack of it.

Homeschool teacher, author, and publisher Jane Williams says:

> We get too focused on conventional academics (reading, writing, history, geography, mathematics). Employers are looking for individuals who are self-starters, who take responsibility, who can be counted on to finish the job within the time frame required, who need minimum supervision, who are honest, who follow through, who are creative, who know how to anticipate and prevent problems, and who are willing to go the extra mile to get the job done with a positive attitude. These are skills seldom taught in traditional academic curriculums, especially at the elementary and high-school levels. And yet these are the fundamental skills that should be taught to all children as soon as a parent knows they are capable of understanding dialog. And if the young child learns these skills, the conventional academics become much easier to teach.

Character Qualities

Desirable character qualities include honesty, diligence, self-control, patience, compassion, kindness, and respect for others.

Students should be honest so that they will not be tempted to cheat, lie, or steal (common occurrences on campuses today). Also, if they have a reputation for honesty, there is less likelihood that they will be falsely accused. Students should be dependable so that others can count on them to keep their promises and to finish what they start. Diligence and persistence are other essential survival skills. The workload in college is a shock to most students, many of whom quit before the end of their sophomore year. If you have trained your young adults to persevere through difficulties, they will be more likely to earn their degrees.

Most homeschool applicants have strength of character and moral values that match our institution. Most applicants love to learn and want to make a positive difference with their lives. There is evidence of strong personal, spiritual, and educational discipline as well as creativity and maturity that comes to mind as I reflect on homeschool students I know who are here.

Lydia Knopf, Director of School and Church Relations, Biola University

Associate Director of Admissions Katherine Hallas has noticed strengths among homeschool students in this area. She says, "Marlboro College's academic program requires an unusual degree of self-motivation, discipline, and independent thought. Homeschooled applicants often demonstrate these qualities above and beyond their peers schooled in more traditional institutions."

Self-control is another desirable character quality for the college student because opportunities for recreation and service abound. Active campus involvement enhances the educational experience, within limitations. Students need to know how to evaluate their options in light of their responsibilities. They need the courage to say no, even to worthwhile activities, but especially to anything immoral, inappropriate, or potentially harmful to themselves or others.

Homeschoolers "tend to be extremely motivated," according to Robert Massa, Dean of Enrollment at Johns Hopkins University. He says, "I have also noticed, though the numbers are much too small to generalize, that they tend to want to compensate for not having convenient access to activities during high school by getting involved in several student organizations early in their college career. I find this to be a positive force on the campus."

The character qualities of patience, compassion, and kindness will help in all relationships your students develop in college, especially with their roommates. Students should be willing to share but still have the wisdom not to allow their generosity to be abused. They may want to help fellow students study. However, make sure that they understand where to draw the line so that they leave enough time for their own assignments and do not deprive others of the benefits of learning for themselves. Obviously, helping someone else to cheat in any way is wrong.

Homeschool students' compassion also should extend to those who are different or who have had fewer advantages. Geoffrey Gould, Director of Admissions at Binghamton University (SUNY), makes a good point. "While much homeschooling is done deliberately to maintain a specific social values perspective, there is a loss of awareness and perhaps appreciation of social and economic diversity to a family whose child doesn't interact with children of other socioeconomic or racial groups outside the home. It wouldn't have to be in a school, of course, as others might congregate in community centers, religious institutions, on recreational or sports teams not affiliated with schools and, therefore, available to homeschooled kids. I am sure most homeschooled children do not live 'in the woods' or in total social isolation, but perhaps the point can be made in a balanced fashion."

Homeschoolers should be grateful for the opportunities and parental devotion they have enjoyed and should demonstrate their gratitude by extending kindness and understanding (but not condescension) to those who have not been so blessed. A superior attitude has no place in a homeschooler's character.

To help your students develop good character, provide examples of moral behavior in the literature you read, the entertainment you watch, and the friendships you develop. Aristotle wrote that the complete formation of moral virtues is the product of habit. Encourage your children to practice desirable moral habits at all times and use loving discipline, when necessary, to keep them on track. Although teens seek increasing independence from their parents, they still need and desire your guidance.

Christine told me that the scariest thing a parent can say to a teenager is, "I'll tell you what I think, but after that, you're on your own." She says, "Sure, we're growing up, but we still need you to be our parents."

The faculty report to me that [homeschoolers] are generally much more well read and that they truly enjoy learning and soak up new information like sponges. Another interesting comment I heard from a history professor is that homeschoolers do not tend to have a negative image about teachers which many high school students come into college with. He said it sometimes takes high school students a while to realize that is not the same in college. He said homeschool students see the professor or teacher as a conduit from which to learn.

Barbara Henry, Home School Adviser, Oglethorpe University

Courage Tempered with Respect

Your homeschool graduates should go to college with the courage of their convictions. However, courage must be tempered with respect, especially for those who are in authority. Most homeschoolers show this respect and relish the opportunity to learn under their professors.

Some students feel that they must defend their beliefs at any cost, even if it usurps a professor's authority and disrupts the class. Instead they should approach those who disagree with them with an attitude of respect and humility.

Christian homeschool mom Beth Vellalos says, "[Teaching the professor] is not your job. However, if the teacher asks you a question, you most certainly can give him the answer that you believe to be true. You want to hold firm to your beliefs, and you want to be able to give an account and a reason for your faith at any time, but it's not your job to take over and teach the class because what your teacher is teaching is wrong."

Serious students who study hard and ask honest, probing questions will learn more and potentially have a greater influence than those who go into the classroom with the agenda to convert professors and students to their viewpoints. Dogmatism is seldom effective for changing opinions; instead it usually alienates people. A lifestyle of moral courage and integrity will have far more impact than classroom confrontations. Students should also be aware that teachers sometimes take an opposing viewpoint in classroom discussions as part of an effective teaching style.

Glenn Lygrisse, Vice President for Enrollment Management at Tabor College says, "[Homeschoolers] do not seem to be able to adapt as readily to various teaching styles, and especially the more confrontive 'prove what you believe and why' style of teaching…. Help the student to know that when their beliefs are challenged (if not in a hostile environment), this can be a learning experience as well. When the parent is both teacher and parent, this does not leave a 'safe place' for a student to bounce off ideas that may be new without fear of rejection." He suggested having exposure to people with different teaching styles or working with schools that offer distance education opportunities. For example, Biola University offers an online great books program for grades 10–12.

One of the most important skills you can teach your children is how to ask a good question.

Jane Williams,
Bluestocking Press

According to Jane Williams, the opposing-viewpoint type of training can be effective in the home setting. She says that you can and should test the strength of your students' convictions. One method, suggested by author Richard Maybury, is to switch to the opposing viewpoint in the middle of a discussion without informing your students. Then see whether they notice that you switched. Williams recommends using this method to see how well-grounded students are in their beliefs.

"Sometimes you can learn more about your own philosophical position by studying the opposing viewpoint than from studying only concepts that are philosophically consistent with your value system," Williams says.

Academic Preparation

Academic preparation, like an upstairs bedroom, rests soundly over the living area of character. Your students should complete a curriculum of challenging courses that fulfill all requirements for high school graduation and college admission. They should read profusely and develop skills in independent study and communication.

Mike Williams of Harding University says, "If homeschoolers have any weakness, it generally lies in communication skills." He specifically referred to problems working in teams, participating in discussion groups, and speaking in public.

William J. Katip of Robert Morris College also emphasizes the need for this type of experience. "I would suggest that you recommend ways to get them to work together on projects…. You might have combined science classes, or music, etc. Some Christian schools allow homeschoolers to be involved in sports or classes. I think this is positive in that it allows the student the opportunity to interact with peers and learn about negotiation, giving in, etc. College courses often involve group projects, and this sort of skill is necessary."

I think it's a great idea. It takes an awful lot of time and effort to do it right. The students we've seen have come out of families that have done it right, in terms of the academic part of it, at least. I just wish there were some way to simulate the social part of school to develop some of the other skills that go along with the academic part…. The ability to compromise in groups. That seems to have been missing.

Robert G. Voss, Worcester Polytechnic Institute

Generally, college professors present the most important material during lectures, so note-taking skills are essential. Students also will have to read voluminous amounts of material. Therefore you should teach them how to read textbooks for necessary information only. Here is a method that might help them save time. Suggest that they first read chapter headings and subheadings and formulate questions about the topics. Then have them read the beginning and end of each paragraph, and read the middle only if the material is not clear or if their questions have not been answered in the text. They may highlight important points for later review. Students are studying correctly if they can answer chapter questions and/or discuss the material satisfactorily after this exercise.

Academic goals should not be limited to course work. Veteran home teacher Marty Bigger says, "I wanted my children to be readers and thinkers. I didn't want them just to reflect what they'd been taught. I wanted them to be able to think and ask questions. To me, learning has nothing to do with four walls and somebody up in front with a teacher's degree. You can learn anything you want. Learning is exciting. It doesn't depend on your surroundings as much as it does on you."

Students who have the opportunity to develop their talents and special interests during high school are excited about learning. This helps them stand out from the crowd of other college applicants and makes them well-rounded and self-confident adults. Thoughtfully chosen extracurricular activities reinforce academic learning. For example, Nathaniel Goggans built on his interest in law by completing an internship with the Home School Legal Defense Association and volunteering for his state legislature. Mark Bigger, also interested in law, signed up as a precinct committee person, worked on elections, apprenticed under a person running a campaign, and eventually (after high school) conducted a campaign for someone running for his state's senate. Catherine Musselman, who planned to major in deaf education, worked with deaf children as a volunteer at the local children's hospital.

Travel also enhances learning and strengthens college applications, especially if you visit museums and historical sites on your journeys. Students who have experienced other cultures offer fresh perspectives that enrich learning for other students.

Although academic strength is the first criterion for determining students' potential success in college, this quality must be complemented by strong social and practical skills if students hope to thrive.

Social Skills

The upstairs room of social skills also must rest firmly on a moral and spiritual foundation and on the first floor of character. To succeed in college and in life, young adults need to be able to get along with both their peers and adults while still maintaining their own identity, beliefs, and character.

Peer Relationships

Although homeschoolers seldom have trouble relating to various ages of children and adults, some colleges report that relationships with traditionally schooled peers can present problems for home-educated college students, especially in group settings. Different levels of maturity sometimes hamper interaction between home-educated college students and their peers. Those homeschoolers who have been completely sheltered by their parents are reportedly immature and have trouble adjusting to college. More often, homeschoolers are maturer than traditional students are because they are used to interacting with adults. As a result, some of them have trouble relating to less mature peers. Although no one would suggest that mature students stoop to the level of immature ones, they need to be able to enjoy the company of their fellow students.

Gary T. Ray of Lee University says, "A lot of parents make provisions for social time within their homeschool structure...then you don't see any difference. But it's when the parent isolates them...that sometimes they get behind socially and have a harder time adjusting because their world is constantly communicating with adults. Then when they get in with people their own age who are not as mature, it's a little tougher as far as having fun and just goofing off [is concerned]. It's called socializing during leisure time."

Alice Dunfey of St. Anselm College warns about other consequences of social isolation. "Most of the students I have spoken with have been involved, interesting, social people. There are a few students who have been educated in a program that has limited their social interaction and these students have not done as well. They write well and speak well (technically) but have no sense of audience. The families are concerned, as we all are, about college issues, but without social development and exposure, students are unlikely to develop the skills they need to be successful in the social arena."

Handling peer pressure is a weakness that Jeff Lantis has noticed among homeschoolers at Hillsdale College, although this admissions director also has found homeschoolers to be strong students and good campus leaders. He encourages home high schoolers to obtain quality leadership experience.

To alleviate potential social problems, encourage your students to participate in activities with others of their own age. However, realize that frequent and prolonged interaction with peers can foster peer dependence, which defeats one of the purposes of homeschooling. Homeschool leader Sharon Grimes cautions parents to limit even homeschool group activities lest your teens begin to rely too much on peer relationships at the expense of healthy family ties. Volunteer work, jobs, sports, and leadership involvement in the community also will develop social skills.

For those students planning to go away to college, dormitory life could be another major adjustment. Many homeschoolers come from large families, so they are used to sharing a small amount of space with others. However, it can be difficult to adjust to living in a community of strangers and sharing a room with someone new.

Kerry Durgin of Hood College considers residential life the biggest issue for homeschoolers. "It's not as if they don't integrate well, but it takes longer than those who have constantly been thrown into both good and bad situations in a high school setting."

> *Our homeschool applicants are interesting individuals—very structured, well-organized, more mature, almost to a 't'. I think a lot of it has to do with the parents. They demand and expect a lot out of their students.*
>
> Jeff Palm, Associate Director of Admission, Hawaii Pacific University

Male/Female Relationships

Another social issue that should concern homeschool parents is the whole area of male/female relationships. Students need to make a concerted effort to stay focused in college, and romantic entanglements distract them from their primary responsibilities. Before your teens enter college, make sure that they know how to handle themselves with members of the opposite sex. Help them learn the importance of respecting others enough not to manipulate or coerce them into getting involved emotionally or physically against their better judgment. Encourage them to have enough respect for themselves that they will not allow someone else to pressure them into relationships with which they are uncomfortable. Help your young adults to realize that if a person really loves someone, he or she will do what is best for that person. Assure them that they are worth waiting for, and only someone who realizes that fact is worthy of their love.

Since most colleges are coeducational, it is important for students to be comfortable interacting with the opposite sex. Most teens learn these skills through group activities and traditional dating. However, a large number of homeschoolers have decided not to date, opting instead for courtship when they are old enough to seriously consider marriage. Up until that time, their interaction with the opposite sex is limited to group and family events. (For resources about courtship versus dating, see Appendix B.) Whatever your family decides on the dating/courtship issue, make sure that your teens build some friendships with members of the opposite sex in order to develop social skills and self-confidence in mixed-gender situations.

Preparation for Real Life

- *Personal hygiene*
- *Neatness*
- *Manners*
- *Time management*
- *Organizational skills*
- *Consistent sleep habits*
- *Efficient study habits*
- *Good nutrition*
- *Regular exercise*
- *Wise money management*
- *Shopping savvy*
- *Housecleaning skills*
- *Cooking ability*
- *Laundry and mending skills*
- *Safe driving skills*
- *Understanding of car maintenance*
- *Dependability*

People who are not accustomed to the homeschool way of life often wonder how seemingly disadvantaged homeschoolers tolerate having to miss out on junior and senior proms. If students have the desire, homeschool groups certainly can plan their own proms. Many, if not most, homeschoolers prefer not to participate in proms because of the dating involved and because of prom night's reputation for encouraging drinking and promiscuity among high school students. Students have numerous other ways to enjoy themselves in group settings.

Many still assume that homeschoolers are isolated. Help debunk the socialization myth by providing opportunities for your students to gain the social skills they need.

Practical Skills

To top off our model house, we need a sturdy roof. Young adults going out on their own should have basic survival skills and know how to take care of personal needs. Teach your students to be considerate of others in their habits, manners, and hygiene. No one should have to pick up after them or straighten their messes, and they should keep themselves and their living areas clean and free of offensive odors. Help them develop organizational skills so that they can manage both their time and their possessions wisely. Encourage good sleep and study habits, regular physical activity, good nutrition, and polite eating habits (also polite gum-chewing habits, if they must chew). Teach them how to budget their money, clean house, shop for necessities, launder and mend clothes, and cook simple meals. (Although colleges offer cafeteria food, some students live off campus and prepare their own food.) Also, make sure that your students are safe drivers and that they practice proper car maintenance.

Especially impress on your children the importance of completing projects and arriving at classes and meetings on time. Timeliness is serious business, especially for college assignments. Often a late assignment will cause a student to lose an entire letter grade. Most of all, teach your students to take all of their responsibilities seriously, insisting that they follow through on their commitments.

Doorway to Success

The doorway of our imaginary house is the preparation you give your students for leaving home to begin their adult lives at college, in marriage, or as independent single adults. Since this book focuses primarily on college preparation, I will limit my discussion to that topic.

When it is time for your students to leave their homeschooling years behind and head to college, the process is usually a bit different from that of traditional students. Much depends on colleges' homeschool policies, which vary. (See Appendix A.) Willingness to cooperate with admissions departments is essential. Eric Synstelien of the University of Dallas noted that a portion of home-schooled applicants show defensiveness about having to document their educational history. If you feel this way, you need to realize that *all* potential students have to provide educational documentation to colleges as part of the application process. Homeschoolers who refuse to cooperate are asking for special privileges. It is unreasonable to expect colleges to guess your student's educational background and academic abilities. They cannot admit all students that apply, so they need some means of determining which ones are most likely to succeed on their campuses. If you expect colleges to admit your students, make sure they are ready and do not refuse reasonable requests for documentation of their high school work.

Dr. Marian Sanders, Chairman of the Department of Classical Liberal Arts and Associate Professor of History at Patrick Henry College, gives this advice: "Because homeschoolers and their parents may not have ready access to the kinds of resources available to students in private or public schools, they ought to develop a plan for choosing a college. They should prepare a package of materials that will highlight the homeschooler's academic accomplishments and other talents. If a student wants to devote four years of his life to college, he should thoughtfully craft a solid set of materials demonstrating his abilities."

Many admissions officers I surveyed expressed interest in learning more about how home-schooling works; therefore *you* have the opportunity to educate *them*.

"In the past five years we have seen an increase in the number of homeschooled students who are interested in Saint Anselm," says Dunfey. "We have a modest knowledge of some programs but would be very interested in obtaining more information on the variety of programs (including self-styled). With this in mind, it would be terrific if families could include a description (formal or otherwise) of the program they use so we may continue to educate ourselves in order to make good decisions."

Most of the admissions people I have dealt with have been friendly, enthusiastic, and helpful. Unless a college proves itself to be unfriendly to homeschoolers, give its admissions department cooperation, respect, and the benefit of the doubt. If a college does not welcome homeschoolers, respectfully try to change its policy or go elsewhere.

While he was Vice President for Enrollment at Geneva College, Katip investigated other colleges' homeschool policies. He says, "I would...encourage your families to go to the colleges that want your kids. I did a survey a few years ago of Christian colleges and found that many had lots of extra hoops to jump through. I would not bother with these schools if I were you. There are enough who want your kids. There has been plenty of research indicating that they are doing as well or better than traditional school kids. So, go where you are wanted and forget about the rest!"

If you follow this model house plan and help your students to develop their character and skills on the foundation of spiritual and moral strength, they will be well on the road to a successful and fulfilling future.

Now that you have the basic blueprint, it is time to fill in the details, roll up your sleeves, and get to work.

By wisdom a house is built, and through understanding it is established;
through knowledge its rooms are filled with rare and beautiful treasures.

Proverbs 24:3–4 NIV

1. Gene Edward Veith, "Christian Higher Education: The Temptations and the Opportunities." Convocation address presented August 27, 1998, at Bryan College, Dayton, Tennessee. Used by permission.
2. Railback, Ph.D. dissertation, UCLA, as quoted on Worldview Academy website, www.worldview.org.
3. Veith.
4. *The Columbia Dictionary of Quotations* is licensed from Columbia University Press. Copyright © 1993 by Columbia University Press. All rights reserved.
5. Veith.

Chapter 3

Planning and Priorities

Think ahead. Don't go into home schooling without some idea of how you are going to explain and justify it to a college several years down the line.

Jonathan P. Reider, Senior Associate Director
of Admission, Stanford University

An excellent home high-school education requires careful planning. You will first need to define your purpose for education and then set your priorities on that basis, keeping in mind that at some point you may be accountable to colleges or employers for the decisions you make.

The Purpose of Education

If you are like most homeschoolers, you probably have more in mind for your students than just meeting the minimum requirements for high-school graduation or college entrance. Discuss with your students what you want to achieve based on your educational philosophy and your students' interests and talents. Is completing a traditional college-preparatory education your goal, or do you prefer a more creative approach to learning? Do you consider it more important to fulfill requirements or to allow students the freedom to develop their individual strengths and interests? How willing are you to cede your decision-making power about what your students should learn to administrators, curriculum writers, and others? Answer these questions before finalizing your high school plans.

Liberal Arts Education

As you plan your home high school, keep in mind the inherent value of learning. Education is gourmet fare that should be sought diligently, savored regularly, and served enthusiastically as nourishment for growing minds. The education I am describing is not the sort of training that often passes for education. Gene Edward Veith notes that the ancient Greeks and Romans employed two types of education: one for slaves and one for free citizens.

> *[Their] goal was to teach slaves to do their jobs well and to serve the economy. They most emphatically did not want slaves to be able to think for themselves. Free citizens, however—those who were to play an active role and exert leadership in the Greek democracy or the Roman Republic—were given what was called a "liberal" education, the term coming from the Latin word* libera, *meaning "freedom." To be free, students*

needed to develop all of their powers as human beings. They needed to learn how to think, how to create, how to contribute to society.

Liberal education as Veith describes it is the type of education I believe every child deserves. No matter what students plan to do for a living, they should be taught how to think. Then they will realize that there is honor in doing all kinds of work if the work is done well by a person of character. However, most young people today care only about climbing the proverbial "ladder of success" and making a great deal of money. Veith says:

Notice that students who come to college simply wanting vocational skills—so that they can, as they say, "get a good job and earn lots of money"—are asking for the education of a slave. In fact, the current trends in education might be summarized as constituting a curriculum of slavery. Such slave virtues as conformity, passivity, the victim mentality, lack of thinking, unquestioning obedience to the dominant culture—these have become endemic in today's mentality. Citizens who think like this—and who have good jobs and make lots of money—have little interest in governing themselves, a process that requires knowledge of the issues, critical thinking, and civic responsibility. They would rather believe what they are told and, as long as their place in the economy is assured, give their leaders high approval ratings, no matter what.[1]

So how can you guide your students away from this trap? Veith promotes classical Christian liberal arts education as the logical alternative to today's "slave education." He notes that classical education is being rediscovered today, as it seemingly is "whenever Western civilization starts to go stagnant." The following is an outline of Veith's description of this method:

A. **Seven Liberal Arts (intellectual skills)—the modes of learning**
   1. **The Trivium**
      a. **Grammar:** basic facts and structure of language; basic knowledge of any discipline.
      b. **Logic or dialectic:** taught by questioning; the Socratic method of discussion and open inquiry; used to achieve understanding.
      c. **Rhetoric:** ability to write and speak in original, persuasive, and creative ways, to apply knowledge and understanding on one's own.
   2. **The Quadrivium**
      a. **Music:** including study of poetry and music theory, listening, and performance—the perception of aesthetics.
      b. **Astronomy:** involving empirical observation and use of mathematical models in the scientific study of the external universe.
      c. **Mathematics:** the study of numbers, involving pure abstract thinking.
      d. **Geometry:** the study of spatial relationships, including drawing, design, architecture, and, by extension, engineering and the visual arts.
B. **The Sciences (knowledge)—the content of education**
   1. **Natural Science:** knowledge of the external, objective world, including chemistry, biology, physics, and the like, but also philosophy.
   2. **Moral Science:** knowledge of human relationships, including history, law, and what we would term social sciences.

3. **Theological Science:** knowledge of God, the study of Scripture and theology, which give us the first principles of every other kind of knowledge; considered the "Queen of the Sciences."

C. **Purpose of Learning**

1. **To develop the God-given powers of the intellect:** aimed toward three absolutes:

   a. **The True:** growing in appreciation for what is true.

   b. **The Good:** growing in moral virtues.

   c. **The Beautiful:** growing in aesthetic sensibility.

Veith explains that "in the classic universities there were no majors, no vocational specialization. This came after the student mastered the arts and sciences. Then and only then would the student study a profession."[2]

Even in high schools today, students are being pushed to make vocational decisions before they have the training and maturity they need. Guidance counselor Judy Rodgers says that job preparation seems to be the main focus in most high schools today, and she finds that situation disturbing. She believes that students are forced to make decisions too soon—for instance, choosing either a university track or a technical track at the age of fourteen or fifteen. She laments the fact that business and industry are increasingly able to dictate how education is conducted in public high schools at the expense of the students. She says that those in power often laugh at learning for learning's sake. Businesses want schools to produce good workers; Rodgers thinks it is more important to produce good citizens who have completed a strong general education and are ready to be trained for work.

Liberal arts education seems to be the perfect vehicle for the preparation Rodgers describes, and you can provide it at home. In fact, Michael Farris believes that much of the traditional liberal arts education can be completed at the high school level by the child's own parents. He sees college as a time to expand upon that good foundation by furthering the liberal arts education. In Farris's view, college is also a time for career preparation after students have received "worldview instruction and broad exposure to…the important ideas that have made our culture and our country what they are."

We feel that [homeschoolers] fit the philosophy of a liberal arts college since they appreciate the true value of learning and are able to demonstrate that through the way they have been educated.
Martha O'Connell
Dean of Admissions
McDaniel College

While a college degree seems to be essential for jobs in many fields, you should still make sure that your students have good reasons for choosing a college education. It is an appalling waste of money and time to attend college just for the experience.

Farris offers this advice to homeschool students: "Go someplace that's going to help you get prepared for an appropriate career. Don't go to college for the sake of going to college. It's a waste of $50,000. If you're going to college just to get an experience, don't do that. Go to the mission field for a couple of years. Take your $100,000 and go buy a Mrs. Field's cookie franchise. But if you're going to college for a specific career preparation course—if that's the best way to do it—then do it. Work hard and be successful."

If you decide to provide a liberal arts education at home, plenty of resources are available to help you do it. However, if you do not feel up to this task or if you want liberal arts courses to be available for your students in college, you will have to search for a college that still offers them. Most colleges used to provide these courses through their general education requirements, but fewer of them do so today. Veith laments the incoherence and gaps in knowledge that he observes in higher education and calls for a return to the high standards of traditional liberal arts education at the college level. He claims that lack of coherence in curriculum and lack of knowledge in today's college graduates are the consequences of a worldview that has rejected God and the "Queen of Sciences," thus losing its unifying foundation.

"Today, it has become a commonplace to say 'there are no absolutes.' And indeed, the three classical absolutes are routinely and systematically rejected. Truth is relative. Goodness is relative. And Beauty is relative. They are all swallowed up into the black hole of subjectivity. Higher Education ends up deconstructing itself."[3]

Veith says that while he is not necessarily advocating a literal implementation of the curriculum he described, he believes that the conceptual structure and philosophy of the classical university offer a proven model for educational reformation.

I believe it is a good model for a high school curriculum as well and that homeschool teachers should strive to give our students this "education for free citizens." Teach your children how to reason, allow them to be creative, and encourage them to contribute to society in their own unique way.

Ultimately, your children must decide, with your help, what type of education they want to have in high school, whether or not they should attend college, and, if so, what type of college they should attend. Navigating them through this process is one of your most important jobs as their parents, teachers, and counselors.

Objective: College

If college is your students' objective and you value educational freedom, finding a balance between autonomy and accountability may be tricky. Most colleges stipulate courses as prerequisites for admission, and when surveyed, a few colleges expressed concern about incomplete preparation among homeschoolers.

We did not fully understand the importance of gearing our curriculum to college entrance requirements until it was almost too late. Early in Christine's junior year, we began to investigate a few colleges that interested me. You read that right: *me,* not *her.* At that point, our daughter had no interest in higher education. However, as her guidance counselor (see chapter 6), I had to make sure she was ready for college, whether she eventually attended or not. So I called and asked several colleges about their admissions policies. Being timid about revealing our homeschooling status, I called the same schools anonymously later to inquire about their homeschool requirements.

> *Because of the individualized and non-standardized curriculum, some students have not completed the desired distribution of courses in college prep areas of math, science, or social studies.*
>
> Myron Van de Ven,
> Assistant Vice Chancellor for
> Enrollment Services, University
> of Wisconsin-Green Bay

I found out that finishing high school is not enough. One state university admissions director told me that his one complaint about homeschooled applicants is that many have not fulfilled the university's minimum requirements for admission. Specifically, the various colleges within the university had different course requirements, and homeschoolers were not paying attention to them. For example, engineering majors are usually required to take more math and science during high school.

Meeting Requirements for College Entrance

To plan high school adequately, it is a good idea to research some potential college choices during the high school planning stages. When you call colleges, be sure to ask whether there are extra requirements in your students' areas of interest. Do your research early so that you can schedule all the necessary courses. Unlike me, you should not be afraid to identify yourself as a homeschooler, but you should find out the colleges' general requirements before you do. Then you'll be able to determine which requirements are for all students and which are specific to homeschoolers. Many institutions' homeschool policies are still being developed, so be sure to check back with the schools periodically to determine whether any changes have been made.

Call more colleges than you think you need to. One of the colleges I contacted is the one Christine eventually entered, but because of its distance from our home, we did not really consider it a possibility at that time. How should you select schools to call? Skip to chapter 7 for some pointers on choosing a college. For your first contacts, though, call a few local colleges, both private and public, and a few appealing out-of-state schools. Pay special attention to more selective ones. If your students are prepared for them, they'll be ready for less selective schools, as well. One exception to this statement is that more of the less selective schools seem to require certified diplomas or the GED.

Table 3A lists the most common curriculum requirements. In general, college-preparatory English courses need to cover writing and literature. Mathematics courses usually have to be at the level of Algebra I and above, and most colleges require at least one or two lab sciences. Social studies requirements often include U.S. History, Government, World History, or Geography. Colleges with foreign language requirements expect students to study the same language for a minimum of two years. Some will allow Latin or sign language to fulfill this requirement; others will not.

If your children plan to attend state colleges, or if they want a state diploma (available in some states), they will need to fulfill state high school graduation requirements as well as college admission requirements. Some out-of-state colleges require conformity with your local state regulations as well.

Homeschooling mother of ten Tamie Goggans suggests contacting your local board of education and asking requirements for a college-prep diploma. "If you can't get it from them, call a local state university and ask what high school credit hours the state requires for a student to be admitted to a state university.... You want to make sure that your children have what they need for you to be able to say that they have a college-prep diploma from your state. And if you meet the requirements of your state, that will be acceptable at other institutions. I suggest beefing it up. Give them extra history and science."

Information about your state homeschooling laws should also be available from your state homeschool organization and the Home School Legal Defense Association (HSLDA). I highly recommend that you join HSLDA so that you can avail yourself of its wonderful resources, receive timely information, support its work, and obtain legal help should you ever require it. (See Appendix B.)

After you have done your preliminary research on meeting college requirements, evaluate your desire or need to use an umbrella school or correspondence school. Many colleges require homeschooled applicants to provide certified grades, diplomas from accredited schools, or GED certificates. Depending on the colleges you choose, you will need to determine whether or not your method of schooling will require your student to take the GED. If taking the GED is not an acceptable option for your student, you might want to consider other alternatives, such as an accredited program, part-time high school, or concurrent high school and college. Keep in mind that qualifying for federal aid requires proof of graduation. Even if the college does not require a GED, state laws or your need for federal financial aid could limit your options. Eligibility for federal financial aid is based on having an acceptable diploma, which

Table 3A
High School Course Requirements

College requirements vary, but usually include:

English	*4 years*
Science	*2–4 years*
Mathematics	*2–4 years*
Social Studies	*2–4 years*
Foreign Language	*0–3 years*
Arts	*0–1 year*
Electives	*to a total of 16–25 credits*

can be a homeschool diploma, or passing an ability-to-benefit test. (See chapter 6 for the definition of an acceptable diploma and for more discussion about both the GED and financial aid.)

College Entrance Examinations

If your students want to attend four-year colleges, they will most likely be required to take college entrance exams. Be sure to make time in your high school schedule for testing and preparation. Most colleges depend on standardized test scores to help them determine how homeschool students compare with other students applying to their colleges. In many cases, test scores weigh heavily in the admissions decision.

At a few colleges, test scores are viewed differently. "Generally, we treat each application as a portfolio of accomplishments, then develop an individualized system for testing knowledge and competencies," says David Hawsey, Associate Vice President of Juniata College. "When the SAT tests comes in, I find that homeschoolers often show scores in the 1200–1400 range, when most other students from traditional systems do not show such consistency as a cohort. SAT tests are probably the worst way to assess a homeschooler, since they will not give you any idea of the skills and depth this individual has, nor of the discipline it took to go down a different path to college." Still, since test scores are so often used to verify the accuracy of homeschoolers' grades and their readiness for college study, it is crucial to prepare for college entrance exams early and continuously. (See chapter 6 for more information about testing.)

Educational Freedom: Going Down a Different Path to College

Home high schoolers have a decided advantage over public school students because they can take a different path and change direction more easily. I realize that when you plan your students' high school programs based on colleges' requirements, you risk losing some of the advantages of homeschooling. For example, the schedule might not allow adequate time for students to pursue their own interests. You might have less freedom to teach subjects that you consider more important than those required by the colleges. Also, you might be forced to teach courses that you feel have no application to real life.

What I am advocating is balance. Realize that your students may want to attend traditional colleges in the future even if they have no desire to do so now. Do not shortchange your students. If you as a family decide to forego required subjects, find colleges that will accept what your students plan to study during high school. If that is impossible, realize that your children may not be accepted into the colleges of their choice before having completed the required subjects. They may have to attend a community college first or take remedial courses. However, this is certainly a viable option and for some students might be the best of both worlds.

Even if working through traditional textbook courses is not your idea of learning, there are alternative methods for completing a college-preparatory program. In her homeschool curriculum, Debbie Musselman followed Charlotte Mason's method of using "living books" and having her students narrate back what they read.

"I hate a lot of textbooks," Musselman says. "They are necessary for some subjects but can be dry and full of busy-work.... I think the most important part of a student's education is reading because it gives them a bigger picture of the world around them and how they can affect that world.... Good literature...motivates us, especially biographies. They show us that one person *can* make a difference."

Musselman tried to make every subject as interesting as possible by having her students read biographies and historical novels "so that in each time period, each person was not just a name on a page but a living, breathing actuality."

Many homeschoolers use unit studies for the same reasons. In the unit study approach, all subjects, except possibly math, are studied around a theme. Unit studies involve more reading, writing, research, and hands-on activities than do traditional methods.

Totally student-directed learning is often termed *unschooling*. Unschoolers pursue their interests with little or no formal instruction. Many have achieved advanced skills and knowledge in their areas of interest using this method. If your homeschool philosophy is along unschooling lines, make sure that your students are at least covering the basic skills necessary for college success and try to find ways to make your students' learning activities fit into traditional course titles. If you decide to go that route, make sure that you document everything that can be considered academic or extracurricular learning. Make special note of anything that develops leadership skills. For more information about this method, consult *Homeschooling Today, Practical Homeschooling,* or *Home Education* magazine. Barbara Shelton's *Senior High: A Home Designed Form+U+La* and Cafi Cohen's *And What About College?* discuss record keeping.

If you prefer a more traditional approach, simply decide which courses your students need for graduation and allow some room for electives and extracurricular activities. For those of you who are philosophically between unschooling and traditional approaches, decide which courses are essential and then brainstorm with your students about other learning opportunities. For some great ideas for adding variety to your students' studies, consult Debra Bell's *The Ultimate Guide to Homeschooling.*

Again, keep good records and be flexible in case your students' goals or interests change. Whatever courses you teach and whatever methods you use in your homeschool, it is important that your students study a variety of challenging materials to prepare for college-level work.

Homeschoolers tend to have a unique world view. They are usually well prepared academically and are eager to learn in a more traditional setting. Many of them are independent thinkers and have used research techniques in their schooling. Homeschoolers seem to come with more direction and a greater sense of ability to accomplish their educational goals.

Randy Comfort,
Dean of Admissions,
Greenville College

For more information about the various methods and materials for homeschooling during high school, consult *The Homeschooling Handbook* by Mary Griffith, Mary Pride's *Big Book of Home Learning*, and Cathy Duffy's *Christian Home Educator's Curriculum Manual: Junior and Senior High.* You should also consider subscribing to at least one homeschooling magazine. Such periodicals provide a wealth of information and will make you feel more connected to the homeschooling community. Some may offer back issues that address specific areas of interest. Introductory packets for those who are new to homeschooling are available from various magazines and homeschool organizations as well.

The HSLDA and state homeschooling groups are other excellent sources of information. Find out if your local or state group holds annual conferences where speakers and fellow homeschoolers will be available to answer your questions. (Check Appendix B for sources of information on homeschooling methods, conferences, and organizations.)

Craig Gould of Rocky Mountain College states, "Strengths of students depend on their homeschool environment. If the curriculum is organized, varied, and demanding, the students do well.... If the homeschool situation is not organized, demanding, and varied, the students have a difficult time adjusting to the rigors of a traditional education setting."

Setting Goals

How can you provide a high school education such as Gould describes while still maintaining some freedom? Defining your educational philosophy and setting clear goals will start you on the right path. Perhaps it will help if I explain how we did it in our family.

43

When we were planning Christine's high school curriculum, we tried to keep in mind our desires for her development as a whole person. Even though academics were extremely important, we needed to keep things in perspective.

To help us determine our goals, Steve and I developed the following definition according to our Christian worldview:

To be educated means
- To know God and His Word
- To love learning and to continuously pursue knowledge
- To think logically
- To express oneself fluently, clearly, and persuasively in both speaking and writing
- To know how to find information, discern its accuracy, and apply it
- To develop the skills necessary to live in adult society
- To value relationships and to treat all others with kindness and respect
- Under the lordship of Jesus Christ, to seek God's will for direction and purpose in life

From the beginning, I realized that one goal, a love for learning, could not be taught. Rather, I knew it would have to come as the result of the educational process. As Christine's teacher, I deeply desired that she would develop a love for learning because those who relish learning are never stymied. For them, each problem is a challenge, and ignorance in an area is a call to adventurous discovery. Suddenly one day when we were in the middle of geometry, Christine exclaimed, "I love geometry. I love everything we're doing. I just love LEARNING!" That was a homeschooling moment to treasure.

There is no substitutes for desire in learning. For the most part, that is not easily taught. But if the teacher, home or not, is enthusiastic about learning, that tends to 'rub off' on the student.

Jack Traylor, Professor of History, Bryan College

Bob Voss of Worcester Polytechnic Institute (WPI) has observed this same love of learning among WPI's home-educated students. "[T]hey have this love of learning for learning's sake that I think is super...something that comes to all of us in time—or most of us in time—but it doesn't come to high school students that easily anymore."

Your attitude about education can have a profound influence on your students. Homeschooling provides the perfect atmosphere for nurturing a love of learning. Perhaps that is one of the best reasons to continue doing it through the high school years.

The next chapter will take you on a tour of Homeschool High, where you will be working as the prime mover in the administration, the faculty, and the staff. Exciting times are ahead for you and your students. Please join me in the reception area to learn more about it.

Commit to the Lord whatever you do, and your plans will succeed.

Proverbs 16:3 NIV

---

1. Gene Edward Veith, "Christian Higher Education: The Temptations and the Opportunities." Convocation address presented August 27, 1998, at Bryan College, Dayton, Tennessee.
2. Ibid.
3. Ibid.

Sample High School Goals

Practical Skills

- Learn practical survival.
- Practice personal hygiene.
- Understand and apply good nutrition.
- Practice good exercise and sleep habits.
- Know how to grow, buy, and prepare food.
- Master cooking skills.
- Master clothing care, including laundering, replacing buttons, and mending.
- Develop wise buying habits.
- Know how to maintain a house and yard and realize the importance of doing so.
- Learn how to grow flowers and other plants to beautify your home.
- Know how to do basic repairs.
- Know whom to call when you need assistance in various areas.
- Realize that evil is in the world. Learn safety precautions and some self-defense.

Communication

- Know how to write letters, using proper forms of address.
- Know how to express ideas, opinions, and complaints in both oral and written forms.
- Understand and practice proper etiquette.
- Know how to read and follow directions.
- Know how to write and give directions.

Automobiles

- Learn to drive responsibly.
- Understand basic car maintenance.
- Know how to change a tire, check the battery, refill windshield washer fluid.
- Understand emergency road procedures.

Finances

- Understand that you are a steward of the gifts God has given you. Give liberally back to Him out of gratitude and love.
- Remember the poor.
- Understand that "the borrower is servant to the lender" (Proverbs 22:7).
- Learn how to live within your means.
- Learn to save money for the future.
- Understand the value of delayed gratification.
- Know how to prepare a budget and stick to it.
- Know how to set up accounts and balance a checkbook.
- Learn how to make change.
- Understand that contracts are binding; read everything carefully before you sign.
- Understand about interest (earned or charged).

Faith, Family, Relationships

- Learn respect for and obedience to God's commandments. Worship God alone. Revere His name. Honor the Sabbath. Value sexual purity, honesty, and obedience. Rejoice when God blesses others. Love others as you love yourself.
- Understand that all relationships take work to keep them healthy.
- Learn that marriage is a covenant relationship that is an unbreakable, threefold cord with God as its source of strength.
- Understand that love in any relationship means commitment, not simply feelings.
- Learn how to resolve conflicts in a compassionate and reasonable manner.
- Look to Jesus as the perfect example.
- Strive to live by the principles set forth in Scripture.
- Learn how to nurture and care for infants and children.
- Realize that children are a gift of the Lord.
- Learn to respect and appreciate people of all ages, abilities, colors, faiths, etc., as those made in the image of God.
- Learn that accepting a person is not condoning his or her bad or sinful behavior.
- Learn that disapproving of a person's behavior does not justify judging that person.
- Learn to use wisdom in choosing friends, realizing that "bad company corrupts good character" (1 Corinthians 15:33).

- Respect the property of others. If a borrowed item is damaged, replace it with a new one. Return borrowed items promptly.
- Do what you should without complaining, arguing, or making excuses.

Academics

General

- Know how to research and find information.
- Learn how to take notes from both oral presentations and written materials.
- Develop the ability to express yourself clearly in both speech and writing.
- Have a general understanding of logic.
- Read and discuss editorials with both peers and adults.

Language

- Develop writing excellence, using proper grammar.
- Know how to write creatively and persuasively.
- Display confidence and skill in public speaking.
- Read great classic literature.
- Write about and discuss literature.
- Read and understand Shakespeare.
- Read and write poetry.
- Learn to appreciate the beauty of the spoken and written word.
- Know how to write term papers, essays, reports, editorials, etc.
- Develop an extensive working vocabulary.
- Appreciate the Bible as a literary work.

Mathematics

- Develop confidence in applying mathematical knowledge to everyday life.
- Complete college-preparatory math to the level required for future goals.

Science

- Recognize the evidence of our Creator's design in everything around you. Wonder at His majesty as revealed through creation.

- Understand that God has given humanity stewardship over the earth and its creatures. Treat them accordingly, but never worship the creature rather than the Creator.
- Look at science as an exciting adventure of discovery.
- Read and study what has been discovered in several areas of science.
- Learn from your own observation and experimentation.
- Use reasoning skills to distinguish good science from bad science and truth from error.

History

- Understand how present world societies developed.
- Understand that history repeats itself and is thus a good indicator of future events.
- Understand the history of the United States.
- Study the history of Western civilization.
- Understand the Jewish roots of Christianity.
- Understand the origins and beliefs of other world cultures and religions.

Geography

- Have a general knowledge of world geography.
- Have a detailed knowledge of U.S. geography.
- Understand how geographic features affect climate and weather.
- Understand how the geographic features of an area affect its commerce, government, defense, self-sufficiency, natural resources, transportation, etc.
- Know how to read several types of maps: political, relief, contour, highway, street, etc.
- Know how to draw maps when giving directions or describing an area.
- Know how to spell the names of countries and major cities.
- Truly understand that people in other cultures think differently, act differently, and speak differently. Respect them and their language. Don't expect them to know English.

- Realize that evangelizing and Americanizing are not synonymous.

Government

- Read the Declaration of Independence and the U.S. Constitution.
- Understand the intent of the Founding Fathers.
- Read as many primary source documents as possible, such as the Federalist Papers, letters, essays.
- Understand how your federal, local, and state governments operate.
- Understand and participate in the electoral process.
- Understand your responsibilities and privileges as a citizen.
- Participate as a volunteer in church and/or community.
- Learn about governments in other countries.
- Know the differences between communism, socialism, capitalism, fascism, etc.
- Understand the differences between the American Revolution and other revolutions, and the philosophies behind them.

Foreign Languages

- Study at least one foreign language for at least two years; become as fluent as possible.
- Appreciate the culture of those who speak the language you study.
- Learn to speak, read, write, and listen with understanding in the language of your choice.
- If possible, correspond with a pen pal who speaks the language you are studying.

Bible and Philosophy

- Be familiar with all of Scripture.
- Utilize Scripture to guide you in life.
- Develop the habit of daily Bible reading.
- Learn to search the Scriptures for answers to perplexing questions.
- Recognize the Bible as an accurate historical record.
- Memorize portions of Scripture.

- Understand what other religions teach and how these beliefs compare with biblical truth.
- Understand the major worldviews, how they are manifested, and how they influence people's thoughts and actions.
- Learn to discern bias in other people's writing or speaking based on their philosophies.
- Realize that knowledgeable people don't know all the answers, just how to find them.
- Develop a genuine love for learning so that you will never want to stop learning.

Physical Education and Health

- Develop the habit of regular exercise.
- Develop skills in at least one sport.
- Learn first aid and CPR.
- Understand the health risks involved with alcohol, other drugs, unbiblical sexual relations, sedentary lifestyles, gluttony, and other risky behavior.

The Arts

- Develop the freedom and confidence to express yourself in creative ways.
- Learn to appreciate great music, art, literature, and theatre.
- Listen to works of classical composers.
- Listen to other types of music: traditional and modern jazz, spirituals, gospel and folk music, music from other nations, etc.
- Understand a little about the history and development of music in the Church.
- Learn at least several traditional hymns and understand their meanings.
- Become familiar with various styles and periods of art.
- View originals of master artwork if possible.
- Learn to sing and/or play an instrument.
- Learn basic drawing skills; do some kind of art or craft for recreation or useful labor.
- Attend live dramatic performances.
- Learn to appreciate drama as a communicative art form that can be useful to your church.

- Understand that music, art, drama, and other art forms are expressions of the cultures and worldviews represented.
- Understand that the arts and entertainment are powerful forces for change in society.
- Learn to discern the messages behind the arts that you experience.
- Learn to use wisdom in choosing forms of entertainment.
- Learn to keep entertainment in its proper place.

Chapter 4

A Tour of Homeschool High

We have begun to see an increase in home school applications and expect this will rise as the movement has grown extensively and the wave of high school age students is now seeking college admission.

Martha H. Moore, Associate Director of Admissions,
University of Illinois at Urbana-Champaign

Welcome to Homeschool High, where parents comprise the majority of the administration, faculty, and staff. Consequently there is no need for an organizational chart. You know who you are. As for job titles, adopt them all. The responsibilities are yours, but you are free to delegate any of them you wish. Let me show you your new offices. Our tour begins in the administration wing.

Office of Planning and Budget

Our first stop is the office of planning and budget, which performs vital tasks to keep the school running smoothly. It is in charge of determining the school calendar—including vacation breaks—as well as overseeing daily class schedules, giving final approval for curriculum and course selection, coordinating schedules with the elementary and junior high schools, and budgeting money to cover faculty and staff stipends, curriculum, and building operations. Most of these tasks are self-explanatory. However, there are a few areas where you might benefit from hearing about the experiences of other homeschool administrators.

Balancing Daily Schedules

Experienced homeschoolers often advise beginners to "homeschool" rather than "school at home." In other words, you should not try to duplicate a typical day at school, with fifty minutes for each subject, unless your umbrella school or state law requires it. Your family's lifestyle and your students' needs and preferences should determine your homeschooling schedule and methods. Stay focused but remain flexible.

Scheduling is especially challenging in large families where parents have less time to spend with their high-school students because younger children require more of their attention. Beth Vellalos, a homeschooling mother of five, believes in encouraging her students to be almost completely independent learners in high school, which she feels helps prepare them for college and adulthood. Since she sees herself more as a tutor for her high schoolers, she does not allow them to interrupt her elementary school teaching in the morning. She makes herself available to the older children in the afternoon.

Begin the school day early if you can. Even though I have always considered myself more of a "night person," homeschooling made it eminently clear that the old adage is true: An ounce of morning is worth a pound of afternoon. Christine and I found that we got much more schooling done when we started early, and our morning hours actually seemed to last longer.

Home high school graduate Christina Musselman describes how her school days were structured:

> *We would begin our day with breakfast together at 7:30 in the morning. Mom didn't allow us to stay in our pajamas, even though we usually stayed in the house. Rather, she expected us to be fully ready to study by the time breakfast was served.*
>
> *Every Monday she gave us an "assignment sheet" that listed the things we had to get done by the week's end: papers to be written, exercises to be done (usually for math), and, most important, books to be read.*
>
> *We spent about two hours together each morning reading books for history and doing math exercises. Then we would go our separate ways, and Catherine and I would work on our assignment sheets until lunchtime…. During the time apart, Catherine and I would read books, write papers, and fill out unlabeled maps Mom assigned to us.*

Debbie, Christie and Catherine's mom, gave her daughters full responsibility for having their assignments completed on time. Her self-designed curriculum required a great deal of reading. The Musselmans held school four days and volunteered one day each week at a local homeless shelter.

If your students have extracurricular activities or outside jobs, take that fact into account in your planning. Your students will need self-discipline to combine school with other commitments. Help them learn how to set priorities and to use their time wisely, studying smart instead of studying long. Encourage them to realize their limitations and limit their activities accordingly.

Your teens also may need your assistance in dealing with their employers about work schedules. Homeschoolers are popular employees because they are usually reliable and available to work during hours when other students are in school. If you are not careful, supervisors might take advantage and intrude on your school time. Your students' most productive hours should be reserved for school, no matter what times employers want them to work. Encourage your teens to be reasonable and cooperative yet respectfully firm about not letting work interfere with their studies. No job is worth sacrificing their education.

I realize homeschooling is very hard work, and I admire those who persist and achieve solid academic results.

Geoffrey Gould, Director of
Undergraduate Admissions,
Binghamton University

Many homeschool families operate home businesses, with the whole family helping, and some students start their own businesses. This is one of the best ways to develop many of the skills necessary for college and adult life, such as responsibility, organization, public relations, money management, marketing, diligence, and persistence. Realize, however, that business obligations limit the time available for studying traditional subjects.

As you plan your daily schedule, pay attention to the needs of your whole family and try to find a balance between being firm most of the time and being flexible when the need arises. The first way to alleviate problems with daily schedules is through wise course selection.

Reasonable Course Selection

Because homeschoolers strive for excellence, we often tend to go overboard, thinking we can accomplish much more than is possible in the traditional four years of high school. For example, I loved to plan but tended to underestimate the time it would take to finish assignments and projects. I was determined to cover the required courses for every college Christine might attend but was not willing to leave out electives like art history, drawing, drama, sewing, and music appreciation. Christine was not any better. She was like a sponge, thirsty to soak up all the knowledge in her path (except for algebra). She never had fewer than seven subjects, and I planned too much for most of them. Consequently, I was continually frustrated when we didn't finish all the wonderful learning adventures I had envisioned in the inadequate amount of time I had allotted.

If you are like me, try to control yourself. There is an abundance of information to discover with your students, but you cannot do it all in four years. Allow your students some time, especially in the afternoons, for reading, exploring, and discovering some gems of knowledge on their own. Not everything they learn has to be for credit, but by all means, give credit where you can. If you cover the basics, instill in your children a sense of responsibility for their own education, and teach them how to learn, you will have done your job.

Now we will proceed to the next office, where the curriculum review committee meets at least once a year.

Curriculum Review Committee

The curriculum review committee is composed of the principal, the homeroom teacher, and the high school students. In other words, parents and teens select all the textbooks and other resources here at Homeschool High. Please read the following guidelines before your first committee meeting convenes.

Finding and Selecting Curriculum

To find the best teaching resources for your homeschool, you need to do some research. Ask the opinions of fellow homeschoolers and read homeschooling magazines for their product reviews. Also refer to homeschool and general school catalogs and curriculum guides. If you would rather design your own courses, refer to Mary Schofield's *The High School Handbook: Junior and Senior High School at Home* or Barbara Shelton's *Senior High: A Home Designed Form+U+La*. (See Appendix B under "Homeschooling Information, Organizations, and Websites.")

I preferred an eclectic curriculum, so each year I reviewed various books and teaching methods for each subject. Excellent high school books are available from many publishers. You also should consider using some books written for the college level, especially during the last two years of high school. Check for used copies at college bookstores and library book sales. A visit to a local community college bookstore may be helpful in developing your curriculum, too. Either you can purchase books there for use in your homeschool or you can use their books as guides to make sure you are covering subjects adequately. The table of contents should list the main areas you need to cover.

Homeschool conferences and bookfairs are good places to find various books and teaching resources. However, it is difficult to thoroughly review books in those settings. If you can, take some time to go over materials at home before you buy them. I used to order copies of several different books to review each year during February. That gave me plenty of time to choose curriculum for the following year. One of the publishers I ordered from used to allow a thirty-day review period for homeschooling customers, but now it charges restocking fees if you return its publications. If

[Students] should strive to present a transcript with the most challenging course of study possible, do well in these courses, be active in extra curricular activities if available, be involved in the community, come to campus for an interview, and write a solid essay/ personal statement. In short, they should do whatever they can to let the admissions committee know that they can successfully balance studying in a rigorous academic program with taking an active role in a campus community.

David Maltby,
Dean of Enrollment,
William Jewell College

publishers will not allow a review period, try to find other homeschoolers or local schools that own the books you want to see. Ask whether you can borrow the materials for a week or two. If not, at least try to review them on location and have your students examine them, too. Then when you attend conferences, you will not have to spend precious time leafing through textbooks.

Also realize that what works for one student will not necessarily work for another. For example, thousands of homeschoolers love Saxon math; others, particularly creative types, find it tedious. If you have doubts about a math curriculum, borrow a book and go through a few lessons with your student. That will tell you more than dozens of reviews. If you cannot find a book to borrow, write or call the publisher and ask for a sample lesson. Some might not be willing to send one, but if you do not ask, you will never know.

Going through a lesson or two will help in other types of curriculum as well. A history book might appear to be fascinating, based on the pictures, captions, and headings. However, the proof is in the actual chapter content and the discussion questions. Some texts discourage a love of history because they bore students by spouting endless facts that have to be regurgitated later. Most students need something on which to hang the information. History is about living, breathing people who made an impact on the cultures of their time. Biographies, original writings, and historical fiction can all be used to help students understand historical figures and periods.

When choosing curriculum, always keep your students' interests, abilities, and learning styles in mind. Our daughter Christine is primarily an auditory learner, which made choosing high school materials especially challenging. (Learning styles are discussed in several homeschooling books, curriculum guides, and magazines, so I will not discuss them here.) Also be aware of your own teaching style in determining the best materials to use.

Share but Beware

Homeschool curriculum review committees need to be aware of a growing problem within their ranks. I want to both caution and admonish you to make sure that you keep track of what you borrow and lend. Homeschoolers are known for their helpfulness and generosity but are notorious for their habit of borrowing and not returning books. I hate to make that generalization, but so many of us have lost books in this way that I feel compelled to say it. We handle so many books that we can easily forget what we borrowed from whom. Keep track of your own books and hold borrowers accountable to return them. If you are the borrower, return what you have borrowed in a timely manner. Write notes to yourself or keep a borrowing and lending log. Do not become either a victim or an offender. As all homeschoolers know, books are expensive, precious, and sometimes irreplaceable. Also, if a book is damaged while in your care, you should repair or replace it.

Following these guidelines should help your annual or biannual committee meetings go smoothly.

Next is our home guidance office. We offer a separate tour of that office, if you are interested, in chapter 6. Right now we will visit the office of special programs. Relax while I describe what happens here.

Office of Special Programs

As with any good school, Homeschool High is dedicated to providing the best education for all of its students. Here you will administer special academic programs for those students who need extra help learning and for those who require extra challenges to remain interested. Here is an article detailing other home educators' experiences with these students. Their insights might help you.

Helping Students with Special Needs

Homeschooling is often the best alternative for students with special needs because parents can give them more personal attention and allow them to learn at their own pace. The problems these students experience vary and have dozens of labels attached to them, such as ADD, ADHD, dyslexic, slow, uncoordinated. Personally, I think the only value in labeling students' *needs* is to determine the best course of action. A *student* should never be labeled.

Often needs go unnoticed. For example, children and teens may have trouble reading or playing sports because of undetected vision problems. Some types of problems with tracking and focusing are not detected in routine eye examinations. One high school student I know—I will call him Jim—still has trouble reading because his eyes do not work together the way they should. Jim's parents have taken him to a behavioral optometrist, who has been able to help him improve his reading through vision therapy. After initial success, Jim suffered a huge setback with his vision after oral surgery and orthodontics. (Apparently, stress to one portion of the facial muscles affects the others.)

Additional therapy and vision exercises are now helping Jim to gain back the ground he lost. His mother has found that giving Jim reading that has immediate, practical application is the best for him. For example, whenever they buy a piece of electronic equipment, Jim reads the directions, sets it up, and teaches the family how to use it. He is also beginning to take classes at the local community college, which is boosting his self-confidence and helping to fill his learning gaps.

Another young man's lack of coordination resulted in an inability to play sports, which prompted incessant ridicule from his schoolmates. He also suffered from an undetected vision problem. After eye surgery followed by therapy, he was just as coordinated as his classmates.

Diet can also affect students' learning and behavior. Before we changed her diet, Christine—an active and extremely creative child—would probably have been labeled ADD or hyperactive if she had been assessed. We discovered that her behavioral and learning problems were entirely food-based. Through eliminating certain foods and then adding them back one at a time, we discovered that she could not tolerate artificial colors, artificial flavors, or preservatives (which are really nonfoods). Now, as an adult, she still has to be careful of these additives. They affect her mood and limit her ability to focus on whatever she is doing. In her teens, she also developed an allergy to dairy products. Consuming dairy products was detrimental to her health and to her learning, so she eliminated them from her diet.

Although schools tend to favor use of the drug Ritalin for students who have difficulty settling down and concentrating, many parents are trying alternatives, such as an altered diet and/or supplementation with vitamins and minerals. Investigate your options and consult health and education professionals to determine what is best if your student suffers from hyperactivity or learning disorders. Many books are available to help get you started. (See Appendix B.)

Students often have learning problems that cannot be helped by altering their diets or solving visual problems. There are many different types of learning disabilities, and they require various kinds of attention. Kyle Hughes, the coordinator of special education programs at a public high school and an instructor at Metro State College, kindly offered her advice for those homeschoolers who are teaching teens with learning disabilities. She identifies four actions as the most important ones to take:

I am dyslexic. I was told in high school that I would never get a diploma.... In my second year of college, it was the same thing...and then again in graduate school. The sad part of dyslexia is that two-thirds will take it. Their dreams are destroyed. But I had a mother who never gave up on me.

Mike Bolinsky, Owner of Science Projects and a former Science Teacher of the Year

1. Get a really good assessment so that you will know the type of learning disability and how it impacts the student academically.
2. Access the people who can tell you the specific strategies for your student's disability (usually those who do the assessment).
3. Teach your students self-determination skills so they can advocate for themselves and be able to access services when they get to college.
4. Be knowledgeable about the resources available to those who are enrolled part-time in a public high school, especially postsecondary options such as vocational training.

A thorough evaluation determines whether or not students are eligible for special education programs. Hughes mentioned that many parents of children with documented learning disabilities will homeschool their children and take them to a local school for special education support or speech-language support as part of the school day. Each student who qualifies for special education will have an IEP (individual education plan) developed. An IEP details the assessments completed to document the learning disability, maps out goals and objectives to support learning for the student, and indicates services to be provided for the student through the special education process.

Some students with learning disabilities will not qualify for special education but will be eligible for a 504 Plan, which is part of the federally mandated Americans With Disabilities Act (ADA) of 1990. Hughes says that a 504 Plan allows students to benefit from accommodations in high school and college. These might include access to notes or a note taker, extra time to complete assignments or work, oral tests or extended time for tests, extended time for ACT and SAT exams, and help in the college's writing center. What colleges will not do for these students is alter the college curriculum so that it changes the learning outcome. (This type of change is called a "modification.") For instance, they will not provide books at a lower reading level or change course requirements.

Students should understand their own strengths and challenges as learners and be able to access the help they need. This is what Hughes calls self-determination. For instance, if students know that they learn best at the front of a classroom, they should sit there. If they need a few extra seconds to process their thoughts before answering a question, they should make their instructors aware of this.

Carla Williams, whose son has a learning disability, notes that students need to be able to express both orally and in writing what their disabilities are and what their needs will be in college. "You won't be there to explain it to every professor," she says. "Students should be able to explain how they have learned to overcome their learning problems and what they're still working on. If they have been tested to verify the disability, have copies of all the paperwork available for colleges." Williams also recommends having your students keep journals to record methods that succeed, such as particular problem-solving methods and why they are successful.

If your students are enrolled part-time in public high school, Hughes recommends considering postsecondary options to supplement your home training and any special education help you may receive. With vocational training so readily available, today's high school students with learning disabilities have a decided advantage over those who grew up twenty years ago. Hughes named several programs that her school's students participate in off campus, including med-prep, auto mechanics, aviation, computer technology, and computer graphics. She says, "There's a whole level of training that's available before students leave high school, if they want to access that."

To aid you in teaching your students with learning disabilities, Hughes provided a list of resources that she recommends. It is included under "Learning Differences" in Appendix B.

With a thorough understanding of your students' learning problems and the right help and information, you should be able to provide a good home education for your teens who have learning disabilities.

Helping Students with Special Talents

Homeschooling offers many benefits for students with special abilities who often feel like misfits in schools where being smart is not considered cool. If you have students who are highly intelligent or especially talented in one area, turn them loose to explore and develop their talents, to build, create, write, or whatever. Give them opportunities to study college-level materials, work with experts in their fields of interest, and sit for AP and/or CLEP exams to earn college credit. However, while giving them this freedom, see that they do not neglect essential parts of their education because of their preferences. For example, do not allow your budding engineers to spend all their time on math and science. See that they learn how to write.

Also make sure that they do not view themselves as superior to others because of their God-given talents. As Sharon Grimes says, "Every child has special gifts, just as all of us have learning disabilities." (See Appendix B for resources.)

Now, if everyone has finished reading, we will continue our tour. The last office we will visit in the administration wing is the office of public relations.

Office of Public Relations

Public relations can be a tough job, especially at Homeschool High, but take heart. If you are new at this, many have gone before you and are willing to offer their advice. Even if you have handled public criticism at the elementary and junior high levels, the following tips on public relations may help you muster your courage again.

Dealing with the Public

As you probably know, most homeschoolers have been reproached by relatives, friends, or perfect strangers for their decision to educate their own children. The most memorable of my own experiences was at a dinner with a large group of people. The conversation turned to recent events at the junior high school, where a teacher had been conducting classes in Eastern meditation, an unpopular girl had succeeded in committing suicide after several attempts, and a drug bust had occurred inside the school. Suddenly the speaker turned to me and stated emphatically, "But you can't shelter them!"

I did not respond, but the words would have been laughable if not for the tragic situation. Not shelter my child from drugs, suicide, paganism, and the other prevalent evils of foul language and sexual pressures? Why would I even consider placing her in such an environment? What seems so clear to homeschool parents is hard for others to comprehend. Just because most of the country educates through public schools does not mean everyone should.

If you have homeschooled for any length of time, I am sure you have faced similar criticism from family, friends, or neighbors. The best way to deal with it is to remain courageous in your convictions. You know you are doing what is best for your children. Somehow you have to get over worrying about what other people think. Give your children the best education you possibly can and ignore the criticism.

Beth Vellalos agrees. "I think it really depends on what your conviction is. Why are you homeschooling? If you're homeschooling because you can do better than the [traditional school] teacher can, at some point it's going to occur that the teacher can do better than you.... If you're homeschooling because you believe it's your responsibility to teach your children and the best environment for them is in the home, that's not going to change."

I realize it is not easy to ignore those outspoken relatives and friends who feel they have a right to interfere. So do what you can to help them understand the advantages that your homeschooled children are enjoying. Contact the National Home Education Research Institute and buy a copy of their latest research to show to doubters. Show your friends and relatives one of the many other good books about homeschooling and tell them what the experts are saying. For example, Michael Farris has observed that not many traditional students are "really ready to go into the adult world." He says that, in his experience, young people who are homeschooled through high school "are much more like adults when they get done than more traditional students are."

> *I do think homeschoolers are an interesting population, but I don't think they're different. Some people really look at them in a different light, as if they're sort of aberrations or they have a problem or something. I think...there's something they can bring to this campus. Their experience enhances. Other students have been in a very strict structure all their lives, so I think it makes a nice little mix....*
>
> Kerry Durgin, Director of Admissions, Hood College

Cara Transtrom, former homeschooler and admissions counselor at Dickinson State University, has noticed the same thing. "Something I frequently observe with homeschoolers is that they usually come prepped for life in the adult world.... I think that in homeschooling you mature emotionally somewhat faster and you are a little less peer dependent, which enables you to be a clearer leader."

If you want more statistics to back you up, use this book to convince your critics that colleges are interested in homeschoolers because they have proven to be excellent students and fine individuals. If nothing convinces your critics, just try to keep peace by avoiding the subject.

What if criticism is causing you to doubt your decision to homeschool? What if you are unsure of your abilities? Read the rest of this book and then take some time to get away from dissenting voices. Read other materials about homeschooling. Talk to some homeschoolers. Attend a homeschool conference. Then visit some high schools, either alone or with your students. Finally, discuss your options as a family. Christians, pray about your decision. Be silent before God, and He will show you His will for the children He has given you to raise.

It may be difficult at times, but be encouraged that public relations is only a small part of your administrative workload, and with the continued success of homeschoolers, the tide of public opinion is turning in your favor.

Now we will proceed to the educational wing, which houses faculty offices and classrooms. Please watch your step.

Faculty Offices

We are now looking at the offices for the various faculty members. Not all of these offices will necessarily be in use at any one time. However, they are available should you need them. You as homeroom teachers will have primary responsibility for coordinating educational activities and delegating various teaching tasks to the rest of the faculty. Now, if you would, please join me in the faculty lounge for a cool drink, and we will discuss Homeschool High's faculty guidelines as a preview to our upcoming discussion of teaching high school subject areas. (See chapter 5.)

Faculty Guidelines

As homeschool teachers know, a great deal of planning and preparation time is required to teach your children. Having to juggle planning, teaching, and grading with other responsibilities is also a struggle.

Unless students are working independently, parents have to stay at least one step ahead of their students in order to teach subjects and correct student work. When I taught Christine geometry, I reviewed each lesson and worked through the most difficult problems myself first to make sure that I could explain anything she did not understand. Then I taught each day's lesson. She worked some of the problems as I watched and then completed the rest independently. The book we used, *Discovering Geometry*, has many problems and projects designed for students working in groups, so it made sense for me to work with Christine, since there were no other students in our "class." Christine and I had so much fun doing geometry together that it became one of our best memories in all the four years of high school. Many parents do not have time for this, and so they use Saxon or another program that can be largely self-taught.

Students who have developed self-motivation and self-discipline may relieve their parents of much of the teaching load by essentially directing their own education. "Then," says Jane Williams, "as learning resource manager, the parent's job is to research and locate the best curriculum materials based on the interests of the student. Determine what subjects your student wishes to study, and together explore all the mediums for learning those subjects: textbooks, supplementary books, documentaries, books on tape, hands-on applications, distance learning, college courses available for the high school student, etc."

Even if your students work independently, try to work through a subject or two with them, especially foreign languages, so that you can practice speaking together. Also, supplement your curriculum with books related to study topics that can be read aloud. Have students practice recounting both orally and in writing what they have learned. Give them assignments that require research in a college library and/or interviews with local experts before they can write a paper or give a speech. As experienced homeschoolers know, all of life presents teachable moments, so include real-life activities wherever possible. You also should try to let your students take a few classes from someone other than yourself.

Adjunct Faculty

To alleviate the homeschool teacher's workload, it is often advisable to hire adjunct faculty. These may be community college or college teachers, private tutors, local experts, instructors for local organizations, the students themselves, and even (excuse the personification) textbooks.

Many colleges recommend that students complete some dual-enrollment classes during high school. These are college-level classes that allow students to receive high school and college credit simultaneously. Beth Vellalos homeschools in Hawaii and has used dual-enrollment courses to supplement her homeschool curriculum, especially in the area of science. However, she does not think it advisable to send your teens to college for a difficult course like chemistry without some prior exposure to the subject. She had her sons view the high school chemistry videotapes from The Teaching Company before they took college chemistry at Hawaii Pacific University. (See chapter 6 for more information on dual enrollment.)

[Homeschoolers] have developed some study skills that are critical to success in college, such as managing their study time wisely and being comfortable with studying on their own outside of class.

Carlos Garces, Senior Assistant
Director of Admissions,
Marquette University

You can find tutors and local experts through your homeschool organization, local high schools and colleges, or your place of worship. Knowing the subject matter is not enough to recommend a tutor or other teacher. Make sure that the candidate knows how to teach. Communicate your expectations clearly, and periodically ask your students how well they think it is working.

One homeschooler I met was being tutored in algebra, but she was not happy with the tutor. When I asked her why, she said that when she had trouble with a problem, the tutor would do the problem for her instead of letting her work through it with his guidance. She said, "I'm not learning how to do it myself." Keep tabs on the tutoring or other learning situation, and change teachers if necessary.

With a little research in the local community, your students should be able to find other interesting classes to supplement their basic high school curriculum and expose them to a variety of teaching styles.

Students might also take advantage of one of the best learning methods—teaching. They can study with friends or help siblings with subjects they have already completed, which will help them to review. While she was in college, Christine learned the value of helping others to study. History comes easily to her, so her friend asked for help. Every week Christine went over the lessons and drilled her friend on them. As a result, both Christine and her friend learned the material thoroughly and received A's in the course. Music theory, on the other hand, was more difficult for Christine, so she sought the help of friends who understood it better. Then she studied with another friend who was struggling. When she explained things to him, they became clearer to her.

Our admissions committee is particularly impressed with those homeschoolers who take courses at their local colleges for high school credit.

Mike Konopski,
Georgetown College

So if your students want to learn a subject better, they should find someone to teach. If they cannot find pupils, suggest that they imagine teaching the subject and then write or record on tape what they would say to teach another. Organizing topics in this way will help them to retain information and to understand concepts better.

Textbooks can also be employed as adjunct instructors. Many home high schoolers use traditional textbooks for the majority of their curriculum. Parents often supplement these with other resources and may eliminate textbook material that is repetitive, irrelevant, or unnecessary. Others require their students to complete textbooks from cover to cover. When you assign a textbook, think about your students' learning goals and give them lists of questions to answer for each chapter or section. At this level, your questions should be thought provoking, and you should require most answers in essay or oral form. Unless a textbook is extremely well written, students shouldn't need to read every word to glean important information. Encourage them to skim where they can and to save in-depth reading for literature, theology, philosophy, and other subjects that require more contemplation.

We are running out of time, so we will not be able to tour the classrooms today. Suffice it to say that Homeschool High has a variety of learning venues. Students study here under all sorts of conditions, both inside and outside the building. Two of their favorite study hangouts are the cafeteria (or kitchen) and their personal study rooms (otherwise known as their bedrooms).

I hope everyone is refreshed. Take your drinks with you, if you like, and proceed through the door at the end of the hall to the gym.

Physical Education Department

Although physical education activities are somewhat limited at Homeschool High, especially in the area of team sports, it is possible to form cooperative arrangements with other home high schools, traditional schools, or community sports teams. Here are our sports guidelines and NCAA (National Collegiate Athletic Association) eligibility requirements. We will continue our tour when you have finished perusing them.

Team Sports and NCAA Eligibility

Would you like your students to play team sports? If you live in an area with a large number of homeschoolers, you can have your own homeschool sports program using volunteer and/or paid help. For instance, Denver has teams in basketball, soccer, baseball, volleyball, and softball. Often students can participate in city or county leagues as well. In some states, homeschoolers can even participate in public or private school sports programs. Contact your local public or private schools to find out whether they will allow homeschoolers to compete on their teams.

For those who are serious about playing competitive sports in college, standardized test scores and course selection are even more important than team experience. The NCAA has strict regulations for athletic eligibility, all relating to academics. Eligibility requirements are the same for homeschoolers as for traditional students, but the certification procedure is different.

Students who want to participate on NCAA Division I or Division II teams must complete the core of courses required by the NCAA if they want to qualify academically for these teams. College coaches will assess athletic ability and eligibility.

According to the NCAA, home-educated athletes must meet initial eligibility requirements by being certified through the initial-eligibility waiver process, which is administered by the NCAA national office. Your students' NCAA Division I or Division II college must submit the waiver application directly to the NCAA. According to the NCAA[1], the waiver application must include

- *Homeschool transcript*
- *ACT/SAT test score*
- *Evidence of outside assessment, if available (tutors, tests graded by an outside agency, etc.)*
- *Evidence that homeschooling was conducted in accordance with applicable state laws*
- *Detailed description of homeschool teaching environment (e.g., name of instructor(s), method of instruction, number of hours of instruction per day)*
- *List of titles of all textbooks for all homeschool courses*
- *Copies of the table of contents for textbooks utilized in core courses (a sampling)*
- *Samples of work completed (tests, papers) by the student*
- *Initial-Eligibility Certification Report (formerly Form 48-C) from the NCAA Initial-Eligibility Clearinghouse (only if student attended some traditional schooling)*

The NCAA seems to be somewhat flexible with students who do not have all of this documentation, but students must complete the required core curriculum, provide ACT/SAT results, and follow state homeschooling laws. It is important to note that certain courses will not qualify for core requirements, according to the NCAA website, including "courses completed during eighth grade, correspondence courses, internet courses, independent study courses and credit awarded through credit-by-exam." For more information, consult the current "NCAA Guide for the College-Bound Student-Athlete" available on the NCAA website and at local high schools. Also refer to the "NCAA Initial-Eligibility Procedures for Home-Schooled Student-Athletes" (available on the NCAA website). For further questions about homeschooling as it relates to NCAA legislation and initial eligibility requirements, contact

Membership Services Department
NCAA
PO Box 6222
Indianapolis, IN 46206-6222
Phone: 317-917-6222
Website: www.ncaa.org

Even if your students lack team experience during high school, they may still succeed as college athletes. Brent Rudin, Director of Admissions at Cornerstone University, reported that the school had one homeschooler who competed in cross-country and became their college's first All-American athlete. He reports, "She never ran on a cross-country team until she arrived here."

Once everyone is ready, we will proceed to our office of nonacademic activities. Follow me, please.

Office of Nonacademic Activities

You may be surprised that I have led you outside. Frankly, Homeschool High is just not large enough to house all the facilities needed for extracurricular activities, so our school participates in the local, and sometimes the world, community. Your job is to help your students discover and tap into some of the many opportunities available to them. Here are some strategies to help you get started.

Well-chosen extracurricular activities serve to enhance the learning process and develop leadership and social skills. Encourage students to get involved in activities, jobs, and community service, especially in their areas of interest. Such experiences can even help students define their goals for the future. For example, Christine thought she wanted to be an elementary school teacher, but after two years as a Sunday school teacher, she realized that five days a week in the classroom was not for her. Then she taught summer classes in children's theatre, which helped determine her major.

Try to guide your students to activities that will help them grow. Encourage them to branch out of their comfort zone by trying something new or by challenging one of their fears. If your students tend to be shy or introverted, get them out serving others. It is amazing how helping someone who is less blessed than they are can make people forget their own fears and problems.

Colleges seek students who are involved in their schools and communities. Craig Gould of Rocky Mountain College says, "Performing well on [standardized tests] greatly improves the chance of acceptance. But I'm also looking for 'what will the student contribute to the college community.' That is where the experiences outside of books, grades, and scores become important."

Without the resources of public schools, homeschoolers have to make a special effort to participate in volunteer, church, club, music, and sports activities. In the community, they might volunteer at homeless shelters, nursing homes, churches, hospitals, political campaign offices, nature centers, etc. They might help elderly couples or widows with yard work, teach reading to illiterate adults, tutor inner-city children, help at food banks, glean fields (collect leftover produce after harvest) for the poor, or volunteer at the county extension service office. The 4-H program and scouting are other popular activities that do not require students to be in a school setting. Both programs encourage students to develop leadership skills. Other possible activities include short-term mission trips or inner-city missions.

Orchestra and choir participation can be arranged if someone is willing to spearhead the project. In the Denver area, where we live, a homeschool choir and orchestra are conducted by professional musicians and coordinated by a homeschool mom. All students pay a fee for sheet music and for the directors' stipends. Singing with the choir was a highlight of Christine's high school years.

Even if group activities are not available in your area, your children can develop skills in music or another area of interest. One student at my daughter's college had become so adept at playing the hammered dulcimer that she won a music scholarship, even though the college had no program for that instrument. The college arranged for the girl to continue studying with an outside teacher and featured her unique talent in musical productions and tours.

If you and your students work together to select worthwhile extracurricular activities, the high school years will be more rewarding for everyone and your students will be better prepared to contribute to society as adults.

The very last stop on our tour is custodial services. You may not find it the most exciting job in the school, but it is your responsibility and a vital link to keeping the institution running smoothly.

Custodial Services

Okay, is everyone here? Be careful not to hit your head on the pail hanging from that hook. This is where all the tools for keeping Homeschool High neat, clean, and in good repair are stored. You will visit here often, but maybe not so often as you did before you came to work here because you will be busy. Just remember that one advantage of being the manager of custodial services is that you have the power to delegate. Be sure to enlist help from the elementary and junior high school as well as from high school staff and students. Here are some homeschool maintenance tips from those who have gone before:

First of all, everyone makes messes, so everyone should help maintain your school in the best condition possible. Delegate jobs based on the interests and abilities of your whole family and rotate unpleasant tasks. Have your children keep their books and supplies in one place, possibly in a bag or bin that they can carry to wherever they will be studying. Young children should be taught to pick up their toys. Clutter, as cleaning expert Don Aslett teaches, is your worst enemy when trying to clean. Get rid of anything you do not really need and organize the rest. Homeschool dads, do your part by helping wherever you can. It is especially important for you to fix anything that breaks (or delegate that task) as soon as possible. Leaving broken fixtures or other objects unrepaired will just make the problems worse and could cause injuries.

Since some may stereotype homeschoolers as being isolated, it's important to be involved in things, both within and without the homeschool circle, that develop and suggest good people skills and interest in being active.

Bruce Campbell, Alumni Director and Internal Homeschool Expert, Houghton College

Needless to say, you are not likely to have a perfect house. When you homeschool, other activities often have to take a backseat.

Tamie Goggans's ten children range from preschool to college age. When I asked Goggans how she does it all, she replied, "That is extremely challenging.... The house ends up coming last. I have to constantly put before me to do the things that are eternal. People are eternal. Souls are eternal. So we deal with spiritual and character matters first." Goggans said that education is also a high priority in her household because of the scriptural admonition to seek wisdom and knowledge.

Other large families have had to make similar concessions. Cara Transtrom, who graduated from her homeschool in 1989, is one of eight children. She believes that her mother's conviction that people matter more than things is a key to her homeschooling success. "We tried to have a picked-up house...and keep our lives in order, and so forth. But anytime that a thing or a person came into conflict, the thing went and the person remained of primary importance."

Transtrom says that her mom also had to learn to say no to many opportunities to be involved outside her home:

> *Sometimes homeschool moms have trouble...with this because they're seen sometimes as model Christian people and therefore churches and individuals try to latch onto them for say, women's ministries or [hosting] women's luncheons.... But Mom, I think, made a decision that God had called her first to her family for that time period.*

Do your best with custodial tasks, and then if things are not as clean as you would like, realize that homeschooling does not last forever. Enjoy your children while you can.

There you have it. Our tour of Homeschool High is complete. Please proceed to the next chapter to receive teacher training from college professionals and homeschool leaders.

Instruct a wise man and he will be wiser still; teach a righteous man and he will add to his learning. The fear of the Lord is the beginning of wisdom, and knowledge of the Holy One is understanding.

Proverbs 9:9–10 NIV

---

1. National Collegiate Athletic Association. "Guide for the Student Athlete." http://www.ncaa.org/eligibility/cbsa/home_school.html (30 Sept. 2003).

Chapter 5

High School Course Work

Areas of math, science, and foreign language seem to pose the greatest difficulty. Even when a homeschool student has a strong background in science, it is often a hard thing to document well. For our application needs, we prefer the students to be as descriptive as possible about what they have been studying. Including a bibliography is also extremely helpful.

Natalie Arnold, Assistant Director of Admissions,
St. John's College, New Mexico

The thought of teaching high school subjects fills many homeschool parents with trepidation. However, most of you should be able to handle it with the right materials, a little extra help, or both.

What should students learn in high school? Whether you use traditional textbooks, unit studies, or another approach, most homeschool and college experts would agree that students should master basic skills from several disciplines, including language arts (reading, literature, writing, grammar, and speech), math, science, social studies, foreign languages, and the arts. Language arts—especially the communication skills of reading and writing—are foundational to a good education.

Literature

At the high school level, students should be reading and interpreting literature, including novels, essays, and poetry. Be sure to give them exposure to the classics as well as to important modern literature. David Crabtree, President of Gutenberg College, has noticed that some homeschoolers have not read enough outside our time period, especially well-known works.

Consider carefully what literature you assign to your students. It is best if you have read it yourself, as then you will know what your students are reading and can enter into lively discussions with them.

Debbie Musselman spent most of her class preparation reviewing books for her "living books" curriculum. She read everything she ever assigned to her children. That way she could discuss the books with them and make sure they had both read and understood what was presented. She timed her own reading in order to estimate the time it would take her daughters to read each book. (She allowed extra time for them.) Besides reading individually, Musselman and her children read aloud every day. This provided not only information but also memorable family times. Christina describes one such day this way:

Snow was falling outside our living room window. Each of us had a hot drink in our hands and were huddled together under a blanket…. Mom was reading to us from

The Silver Branch, *a historical novel set in ancient Greece. My sister and I listened as Mom's voice painted the scene with the words she read…. Suddenly, [we] were transported from within the four walls of our living room to faraway Greece. We watched as history took its course. No longer names and dates and places on a page, but living beings and real events we could see and feel.*

Reading aloud does not have to stop when your children grow up. No matter what your children's ages, you should take time to read aloud as a family. Infants enjoy the rhythmic music of well-written words. I began reading to Christine when she was four months old, and from her response, I realized that I could have started sooner. Because she had always been read to, Christine learned to express herself well while still very young with a vocabulary that was larger than that of most children her age. Reading together was still one of our family's favorite activities even when Christine was in college.

Those who have been admitted have had very high SAT or ACT scores, indicating strong academic preparation, particularly in English literature. Those who have not been admitted have shown a very narrow focus in their high school curriculum, especially in the material they read while in high school.

Suellen Ofe, Vice President for Enrollment Management, Huntingdon College

Musselman says, "I like what we did in terms of reading and narrating back and not focusing on a lot of memorization, because it made the children read carefully and think about what they were reading. It made them interact with the literature as opposed to just parroting back. We really tried to emphasize 'read it once and read to learn.' And Christie found as she went through her first year of college—even with the honors program classes—that that training has stood her in good stead. It eliminates a lot of work in the long run." Musselman is referring to Charlotte Mason's method of having children repeat to the teacher in their own words what they have just read.

Literature anthologies give students a sampling of great writing, but it is more important for them to read entire works at the high school level. Find out which longer works are represented in the best anthologies and choose from among them. Also, see Appendix D for recommendations from a veteran English professor and fellow homeschoolers.

Tamie Goggans has her children go through one literature anthology from a textbook company so that they become familiar with literature terminology and methods of interpretation. "But we try to make them read literature in its entirety rather than literature collages," she says.

From my experience teaching British literature to groups of homeschool students, I agree that reading whole works is important. I want to help my students learn to enjoy reading great literature and to appreciate the artistry of the writers who produced these works. Except in rare cases, such enthusiasm only comes after thorough reading, discussion, and participation in related activities, such as creative projects or thoughtful written analyses. This kind of learning takes a great deal of time, so it is important to choose a sampling of the best works for comprehensive study and do an overview (perhaps from an anthology) of other important works.

Writing

In all walks of life, writing ability is essential. College students are required to write numerous papers, reports, and essays each semester or quarter. Yet more and more students are graduating from high schools and entering colleges without this fundamental skill. In 2003, in fact, the College Board's National Commission on Writing found writing preparation to be so poor among students entering college that it called for a five-year Writing Challenge to improve writing instruction in every subject area and at all grade levels. In its report, *The Neglected "R": The Need for a Writing Revolution,* the commission cited studies showing that "more than 50 percent of the freshman class are unable to produce papers relatively free of language errors or to analyze arguments or synthesize information."[1]

Rachelle Reitz, homeschool graduate and Associate Director of Admissions at Patrick Henry College, reports that professors find this lack of preparation disconcerting. She witnessed an appalling lack of English skills in high school graduates when she was an admissions counselor at Concordia University in Oregon and taught part of an English class there.

Some homeschoolers have also shown weak writing skills. Ben Jones, Dean of Admissions and Financial Aid at Bennington College, says, "We have had many excellent homeschooled students here. When they struggle, we often find the area of trouble to be formal, structured writing, so we pay particular attention to that in an applicant's file."

Most homeschool teachers consider teaching writing a formidable task, and many feel inadequate even to attempt it. I asked two college professors whose writing and teaching I admire for their advice. Dr. Richard Cornelius was Professor of English at Bryan College in Tennessee at the time of the interview and has since retired. Dr. Leland Ryken is Professor of English at Wheaton College in Illinois.

The Writing Process

According to Ryken, a writing teacher is a coach and therefore cannot make a student a good writer, any more than an athletic coach can make an athlete a good athlete. Instead, coaching influences student writers to improve. As "coach," your two main responsibilities are "telling your students how to do it, and critiquing (both positively and negatively) what they write."

Cornelius encourages students to have a target audience in mind when they write and to have a clear purpose and stick to it. He says, "Writing is hard work. Most writing can be cut down 30 percent without loss of important ideas. Interesting writing contains specific details but not too many." He expects incoming students to be able to write a clear, logical topic sentence; a thoughtful thesis statement; and a unified, clear, logical, and adequately developed paragraph.

Ryken expects his college students to have a grasp of grammar and to know how to write coherent sentences. The following writing skills he stresses are also important at the high school level.

1. Structuring an essay around a single controlling thesis and maintaining a unified and coherent line of argument.
2. Beginning every paragraph with a topic sentence that announces what the rest of the paragraph will prove and that at least part of the time reminds the reader of the main thesis.
3. Supporting every topic sentence with valid and relevant supporting data.

Once your students have attained basic writing proficiency, you should consider preparing them for college-level writing in what Cornelius calls a "process approach." The first step in this approach is for students to study the rules, theories, and principles of

1. Thinking
2. Language in general
3. Grammar
4. Composition

Good English handbooks usually supply this information. Then students should study literary models that exemplify these rules. (Models might also suggest ideas for papers.)

Ryken also stresses the value of models. He says, "I believe that student writers are hungry for models—specimens of (a) the specific genre for a given assignment and (b) examples of student writing that did it well. If the specimens can illustrate a certain range of ways in which to do an assignment well, so much the better, so as to free students from thinking there is a set formula for completing an assignment."

Before giving an assignment, provide models for your students by selecting two or three examples of the type of writing you want your students to complete. Select your samples from published writing in magazines, newsletters, and books. Try to choose authors with different writing styles so that students will not try to imitate anyone else's style.

Cornelius says that students should attempt to "appropriate and practice the information gained from the study of rules and models" by using the following five steps:

1. Preparation (thinking, reading, defining terms, etc.)
2. Investigation (research, interviews, observation, preliminary outline)
3. Incubation (just thinking about the project and letting it simmer)
4. Inspiration (when ideas come, jotting them down quickly)
5. Completion (revision, data evaluation, outline revision, rough draft, final proofreading)

As the writing progresses, Cornelius encourages students to correct and chart their errors and review their writing in conferences with their instructors.

Reviewing your students' writing as it progresses is a good idea, especially for long assignments. Ryken says that since many college students have the bad habit of dashing off a paper the night before it is due, college English professors have begun to require students to turn in various stages of their papers.

> *[Homeschoolers are] taught expressive writing but not persuasive writing.*
>
> Dr. David Crabtree, President, Gutenberg College

Ryken says, "I currently follow this format so that for virtually every paper, students (a) engage in some rudimentary prewriting exercise slanted toward the specific topic of the assignment, (b) hand in a 'discovery draft' (first draft) that I critique, and (c) hand in a finished essay. This requires students to be working on the essay over a period of time. I critique the finished essay but do not give it a grade. Students must correct errors and sometimes revise sentences or paragraphs or whole essays as a prerequisite for passing the course. Half of the essays must be revised in keeping with my critique for inclusion in a final portfolio. Grades consist largely of the grades earned for the final portfolio."

Since homeschoolers are not as used to meeting deadlines as traditional students are, you should consider using this method at home. Accept no excuses, other than legitimate ones (such as illness, accident, or death), for late work. College professors and employers will not tolerate tardiness, and neither should you.

Professors often require college students to write complete essays during single class periods or for exams, so Cornelius suggests having your students practice writing under timed conditions. He says that in fifty minutes they should be able to write a 300- to 500-word essay that is clear, adequately developed, and thoughtful.

Practice Makes Perfect?

Because so much writing will be required in college, have your students write as much as possible, but do not overwhelm them with assignments. Allow enough time for them to revise their work, since revision is the most important part of the writing process.

Cornelius believes that practice plays a large factor in learning the art of writing and that students learn to write by writing, correcting, revising, and rewriting. This kind of practice, he says, "can lead to perfection." Many English teachers require their students to practice by writing regularly in journals. Ryken believes that writing papers is a better way to practice writing than mere journaling, although he admits that journaling holds high appeal for some of his colleagues. He does not believe that writing improves simply by the act of writing, as one would practice free throws. He considers the composition of a complete, coherent piece of writing to be more worthwhile practice than simply jotting down whatever strikes you at a given moment, as you would in a journal.

Journaling is not finished writing; it is just one step in the process of writing. This process is often used to encourage reluctant writers or to help those who have trouble finding ideas. Professional writers espouse journaling for recording impressions and memories that they can use later as both springboards for ideas and anecdotes for future writing projects. Some use it to get their creative juices flowing. However, few, if any, writers would consider their journaling to be finished writing. To make a piece marketable, professionals usually labor through several rewrites, some up to fifty or one hundred times. If your students enjoy journaling, that is fine. Just encourage them to take some of their ideas beyond the journaling stage to polished pieces of writing.

Most public schools right now are demanding a senior project from their students. That's something homeschoolers really need to consider, because it prepares [students] for big, lengthy projects in college. Have them do a senior project or a senior paper that is well researched.

Rachelle Reitz,
homeschool graduate and
Associate Director of Admissions,
Patrick Henry College

Homeschooler Tamie Goggans recommends assigning your students "real-life compositions that are meaningful accomplishments," not things that will make students "feel like they're running on a wheel." Her writing assignments have included pieces for 4-H and volunteer activities, letters to editors, and reports about research her students have done "for a purpose."

What to Write

What types of writing should your high school students be doing? In college English classes, students will have to write many papers about the literature they read. In other classes, they will be required to write a variety of papers about the topics covered in their courses. Some of these will be only a few pages; others will be long papers requiring research and cited literature.

Cornelius mentioned that high school seniors should be able to evaluate a book, film, or speech for its central idea and significant strengths and weaknesses. Ryken considers the expository essay to be the only essential type of writing for high school students to learn before college. Examples he cited include analysis of a cultural trend, social problem papers, research papers, and persuasion papers.

Because writing about literature will be so important in college, I asked Dr. Ryken what he expects from his students when they write about literature. Ryken prefers to assign explications, which are synonymous with "reliving the text," because, he says, "A general reading of a work is the most universal type of analysis that people will do later in life." The following are the three types of explication he assigns:

1. **Straight explication,** a detailed explanation of what the author said, how it was said, the structure, unity, texture, literary devices, etc.

According to Ryken, if you were writing a straight explication of a poem, for example, you might begin with general things like topic, theme, implied situation, occasion, and genre. Discuss structure and unity and then go through the poem line by line or stanza by stanza, describing its texture—what is said, what is going on, what is implied, what effect is created, what is compared or contrasted, what allusions are made, etc. Everything must be supported with portions of the text, which may be either quoted or referenced in the paper. Include the poem's versification, meter, and sound effects as part of the texture discussion if they contribute directly to the poem's meaning. If not, place them after the texture discussion. Ryken says, "Round off your explication with a note of finality by casting a retrospective look back over the poem as a whole or by fitting the poem into some broader context."

2. **Explication slanted around a specific thesis or focus,** such as *Emma is the story of a well-intentioned but unsuccessful matchmaker.*

Ryken offers these rules for writing a good paper of this type:

   a. You must have a unifying thesis or focus to which everything in the paper relates.
   b. You need a framework of supporting generalizations that form the topic sentences of the paragraphs in the body of your paper.
   c. You must support your topic sentences with data (usually from the literary text about which you are writing).
   d. You should surround the body of your paper with an opening paragraph that introduces the general topic and ends with a clear statement of your thesis, and a concluding paragraph that summarizes the paper.

3. **A brief thesis paper (or literary criticism).** In this type of paper, a writer presents a premise and then supports it with evidence from the literary work. Ryken writes, "In literary criticism, the supporting evidence includes the critic's commentary on what the data show." An example of a premise is, Poe's poem "The Bells" is an analogy of life from the perspective of hopelessness beyond the grave. Thesis papers are probably beyond the scope of high-school-level English. However, students who intend to major in English might wish to try writing one or two of them.

This is the way Ryken instructs his college students to write this type of paper:

   a. Your essay must have a thesis that provides the unifying focus of the paper. A thesis need not be argumentative. It can simply state the unifying topic of the paper.
   b. Any thesis must be supported by references to the literary text.
   c. In literary criticism, the supporting evidence includes the critic's commentary on what the data show.
   d. Some paragraphs illustrate rather than prove the general thesis. They win the reader's assent not by a wealth of quotations from the work but by illuminating the work.
   e. Sooner or later a critic must answer the question, How do you know? The answer will ultimately consist of references to the literary text.

f. The ultimate test of literary criticism is whether it illuminates or helpfully describes the text.

Besides having your teens write about literature, have them write persuasive essays, short stories, formal letters, analytical essays, speeches, directions or instructions, and other practical types of writing. Be sure to assign at least one term paper on a topic that appeals to the student. Giving your students a variety of writing assignments should help keep them interested in writing and give them adequate practice.

Writing Resources

Besides traditional high school textbooks, dozens of resources can help your students learn to write better. Libraries usually carry a good assortment of books for aspiring and professional writers. Some of the books will help with the mechanics of writing, like punctuation, usage, and grammar. Others deal with the writing process and will offer inspiration and encouragement. If your students are interested in publishing their writing, books about marketing are also available.

Writing books that Ryken has used with his students include Sheridan Baker's *Practical Stylist* and a barebones handbook by Diana Hacker entitled *A Pocket Style Manual*. Cornelius recommends using "a good recent grammar and rhetoric such as *The Harbrace Handbook* (13th edition); Strunk and White's *The Elements of Style*; Berke and Woodland's *Twenty Questions for the Writer*; Burack's *The Writer's Handbook*; and a good, recent collegiate dictionary" such as *Merriam Webster* or *American Heritage*.

The Grammar-Writing Connection

Where does grammar fit into the writing picture? Although competent writing involves much more than simply mastering the mechanics, correct grammar is an essential component of good composition. It is difficult to lead students to higher levels of thinking and writing before they have mastered the basics of how to express themselves clearly and concisely.

[Homeschooled students] are interesting applicants who can clearly demonstrate their love of learning....Many have strong verbal and writing skills. Most are very well read and know how to make connections between ideas [and] disciplines rather than simply memorizing names, dates and facts.

Renee Wruck Bischoff, Senior Assistant Director of Admission, Lake Forest College

Patrick Henry College's Michael Farris encourages homeschoolers to master grammar because it fosters excellent writing. He reports that the study of grammar was instrumental in making his daughters good writers. He told me that his wife drilled their girls for twelve years in grammar using the A Beka language program, which he says is "really tough."

Ryken agrees that grammar is essential. He says, "One cannot write a good essay if one does not know the rules of grammar." Nevertheless, he contends that the mere mastery of grammar is too abstract to be of much use, so students should be writing while they are mastering grammar.

Cornelius agrees that people can improve their grammar as they practice writing. He says, "A correction and revision system enables one to do both grammar and writing. Grammar divorced from writing or reading is dry and boring to many people and need not be studied that way."

Make sure that your children use correct grammar in their writing assignments, and refer them to appropriate sections in a college-level English handbook, such as *The Bedford Handbook* or Hacker's *Pocket Style Manual,* when you correct their work. When you see the same mistakes occurring repeatedly, it is time to do a thorough review of those concepts. Errors I see most often in my students' writing involve subject-verb agreement in both tense and number, lack of parallel structure, dangling modifiers, incorrect usage, split infinitives, and ambiguous or remote reference. My students are also overly dependent on spell-check, witch as ewe no does knot all ways ketch e very thing. Even if your children are strong in grammar, review periodically to help them stay strong.

If your students are struggling to master grammar, show them how to use their English handbook to find answers to their grammatical questions. Study the handbook yourself first if you need some review. Sentence diagramming may help, too. Diagramming is a skill that is not generally taught in schools anymore, but it should be. A diagrammed sentence is like a map of language and is beneficial in helping especially kinesthetic (hands on) and visual learners understand the reasoning behind grammar rules. When Rachelle Reitz was homeschooled, she learned to diagram sentences and found it to be valuable in preparing for graduate school admission tests.

Although understanding grammar is important, Cornelius cautions, "[grammar] is not more important than ideas. A person can have perfect grammar and yet nothing to say…. A writer needs to live well, so that his writing is honest and genuine and sincere. His goals should not be mere money or fame but to minister and glorify God."

The Reading-Writing Connection

Most people extol extensive reading as the road to excellent writing, and with good reason: Most good writers are avid readers.

Cornelius thinks that familiarity with good literature has a great deal of influence on a student's ability to write. He claims that writers first need to be readers to notice technique and style as well as to pick up ideas.

Although Ryken believes that there is a correlation between reading literature and writing well, he does not think that the reading itself produces good writing. He says, "I believe that readers are simply more literate and more adept at using language. Even here, though, I do not believe that one needs to be reading literature specifically for the facility with language to emerge."

Whether or not it directly affects your students' writing ability, the literature your students read can certainly influence their use and appreciation of the English language and widen their pool of knowledge and ideas. Try to expose them to the best writing, including poetry and drama. Assign classics as well as works of excellent contemporary authors. Have your high school students read more difficult works on their own, but if your schedule allows, read at least one difficult work aloud together each semester or each year. At the end of books or chapters, consider having your students narrate back what has been read. Verbalizing what they have read or heard will help them learn to form well-organized, coherent thoughts that translate into good writing.

The benefits of reading good literature never end. As children grow older, they learn to understand character motivation, plot, and themes. They can glean authors' messages and determine their worldviews. Eventually they realize the power inherent in the written word. Sometimes this realization motivates them to use that power to promote positive changes in their culture or simply to express their deepest thoughts on paper.

Michael Farris says that writing ability in college is "critical." He attributes much of his daughter Christy's success in college to the fact that she could write "like a mature adult—since the day she walked into school."

"I was a bar examiner in Washington state," Farris says, "so I wrote test questions and graded them for potential lawyers. And I'll tell you there's just not enough preparation—even for the doctorate—in writing, even in fields where writing is very important. So I just can't overstate the importance of writing."

Speech

Learning to speak in public is another important part of high school education. As students mature and take on leadership responsibilities in community, church, school, and work situations, they will have more and more opportunities to speak in both formal and informal settings. The earlier they become comfortable speaking, the better.

Call It Courage

Students often cringe at the thought of having to speak in front of groups, although I think homeschooled students are less fearful than most. When I was a sophomore in high school, a friend of mine grabbed me in the hall and asked me to make an announcement to my class. She was gone before I could protest. For several minutes before class, I tried to gather the nerve to do it. My throat went dry and my stomach cramped at the thought. Finally I asked a member of the student council to make the announcement for me. I was shocked to find out that she was just as nervous and reluctant as I was. She forced herself to do it; I did not. Because she was willing to take the risk, she learned public speaking and leadership skills years before I did.

The difference between those who will speak in public and those who will not is courage. It is not the kind of courage that says, "I'm not afraid." Rather it is the attitude that says, "I'm scared to death, but I'm going to do it anyway because what I say might help someone listening." When people repeatedly force themselves to speak in public, they find that it gets easier. Eventually, many lose their fear, but most speakers usually feel a twinge of nervousness every time they speak.

If your students feel nervous, coach them to get the focus off themselves and onto others. They need to train themselves to stop worrying about what others might think of them or about how they might look or sound. Encourage them to care enough about their audience to try to make their speeches enjoyable for their listeners. Christians should also try to remember to "do all for the glory of God." I have found that focusing on Him instead of myself makes everything easier.

At the high school level, students should write persuasively about issues they care deeply about and then find opportunities to present their ideas to groups of people that can do something about them. Issues can be as simple as why they think the family should adopt a new pet or as complex as the effects of foreign trade on religious persecution. Just make sure that their points are concise, that they present their cases clearly and convincingly, that they speak in the proper tone of voice for their audience, and that they avoid any distracting body movements.

Students might also recite memorized poems or present the speeches of famous historical figures to your family, friends, or homeschool group. Monologues from plays, portions of novels, or lessons from textbooks also provide speaking material. Encourage your students to become familiar enough with their speeches that they can present them without reading word for word. Also have them give some speeches without having written them out, using only notes on cards. Have them practice their speeches several times before delivering them. Even if it is simply to make an announcement, encourage your students to take every opportunity to speak in front of groups.

The Bigger family participated in homeschool get-togethers each Friday. The group had guest speakers and then allowed time for students to do oral reports. This provided students with an audience for their memory work and speeches. Afterward, they ate sack lunches and played basketball, football, and other games with their homeschool friends.

Michael Farris encourages students to be involved in Toastmasters' Youth Leadership Program. You will have to gather a group of students to make this training possible. Besides helping students learn public speaking, Farris says that this activity looks good for college admissions. Also, the National Christian Forensics and Communications Association, in cooperation with the Home

School Legal Defense Association (HSLDA), sponsors a national debate tournament for home-schoolers. "These are students who come to us after they've competed in their state disqualifying tournaments," Farris adds. (See Appendix B.)

Farris says, "No matter what your career…the ability to present what you're trying to say in a cohesive fashion is very good for your job…. If you're going to be a politician, a pastor, a house-wife who's concerned about politics…it's hard for me to imagine how any person couldn't improve his or her adult life by learning to do oral presentations. So I would encourage students to partici-pate in debate and speech activities."

If students force themselves to get up and speak over and over again, they will soon realize, if they have not already, that the toughest things we do in life often bring the greatest rewards.

Whatever your students plan to do in the future, language arts courses are probably the most important, which is why virtually all high schools and colleges in the United States require four years of high school English. Even coaches, scientists, and mathematicians have to be able to read, write, and speak coherently.

Mathematics

After language arts, mathematics is probably the second most basic academic discipline. When planning your high schoolers' curriculum, do not neglect mathematics. Many careers require profi-ciency in advanced math. Even if your students have no interest in those careers, a certain amount of mathematical competency is necessary for adult life. Many high school graduates cannot even make change or balance a checkbook, let alone compute sales taxes, interest charges, or tips. If they cannot do even these simple calculations, they can easily be exploited by slick mer-chants, unscrupulous loan officers, and dishonest employers. If your chil-dren have no interest in college, make sure they know at least enough math to take care of themselves as adults.

Verbal skills and writing are usually very strong. Some-times math skills are weaker than verbal skills, and social skills sometimes are less well developed.

Jon Henry, Director of Admissions, Johnson State College VT

Higher math, like algebra, geometry, trigonometry, and calculus, helps students develop their mental acuity. Most colleges require high school students to complete courses through Algebra II and will not count general mathematics for college-preparatory credit.

Bob Beavin, Director of Admissions at Patrick Henry College, says:

When Patrick Henry College opened, there were few surprises, but one emerged as we began receiving applications: a general weakness in mathematics. It became evident from transcripts, as well as SAT/ACT scores, that this was an area where high school preparation was less than adequate. All too often, young people were applying to PHC's rigorous academic program insufficiently prepared, having taken, for instance, only Algebra I and Consumer Math. We like to see applicants who have completed at least Algebra II, Geometry, and Trigonometry, and advanced math courses always make a good impression. The encouraging thing is that now, a few years later, we're seeing home schoolers creatively and effectively addressing this situation through co-ops, umbrella schools, tutors, and community college courses.

When it comes to teaching higher mathematics, many homeschoolers feel inadequate. However, advanced math is nothing to fear. You simply need to avail yourselves of the excellent resources available. There are several alternatives you can consider:

1. Buy a user-friendly, largely self-instructional curriculum with solution guides and answer keys, and either learn or relearn the material yourself. Then teach your students. You will need to stay at least a lesson or two ahead of them.
2. Buy a largely self-instructional curriculum with solution guides and answer keys, and allow your students to complete the course independently. Use the answer keys and solution guides to check their work.
3. Use math video courses or computer programs.
4. Enroll your students in online classes.
5. Find a fellow homeschooler who is strong in math to teach your children along with his or her own. You might trade services and teach his or her students in your area of strength.
6. With other homeschool families, hire either a professional or a college student to teach a group class.
7. Hire a tutor to teach your own students.
8. Enroll your students part-time in high school or community college for the courses they need.

Self-teaching is a good alternative for bright students, especially in large families. Beth Vellalos chose option two for her sons, using Saxon math. Like most homeschoolers who use Saxon, her sons have excelled in math. Sharon Grimes, mother of six, also advocates using "Saxon all the way."

Our daughter's Algebra II course was a combination of options two and three. Christine used *Intermediate Algebra,* available from Bluestocking Press, and its optional peripheral materials. Using the textbook and peripherals, she was basically able to teach herself. This math series from Bluestocking Press begins with *Basic College Mathematics* (appropriate for ages 10–12 and up) and also includes *Introductory Algebra* and *Intermediate Algebra* (equivalent to Algebra I and Algebra II). The optional peripherals include student and instructor solution manuals, answer books, and video tutorials. The peripherals can change with new editions, so contact Bluestocking Press for current information.

Mathematics resources are becoming more sophisticated and more available every year. Both The Teaching Company and A Beka offer video courses taught by classroom teachers. There are also several computer programs. To find out about the latest resources, subscribe to homeschooling magazines and check curriculum guides and homeschool vendor catalogs. (See Appendix B.)

David Crabtree, President of Gutenberg College, has observed that some homeschoolers can do mathematics manipulations but don't understand concepts. Make sure that your students are comfortable with both. To help students learn concepts, search for math curriculum and/or enrichment materials that utilize manipulatives, games, and plenty of practical application. Mathematics training is especially important as preparation for science classes.

Science

You can take many different avenues for teaching high school science. High school textbooks are available, but you might want to consider using well-written college textbooks. According to Wayne Jones, chemistry professor at Binghamton University (SUNY), some high school chemistry textbooks teach students shortcuts that they would be better off not learning. Also, encourage your students to read articles in scientific journals on specific topics that interest them. Journals are usually available at large city or county libraries and in college libraries.

Science should be an exciting adventure of discovery, not just the tedious memorization of facts, or what are purported to be facts at the time. Mankind's science changes with new discoveries, but the intricate design of creation remains constant. So whether you use traditional high school textbooks, college textbooks, readings from scientific journals, videos, or lectures by working scientists, make sure you include plenty of application. This can be in a laboratory, outdoors, at the zoo, in a museum, etc. For example, when we studied biology, we collected our own specimens for microscope study; practiced life drawing at the zoo; participated in a park-sponsored bird walk; performed plant growth, bacteria, and osmosis experiments; and dissected four different animals.

Taking a community college course is particularly helpful in the lab sciences.

Robert J. Massa,
Dean of Enrollment,
Johns Hopkins University

Several colleges consider laboratory science experience an essential part of the high school curriculum. However, laboratory sciences—especially chemistry—pose some of the greatest challenges for home high schoolers. Approximately 12 percent of colleges responded with concerns about laboratory sciences in regard to homeschooled students. Some named it as a weakness; others mentioned the need to include laboratory experience in science courses. If you want your students to be competitive in the college admissions game, it is imperative for them to gain some type of laboratory experience during high school. Laboratory resources are readily available to homeschoolers. For instance, Bob Jones University Press sells a nice dissection kit with four animals, and Tobin's Lab sells a kit with five. Blue Spruce Biological Supply and Home Training Tools are other excellent sources for animals and science equipment. (See Appendix B for these and other resources.)

Biology

Biology poses comparatively few problems for homeschoolers. You can provide an adequate biology laboratory with an inexpensive microscope, a slide kit, and some dissection tools. Household items like paper and plastic cups and aluminum pie plates can substitute for most of the other tools you will need for experiments.

Have your students write detailed descriptions of experiments they conduct, complete with hypotheses, methods, observations, and results. They should also keep a lab notebook in which to draw and label the specimens they dissect or observe through the microscope.

Your students need access to a microscope for biology. If you cannot afford a microscope, perhaps your homeschool group could buy one that its members could either rent or use in a central location. If you have to use a microscope away from home, you might find it more convenient to complete the microscope sections of your lab all at once over a few weeks instead of spreading them out over the whole year. We did our microscope work and plant dissections during the summer, when fresh specimens (flowers, insects, pond water, leaves, vegetables, etc.) were readily available. We did preserved animal dissections after the weather turned cold. If using a microscope is impossible for you, check the Internet for photos of microscope specimen slides.

You can tell kids that water pollution is bad, but there's a visible way to show them. We hand them fouled water and have them clean it up. They start with a cup and end up with a thimble, and that's the point.

Mike Bolinsky, Science Projects

Most people think of animal dissections whenever biology is discussed. At the thought of cutting into dead animals, students often recoil, as did my daughter and the two girls who studied biology with her. They winced at the first cut, but they were soon intrigued. I will never forget my own amazement at discovering the intricate structures packed inside a tiny earthworm and the artistry of color and form concealed under the shell of a crayfish. If your students are squeamish or lack the necessary supplies, they may opt to do virtual dissections on the Internet instead of performing dissections at home. Search through your browser or a search engine to find dissection sites. As technology improves, online dissections will likely become more sophisticated, but I cannot imagine that videos or photographs will ever take the place of discovering firsthand the creative wonders hidden inside an animal's body.

When your students are studying a science, assign some challenging questions that require library research. I required my students to answer research questions every week, which helped develop their research and library skills. We used *A+ Projects in Biology* for most of our experiments and research questions. We also visited a state college library so that the students could learn how to use scientific journals in their research.

If you prefer to do biology by correspondence, Oral Roberts University offers a program to homeschoolers who want to earn college credits while in high school. It offers a lab course called Principles of Biology as part of this program. Northwestern College in Minnesota offers an on-campus Science Academy, a program especially for homeschoolers. Director of Recruitment Ken K. Faffler says that many colleges offer similar programs in various subject areas.

Chemistry

A proper chemistry lab is harder to come by than a biology lab. A chemistry set like those sold in hobby shops will give your student some basic lab experience, but it might not be adequate to go with the textbooks you are using. Some curriculum providers and correspondence schools might offer lab equipment and/or chemicals in packages to go with their chemistry courses. (Request information from suppliers in Appendix B.) Another possibility is to get permission to use public or private school labs either while classes are in session or after school hours. Many families spend the money to assemble their own home laboratories and then proceed to teach science courses as they would be taught in traditional schools. However, that option is prohibitively expensive for most homeschoolers. With young children in the house, chemicals, flasks, and other equipment could be dangerous. Using some chemicals might violate fire and safety codes.

> *Homeschoolers need to be aware of the disadvantage of underdeveloped laboratory skills if they do all their work at home. Taking some lab science courses either in the local high school or community college would alleviate what might be a serious disadvantage for students planning to study science in college.*
>
> Geoffrey Gould, Director of Undergraduate Admissions, Binghamton University

Because of these difficulties, increasing numbers of homeschoolers take lab sciences through co-ops, community colleges, or high schools. Other options also might be available. For instance, if your local homeschool association has a central location, it might be able to set up a lab that homeschoolers can use for a fee. Another alternative is to find a professional teacher or scientist who is willing to teach a group chemistry class one or two evenings per week, using facilities at a school or laboratory.

If you cannot provide a chemistry lab, consider teaching other sciences that require less sophisticated lab equipment. However, if your students' intended majors are in the physical sciences or engineering, chemistry is most likely a required high school course. In that case, I encourage you to enroll your students in a chemistry course at a high school or college. If that is not possible, they can probably take introductory chemistry when they get to college.

Wayne Jones, a chemistry professor at Binghamton University (SUNY), offered several suggestions for homeschoolers who want to complete a chemistry laboratory at home:

> *At a minimum, I would like students to have experience with a gram balance (diet balances should work and be relatively inexpensive) and some volumetric glassware [flasks and cylinders] that are calibrated in metric units of volume such as liters. Finally, a buret would be valuable for titrations. Titrations are relatively easy to do, and you can*

Table 5A
General Chemistry Laboratory Equipment List

Item	Number
Beakers	
20 or 50 ml	*1*
100 or 150 ml	*1*
250 ml	*1*
400 ml	*1*
Droppers with Bulbs	*4*
Evaporating Dish	*1*
Erlenmeyer Flasks	
25 ml	*1*
50 ml	*1*
125 ml	*1*
250 ml	*1*
Funnel (Plastic)	*1*
Graduated Cylinders	
10 ml	*1*
50 or 100 ml	*1*
Test tubes	
large	*6*
small	*6*
Watch Glasses	*2*
Spatula	*1*
Test Tube Holder/Rack	*1*
Stirring Rod	*1*
Weighing Vial with Cap	*1*

Graduated pipette (2 or 5 ml)
with a pipette bulb (NO
MOUTH PIPETTING)

Wayne Jones,
Binghamton University
(SUNY)

prepare indicator dyes from readily available ingredients such as purple cabbage. (A web search of "purple cabbage indicator" will give you several reasonable recipes.) Frankly, if you can get your kids to do titrations and understand concentrations, you would be achieving great success. If they really knew that stuff coming out of homeschooling, they'd probably be better off than half the kids that make it to general college chemistry anyway.

I would recommend that you concentrate on the concept of the mole and make sure the students can handle those basic calculations in the context of typical classes of reactions, including acid-base, precipitation, and oxidation reduction. If your students can handle balancing those reactions and appropriately doing g-mole conversions [grams to moles, moles to mass], you will be in great shape…. If the parents were to pick up any general, freshman-level, college chemistry text and look at the first six to ten chapters, those are the ones I would concentrate on if I were homeschooling my child.

As I mentioned earlier, Jones recommends using a college textbook. He says that high school texts "water things down and teach some habits…some shortcuts that I'd rather they didn't learn."

Jones also mentioned a wonderful opportunity, if you can arrange it. He said that the American Chemical Society sponsors a National Chemistry Olympiad. Participating students receive some laboratory experience and, in some of the larger districts like Detroit, participate in training sessions that include laboratory experience. There is no charge to the students; expenses are covered by the American Chemical Society. Jones suggests that you contact the coordinator of your local section of the American Chemical Society—he happens to have been the coordinator for the southern tier region of New York—and ask if they run the National Chemistry Olympiad. Explain that you have a certain number of homeschooling students in your area who would be interested and ask if it would be all right if these students participate as independents. There is nothing in the rules that would preclude that, according to Jones, but you would need permission from the local coordinator. You can find a list of local section events at www.acs.org by searching for "chemistry Olympiad."

One of the challenges high school chemistry teachers face is finding good in-class demonstrations and laboratories that students can do in brief periods of time, according to Jones. He mentioned that homeschool parents have an advantage in that they don't have to complete the work within a one-hour block but can spend a whole day doing a lab, if they choose. Therefore, they can potentially do something more complex. He told me that demonstration sites have started to appear all over the Internet that offer instructions for doing demonstrations. Examples include driving a battery-operated wall clock using only an orange, a nail, a penny, and a couple of wires; testing the pH of different household acids and bases using red cabbage as an indicator; oxidizing sucrose directly into carbon; blowing up balloons using acetic acid and baking soda; etc. Jones suggests that you investigate web-based resources by searching at Yahoo.com or Google.com. A particularly good site for demonstrations for the home can be found at http://www.thecatalyst.org/m05demos.html.

Internet-based simulation laboratories are the wave of the future in chemistry education, Jones believes, and several colleges are developing them. Binghamton University (SUNY) has a complete set of simulation laboratories on the Internet, including titrations, pH meters, and spectrophotometers. The site is password protected, but you can purchase simulations as part of a complete electronic chemistry curriculum from Houghton Mifflin. The CD includes a general chemistry text. Jones describes it as a web-CD-ROM hybrid costing less than most textbooks. Ordering information can be found at http://hmchemdemo.clt.binghamton.edu.

Other universities may offer similar plans. Jones believes that all will require some form of payment, through purchasing a textbook or paying a fee to be able to access simulation sites because simulations are time intensive and expensive to create. At this point, he estimates that one chemistry site in seventy-five has simulations on it. Two other publishers with chemistry programs you might want to investigate are Peregrine Publishers and Thomson Learning. Peregrine has websites for both chemistry (www.chemplace.com) and biology (www.biology.com), and Thomson offers an interactive general chemistry CD-ROM (www.brookscole.com/chemistry_d).

Jones also mentioned opportunities in distance education from places such as SUNY Learning Network. There are dozens of accredited institutions that offer a general chemistry course online suitable for students interested in AP credit.

Jones says, "I think that if I were a homeschooling parent, I would be thinking to myself, 'Okay, all I have to do is find a publisher whose textbook I can buy that has access to this kind of stuff.' And I think that publishers are seeing that coming down the pike and seeing that that's going to be a requirement."

To find online chemistry information and education, Jones suggests going to university and college websites and checking their chemistry department pages. He mentioned that some other wonderful sites include: University of California San Diego, University of Massachusetts Amherst, Virginia Polytechnic, Cal Tech, Clemson, and University of Wisconsin.

Another great suggestion Jones made was to have students design a chemistry demonstration show—a kind of chemistry magic show—to perform for a second- or third-grade class or a church, YMCA, school, or community function. Students can also use this project to earn a Boy Scouts or Girl Scouts chemistry merit badge. Jones believes that students often learn more in this type of creative endeavor. "Just make sure they can explain things mathematically as well as visually," he says. "If they're going to do a good job, they have to really understand what is happening." Libraries, especially college-level ones, should have books to help students plan chemistry magic shows. College-level science books are great sources of experiments to enhance student understanding.

Dr. Jones was kind enough to supply a list of what he considers essential equipment for a home high school chemistry laboratory. (See Table 5A.) He did not supply a list of chemicals, however, because he notes that you can accomplish a lot of interesting chemistry with items available at the grocery store. "Besides," he says, "with chemicals comes liability." He recounted the story of how the Open University in England, one of the largest distance education universities in the world, ran General Chemistry and supplied kits for accompanying labs. Apparently they discontinued their "lab in a box" because the school would be liable if students injured themselves while using the kits. If you want to purchase chemicals, contact your local chemical or scientific supply company or a well-known company such as Fisher Scientific. Science Labs-in-a-Box offers a more recent version of mail-order science labs. Homeschoolers rent equipment and pay a monthly fee to use this Bible-centered program. (See Appendix B.)

Jones says, "I would say if you had that core set of glassware at home, the only thing you'd need is the chemicals.... You can pick up some at the grocery store, some at the pharmacy, and if you really needed something fancy, you could call up Fisher Scientific and probably get it.

"Of course, the key to the laboratory experience is encouraging students to ask the question WHY something is observed. It is not enough to just reproduce a known phenomenon; challenge them to do something different. Design a new experiment that supports, or disproves, their description of why something happened. That is real science and the students will learn more than just chemical manipulation."

Physics

Another Binghamton University (SUNY) professor, Bob Pompi, Chair of Physics, offered his insights about high school preparation for college physics:

> The problem of success in physics at the college or university level does not involve laboratories or the lack thereof in the background of the graduating high school student. The problem involves mathematical skills and/or tools. Can the student solve word problems? Can the student translate the verbal statement of a problem into an appropriate mathematical form? Does the student have a good working knowledge of algebra, geometry, and trigonometry? We find the best correlation of success is the existence of AP calculus in the background of students entering introductory physics. Although calculus is not required for all of our introductory physics courses, the students who have succeeded in AP calculus know geometry, trig, and algebra. If a student has the appropriate mathematical skills, we can teach him or her. If not, all the laboratory experience in the world will be of little use. I frankly would not worry about the absence of laboratory experience in the study of high school physics. I would worry about such a lack in chemistry or biology.... [High school physics laboratories] have never been much of a factor in predicting the success of a student at the college level.

Like Pompi, Uwe Greife, Associate Professor in the Department of Physics at the Colorado School of Mines, expects incoming students to have developed strong mathematical skills, especially the ability to show the process they use in reaching their answers. He reports that about 20% to 30% of new students at Mines struggle in the first few semesters with both math and "putting their thoughts on paper in a structured way while developing the solution to a physics problem."

"Many still try to develop the solution in their heads, as with simpler math problems," he says. "But at a certain point, this is just not possible anymore."

Greife recommends doing the laboratory component of high school physics because it "gives the hands-on experience and the feeling for the physics involved. It also trains students in lab report writing and the determination of experimental errors, which are the basis of experimental science."

To help you determine what might be needed for a physics lab at home, I asked Debbie Shope, who teaches physics to classes of homeschoolers, for her recommendations. She kindly provided a list, which I have reproduced in Table 5B. She also recommended several books and websites, which have been incorporated into Appendix B. (See under Math and Science.) When looking for materials for physics experiments, Shope usually goes to a hardware store first. She says, "The heart and mind of a scientist is nurtured when you encourage your student to use basic materials to 'rig up' an experiment."

For curriculum, Greife recommends getting a head start by looking at the textbooks used at the universities or colleges where students plan to apply. "Most of these books now have websites and links to other interesting materials," he says. For example, Greife suggests that students intrigued by astronomy start by exploring websites about the Hubble Space telescope. "From there one can work a student into all kinds of problems. How did the [telescope] get up there, how does it work, what keeps it from falling down...?"

Although some future scientists and engineers believe that they do not need English skills, Greife stresses the importance of writing ability for these students:

> *Both scientists and engineers need to communicate with others in an effective manner. There are very few projects in our day where you can work out an important problem hidden in a basement laboratory on your own. You need to work and function in a team and communicate your results to the larger science community. If you are working in industry, the chances are very high that after a few years in the research lab or on field work you will actually enter the management level where effective communication is necessary for your survival.*

(In fact, the Colorado School of Mines is required by its accrediting agency to offer writing-based science courses.) Greife also recommends that students practice giving presentations, just as they would for a science fair, which would include reporting on the lab work they do for the project. He notes that high schoolers can also gain valuable work experience at some national laboratories that offer summer employment.

Since Mines is an engineering school, all of Greife's comments also apply to future engineers.

Table 5B
Basic Equipment for a Home Physics Lab

Motion
- *Mass set (For some masses, you could use a jars of beans and weigh them at a grocery checkout.)*
- *Mass hanger*
- *Pully with tabletop clamp (adjustable)*
- *Spring scales, 1 50N, 1 5N*
- *Dynamics cart set (friction-free wheels)*
- *Stopwatch (A sports watch works fine.)*
- *Ramp (Aluminum channel from a hardware store works great.)*

Sound and Light
- *Many simple experiments can be done with household items.*
- *Laser pointer*
- *Color mixing: 3 track lights (bulbs same wattage) with good quality color filters in red, green, and blue. You could use 3 flashlights, but they must be the same brand with the same types of batteries and bulbs.*
- *Resonance: 2 timing forks of same frequency; "Beats": 1 tuning fork about 3–4 Hz difference from the other two. Small tuning forks from music store can be amplified by setting the ends on a tabletop, but don't strike them on hard surface. Larger ones from lab supply companies emit more sound.*
- *Mirrors: 1 concave, 1 convex*
- *Lenses: 1 concave, 1 convex*
- *Optics bench*

Electricity and Magnetism
- *Household items*
- *Batteries*
- *Battery holder or toilet paper and paper towel rolls and tape*
- *Coil of 22-gauge wire or twisted aluminum foil*
- *Small light sockets with bulbs (3 minimum)*
- *Multitester to measure voltage & amperage*
- *Magnets*
- *Compass*

Heat/Thermodynamics
- *Burner*
- *Pyrex containers*
- *Thermometer 0–220 degree F. (12" or longer)*

From Debbie Shope,
homeschool group teacher

For Future Engineers

Students who plan to major in engineering must take chemistry and physics and should complete a biology course in high school, according to Dr. Larry Zavodney, a homeschooling father who is Professor and Chairman of the Department of Engineering at Cedarville University. Various providers can supply the equipment for students to complete what he calls a "surprising number" of laboratory experiments at home. Zavodney adds that science and laboratory experiences develop other skills that are necessary for success, such as critical thinking, information processing, data reduction, and laboratory report preparation.

Homeschooled students, anecdotally, possess independence and initiative to succeed in a college environment. Frequently, the biggest difference between high school and college is not necessarily curriculum but the responsibility for time management without the structure of the school day.... However, there can, at times, be an incoherence to the curriculum of a homeschooled student. Generally, the homeschooled student may not have opportunities to develop the curriculum the ways a student educated in a school system may.

Ryan J. Hagemann, Admission Officer, Whitman College

"The most important aspect is to not quench the natural curiosity that children have," Zavodney says. "The TV and computer [games and Internet] are good at doing this with their entertainment ability. The content is not as important as the process of learning the scientific method of discovering truth, processing the data, and presenting it in a meaningful manner that is understandable to someone knowledgeable in the field."

By far, the biggest deficiencies Zavodney sees in incoming students are math reasoning and algebra skills. He says that students who want to major in engineering need to be ready for calculus with preparation in Algebra I and II, geometry, trigonometry, advanced math, including functions, functional analysis, series, logarithms, exponentials, trig and hyperbolic trig functions, and even an introduction to calculus. The primary reason students do not do well in calculus is poor algebra skills, according to Zavodney, so be sure that your students have mastered (and reviewed) algebra before they leave for college. He notes that students who have taken AP calculus in high school can get college credit and move on to other classes.

Budding engineers tend to take things apart to see how they work, according to Zavodney, who recommends kit building, such as construction kits from electronics stores, Fischertechnik, or others. When he was in high school, Zavodney designed and built his own computers. He suggests that high school students leave the TV off and use the computer for learning a programming language and writing programs instead of playing games.

"Find people who are working in the engineering field and see if you can go to work with them some day and just follow along with them to see what they do. Study hard in school and take all of the math, science, and computer programming classes you can," he advises.

He refers parents who do not have the knowledge base to teach these subjects to video series and good homeschool support groups for resources and recommendations.

Other Sciences

If your students want to complete other science courses, here are a few suggestions.

For a geology lab, you could do a rocks and minerals lab, erosion studies, etc. You can find laboratory activities in textbooks and other science books. Also check curriculum guides for suggested resources.

For entomology you would need a microscope, stereoscope, or a strong hand lens; a butterfly net; a few collecting bottles; some alcohol for larvae preservation; and a tiny bit of nail polish remover to asphyxiate adult insects before you study them. If your students want to make an insect collection, they will need pins, labels, a box with a lid, and an insert that will hold the pins.

For botany, you would need a microscope, soil, seeds, live plants, containers for growing plants, etc. Supplies would be similar to those needed for biology, minus the animals for dissection. You will need dissection tools for leaf, stem, flower, and seed dissections, etc.

Social Studies

Although the high school study of science is critical for college preparation, the "science" or study of human actions and relationships is just as important. Grouped together these disciplines are called social studies, and at the high school level they include primarily history, government, economics, and geography.

Colleges differ on their social studies requirements, so make sure that you find out what your students need for their top-choice schools. Most American high school students complete at least one year of United States history and one year of world history. Government, economics, and geography courses are also popular, and some students do in-depth studies of regional history, such as European history or their state history. Although social studies courses are usually divided into different areas, you will find that each course incorporates information from other social studies disciplines. For example, governmental actions and economic conditions usually determine major historical events. Geography is closely tied to the other areas because of exploration, political divisions, people groups, defense, economics of location, etc. Perhaps history incorporates the other areas best, so I will discuss social studies courses in that context.

History

Students need to know what happened in the past to understand the present, so the study of both national and world history is essential. George Santayana said, "Those who do not learn from history are doomed to repeat it." People who are misinformed about the past or who refuse to believe the truth about historical events cannot make wise decisions in the present. We have seen evidence of this principle in U.S. court decisions about the supposed constitutional "separation of Church and State," a phrase that is not mentioned in the U.S. Constitution at all. Our Founding Fathers had experienced government control of religion in Europe, and they wanted to keep their new government from wielding the same power. The phrase "a wall of separation between Church and State" is found in a letter written by Thomas Jefferson assuring the Danbury Baptists that their free exercise of religion would not be hindered by the federal government. This "separation of church and state" phrase has been misinterpreted to mean the opposite of what Jefferson intended, and this has allowed our constitutionally-guaranteed religious freedoms to be stripped from us one by one.[2]

When one observes modern dictatorships, it is easy to see how a misinformed populace can be duped into believing false accounts of historical and current events. Citizens in such countries believe what their governments want them to believe, and as long as a dictator controls the media, the military, and education, his power continues unabated. Both those seeking freedom and those desiring to remain free must seek out the truth.

The misinterpretation of historical events can also lead to naïveté. For instance, Christians need to be careful that they do not whitewash history simply to justify national patriotism or prove providential guidance. Patriotism needs no justification in a country that honors God and attempts to treat its citizens and the rest of the world honorably. According to the Bible, no leader rises to power without divine sanction. Sometimes God blesses nations through their leaders; sometimes He blesses in spite of them. Other times he selects rulers to punish nations (such as King Nebuchadnezzar—see Jeremiah 25:9). If those in power seek God's guidance and obey Him, the result is usually blessing, but often good leaders become corrupted—through their own pride, outside influences, or general human weakness—and their people suffer for it. America's founders understood human depravity and designed a government with checks and balances in an attempt to keep it under control. We do our high schoolers a disservice if we do not help them understand the role mankind's greed, hatred, and dishonesty have played in directing the course of history, especially that of our own country.

Bryan College history professor Jack Traylor expressed concern about this issue.

Sometimes [homeschoolers] seem to have been taught from a perspective that throws out most or all secular knowledge as evil in an attempt to gain strictly a biblical perspective. I think some of the books for homeschoolers are geared to a market that expects certain things. In history, for example, this point of view often creates American history as some Christians think it should have happened, even though it may not have happened that way.

The writings of two historians, possibly three, stand out as examples of great, enjoyable historical writing. Stanley Vestal (a pen name for Walter S. Campbell) wrote about the American West (e.g., Dodge City: Queen of the Cowtowns*); William Manchester writes about a variety of subjects (my favorite is* American Caesar, *a biography of Douglas Mac-Arthur). Also, Barbara Tuchman is quite good (her* The Proud Tower *comes to mind).*

Jack Traylor, Professor of History, Bryan College

Debbie Musselman agrees. "I've read 'Christian' history books that leave out whole chunks of history because they consider it 'secular' material. How are our kids supposed to learn from our mistakes if they don't know what happened? We can't gloss over, change, or ignore something simply because it's embarrassing to us as a nation."

Students and teachers need to realize the subjectivity and selectivity that go into reporting history. Each period of history was the present to those who lived it. If you had to record the history of the past five years for future generations to read, what would you include? What would you omit? How would your perception of events change if you were living in a different area or country, belonged to a different race or economic group, or held different beliefs or values? When you think about it that way, it is easy to see that history is not simply cut-and-dried facts. Four witnesses reporting the same event will report and interpret it four different ways. As time passes, other people (historians) write their impressions of what happened based on either these eyewitness accounts or other historians' impressions. So no version of historical events can be considered the definitive one.

We are now seeing more historical information presented from the perspectives of ethnic minorities, women, the poor, and the powerless. In the interest of political correctness, the pendulum has swung way too far in many cases, for instance, discounting anything positive done by white people of European descent. However, it is good for students to "walk in the shoes" of those who were involved on all sides of an event, and it is only right—in the interest of truth and fairness—that all our stories be told.

Most of all and especially considering all the changes being made to history books today, it is important not to rely on any one source for your understanding of history. Jane Williams, whose Bluestocking Press specializes in resources for studying American history, says:

All history is slanted based on the facts historians choose to report. This is not usually a deliberate attempt on the part of the historian. It results from the need to write history to fit within a one-volume semester of study. It is impossible to report all the data available, or history books would be several volumes and thousands of pages long. For the sake of brevity, historians are forced to select what they believe to be the most important events. The author's viewpoint can influence those selections. In teaching children, the most important thing we can do is to teach them how to identify the biases of authors, news commentators, talk show hosts, etc. The goal is that by the time they are upper level high school students, they will be able to identify the bias of almost any material that is presented to them.

One effective way to identify biased reporting and keep historical events in proper perspective is to study history through a model. Williams recommends this approach for the study of high school history.

The model that we promote at Bluestocking Press is called Uncle Eric's Model of How the World Works. It is a model consistent with free market economics, limited government, and political neutrality as well as with the principles of America's founders. Models are how we think. Models help us sort the incoming data to determine what is important and what is not. There are lots of models out there…. [High school students] are old enough to do much of their own research to determine for themselves which models make sense and which do not. The most important thing to remember is that while a student studies history, the newly acquired historical data are used to test the model, to determine whether the model can stand up to the facts. If not, the student must question the data and/or question the model. If the model doesn't hold up, then a student must reevaluate the model. In the information age, with the Internet, TV, media coverage, etc., we are becoming loaded down with data, which is why it's extremely important to develop tools to help us determine what data are important and what data are not—a model.

Many also tout the value of using primary source material in the study of history. These are the writings of those who actually lived at the time of specific historical events. Nothing makes history come alive better than reading first-person accounts (or historical fiction based on those accounts). However, Williams cautions teachers to keep the significance of these documents in perspective.

Primary source material is an individual's account of what took place—his/her thoughts and observations as a witness to, or participant in, an event. A person's bias can color his/her account, so primary source, like secondary source, must be read with the understanding that other sides of the story also exist. When an individual tells a story, s/he usually presents the facts that place himself/herself in the best light. S/he might not choose to report all the facts, but what is reported will be true. So, to understand the events of history, read many opposing viewpoints in an attempt to sort through the biases and find some sense of what really happened. Since America's founders established the government on their own principles and philosophies, their writings provide essential insights into the original American ideology. For example, many people today do not understand the difference between a republic and a democracy. However, there is a distinct difference between these original concepts and contemporary understanding of them. I encourage all students to read as much of these primary sources, the writings of America's founders, as they possibly can.

History in Relation to Government

In the political or governmental arena, the history of mankind is the study of peace and war—of who was in power where, why, how, and for how long before someone else took over. Studying the government of our own country and comparing it with forms of government in other places and times helps students understand how history is made today and why things happened the way they did in the past. We Americans are so used to freedom that we often do not realize how little power the populace in other countries may have. When I was in high school, our government teacher required each of us to write a term paper comparing the form of government in the United States with that of another country. It was an enlightening experience that you may want to duplicate with your students.

Williams encourages students to approach the study of government in two ways. She says:

> Government is generally a required course of study for high school students. However, there are two aspects of the study of government that we encourage at Bluestocking Press. One is the blueprint definition of how government works (understanding the separation of powers, how a bill becomes a law, elections, etc.). The second aspect, the one America's founders were most concerned with, is the nature of government. The system of government originally constructed by America's founders was implemented to curb the nature of government. At Bluestocking Press we provide materials that inform students about both aspects of government. The Uncle Eric books by Richard Maybury provide an excellent introduction to the nature of government, as will the original writings of America's founders.

History in Relation to Economics

Economics is more important for understanding historical and current events than most people realize. Money runs countries. For instance, in the former Soviet Union, the state controlled jobs, land, housing, food supplies, and medical facilities. Consequently it controlled the money and the people. In medieval times, the manorial system, feudalism, and guilds were all based on economics. Economics has also been responsible for most wars, because somebody wanted what someone else had: land, wealth, power, resources, or material possessions.

As important as it is, the economic side of history is missing in most textbooks, according to Williams. "Students study historical data. They study the cultures, chronology, place names, key players, and dates relative to historical events, but they will learn little about the economic history that explains why it happened. Usually, in the study of history, if you follow the money, you'll follow the course of history," she says.

Even if your students do not study economics as a separate course, be sure to supplement their study of history with some basic information about this topic.

History in Relation to Geography

Everything in history happened somewhere. Sometimes historical events happened in certain ways or at certain times specifically because of the geography of the areas involved. For instance, Hannibal and his elephants would have had an easier time defeating Rome if he had not lost so many troops crossing the Alps. If he had not been from northern Africa, he would not have used elephants at all.

Though most high schools have abandoned geography as a required course, knowledge of it is essential in today's global society. Traylor reports that geography, especially U.S. geography, is a common weakness of today's college students. Make sure that your students have a working knowledge of the topography, political divisions, and people groups of the world. At the very least, students should know the geography of their own country. I will never forget my shock when a high school senior in Maryland asked me if Colorado is next to Ohio.

Even if you do not teach geography as a formal high school course, there are many ways to incorporate it into your curriculum. Take advantage of opportunities to learn about places that are mentioned in newscasts or in your study of history and literature. Have your students look these places up and learn about their history, languages, and cultures. Play geography games or challenge each other with geography trivia. Draw maps. Read novels or biographies that take place in other parts of the world. Also, make sure that your students can read various types of maps, including street maps and highway maps. Geography is fun and can help us to understand history and other cultures better, so take some time to explore the world with your high schoolers.

Social Studies Resources

There are several ways to learn high school history, government, economics, and geography at home. One way is to study each course separately, using traditional textbooks. However, many homeschoolers use primary source materials, historical fiction, texts of speeches, movies, documentaries, and other resources, either for their curriculum or as supplements to textbooks. Also, make a point to visit local, state, and national historical museums, battlefields, and other historic sites during family vacations to reinforce learning. Richard Maybury's Uncle Eric Books (available through Bluestocking Press) provide an enjoyable way to learn about the connections between economics, government, history, law, and current events. Our daughter loved these books, and she is not alone. Mary Pride says in *Practical Homeschooling Magazine,* "None of my kids are graduating from high school until they've finished reading all these books. Very highly recommended (5 hearts)." William P. Snavely, Emeritus Professor of Economics at George Mason University, comments, "The entire series should be a required, integral component of the social studies curriculum in all public and private schools. This would bring a quantum leap upward in the quality of citizenship in this country in a single generation." I agree with them both.

Another way to teach social studies is through an integrated approach, such as unit studies. Social studies courses combine well because they are so closely related. You could easily integrate your study of world history, world geography, and economics or U.S. history, U.S. geography, and U.S. government. Unit studies are also wonderful for studying social studies in conjunction with literature, art, music, crafts, and other learning activities.

In choosing your social studies curricula and teaching methods, do not do what is popular with your friends or use a book simply because the local school uses it. Do what is best for your students. Williams says it is important to determine what type of learner you are teaching. It's also important to realize when a student is ready for abstract, philosophical discussions. "Students mature at different ages and have different learning styles," she says. "This will influence one's approach to teaching. If a student is not yet interested in or ready for the philosophical aspects of history, a teacher might encourage the student's study of history through interesting historical fiction, historical music (ballads, for example), hands-on activities, historical movies, documentaries, etc. These will give a student a sense of chronology, key players, and geographical places of importance."

Foreign Languages

The study of human history and society would not be complete without some exposure to the various languages we speak because many ideas and statements can be clearly understood only in the language in which they were originally conceived. When we understand a culture's language, we usually understand its people better.

Since our world community comprises people who speak various languages, it only makes sense for students to study at least one language besides their native one.

Foreign language study presents challenges of its own because students have to learn how to speak a language without being able to hear it spoken every day. Many homeschoolers opt for Latin, Biblical Greek, or Hebrew because learning to speak these languages is not essential, as it is in the study of modern languages such as French, Spanish, German, Russian, and Japanese.

Weaknesses can include the lack of lab science, poor foreign language speaking skills, and depending on the student, a noticeable lack of social skills when dealing with other people in the same age group.

Renee Wruck Bischoff, Senior Assistant Director of Admission, Lake Forest College

Learning biblical languages and Latin is definitely worthwhile. Understanding biblical languages helps to clarify points of Scripture, and learning Latin expands vocabulary and enhances the understanding of literature. Textbooks are probably sufficient, and generally they are all that is available for teaching ancient languages. However, *Artes Latinae*, a Latin program popular with homeschoolers, includes training in speaking the language. It offers three pronunciations: restored classical, continental, and ecclesiastical.

Modern Languages

In a world that is becoming more globalized, students should be able to speak at least one modern language besides English. While traveling in Europe, I realized how arrogant we Americans can be about the English language. Many of us visit foreign countries fully expecting the people there to speak and understand English. Yet when people from other countries visit the United States, we do not return the favor. We still expect them to understand English. It is only common courtesy to make an attempt to speak a country's language when you visit. Once you have learned a language, you can help visitors who speak it to feel welcome when you encounter them at home. Also, for students planning to participate in foreign service organizations or short- or long-term missions, learning the native language will increase the impact of their activities.

When we visited France, Austria, and Italy several years ago, we thought we had prepared fairly well for the different languages we would encounter. However, there were some surprises we hadn't expected. For example, in Paris we found that the people spoke much too fast for us to pick up individual words and phrases. I had studied French in high school, so after a few days, it was getting easier for me, but by then it was time to leave.

None of us had studied German, except with audiotapes for travelers. We had those travelers' phrases down perfectly. I made the mistake of using one in a shop. "Was ist das?" (What is this?) I asked the shopkeeper, holding out an item. Naturally the shopkeeper answered in German, and I had no idea what she said. I thanked her and placed the mystery item back on the shelf, too embarrassed to let her know that I had not understood. What good is it to know the questions if you cannot understand the answers?

These experiences have made me quite opinionated about the study of modern foreign languages. If you cannot understand the language when natives speak it at normal speed, you have not learned the language. Listening and speaking are the essence of language. Traditional foreign language courses in the United States stress grammar and writing. Although these skills are important, they are not enough when you need to communicate with native speakers.

Many experts claim that the ideal way for students to learn foreign languages is in the same general order that they learned their own. They should listen, mimic, gradually understand, read, and then write. They will pick up some basic grammar along the way and then study grammar in depth when they learn to read and write. Obviously, high school students cannot take as much time to learn a new language as they did to learn their own language. Still, they should begin with an emphasis on listening and progressively add other skills.

Resources for Teaching Modern Languages

Dozens of foreign language programs are available for teaching most modern languages. Try to find a course that includes videotapes or audiotapes featuring native speakers from several regions. This will help students learn both to hear with understanding and to speak with proper pronunciation and correct grammar. Textbooks alone will not provide this training. Learn along with your students and immerse your family in the language as much as possible.

Also, take every opportunity to hear the language being spoken. For example, try to find a native speaker who will meet with you and your students on a regular basis. When you are together, speak only the new language. One homeschooler in our area met once a week with a French student who was studying at a local college. They talked, played board games, and just spent time together speaking nothing but French. The arrangement benefited them both. The French student made a new friend and learned more about American culture, and the American girl got to practice her French with an expert.

If you decide to use a foreign language teacher instead of teaching the language yourself, try to find a native speaker or someone with an accurate accent. It would be better to use tapes than to learn to speak the language incorrectly. If no one is available, find other ways to expose your students to the language. For instance, in addition to using a course that is heavily audiovisual, I bought some videos and children's books and magazines in French. One of the books was a translation of one we had in English, so we were able to compare the way things were said in both languages. I found most of the books at library used-book sales. If you have access to radio or television programs in the target language, have your students listen in as much as possible. In the United States, Spanish-language materials and media are probably the most readily available, whereas in Canada you are more likely to have access to French.

It is difficult to generalize, but we are concerned that home-schooled students tend to focus on one or two areas and ignore others—more often than not, they are well-read, big in humanities, with little hands-on experience in the sciences, and a whole bunch of things in between. We would also like to see more experience with non-English language.

Bill Swain, Central
Washington State University

As they work through audio or videotapes, students should spend time learning grammar and memorizing vocabulary, especially verbs and verb forms. Buy a phrase dictionary for common phrases and have students learn how to read signs they might encounter in countries where the language is spoken. If you visit a country before you have mastered these, utilize time in subways, buses, and other public places to copy down signs so that you and your students can learn what they mean. Students should learn how to read handwritten signs as well. Native speakers might form some letters differently than Americans do, as is the case with the French.

I also recommend reading the New Testament or the Bible in your target language. (These are available from the American Bible Society or in the native countries. I bought a New Testament at Notre Dame Cathedral in Paris.) I suggest reading a passage in English, then in your target language, then in English again. Realize that you cannot translate sentences word for word. The word order may be different, and one of the languages may use idiomatic expressions that are not in the other language.

In addition to curricular materials, Susan Richman of Pennsylvania Homeschoolers had her children read foreign children's books and magazines, eventually progressing to works written for teens and adults. They also used videos of "real movies" and audio tapes of songs. Richman also recommends participating in language nights with other homeschoolers, having your students take the national language exam each year for the target language, and preparing your students for the AP exam in that language.[3] Pennsylvania Homeschoolers offers an AP preparation course online for French. Contact your local high school for information about national language tests.

Whichever language you choose to study and whatever program you use, do as much as you can to hear the language as natives speak it and to read the language as they read it. Then you will be more successful than those who settle for mediocre, traditional foreign language textbooks.

The Arts

Although language is the vehicle by which most human communication takes place, the soul of a people is expressed through its art. In this context, I would include literature as an art form, but the arts as a curricular area usually include only the visual and performing arts. A well-rounded education should include some exposure to these creative forms.

Regrettably, the arts are often neglected during high school in favor of more "academic" subjects. However, art, music, dance, theatre, and—in this century—movies and television are integral to the cultures of various places and times. The arts not only help to explain cultures but also serve to effect change in cultures. If we study the art of another century or another country in conjunction with our study of its history, we will have a better understanding of its people.

Art and music, both appreciation and history, are worthwhile areas of study. If you can fit them into your high school schedule, I highly recommend that you do. Your students also might enjoy classes in applied art, piano or another instrument, voice, ballet, liturgical dance, theatre, etc. Participation in the arts allows us to express and develop the creativity that was instilled in us by our Creator. If your students become leaders in the arts, they can influence their own culture, one would hope, for the better.

Several homeschool arts programs are available. David Quine has designed an art history and appreciation course for Cornerstone Curriculum called *Adventures in Art* to help teach worldviews. Applied arts programs are available from Artistic Pursuits, the Gordon School of Art, and How Great Thou Art. The Artistic Pursuits program covers drawing, painting, color, composition, and art history, while Gordon's New Masters Program teaches the drawing and painting methods of the old masters. Also, *Homeschooling Today* magazine features a famous work of art and art instruction in every issue. (See Appendix B for contact information for these and other programs.)

Christians have varying viewpoints on the amount of viewing and participation that is advisable in the arts. It is difficult to erase pictures from the mind and impressions from the heart. One does not have to see a lewd picture to understand the statement it is making or to observe its cultural effect. As a guideline, why not resolve, like King David, to set before your (and your students') eyes no vile thing (Psalm 101:3). Conversely, Christians should resolve not to be instrumental in producing evil for others to experience.

Where should students develop the discernment and the values that will help them to make wise decisions in their participation in the arts? They should learn from you in your home.

Religious Education

According to the Bible, God has given parents the primary responsibility for their children's spiritual education. Religious institutions can support parents in this training but should not supplant them.

Christian students should have a thorough grounding in Scripture. This and a close relationship with Jesus Christ are the best assurances that they will remain pure and ward off the evil influences of the world around them. They should be able to explain—to anyone who asks—the reason for the hope they have in Christ. (See 1 Peter 3:15.) The best textbook for Bible study is the Bible itself. However, a concordance, commentaries, a Bible atlas, an amplified or parallel Bible, and other resources that help you understand the text in the original languages are all worthwhile tools for Bible study. Your students might want to study your denomination's doctrinal teachings as well. If your denomination has a publishing arm, contact it for a catalog of available resources or visit your local Christian bookstore.

It is quite possible that your teenagers will go through a season of doubting, of wondering whether what they know about God is true. This time is crucial in their religious education. Doubt often occurs when people see injustice or suffering that makes no sense or when they experience a severe personal loss. If your teens begin to doubt their faith, dogmatism on your part might serve only to drive them away. At this age, children begin to think more independently, and this is natural. Give your children the chance, in the safe environment of home, to question, investigate, doubt, and finally embrace their faith. Encourage them to share their doubts, fears, and ideas openly with you, but only if you can truthfully promise to respond with love, compassion, and honesty. If you cannot do this, try to supply godly mentors who can provide compassionate guidance from a biblical perspective. Also have your children read books like C. S. Lewis's *Mere Christianity* and Josh McDowell's *Evidence That Demands a Verdict* and *More Evidence That Demands a Verdict.*

Realize that if your teens do not feel free to express their doubts and feelings at home, they will find another place to do it. For many students, this happens at college or in the work environment with peer advisers who may be just as confused as they are. Sometimes professors whose principal objective is to destroy the Christian faith lure unwary students into humanistic or atheistic philosophies. This can even happen on Christian campuses, so investigate colleges thoroughly before entrusting your children to them.

Wonderful professors who care deeply about students teach on both secular and Christian campuses, and many Christian colleges stick firmly to the truth of Scripture. You simply need to seek them out. Also, bathe your children in prayer every day. Ask the Lord to guide their steps and help them to stay firmly on the path He has set for them.

Elective Courses

By completing the core academic courses and spiritual training I have mentioned, most students will be ready for college. For many high schoolers, though, this preparation is not enough to satisfy their curiosity about the world or to prepare them for their future goals. This is where electives come in.

Students should choose their electives with their interests, goals, and talents in mind. Other courses your students might select include accounting, other business courses, home economics, or nutrition. Students might even want to design some unique courses of their own. If they do, make sure to document everything and try to give each course a name that clearly describes the course content. (See chapter 9 for information about naming courses.)

* * *

Now that we have discussed high school subjects, you may want to start planning your students' preliminary high school course list. After you have done that, you may proceed to the high school planning checklist if you like. However, to help your students set their goals and determine their options, you will need to put on another hat. As a home high schooling teacher, you are also a guidance counselor. Your job description is in the next chapter. Regrettably, the added responsibilities bring with them no increase in salary.

For the Lord gives wisdom, and from his mouth come knowledge and understanding.

Proverbs 2:6

---

1. National Commission on Writing, "National Commission Calls for a Writing Revolution" press release, 4/25/2003, http://www.writingcommission.org/pr.html.
2. For more information on this topic, consult Wallbuilders materials from David Barton, especially his article called "The Separation of Church and State." See http://www.wallbuilders.com/resources/search/detail.php?ResourceID=9.
3. Richman, Howard and Susan, "Learn a Living Language," *Practical Homeschooling* # 34, March-April 2000.

High School Planning Checklist

Before your high school planning is complete, you should be able to answer the following questions. If possible, your answers should be yes to most, if not all, of the yes or no questions. Do not let this list discourage or overwhelm you. Use it simply as a reminder of those areas that you should consider when you are planning your home high school. Use the high school planning grid and course schedule forms (following the checklist) to map out a few potential programs, if you wish.

General Requirements

- Do you know the requirements of your state homeschool law regarding high school courses and requirements for high school graduation (if applicable)?
- Have you filed a copy of your state law where you can readily find it?
- Have you checked with some potential college choices about their general requirements?
- Have you asked for specific homeschool requirements?
- If your student has a specialized interest, have you looked into colleges that offer that major? Do you know their requirements?
- Will your student complete at least four years of study in English? Will the courses you have planned fulfill state and college entrance requirements?
- How many math courses will your student take? Will these math courses prepare your student for adult life? Will they fulfill the requirements of your state and your student's potential college choices?
- Which social studies classes will your student complete? Will they fulfill your state requirements and potential college requirements?
- Which science courses will your student complete? How many of them will include a lab? How do you plan to provide the lab? Will these courses fulfill requirements? Have you planned how you will keep detailed records of lab work?
- Which foreign language(s) will your student study? How do you plan to teach it (them)? Will you use an outside instructor? Will you use video or audio courses? Will these courses fulfill requirements?
- Have you planned any courses in the arts? Are any required by potential colleges?
- Would your student benefit from business classes? If so, which courses will he or she take?
- Have you provided a course in keyboarding and basic computer use if your student is not already proficient in these areas?
- Will your student complete the minimum number of credits required for high school graduation (according to your state or colleges of choice)?
- Have you recorded your high school plans in an organized, legible form that can be revised as necessary? (See chapter 9.)

Homeschooling Specialties

- Have you allowed enough free time for your student to pursue special interests?
- Are you choosing what is best for your student regardless of what others think?
- Are you directing the education of your student, or are you allowing textbooks to do it?
- Will the literature your student reads include many of the great classics and eliminate inferior, albeit popular, literature?
- Are you encouraging your student to help plan his or her own course of study?

- Have you provided chances for your student to be self-taught in some areas?
- Will your student have the opportunity to tutor or teach younger or slower students?
- Have you planned time for family discussions and recreation?
- How do you plan to expose your student to some of the greatest historical and modern thinkers?

Specialized Skills

- Have you planned opportunities for your student to take notes from a lecturer?
- Have you included opportunities to discuss literature, current events, and philosophical or religious issues in group settings?
- Will you require speeches? Have you included persuasive speeches as well as informational speeches?
- Have you planned for at least one formal term paper?
- Have you included instruction in essay writing?
- Will you provide ample opportunity for your student to write essays and shorter papers on various subjects?
- Will your student take at least one "enrichment" class like art, music, or drama?
- What extracurricular activities are planned? Will any of these activities develop leadership skills?
- Are any sports activities planned?
- How will you fulfill physical education requirements (if any)? If none are required, how will your student stay physically fit?
- Will these academic, extracurricular, and recreational activities develop your student's skills in group leadership and cooperation?
- Will your student have the opportunity to interact with the public?
- Will your student be exposed to people of all ages?
- Have you planned activities that will help your student understand people of different backgrounds, races, abilities, or beliefs?

High School Planning Grid

Courses and Semester Planned

Requirements

Language Arts	Math	Science
Social Studies	Foreign Languages	The Arts
Business	Health and Physical Education	Life Skills
Bible/ Religious Education	Other	Total Credits Planned

Total Credits Required

Extracurricular

High School Course Schedule

Grade 9	Grade 10	Grade 11	Grade 12
Total Credits	Total Credits	Total Credits	Total Credits
Extracurricular Activities, Volunteer Work, Job Experience			

Chapter 6

The Home Guidance Office

[The] one thing these students miss out on is all the information that a guidance counselor would normally provide to you. (That's why you're doing the book, right?) It's really hard to figure this all out on your own, when somebody's been trained professionally to do this and gets paid to do it.

Jeff Palm, Hawaii Pacific University

In addition to being facilitators of your high schoolers' education, you will most likely act as their guidance counselors. Your wisdom and counsel will be of great benefit in helping them assess their strengths and determine their goals. Also, guiding your students through the process of determining the best plan for their future can be enjoyable for all of you.

Mom and Dad: Information Central

One of the primary jobs of a guidance counselor is to provide information to help students make wise decisions and stay on track during high school. Students need direction in choosing courses to fulfill requirements for high school graduation, college entrance, and other postsecondary options. (Refer to chapter 3.) They also need timely information about college entrance exams and deadlines for scholarships, financial aid, and admissions. Home high schoolers can and should be responsible for gathering much of this information themselves, but parents should oversee the process to make sure that important steps are not being skipped inadvertently. High schools have trained guidance counselors to help students in this way, and in some school districts, you are welcome to tap their expertise and use their resources. However, as a home educator, you carry most of the responsibility.

High school and former college counselor Donna Poole encourages homeschoolers to link up with an umbrella school or a local public school willing to share resources such as test registration packets, scholarship books, and other reference materials. "The public school has an obligation to share those resources with taxpaying citizens," she says. "Don't spin your wheels trying to get what is already available to you."

Responsibilities of Home Guidance Counselors

- *Provide timely information to your students.*
- *Help them discover their strengths and define their goals.*
- *Guide curricular and extracurricular choices.*
- *Monitor their progress.*
- *Maintain their academic records and either issue your own or obtain an outside diploma (optional).*
- *Help them determine their best options for post-secondary education and/or employment.*
- *Guide the college search, admissions, and financial aid process and prepare them for standardized testing.*
- *Provide information about the students to prospective colleges and employers.*

Monitoring Educational Progress

Each semester—or at least once a year—take time with your students to review their high school program and to assess their progress. First, review the goals you set to see whether they are being met. Next, make note of any weaknesses that you or your students have observed that need to be addressed during the following term. If the students have taken standardized tests, analyze the results to see where you might strengthen your curriculum or test preparation. Finally, if student goals or interests have changed dramatically, use this time to make any necessary changes in your master plan.

During these times of reevaluation, offer your wisdom freely and assert your parental authority when necessary. For example, do not allow your students to quit a subject that is difficult. Encourage perseverance, at least to a reasonable level.

Is Quitting Ever Allowed?

There may be times when you should consider allowing your student to quit or postpone a course. If one of your principal goals is to foster a love of learning, don't stifle that love by pushing too hard. At the same time, don't encourage laziness.

Sometimes lack of mental or emotional maturity is a good reason to give up on a course. For example, Christine simply could not understand algebra at the traditional age for studying it. After trying three different books (and Saxon twice), we decided to have her complete geometry first. She surprised us by being a whiz at geometry. I was a little worried when we came to geometry problems that required algebraic calculations. However, using algebra in geometric applications that she understood made algebra clear to her. Midway through her geometry course, she began Algebra I again and completed it successfully. Although she had to work hard to understand it, she also mastered Algebra II. So if you have a student who has sincerely tried to understand a subject and cannot, give it a little time. Proceed to something else and return to the troublesome topic later.

Homeschool mom Risa Killingsworth advises, "Don't push to go forward because everyone else is doing it. Do what's best for your child."

If a family decides not to use any grade system we will not be able to consider them for our scholarship (whether they come from a homeschool or a private school system that does not grade their students). So a no-grade system can very much disadvantage a student from college scholarships.

Jeorge Fierro, Assistant Director Admissions, Western Michigan University

Keeping Complete and Accurate Records

There is no reason to wait until your children apply to college to begin writing their transcripts. In fact, it is much better to begin during the first semester of high school and then keep the transcript up-to-date as each course or semester is completed. This will save a great deal of time during the busy junior and senior years. Chapter 9 will give you more information about keeping high school records. These usually include student course titles and grades; course descriptions; school and teacher information; test scores; recommendations from teachers, employers, etc.; samples of student work (possibly graded); and optional photos of students and their projects during labs, speeches, performances, etc.

The No-Grades Option

If you do not give grades, documentation is even more important. Debbie Musselman chose not to grade her children's work. She and her husband, Jim, did not want their girls falling into the trap of working to achieve grades. They wanted them to learn for the sake of learning. The lack of grades posed only minor difficulties for her older daughter, Christie, when she entered college. Younger daughter Catherine's ACT scores were so high that she had no trouble being accepted everywhere she applied.

Musselman says, "I think people need to be aware that if they do things differently, there could be a price to pay, and they need to decide whether they're willing to pay that price or not."

Although several admissions directors mentioned the importance of keeping good records, including grades, Houghton College's Bruce Campbell recommends checking with individual colleges on their policies. He says that schools differ on whether or not they want to see parent-assigned grades. (Houghton does not require them.)

The Importance of Records

Whether or not you assign grades, you need to keep good records. Wayne R. Wood, Director of Admissions and Financial Aid at Goddard College, asks for "as much supporting documentation as possible." He feels that this gives admissions counselors a better appreciation for students' capabilities and accomplishments. "Grades often reflect only a student's ability to memorize," he says.

Michael Farris encourages homeschoolers to keep good records of their studies to show that they have covered the appropriate courses and have completed work at a high level. "Keep writing samples," he says.

> Keep every achievement test that you've done. We [HSLDA] recommend that you take an achievement test every year at the high school level, even if your state law doesn't require it. Keep really good records of what you do outside of school as well so that you can show that you've really done a good job of being a well-rounded person.
>
> If colleges are given a choice between two valedictorians from public schools and one of them has been a candy striper and the other one has just sat in the library and read schoolbooks, they're going to take the person [who's] valedictorian and a candy striper. The same thing is true with homeschoolers. They need to get out and serve....

Another advantage of good record keeping is that your planning will be easier when younger children reach high school, especially if you have noted which methods and resources worked and which did not. Even though each student has different needs and interests, your records for the older students will help you get started.

So keep track of your students' curriculum, goals, academic progress, activities, and anything else you think may be helpful to remember or necessary to show someone else later.

College and Career Planning

As your students progress through high school, they should begin to consider what to do after graduation. Poole recommends having your high schoolers take the Strong Interest Inventory, which many colleges and community colleges administer for a fee. She calls it the "Cadillac of career tests."

A resource I like for those who are unsure of their strengths and unclear about their interests is *Discover Your Best Possible Future* (out of print, but you might be able to find it used). This book was written from the premise that one's passion for certain activities is most likely God-given and can provide the key to unlocking His plan for a fulfilling future. Through a series of questionnaires, the author helps readers evaluate their past activities and discover their areas of strength and weakness.

Completing this book helped Christine realize that she had previously excluded her greatest interest—drama—as a possible major because she could not see its marketability or application to her future life as a wife and mother. On completing this book, she knew exactly what she wanted to do. She majored in communication arts with a theatre emphasis and now teaches children's drama and directs theatre for all ages—work that she can continue doing part-time when she becomes a mother.

Help your students unearth their deepest passions, and it might reveal the best plan for their futures as well.

Students Not College Bound?

Perhaps your students do not plan to pursue a college degree. That may indeed be the best plan for them, but make sure that they weigh the decision carefully. Most careers require more than a high school education, and unless students have superior entrepreneurial skills, they might not be prepared to support themselves or a family through self-employment. Statistically the odds are against them if they want to start a small business. However, homeschoolers have generally been quite successful with home-based businesses. If your students want to try it, make sure that they are well prepared. Taking a few business classes at a community college during or after high school would be a good idea.

College is the answer for a lot of kids, but a lot of other kids would be better served in really preparing themselves to do a good job in life. There are well-paying jobs out there that don't require a college education.... Homeschool kids have a work ethic that's miles above other kids, and the work ethic is going to take them to the top of whatever they want to do.

Mike Bolinsky, Science Projects

Encouraging Higher Education

Poole believes that you should give your students a taste of college while they are in high school so that they will realize the importance of getting a college education. She told of a homeschool mother whose son was a "hands-on, mechanical type of person." He worked construction in the afternoons and had no interest in attending college. During his senior year, his mother had him enroll in freshman English and speech classes at the local community college. He enjoyed it so much, he decided to attend the following fall.

Ralph Green, formerly a high school and community college counselor for many years, says that you should look at a student's aptitude and interests to determine whether college is the best choice for that student. He says, "I think college is not a bad place to make up your mind.... Very few students are really mature enough at the end of the high school years to make wise vocational decisions." He mentioned that vocational experiences, often unavailable during high school, are readily available in community colleges and four-year colleges and that exposure to such activities can help students decide on careers.

Postponing College

Your students also might consider taking off some time between high school and college to work and evaluate their need for more education. Christine waited a year before entering college. She spent that year reading, working, and praying about her decision. One advantage was that she had time to concentrate on the college application process without having to complete senior courses at the same time. She also saved money for college. A disadvantage was that not being a high school senior made her ineligible to apply for some private scholarships.

Alternative Routes to Higher Education

There are other alternatives to traditional higher education. They include correspondence college, online courses, technical or occupational training, and apprenticeships. Continuing a home education through correspondence college could be a good use of time while students are making up their minds.

Marty Bigger encourages parents and students to weigh all their options. "Things are changing so fast. Apprenticeship is becoming popular in health care fields and engineering—so many things can be done through apprenticeship that are more directed, more 'real-life,' and a lot less expensive than traditional college. I think you need to stay in touch with education and stay in touch with your children and their needs and what they really want. Of course, I would really say you need to pray for wisdom. It's a tough world out there." If students are confused, just give it some time. Let them go to work or continue to study on their own for a while. Eventually they'll know what to do. Many homeschoolers have opted to forego college or to pursue degrees at home by correspondence.

Poole says:

> *I probably would not push a child who had not shown some initiative in learning.... I see homeschooling as a wonderful opportunity for individual seeking of knowledge. If you haven't seen that [interest] as a parent, I don't know that I'd be pushing college.... I think a parent just has to be sensitive to how his or her child has received learning all along and be patient. Just because children don't want to go to college now doesn't mean they won't want to in the future.... Sometimes the eagerness to learn more will come later because they will see that life has more options for them if they have been better educated than high school.*

In today's world, it's almost impossible to draw the line between academics and careers. My younger son is an electrical engineer with a master's degree from Georgia Tech. Of course this is extremely math oriented, but the reason he's an engineer is he likes to accomplish tasks. He likes to work on things, and so this is really vocational training.

Ralph Green, former high school and community college counselor

Why Would a Homeschooler Go to College, Anyway?

About 91 percent of the over 260 colleges that responded to my survey have accepted homeschoolers, so it is obvious that homeschoolers are choosing to attend four-year colleges and universities. You might wonder why other homeschool parents would entrust their children to colleges after shielding them from the traditional education system for so many years. Actually, there are several possible reasons. The most obvious is career preparation. Also, many parents feel that their children's education can be enhanced in a carefully chosen college. I suppose it is likely that some students go on to college simply because it is expected of them, but I like to think that most homeschoolers weigh this decision extremely carefully.

Although Beth Vellalos has strong conservative Christian beliefs, foregoing college is not an option for her sons. "They're going to be responsible to provide for their wives and their children should they be married.... In this day and age, if you don't have a college education, the type of job you're going to be able to get is not very good.... I want my daughter to be a wife and mom. If she's interested in college, that's fine. If she doesn't have an interest in college, I'm not as concerned. She's not going to be the head of her home."

Steve and I wanted Christine to receive a college education despite her goal to become a homeschooling, stay-at-home wife and mother. We believe that higher education, especially a Christian liberal arts education, is inherently valuable for encouraging students to reason independently and to evaluate, in light of their own worldview, the ideas and beliefs of other people, both past and present. Higher education also gives students the opportunity to obtain a more in-depth education taught by specialists in areas that are not typically part of a high-school curriculum. Christine's college degree gives her more credibility as a drama instructor and could potentially enhance her abilities as a homeschool teacher.

Christine felt that a college education was important to give her something to fall back on should anything happen to her husband. After hearing about a recently widowed homeschooling mother of four, she said, "It's great to be optimistic and to trust the Lord, but one needs to be realistic too. If something happens so that a husband cannot work or if he is not there to work anymore, a woman should be able, in some respects, to support herself and her family. I think it's best for a woman to stay at home, but sometimes you don't have that choice."

Because she wanted to receive her college education from a biblical perspective, Christine chose a small Christian college with a home-like atmosphere and a strong commitment to a biblical world-view. Living away from home in a Christian setting was a valuable part of her maturation process. The friendships she made in college helped to develop her relational skills and added richness to her life. However, since not all "Christian" students lived up to their name, college was also a testing ground where she learned to live out her beliefs before her peers and professors in a fairly safe (spiritually speaking) environment before she had to do it alone as an adult in secular culture.

Guiding the College Search Process

Finding the right college can be a lengthy process. As guidance counselors, your job is to help your students find information about colleges that might interest them. You should not do all the work for them; instead do what you can to direct them to resources that will help them do it themselves. Poole says that parents should help students interpret college catalogs, which are tricky to read. She suggests starting to compare catalogs in tenth grade.

Voluminous college guides are available in libraries and bookstores. The Internet also has several college search services. (See Teaching and Home Guidance Counseling in Appendix B.) I will discuss the college search process in more detail in chapter 7.

One of the things we see a lot is that students... finish early in a home school. I've had several over the past few years who have been 16 and have finished high school. That brings great scrutiny, especially if the test scores don't match.... If the ACT is strong, certainly we don't scrutinize the high school transcript as much because we know they're ready.

Gary T. Ray, Director of
Undergraduate Admissions,
Lee University

College Entrance Exams

High school guidance counselors spend a large percentage of their time administering tests and informing students about upcoming ones. When homeschool students lack a certified diploma, many colleges rely on standardized tests to verify their achievements.

Types of Tests

Unless your state has other mandatory testing, the two major college entrance exams, the ACT and SAT, are the ones that most concern you. Many students take both tests. Check with colleges to find out which one they require or prefer. The majority will accept scores from either test, but East and West Coast colleges historically tend to prefer the SAT, while most Midwestern, Central, and Southern colleges prefer the ACT. Some require on-campus testing with their preferred test (for students without those scores) for placement into freshman classes.

The College Board and the ACT also provide preliminary exams that students take earlier in high school. Students may take the PSAT in October of their sophomore year (tenth grade), but most take it in their junior year (eleventh grade). ACT offers the PLAN test, usually taken in the fall of the sophomore year. Neither of these tests is a prerequisite for college entrance examinations (ACT and SAT); however, they provide good practice—the PLAN for the ACT and the PSAT for the SAT. The junior year PSAT has the added advantage of being the National Merit Scholarship Qualifying Test (PSAT/NMSQT). Top scorers on this test may win college scholarships. (Students will be notified automatically if they are chosen as semifinalists.) At the very least, your students should plan to take the PSAT in October of their junior year and the SAT and/or ACT in both the spring of their junior year and the fall of their senior year (twelfth grade). Some colleges also require or encourage students to take some SAT II subject tests. The College Board provides these tests. When you are planning your curriculum, include college entrance examinations in the schedule. Then see that students know the test dates at least a few months in advance. Preregistration is required, and students who miss the registration deadlines will have to wait until the next testing date. Timing becomes especially important during the junior and senior years. Without timely test scores, your students might miss out on scholarships and could even lose opportunities for admission. You may register online or obtain test registration packets from a local high school guidance counselor. ACT will also accept requests by telephone. Besides offering information about preparing for and taking their various tests, the ACT and SAT websites contain information about career planning, the college search, and financial aid.

High school counselor Judy Rodgers recommends that students also take the Armed Services Vocational Aptitude Battery (ASVAB). "We give that to all juniors, mainly because it's free. The military administers it. It's a very good aptitude vocational battery, and it's absolutely free to the kids. The military uses it then for recruitment purposes. That's up to them, but we use it, and then they supply a person who comes in and talks to the kids about what their testing showed about them and their possible careers. We think that's good."

If your students plan to enter the workforce immediately after high school, they might consider taking the ACT WorkKeys test. According to Judy Rodgers, "ACT WorkKeys is an assessment of readiness for the workplace. Employers use it as an assessment of potential employees." She explains that it tests basic math and communications skills and "supposedly gives an employer an idea of the student's readiness to go to work." Check with your local high schools to see whether they offer the WorkKeys and/or ASVAB tests.

Test Preparation

You should begin preparing your students for college entrance examinations early in their high school years. Libraries and bookstores have dozens of guides for test preparation. Our daughter found that the best preparation for the ACT, other than having a strong curriculum, was to take timed practice ACT tests. The ACT's official guide was the best resource we found for this. Taking practice tests for the SAT is valuable, too, although learning SAT testing tips from test preparation guides might be even more valuable. Strong vocabulary, math, and reasoning skills are important for the SAT. The College Board publishes *10 Real SATs* (also available with a CD-ROM) so that students can practice on past examinations.

Poole encourages students to practice with test-preparation CD-ROMs. These programs give students the chance for practice with immediate feedback. She says that SAT and ACT results are

Contact Information

For PSAT, SAT, SAT II:
College Board Headquarters
45 Columbus Avenue
New York, NY 10023-6992
212-713-8000
www.collegeboard.com

For PLAN, ACT, WorkKeys:
ACT
PO Box 168
2201 N. Dodge Street
Iowa City, IA 52232-0168
319-337-1000
www.act.org

ASVAB information
www.todaysmilitary.com

a good indication of how well you have prepared your students, "especially the ACT, because it is very content driven and even provides subscores in broad areas of learning. For example, the mathematics score includes subscores in algebra and geometry…so you can see how well your children stack up nationally with people of their age."

Make test preparation a regular part of your high school curriculum from the freshman year on. Have students complete timed sections of sample tests or review parts of test preparation books or computer programs on a regular basis, possibly once every month or so. During junior and senior years, practice should be intensified, especially as test dates approach. Many homeschoolers use James Stobaugh's *SAT Preparation Course* to help their children build critical thinking skills over time. To help students become comfortable with the bubble answer sheets for these tests, Tamie Goggans suggests copying some from test preparation books and using them for other multiple-choice tests in your curriculum. Otherwise students might take too long filling in those little circles or might not fill them in completely.

I would recommend that they take the PSAT or ACT pretest starting in their SOPHOMORE year.

William J. Katip,
Robert Morris College

Christine found that taking a complete sample examination, just as if she were at the test center, was the most helpful preparation. She started at the same time that the real test would be given and followed the exact testing schedule. Later, when she analyzed her scores, she realized that her weakness was not an inability to answer the questions but her lack of speed. So she worked with other sample tests for the next few weeks on one section at a time, forcing herself to increase her speed.

ACT/ SAT Score Reports

The College Board and American College Testing (ACT) report scores differently. ACT will send colleges only scores for the most recent test or whichever one you specify. This can be a decided advantage, especially if you are concerned about test results. Your student can take the ACT more than once and have only the best scores sent to colleges and scholarship agencies. To take advantage of this, opt for no reports to be sent directly to colleges when your student registers for the test.

Occasionally we will see a student who has strong grades but weak standardized test scores which raises questions about inflated grades, but this seems to be increasingly rare.

Marc G. Williar, Director of
Admissions, Flagler College

Conversely, colleges receive test scores for every SAT and PSAT your student takes. If your child does poorly on one of the tests, this could be a disadvantage. However, one admissions adviser said that colleges generally take the highest score in each subject area from the different SATs a student takes. Another admissions director told me that his college takes the scores from the test with the highest composite scores. Both SAT and ACT offer the option of ordering a copy of the actual test your student has taken with his or her answers. Students can use these to see where they were weak and then work on those areas before they retake the test. You may sign up for this question-and-answer service when you register. Read your test bulletins carefully because it is available only for specific test dates.

How can you be sure that your students' test scores are high enough to support the grades you give them?

"If [an A-B average] is matched with a solid score, there's a high probability they'll do as well as or better than their peers from public schools," says Gary Ray, Director of Undergraduate Admissions at Lee University. He estimates that the ACT score should be 23–24 and up and the SAT should be about 1100 to match an A average. However, highly selective schools will expect ACT scores of 28–30 and above and SAT scores of at least 1200.

Geoffrey Gould, Director of Undergraduate Admissions at Binghamton University (SUNY), suggests that you use old SAT, ACT, and SAT II tests to help build basic skills. He says that by giving those public-edition tests on your own, you can gauge your students' progress with materials intended to reflect the current academic substance taught in many high schools. He says that "taking the tests without having to share the scores can at least provide the homeschooled students with feedback which may help them anticipate the reactions of colleges to their preparation."

Taking standardized tests is only one prerequisite for acceptance to most colleges. Applying to college involves many steps, and guidance counselors play a key role in guiding students through the process.

College Application

Guidance counselors help students through the college application process by providing transcripts and guiding students as they write essays and complete applications. (I will cover these topics in chapter 10.) Students also need help in making decisions about diplomas, GEDs, and financial aid.

Although the number enrolling has been small, the quality of students as evidenced by their course selection and ACT/SAT scores has been excellent.

Dennis Hendrickson, Associate Director of Admissions, University of Northern Iowa

High School Diplomas

Issuing or obtaining high school diplomas for your students is optional. Some colleges require students to have them; others do not. Correspondence and umbrella schools usually award diplomas. If you want to issue your own, HSLDA sells an attractive one for you to fill out and sign. They even offer a package that includes a cap and gown. You need to be aware that by offering the diploma, HSLDA is not endorsing your homeschool program. Christine received an accredited diploma from Summit Christian Academy, but we still gave her a diploma, indicating that she had fulfilled our homeschool requirements in addition to those that were imposed by Summit. In some states it may be illegal to issue your own diploma, so make sure you know your state homeschooling laws.

To GED or Not to GED?

Nearly one-third of the colleges that responded to my survey require either a certified diploma (one endorsed by a school or another authority) or a GED for admission. At the time of the survey, several others required one of these documents for financial aid eligibility because of federal requirements. However, now that ability-to-benefit rules have been changed to accommodate certain homeschool programs, fewer colleges have this requirement. A few colleges will not accept a GED at all, and some will disqualify GED holders from receiving scholarships. Therefore it is important that you decide where you stand on the GED issue. Some homeschool parents have no qualms about having their students take it, while others are adamantly against it.

Tamie Goggans refused to allow her sons to take the GED, even though a college was trying to force one son to take it. "I wouldn't do it for two reasons. The fact that it disqualified him for scholarships really cemented me. The other reason is there's a stigma attached to the GED, and I want to avoid it ever getting on their educational records...even if it's just a procedural thing to get around because we're homeschoolers. Somebody looking through their files will see GED [with an] automatic attitude that this kid is not up to snuff, either in character...or in academic ability." Tamie's oldest son is a National Merit Scholar and a presidential scholar at his college. Her second son is also a scholarship winner and college honors student.

Christine had an experience that convinced her not to take the GED when she borrowed a GED preparation book from the library. In the book's introduction, the author enthusiastically dropped the names of several famous people who had completed the GED. He assured the reader that those people were "high school dropouts, too."

"I'm NOT a high school dropout!" Christine told the absent author emphatically, and promptly returned the book. As a result of this experience, she was afraid that earning a high school diploma through an equivalency exam might falsely stigmatize her as a dropout.

Apparently Christine's fears were not unfounded. Rodgers, who has been a high-school guidance counselor for more than twenty-five years, cautions students about taking the GED, particularly if they have an interest in the military. "[Military] statistics have shown that [nontraditional students] are more likely to drop out of basic. I always tell kids, if you're going to drop out and get a GED, you can go to college. You could probably go to Harvard on a GED, but there could be individual employers who might be a little biased against you, and I can guarantee the military will…but if you get 15 semester hours of college work, they [the military] consider you a [high school] graduate."

In this day and age, a high school diploma/certificate is important. And while we hope a student will ultimately graduate from Goddard with a BA, occasionally a student will withdraw. As a counselor interested in advising a student, I think we would be remiss if we did not stress the need for a GED."

Wayne Wood, Director of Admissions and Financial Aid, Goddard College

My survey results suggest that fewer of the highly selective schools require a GED than do less selective schools. Competitive colleges are more interested in high college entrance exam scores, leadership involvement in the church or community, and AP classes or dual-enrollment classes that demonstrate a student's ability to handle a challenging academic environment.

Jonathan P. Reider of Stanford University says, "A GED is such a minimal demonstration of proficiency. It would tell us nothing useful."

Military Requirements

The Department of Defense conducted a pilot program (extended to September of 2004) where homeschool applicants meeting specific criteria were placed into Tier 1, the preferred candidate category, instead of Tier 2, the category from which only a small percentage of candidates are accepted each year. If the pilot program is not extended or made permanent, then homeschool graduates will again be placed into Tier 2 with GED and correspondence-school graduates. At this writing, my understanding is that recruiters look for the following from a homeschool applicant:

- A full 12 years of education, with a minimum number of days and hours of instruction;
- Parent-taught courses (self-taught courses and correspondence school courses place a student into Tier 2);
- An academic environment inside the home (teacher-student interaction for the required numbers of days and hours);
- Fulfillment of state and service (Air Force, Army, Coast Guard, Marines, Navy) requirements;
- Consistent, accurate record-keeping and a transcript in traditional format.

If your children have an interest in the military, be sure to contact recruiters early in high school for up-to-date, specific requirements for military service applicants.

What Is Ability-to-Benefit, Anyway?

Students, according to the U.S. Department of Education's ability-to-benefit regulations, have to prove that they have the aptitude and educational training that will allow them to benefit from a college education. Strict guidelines determine who will and will not be eligible to receive federal financial aid. The first requirement for eligibility is a high school diploma or "its recognized equivalent," such as a GED or state certificate. (Check with your state Department of Education or state homeschool organization to find out whether a state certificate is available.) The regulations for homeschoolers state that a student:

> (a) *must have obtained a secondary school completion credential for home school (other than a high school diploma or its recognized equivalent) provided for under State law; or*
>
> (b) *If State law does not require a home-schooled student to obtain this type of credential, has completed a secondary school education in a home school setting that qualifies as an exemption from compulsory attendance requirements under State law.*[1]

If students cannot meet one of the above qualifications, then they must pass an ability-to-benefit test. The approved ability-to-benefit tests as of this writing are:

1. ASSET Program: Basic Skills Tests (Reading, Writing, and Numerical);
2. Career Programs Assessment (CPAT) Basic Skills Subtests (Language Usage, Reading, and Numerical);
3. COMPASS Subtests: Prealgebra/Numerical Skills Placement, Reading Placement, and Writing Placement;
4. Combined English Language Skills Assessment (CELSA), Forms 1 and 2;
5. Computerized Placement Tests (CPTs)/Accuplacer (Reading Comprehension, Sentence Skills, and Arithmetic);
6. Descriptive Tests: Descriptive Tests of Language Skills (DTLS) (Reading Comprehension, Sentence Structure, and Conventions of Written English);
7. Test of Adult Basic Education (TABE): (Reading, Total Mathematics, Language);
8. Wonderlic Basic Skills Test (WBST)—Verbal forms VS-1 & VS-2, Quantitative Forms QS-1 & QS-2.[2]

Students also must provide documentation to prove that they meet the college's admissions standards and must "maintain satisfactory progress in [their] course of study according to the institution's published standards of satisfactory progress" in an eligible program that offers at least an associate's degree. Other requirements include a valid Social Security Number and Selective Service registration for males between the ages of 18 and 25.

Qualifying under the ability-to-benefit regulation opens the door to federal financial aid—if students are otherwise eligible—and even to some forms of institutional aid.

Saving on College Costs

Scholarships, grants, and loans are available from the U.S. government, colleges, and other public and private organizations. College admissions offices can provide information about the financial aid available through their institutions (which often includes federal aid). Also check your local library, high school counselor's office, or local community college for information about private scholarships and federal aid.

Federal Financial Aid

The federal government has several types of aid available—most of it need-based. To find out about federal aid, get a copy of the Student Guide at a local high school or at http://studentaid.ed.gov/students/publications/student_guide/index.html. To apply for federal aid, you must complete the Free Application for Federal Student Aid (FAFSA) as soon as possible after January 1 of each year that your child will need money. FAFSA forms are available from local high school guidance offices, college financial aid offices, public libraries, online at www.fafsa.ed.gov, or from the Federal Student Aid Information Center at 800-433-3243. The FAFSA uses detailed information about parent and student income to determine the family's required "contribution" to the student's higher education. Any amount above that number can be (but will not necessarily be) supplied through federal aid. Students' assets count against them, so the system essentially punishes those who have worked and saved for college. If you want to preserve your students' eligibility for federal aid, consult an accountant, a financial aid specialist, or a financial/investment specialist about the best ways to save for college. Also check your library or bookstore for the latest books on the topic.

I have a system for assessing non-traditional experiences, assigning traditional scaling to these experiences, and making the full course of financial aid and merit scholarships available on an equal basis with all other students.

David Hawsey, Associate Vice President, Juniata College

When it comes to accepting federal aid, homeschoolers hold differing opinions. Some equate taking federal aid for college with accepting welfare and therefore refuse to apply. Many others feel that they have no choice but to accept it because of the exorbitant cost of higher education.

The whole concept of federal aid presumes a state's obligation to educate its citizens, or at least to bail them out when they cannot afford to educate their children. While that sounds admirable, federal money inevitably leads to federal control. Most homeschool parents feel that the education of their children is their own responsibility. Both constitutional law and Scripture back up their opinion.

The federal aid process also assumes that state bureaucrats not only know what parents can afford but also can dictate what families will pay. Many disagree with these premises and find the federal financial aid process an intrusive invasion of privacy. Much federal aid is in the form of loans. Families should think long and hard about whether they (or the students) should take on such a large amount of debt. It is up to you to decide whether or not you want to apply for federal aid. If you can send your students to college without it, you should consider doing it.

Some would argue that the federal financial aid system is at least partially responsible for today's skyrocketing college costs, claiming that prices have continued to rise in proportion to the availability of federal money. They also claim that federal aid can lead to federal control. To maintain their independence, both Grove City College and Hillsdale College refuse to accept even one dollar of federal money. This includes financial aid in the form of student loans and grants. These two colleges depend instead on private aid to supplement student tuition, although Grove City students may receive state aid.

Although being able to refuse federal money is the ideal, most colleges have to depend on federal funds to survive. People who care about keeping education free from government control should consider supporting good colleges so that they have the option to follow Grove City and Hillsdale's example.

Institutional Aid

One way to avoid the need for federal aid is through institutional scholarships. Colleges usually offer academic or merit scholarships, and many grant scholarships for participation in sports, music, or other specific programs. Your students ought to develop at least one talent or skill that would qualify them for this type of scholarship. Colleges also might offer need-based aid and work-study programs. Check with their admissions or financial aid offices for details.

Often private colleges will have higher scholarships than public institutions, so do not make the mistake of eliminating private schools, thinking that you cannot afford them. Scholarships can make private schools as affordable as or more affordable than public ones.

As a matter of fact we have made changes to our scholarship processes to accommodate home-schooled students.

Bill Strausbaugh, Dean of Enrollment Management, Messiah College

In awarding merit scholarships, colleges take into account students' high-school course selection, grades, AP or dual-credit classes, recommendations, and extracurricular activities. Caution your teens not to be tempted to follow the lead of some traditional students who take easy courses during their senior year, knowing that acceptance letters and scholarship offers arrive before senior grades are reported. This practice is foolish. Students should continue taking challenging courses throughout the senior year, not only to impress colleges but also to keep their study skills current and to invest their time wisely. Homeschoolers should also be sure that their activities and community service projects are well documented because many admissions people have the impression that homeschoolers lack these opportunities. Leadership activities are especially important for scholarship consideration.

Many in-house scholarships are automatic. However, your student must still meet all deadlines and complete all required forms. Check early with the college admissions office or financial aid office about scholarships and requirements. Generally, the earlier students apply, the better their chances. Even the best late-applying candidates cannot receive scholarships once the allocated money has been awarded. For some scholarships, students are required to write essays. This is one reason that writing is so important during high school. Be aware that colleges might count scholarship money as part of your student's income when they award financial aid. So if you plan to combine scholarships with federal aid, be sure to ask whether the college scholarships will raise your "expected contribution."

As early in high school as possible, you should investigate particular colleges' scholarship requirements because meeting these requirements may necessitate changes in your homeschooling plans. Nearly 50 percent of the colleges in my survey award academic scholarships to homeschoolers on an equal basis with traditional students. However, some of these require a certified diploma, a GED, or another ability-to-benefit test for scholarships and/or financial aid.

Several colleges now accept homeschool GPAs for scholarship consideration, but when we began our college search, most of the colleges our daughter was considering awarded scholarships on at least two of the following criteria: class rank, GPA (grade point average), and ACT or SAT scores. As a homeschooler, Christine had no class rank, and it was questionable whether the colleges would accept our grades for scholarship qualification, so Christine's test scores were potentially the only acceptable measurements of her academic ability and achievement. For this reason, and because she did not want to take the GED, we opted for an accredited correspondence school for her senior year. This allowed her to be considered for scholarships because her GPA was verified by placement testing and by the grades she earned while enrolled in the correspondence program.

If colleges ask for a class rank, you should make sure that they really want one from home-schoolers. One out of one is not a rank, and lower rankings could prove disastrous. For example, confusion was caused one year in the admissions department at Worcester Polytechnic when the computer reported a student at the bottom of the high school graduating class. Upon investigation, they found that a homeschool mom had ranked one of her twins two out of two. Learn from her mistake, and do not rank your students unless required to do so.

As the number of home-educated students entering college increases, more scholarships should become available. For merit scholarships, many colleges consider homeschool graduates on an equal basis with other applicants. Some colleges even offer scholarships specifically for home-schoolers.

Private Scholarships

Finding private scholarships requires extra research, which should begin as early as the sophomore year. Libraries and high school counseling offices have books and electronic resources to help students find potential scholarships. Once students have found possible matches, they need to write for applications, follow guidelines, and meet deadlines.

Through experience with club sports, community service, civic fine arts programs and religious organizations, home schooled students can build an impressive resume of activities and leadership.

Brad Chambers, Co-Director of
Admission, Truman State
University, Missouri

You have probably seen advertisements claiming that certain companies can help students win some of the "thousands of dollars in scholarship money that go unclaimed each year." Should you spend money on one of these college search services? The guidance counselors I interviewed do not recommend it. Apparently, search services only provide addresses to write for applications, information that you can obtain easily on your own. Rodgers recommends that you never spend more than fifty dollars, and if a service promises you scholarships, forget it. They do not have the power to promise anything unless they supply the scholarships themselves (which they do not).

You can find free scholarship search services online. These services supposedly match a student's profile with available scholarships. We found that our daughter was ineligible to apply for most of the scholarships with which she was matched, since she took a year off between high school and college. Most of the scholarships were for high school seniors. I have listed some scholarship services in Appendix B.

Advanced Placement and CLEP Tests

Another way to save on college costs is for students to earn college credit during high school either through AP or CLEP testing or through dual enrollment. With enough credits, they may be able to graduate from college a year or two early.

Advanced Placement (AP) examinations are offered each May in local high schools for a fee. Students prepare for the tests by taking intensive, advanced courses equivalent to those offered at the college level. Tests are offered in over twenty subjects. Check with your school district for information about having your children take the exams.

Poole suggests having your students prepare for AP exams in areas where they are gifted. "Anybody can order the syllabus—basically the descriptions of the courses and what's covered.... AP curriculum is pretty rigorous, but it can be done by a parent."

Many review books are available to help with AP test preparation, and the College Board sells AP CD-ROMs containing old tests and other study helps for students to use at home. (See Appendix

B.) By achieving high enough scores, students may either exempt themselves from some course requirements or receive college credit. The highest AP grade is 5. Colleges might grant exemptions or offer credit for scores of 3, 4, or 5. Check with individual colleges for their policies on these exams.

Students also can earn college credit through taking CLEP (College Level Examination Program) tests. These are offered at colleges and other locations all over the country. They measure student knowledge in many subject areas, including English, foreign languages, science, math, and economics. It is essential that you check with your student's college choices about which tests, if any, they will accept for credit before your student completes the examinations.

Dual Enrollment

Dual enrollment (also called joint enrollment or cooperative education) may be a better alternative than AP courses, according to Rodgers, because if students take AP courses and do not score 4 or 5, they do not receive college credit. If they complete dual-enrollment classes, they receive both high school and college credit if they pass the course. AP tests usually cost less than college tuition, so you will have to decide whether dual-enrollment or AP tests are more cost effective for your situation.

Sometimes students cannot participate in the regular joint-enrollment program. In Tennessee, for example, dual-enrollment courses are offered at public high schools, and only enrolled students are allowed to participate. However, students may enroll at community colleges. If a college is not initially open to a joint-enrollment arrangement with your student, Tamie Goggans suggests that you find out what their requirements are for private school participation. Then contact the person in charge of that program and plead your case.

Many admissions directors encourage applicants to make use of internships and dual-enrollment courses during their junior and senior years. Barbara Henry, Homeschool Adviser for Oglethorpe University, reports that most homeschoolers begin their college careers there as joint-enrollment students.

I would suggest that homeschool students take at least one and preferably two courses per "senior-year semester" (pardon the traditional reference) at a local community college—more to ease them in to college but also (secondarily) to validate their performance in a home-based curriculum.

Robert J. Massa,
Dean of Enrollment,
Johns Hopkins University

Although some schools offer the option of taking college classes for high-school credit only, your students might as well earn college credit at the same time, as long as it will not make them ineligible for freshman scholarships. When homeschooler Nathaniel Goggans entered college with several dual-enrollment credits, he still qualified for a freshman presidential scholarship. If he had been enrolled in the community college as a regular student, he would have been considered a transfer student, ineligible for freshman scholarships. So before your students enroll in college-level classes, check with colleges about their policies on college credit and freshman scholarships.

Reporting to Colleges and Employers

One of your most important jobs as guidance counselors is to supply your students' academic records to prospective colleges and employers. Chapter 10 will show you how to complete a professional-looking transcript and will discuss what you should send to colleges. Depending on the college, this may include a transcript of all high-school courses completed, course descriptions, test scores, information about extracurricular and service activities, and documentation to support your claims. You also should make sure that your students are able to describe their homeschool program if asked.

It is obvious that colleges seek homeschool applicants. Of the over 260 colleges that responded to my survey, only one mentioned that it does not actively seek homeschoolers. A handful of others were noncommittal or less than enthusiastic. Most are either interested or enthusiastic about receiving applications from homeschoolers because they have found them to be strong students that contribute to the college community. So if your students are college bound, there is an open door. You just have to help them walk through it. In the next chapter, I will give you some pointers on finding the right door.

Plans fail for lack of counsel, but with many advisers they succeed.

Proverbs 15:22 NIV

---

1. 34 Code of Federal Regulations, Chapter VI, part 668.32.
2. Federal Register, Vol. 67, No. 171.

Chapter 7

The "Perfect College" Pursuit

Since there are a variety of methods to measure or predict success in college, we place a higher emphasis on "the match." In other words, whether the student "fits" at Kansas Wesleyan University. Over the years I have seen valedictorians fail in their first semester of college because they didn't focus on "the match."

Jeffery D. Miller, Director of Admissions

Each college has a spirit or character uniquely its own. This chapter will help you find a college that is a "good fit" for your student by using various sources of information, making college visits, and using the college search evaluation form provided.

Preliminaries

As early as your student's eighth- or ninth-grade year, you should begin researching colleges. Libraries and bookstores are filled with resources about the thousands of higher-education options available. Most guides are updated yearly. Look especially for directories of colleges and for magazines with special college issues. Some periodicals and websites feature specific colleges and give general information about the application process. (See Appendix B or search the Internet for websites.) When reading reviews, keep in mind that ratings and recommendations are based on other people's opinions; you might not agree with them.

You may request information directly from colleges by calling or writing them. Many have toll-free admissions hotlines. Ask what they require of applicants and *especially whether they have additional requirements for homeschoolers*, as many colleges do. During tenth or eleventh grade, narrow the field of choices to four to eight colleges. Then check every year to see whether the colleges' requirements or homeschool policies have changed. By December of the junior year, decide how many colleges you can afford to visit and pare down the selections to that number. Plan your visits for the winter and spring of the junior year and early fall of the senior year, if possible. To save money, we visited colleges after Christine had applied and been accepted. However, it would have been wiser to visit at least local schools while they were in session before she applied. She would have saved the trouble and cost of applying to one school if we had done so.

When you make your list of schools, keep in mind the costs involved in applying to each college. Take into account application fees, visits, and copying and mailing costs. Most counselors advise students to apply to one school that is sure to admit them, one or two schools where they compare well with the average student, and one or two schools that would be more challenging—often called "reach" or "dream" schools—where they have less chance of acceptance. If you and your students do your research well, you will probably have a good idea where they will fit in best.

Several of the homeschool students I interviewed applied to only one college. That practice is generally discouraged unless the college has a guaranteed admission policy and students meet the criteria. It is better to have some other options open so that if the students are not accepted to their top-choice schools, they will not have to scramble at the last minute applying for late admission to other colleges (and losing scholarship opportunities as well).

Criteria for Choosing a College

Before you begin a serious search, discuss as a family what you want in a college. Then rank these qualities in order of importance. A biblical worldview and an excellent education topped our list. Important factors for you may include: price, scholarship and financial aid availability, location and surroundings, variety of majors, selectivity, size, average age of the students, ministry opportunities, foreign study options, internships, school calendar, and extracurricular activities.

Count the Costs

When evaluating the cost of attending a college, you need to consider several factors. First of all, you need to know the rates for tuition, room and board (if needed), and fees. Also, ask the estimated cost for textbooks and materials. Realize that all costs will most likely increase each year. Find out which scholarships and other financial aid your students might qualify for and determine whether the amounts are high enough to make the school affordable for you. Do not forget to ask whether it has homeschool scholarships. Also check the availability of part-time jobs, either on campus or in the surrounding area.

[College] is such a long-term investment. You want to make sure it's a good fit.

Rachelle Reitz,
homeschool graduate and
Associate Director of Admissions,
Patrick Henry College

Take into account costs for transportation and supplies as well. For colleges that are far from home, determine your students' options and the prices for transportation to and from school. Do not forget to include midyear breaks. Estimate costs for any new bedding, towels, and supplies that your students will need and the costs for transporting them. Note that many college dorms have mattresses that require long twin sheets, so standard twin sheets will not fit. Also ask colleges whether they provide returning students with storage space, which will alleviate the need for shipping items back and forth.

If the college is within commuting distance of home, estimate costs for transportation and those meals that will be eaten at school. (These will probably be higher than you expect.) Include expenses for commuting to extracurricular, evening, and weekend functions.

Make sure that the degree a school confers is worth its price. How successful are the school's graduates? What is the likelihood that your students will earn enough money to repay college loans and still be able to support themselves? Is the college accredited? If so, what type of accreditation does it have? If not, will it matter when your students seek employment or apply to graduate school? Some colleges, such as Bob Jones University and Whitefield College, have chosen not to seek accreditation, for reasons they will be happy to explain. Students who choose to attend nonaccredited schools should carefully investigate the success of graduates. If a college's graduates readily find employment and acceptance to graduate schools, the accreditation issue may not be a problem. The key is to know what you are paying for.

The Cost of Money

Some students work to save for college or choose less expensive schools that their families can afford, but the majority of college students take out college loans to help finance their education.

Decide ahead of time whether or not you or your students are willing to carry large loans. Is it a necessity or a convenience? Based on your students' goals and their projected earning potential, would they be wise to go into debt for a college education? Would they be investing in their future or mortgaging it? (A good math exercise would be to have them figure the cost of a college education, including the interest they would pay on loans.)

Wise Solomon wrote that the borrower is servant to the lender (Proverbs 22:7b). Are your students willing to indenture themselves to lenders for several years after college? How much debt are they willing to carry? Compare this amount to the average indebtedness of graduates at each of the colleges that they are considering. (Some college guides provide this information, or you can ask the schools.) If the average indebtedness of graduates is extremely high, the school should have an extremely high percentage of graduates placed in high-paying jobs or accepted to graduate schools shortly after graduation. Even if your students' financial prospects look good, make your students aware that no college major is a guarantee of a successful financial future. For example, the need for engineers fluctuates regularly, and many engineers are laid off, rehired, and laid off again. Changes in Medicare rules have affected other fields, such as speech therapy. Proceed to the lending table with caution.

When considering your options, do not underestimate God's power to supply the resources necessary for college. Jennifer Musselman, a homeschooler from Georgia, was not sure she would be able to attend her top choice college, even with scholarships. "God provided," she says. "It was amazing."

Another homeschooler, Charlotte Revell, was thousands of dollars short of her need, but an anonymous donor paid the difference.

Time Costs Money

On some campuses, students have trouble getting into the classes they need to graduate on time. Extra semesters are costly. Ask colleges what they do to ensure that students who stay on track will be able to earn their diploma in four years. For instance, if classes are full or unavailable, do they offer tutorials or open extra classes for juniors and seniors to complete their requirements? Be aware that colleges cannot be held responsible if students have to attend extra semesters because they changed majors or neglected to take required courses when they were available.

Count the Spiritual Cost

Do not forget to count the cost of higher education in terms of eternal value. How much money is it worth to protect the investment you have made in your children's faith, character, and morals? Decide now whether you are willing to pay more for a private or Christian college if that is the best choice for your student. How much time and money are you willing to invest in college visits to make sure that the education and environment are what you expect? Do not be tempted to skip visits, even to local colleges. Reputation and actuality are not always the same, as we discovered. Even a great reputation is still no more than other people's opinions.

When Christine and I were visiting campuses, we met a fellow homeschool mom and her daughter. The mom was concerned about turning her child over to the care of strangers and worried that all the good she had done could possibly be undone by a college. She asked me how she could know that a college is worthy of her trust. Hers was a difficult question. I think that much of the answer depends on the young people involved. Students with strong personalities, faith, and character and who are not peer dependent will most likely fare better than those who do not possess these qualities. Some will be easily influenced. Many young people are just waiting for the chance to unleash their cravings away from parental knowledge and supervision. Make sure that you know your children well, and then research colleges carefully. Your children still have free will and may go astray, but I believe that seeking God's guidance throughout the process is the best way to assure success.

Rachelle Reitz recalls that some homeschool friends who had never had any freedom to make their own decisions floundered when they were away from their parents. "They weren't making good choices because they weren't used to making good choices. But I wasn't raised that way. I had to make some decisions for myself. I knew how to analyze, and I knew right from wrong."

Even students who know right from wrong and who have been given freedom for making choices during high school may rebel against the way they were brought up. When they reach the ages of 18 to 21, they are free to make most or all of their own decisions. If you have done your best to guide them and they still choose to go astray, you might wonder where you went wrong as a parent. Try not to blame yourself, and do your best to keep the lines of communication open. Be assured that you *are* a good parent, and remember that your grown children are ultimately responsible for their own actions.

Do not underestimate the influence that peers and educational institutions can have on your adult children. If you are Christian, you need to realize that not all "Christian" colleges live up to their name. Even on the best campuses, there will be people, policies, or programs with which you disagree. That is just part of life. Decide ahead of time where you are willing to compromise and where you are not. Then scrutinize colleges before entrusting them with your precious children. Sometimes a secular college with a strong contingent of Christian students and teachers proves to be a better choice than a nominally Christian one, as long as students are actively involved in Christian campus activities. Some of the strongest Christian students we met were on a secular campus. Learn what you can about your students' major departments as well. Some departments may be acceptable, while others on the same campus are not.

Type of College

With your students, discuss what type of college would be most desirable. Four-year colleges come in many sizes and types, including various-sized state colleges, small universities, major research universities, Ivy League schools, and specialized schools for fields such as music, art, and engineering. These institutions may be public, private, nondenominational, or denominationally affiliated. School terms may be semesters, quarters, or shorter periods of time, such as in those colleges that teach one course at a time. (Only a few do this.)

A university includes both undergraduate and graduate or professional schools. The undergraduate divisions of large universities are usually divided into several colleges. For example, they may have a college of arts and sciences, an engineering school, a business school, and a school of education.

Because they are used to individual attention, many homeschoolers prefer small colleges to large state universities, although they choose schools of all sizes.

Jeffery D. Miller, Director of Admissions at Kansas Wesleyan University, believes that students "who are used to a very intimate, home-school setting will transition better into a small, private college or university where the personal attention begins at the campus visit and continues throughout their four years of college."

Check out the various annual college guides that are published by Peterson's, Barron's, and others for information about the size of campuses, types of students, strength of various majors, and other details about the colleges your students are considering. If they are interested in Ivy League schools, they should pursue a rigorous curriculum or an extremely innovative one, be heavily involved in leadership roles in their communities, and perform brilliantly on standardized tests. Check the library for books that explain what these elite schools require.

Majors Offered

Preferences, personalities, and interests usually determine what type of school is best for particular students. However, sometimes students' choices of majors force them to choose larger schools than they would like. For example, there are fewer colleges with majors in preveterinary medicine, piano pedagogy, and other more specialized fields. Your students will probably have a list of at least four possible majors and a few potential minors. Make sure that their top-choice colleges offer those majors, but realize that many students change majors at least once before graduation. Most freshmen register as "undecided," so it is not essential for your students to know their majors before applying to college. They should have a good idea of their strengths and preferences, though.

> To me acceptance is not as important as persistence. I want to recruit a person who will graduate.
>
> Glenn Lygrisse, Vice President for Enrollment Management, Tabor College

Former counselor Ralph Green believes that we tend to want to narrow our students' perspective too soon. "I went to college expecting to be a chemistry major. I majored in history. You can't miss it more than that," he says.

Try to weigh the attributes of colleges a little more heavily than the majors they offer, unless your students are sure of their future goals. Realize, too, that students may complete some general education courses at one college and then transfer to another college later, if necessary. Some credits may not transfer, though, and a drastic change in majors may require students to take several extra courses.

When considering the majors offered at various colleges, bear in mind that similar majors often have different names. Christine planned to major in drama, but at that time Bryan offered only communication arts with a theatre emphasis, which proved to be a better choice for her. If she had looked only for a drama major, she would have missed Bryan.

Faculty and Class Sizes

Low student/faculty ratios are big selling points for colleges, but these numbers can be deceiving. The ideal college has a low student/faculty ratio and a high percentage of faculty members who have earned top degrees in their fields. In the best colleges, professors teach even freshmen in reasonably small classes. As homeschoolers know from experience, students learn better when they can interact closely with their teachers.

Do not be enticed by low student/faculty ratios until you find out what they actually mean. For example, at one particular public university, general education classes meet in huge lecture halls with 200–300 students, making it difficult or impossible to ask questions or meet with professors. These lecture classes break into groups of about twenty each week with graduate assistants as teachers. Yet that school had a 13:1 student/faculty ratio at the time of the interview. (The college had one undergraduate faculty member for every 13 enrolled students.) In contrast, Bryan College, where Christine attended, had a supposedly less favorable ratio of 14:1. Yet her largest freshman general education class had about forty students, and the smallest had eight. No graduate students taught at her school, and 90 percent of the faculty held earned doctorates. When you compare the two schools, which student/faculty ratio was really better? Clearly, Bryan's was. At large universities, those who spend most of their time on research and little time on teaching are included in the student/faculty ratio, so when you are researching schools, ask for the size of the largest classes and whether or not graduate students do any of the teaching.

Activities and Adjacent Areas

Campus activities and the proximity of colleges to towns, cities, and recreational areas are other factors to weigh in your decisions. Students need convenient places to buy reasonably priced toiletries, clothing, and supplies. They also need places to go off campus. Ask your students how they want to spend their free time: in a large city, at the beach, in the mountains, at a mall, in the woods, etc. Encourage them to enumerate the activities they presently enjoy and those they would like to try. Are these available either on campus or nearby? For on-campus activities, are freshmen allowed to participate in meaningful ways? Find out which intercollegiate and intramural sports the college has. Are there facilities for swimming, tennis, volleyball, and working out? If a college and its community do not have all your students' favorite activities, ask students which ones they are willing to live without during the school year.

Investigate the possibilities for internships and foreign study. Most colleges provide opportunities for service in the local community and through mission or service trips. Inquire about the institution's relationship with the local neighborhood. How do the people in town view the college? Are students welcomed into their homes and churches? Is there an acceptable church reasonably close to campus?

If you are considering Christian colleges, ask whether the colleges conduct regular chapels and how often. Find out what sorts of speakers they invite and whether student attendance is required.

College Companions

The students on campus are important to consider, too. How many are there, and what is their average age? What is the male/female ratio? How do most students compare academically with yours? The selectivity of the college gives an indication of this. Highly selective schools will have more academically gifted students. Compare your students' SAT/ACT scores with those of average freshmen in each college. This information is readily available in college guides. The ideal is that your students will be challenged but not overwhelmed.

Many college communities include students from several states and countries, which adds to the value of the educational environment. Find out where students come from and how their moral standards compare to yours.

Serious Sleuthing

The college search process can be overwhelming at times, but it is worth doing a thorough job.

Natalie Arnold of St. John's College, New Mexico, advises, "I would like to encourage any interested home schoolers to approach the whole college selection process as you would any academic discipline; study it broadly and thoroughly. Try to use many different elements, such as visitation, talking to current students at the college, reading different guidebooks, and sending away for information. Also try to make the process as individualized as possible. Develop communication with your designated admissions officer. It is easier to do this at smaller liberal arts colleges, but it is possible anywhere."

Mail Glut: Eliminate the Obvious

After your students take the PSAT, ACT, and SAT, they will be inundated with college literature, especially viewbooks, which are really glorified advertisements. If you have discussed what you and they want in a college, they will be able to eliminate most of these colleges quickly.

However, do not end the search there. Many wonderful colleges do not participate in these mailings, so you will have to make the first contact. Large colleges advertise extensively, but smaller (and often better) colleges may take more work to discover.

As college information comes in, decide what to keep and then file it so that it is easily accessible, because you will refer to it many times. You may organize information alphabetically by college name, by state, in order of preference, or by categories such as type of college and cost. Just be consistent in your filing method. When you have eliminated a college, discard the information or pass it on to friends or a local high school. Automatic mailings will eventually stop, so make sure that your students contact the colleges that interest them. Have them request current literature, videos, and especially catalogs if they are seriously considering the schools.

Viewbooks: Search for Clues

In reading flashy college literature, watch for keywords that can clue you in to the mindset or worldview of the faculty and students. For instance, do you understand terms like *diversity*, *liberal education*, or *Christian humanism*? Do their definitions vary with the institutions involved? Ask colleges to clarify and define their terms for you. If their admissions office cannot do it, call or write their philosophy or Bible department.

Many schools proudly proclaim that they will lead students to new vistas and help them discover their potential—typical advertising jargon. What you need to discern is whether colleges plan to guide students or remold them. If they promise to help students "discover" values for their adult lives, what will they do with students whose values are already formed? Will they automatically assume that these students are closed-minded or misguided, or will they consider them an asset to the campus? Will they tell students *what* to think or challenge them to reason for themselves? Often the answers to these questions depend on the individual teachers or departments involved. You have a right to know what you are paying for and have an obligation to your children to understand the philosophies they will encounter in the classroom. However, colleges are not all striving to undermine the influence you have had on your children. Many will reinforce good values and help students to mature in their convictions while expanding their knowledge and understanding of the world.

Don Crandall, Vice President for Enrollment Management at John Brown University, says, "[Homeschoolers] tend to fit our family profile (conservative Christian backgrounds) well, although they have also been inflexible on some 'fringe' Christianity issues." Can you and your students be flexible on so-called fringe issues? Decide now what is negotiable and what is not. If you are like most homeschoolers, you are intensely independent with strong convictions, so find out where colleges stand on any issues you and your children consider nonnegotiable. Then seek out institutions that either teach what you believe or at least will not undermine your beliefs. At some colleges, faculty members are required to sign and adhere to a mission statement or statement of faith. If this is the case at schools where your students apply, ask for a copy of the statement and try to discover whether faculty members are living up to it.

To really know a college, do not simply ask questions of the admissions staff. Often they will not be aware of the mindsets of all the professors, counselors, and others that deal directly with students once they enroll. Instead, look for clues in college viewbooks, videos, catalogs, student newspapers,

I think an interview is very helpful. Often homeschoolers are admitted to Oglethorpe at a younger than traditional age. [An interview] helps me to judge the emotional maturity of the student and the family's readiness for the transition to college student.

Barbara Henry, Home School
Adviser, Oglethorpe University

and student handbooks. Then question current students and their parents, talk with professors, and visit classes. Also, examine the list of campus organizations—both those that reflect your standards and especially those that do not. Whether you are looking for those who share your beliefs or you are seeking a diversity of beliefs, campus activities will clue you in to the beliefs, morals, and interests of students and faculty.

Arnold says, "Going from a homeschooling environment to a college, one doesn't always necessitate a drastic shift in beliefs. There are many wonderful and educationally minded colleges. A book I recommend for homeschoolers who are embarking on the college selection process is *40 Colleges That Change Lives* by Lauren Pope."

Read our catalog back to front because our program is so unique. Also, visiting campus and sitting in on classes helps applicants decide whether or not they want to attend St. John's. Our application is highly self-selecting, so we try our best to give as much information as possible to applicants so they can make the best decisions for themselves.

Natalie Arnold, Assistant
Director of Admissions,
St. John's College, New Mexico

Catalogs and Handbooks: Conclusive Evidence

While viewbooks present the highlights about colleges, catalogs spell out the details. Peruse them carefully. Here you will find information about admissions requirements, academic programs, individual courses, financial aid, expenses, and faculty.

The May 1996 *Education Reporter* quoted a report by the National Association of Scholars on the "dumbing down" of the top fifty undergraduate colleges and universities in the United States. According to the *Education Reporter*, this report concluded "that students no longer learn the common core of knowledge once taken for granted as essential to a liberal-arts education. The universities have simply purged from the curriculum many of the required courses that formerly taught students the historical, cultural, political and scientific basics of our society."[1]

When you explore a catalog, note what types of subjects are required for graduation. Are important basics like English, mathematics, history, science, and the arts covered? Also, read the descriptions of courses required for various majors. Do they have valuable substance? Read faculty profiles. Are their degrees from reputable institutions? If your students want to work with researchers, find out whether professors are involved in interesting research and whether undergraduate students can actively participate.

Request a copy of the student handbook to find out the rules and the consequences for breaking them. Ask how well rules are enforced. Is there a dress code? What is the college's position on alcohol, smoking, and other drugs? Are there rules about dating, public displays of affection, premarital sex, and cohabitation? Is there a curfew?

Find out where most students live, either on or off campus, and whether the dormitories are single-sex, entirely coed, or coed with males and females on every other floor or in separate wings. Ask how roommates are assigned, whether students can request a roommate, and whether roommates can be changed. Is there a cost for requesting a roommate change? What are the rules for visitation in rooms by members of the opposite sex? Are overnight visits permitted? At many colleges, students have to endure overnight visits from their roommates' "lovers," of the same or the opposite sex, because either there are no rules forbidding it or the rules are not enforced. In some cases, these students are charged a fee if they want to change roommates to maintain their privacy. Make sure that you and your students are aware of the conditions they may have to face.

Also, ask for statistics on campus crime, including the frequency and types of crime, and obtain information on the procedures that the college employs to ensure campus safety. Find out whether there is a night escort service available.

Student newspapers are another good source of clues about a campus. It might even be worthwhile to subscribe to newspapers at colleges that are high on your students' lists. Letters to the editor are especially revealing.

Calling Dr. Watson

Another way to learn about good colleges is through networking with other parents and students. This will save you much time and money in your college search. If you know families who have sent students to college, discuss any changes (both good and bad) that they have observed in their children. Find others who are going through the college selection process, and ask their impressions of the colleges they have investigated. Borrow their copies of college literature and videos and question them about their campus visits. Just bear in mind that other people's impressions can differ dramatically from your own. Do not make the mistake of eliminating a college based on one unfavorable report.

High school counselor Judy Rodgers says, "I am amazed how kids know whether they belong in a place if they visit the campus. That's why I say VISIT. Two kids, two best friends will visit the same college campus. One has found a home; the other one absolutely loathed it—two kids seeing the same thing—go figure."

A Visit Is Worth a Thousand Viewbooks (and Videos!)

College viewbooks are slick booklets filled with pictures of stately buildings and either deliriously happy or coolly sophisticated students, depending on what image the college wants to portray. Glowing descriptions inspire thoughts of how college should be. They make you want to do everything in your power to give your child this wonderful opportunity.

But do viewbooks represent reality or simply portray an image? From our experience, it is more image than reality. That is why I believe that college visits are essential. It is better to spend extra money now than to feel later that you have wasted tens of thousands of dollars. It is better to invest time now than to discover later that the college has undone years of your good training. And it is better to do your research now than to find out that your students have missed out on the best schools for them.

Videos, viewbooks, and catalogs cannot describe campus atmosphere, the general character of the student body, or the rapport students have with their professors. Promotional materials will not tell you about where the colleges fall short, either. They will not tell you about professors whose agenda is to destroy your child's beliefs or about students who are morally bankrupt or about crime on campus. They might not even tell you that the academic program is not challenging enough for your student. You will have to seek out this information yourself.

I applied to only one school, and I didn't visit that school. I was not happy, and I left after a year, even though I did fine academically.... Now, as an admissions [director], I can say it's so important for students to visit schools to really know what they're getting into and to apply to more than one school and compare financial aid awards.

Rachelle Reitz,
homeschool graduate and
Associate Director of Admissions,
Patrick Henry College

Jim Turcotte, Dean of Enrollment Services at Mississippi College, encourages homeschoolers to "be more open minded about college choices." He says, "It seems they have formed opinions before visiting the campus."

Forming incorrect opinions is a real danger in the college search process. We had done extensive research on Christine's college choices and had asked countless questions by telephone, so we thought we had a good idea of what to expect on each campus. However, we were surprised by what we found. Some surprises were pleasant ones, but many were not. After our visits, Christine's first-choice school became her last, and her third-choice school became her first.

Campus visits are essential. *Do not* skip this important step in the college search process. You may think you cannot afford college visits. However, with the skyrocketing cost of college today, you cannot afford *not* to visit your student's top choices. Sending a student to a school that he or she has never visited is like buying a house from a newspaper advertisement. It could be a costly or even a tragic mistake.

When to Go, What to See

When you visit colleges, try to go when classes are in session. Although schools usually have special weekends with planned activities for prospective students, we were able to discern more about colleges by visiting at other times. Make arrangements at least one month in advance for your college visits. That will give admissions departments enough notice to provide you with information and to accommodate your student in a dormitory. Plan to stay for at least two days if you can. Most colleges provide housing and some meals for prospective students who visit. (There is usually a small charge for the special weekends mentioned above.) Parents generally stay in hotels or campus facilities for a fee.

Beauty and the Eyes of the Beholder

No matter what initial impressions students form from promotional materials, campus visits usually determine their college choices. The beauty and appeal of campuses often play a major role in these decisions. Some students prefer urban or suburban campuses, while others would rather attend college in the middle of a cornfield or woods. Still others are partial to ocean or mountain views. Do not underestimate the natural environment, because beauty can help inspire and energize students as well as provide a soothing balm for homesickness. While you are on a campus, keep in mind that it will look different during other seasons of the year. If everything is in bloom, try to imagine the trees bare and the lawn brown and crusty. If you visit in winter, think of how it will look in spring and fall.

> [Homeschoolers should] develop a portfolio, write a really good cover letter, visit the college, and learn to "market" themselves as highly capable, young academicians who didn't lead, didn't follow, but went their own way and did it well.
>
> David Hawsey, Associate Vice President, Juniata College

Make Yourself at Home

Staying at least one night in a dormitory and eating meals in the cafeteria will be more enlightening for students than staying with you in a hotel. This will give them a chance to get a real feel for campus life. Also, the best way to find out the truth about a college is from other students' candid conversations when there are no parents, faculty, or staff around. Prospective students should seize this opportunity to ask probing questions about classes, professors, social activities, food, etc.

While on campus, you and your students should attend several different classes (separately, if possible), taking notes from the lectures. When you have time, or after you return home, compare notes. Observe professors and students carefully in class. Notice how well the teachers respond to questions. How enthusiastic are the students? Ask questions after classes. Also write down the names of the professors and your impression of their teaching styles. This will be useful later for class registration if your students attend the college. Try to include a science lecture, an English class, and a philosophy, history, or Bible class, as well as classes in your students' major area of interest. Before your visit, try to arrange an appointment to talk with a professor in your students' major department, and for athletically inclined students, with a coach. Music majors may be able to arrange scholarship auditions during their visits as well.

If you can, attend a sports or music practice or event or sit in on a club meeting. If there is a fine arts performance, especially a play, attend it. Do everything you can to immerse yourself in the life of the campus. At one college, we enjoyed a choir rehearsal, and at another, a play. One of our most memorable times was during a campus visit to a secular campus with a large Christian student population. A few students invited us to their missions group meeting one evening. It was a wonderful experience that helped us get to know the students better.

During your visit, note how the campus community relates to one another. What are the male/female relationships like on campus? Do the faculty take a sincere interest in students' ideas and questions? Do they recognize their students outside of the classroom? Is there a sense of belonging and school loyalty? Visit the bookstore and thumb through a few textbooks, especially for classes like philosophy, science, and literature. If the president of the college has written a book, buy it or note the title and read it after you return home. Pick up or read at least one issue of the student newspaper and any other student publications. Seek out an English professor and ask for college-preparatory reading recommendations. The books recommended will reveal much about their English program.

Believe me, I get excited when I meet a new homeschooler considering attending WMU, because I know [he/she] will make a difference on this campus in many ways.

Jeorge Fierro, Assistant Director Admissions, Western Michigan University

Hound the students with questions. Ask what they like and what they do not like, and why. Find out why they chose the school and whether it fulfilled their expectations. Ask them in what ways they think they have grown or changed since beginning college.

Take Notes

Above all, take copious notes. Write down everything that you might need to remember later because your memory will blur, especially when you go to another campus. Also, take pictures of a dorm room, a classroom, the cafeteria, and a few other spots on campus as memory aids. Then you will have reliable information on which to base your decisions. You might want to take along some college search evaluation forms for both you and your students to complete.

After the Visit

After each visit, students should write to thank the college admissions department, the student ambassador, and any staff or faculty with whom they had appointments. They should do this as soon as they return home while their memory is fresh. Better yet, take some note cards with preaddressed envelopes for admissions departments and some blank envelopes for other notes. Write the notes immediately and mail them the day you leave each campus. Then you will be sure not to forget.

Having completed all this research, your students will most likely know where they want to apply. If they are still unsure, have them make a list of pros and cons for each college and then compare them. Once your students know where to apply, what chance do they have of acceptance? Colleges seek students who are academically strong with a proven potential for leadership and social compatibility. Find out how homeschoolers measure up to college standards in the next chapter.

Wisdom reposes in the heart of the discerning.

Proverbs 14:33

---

1. "'Best' Colleges Are Dumbing Down," *Education Reporter*, May 1996, http://www.eagleforum.org/educate.

College Search Evaluation Form

Use this form in conjunction with the general college facts form (on page 130) for a complete summary of the information you have compiled for each college. Complete a form for each college that your students seriously consider, filling in responses as you obtain the information. Be sure to bring copies of your partially completed forms with you when you visit colleges. That way, you can compare the information you received with what you observe. (Do not bring your originals in case you misplace them.) You might even consider having two forms for each college so that you and your student can record your individual reactions. It should go without saying, but do not expect colleges to complete this form for you. This is your worksheet, and you have to do your own homework.

General Information

Name of college _____

Address _____

Telephone number _____

Admissions office contact person _____

Private / public

Denominational affiliation, if any _____

Statement of faith _____

_____

Evidence of it on campus _____

Does the college have regular chapels? How often? Is attendance required? _____

_____

Is the college accredited? _____

Does the college have an early action or early decision plan? _____

Dates of visit _____

Is an admissions interview required? _____

When is it scheduled? _____

Other appointments scheduled _____

Financial Matters

• Tuition _____

• Room _____

• Board (Are there options here?) _____

- Fees _____

- Books _____

- Does the college have a payment plan? _____

- Scholarships _____

  _____

  _____

- Financial aid _____

  _____

  _____

Getting There

- Distance from major airport(s) or driving distance from home _____

  _____

- Can you travel through more than one airport? _____

- Is there competition between airlines in the area (keeping fares low), or will you be dependent on one or two carriers (keeping fares high)? _____

- Means and costs of ground transportation to college _____

  _____

Climate

- Comment on weather during your visit. Ask students about weather at other times of the year. Especially note comments of students from your own part of the country. Students from the upper peninsula of Michigan have a different definition of cold than do those from Atlanta, Georgia. _____

  _____

Campus

- Initial impression of campus _____

  _____

  _____

  _____

- Is the campus wooded? By a lake? In the middle of a cornfield? Describe the campus and how it feels to you. _____

_____

_____

- How many buildings are there? Are they a reasonable walking distance from one another?

  _____

- How far are the dormitories from the classrooms? From the dining hall? _____

  _____

- What recreational facilities are available? Can they be used year-round? _____

  _____

- How noisy are the buildings during and after classes? _____

- Describe the bookstore. _____

  _____

- Where do students go to relax? _____

  _____

- What stores and restaurants are nearby? _____

  _____

- Are there nice, reasonably priced hotels close to the campus for visitors? _____

  _____

People

- What type of atmosphere does the college have? Highly intellectual? Family? Businesslike? Countercultural? _____

  _____

  _____

- Overall impression of people on campus _____

  _____

- Size of student body _____

- Were students friendly? Did they make an effort to welcome you or help you find your way?

  _____

- How do men and women students relate to one another? Are you comfortable with this?

  _____

- What kinds of rules are enforced on and off campus? (Obtain a copy of the student handbook, if possible.) How are infractions handled? _____

_____

- Were professors friendly? Did they welcome you? Did you have any favorites? _____

_____

_____

Academics

- Who teaches classes, professors or graduate students? _____

- Describe the classes you visit, giving class titles, names of professors, class sizes, and your observations, or fill out a college class evaluation form for each class you attend.

_____

_____

_____

_____

- Are teachers enthusiastic about teaching? _____

- Are students enthusiastic about learning? _____

- Describe the interaction between students and professors. _____

_____

- How do your academic ability and test scores compare with those of average students here?

_____

- Describe typical classrooms. _____

_____

_____

- How much do students study? _____

- What majors of interest are offered at this college? _____

_____

- Do course selections seem adequate for your needs? _____

- Is there an honors program? What qualifies students to participate? _____

_____

- How good is the library? _____

- Describe computer availability. How far are computer labs from dormitory rooms? Are there limited hours? What are these hours? _____
_____

Campus Organizations

- Which organizations are the most popular? _____
_____

- Do any organizations especially interest you? How large are the memberships?
_____
_____

- How much opportunity is there for freshmen to participate in leadership roles? _____
_____

- Do any organizations bother you? Why? _____
_____

Dormitories

- Are all students not living at home required to live in dormitories? If not, is anyone required to live in dormitories? _____

- Are there enough dorm rooms for all students who wish to reside on campus? _____

- Do the dorms have curfews? Are the dorms locked at night? _____

- What sort of supervision is provided in the dorms? _____
_____

- Is someone available 24 hours? _____

- What are the rooms like? Are they individual rooms or suites? How large are they? How many students share each room? _____
_____
_____

- What arrangements are made to charge individual students for their long-distance calls?
_____

- Where are the bathrooms? How many students share each bathroom? _____

- Are students responsible for cleaning their rooms/bathrooms? _____

- Are freshman dorms different from upper-class dorms? _____

- Are the dormitories clean? _____

- How is the noise level? _____

- Are students able to study in their rooms or on their floors, or do they have to leave the building for quiet? _____

- Are the dormitories single-sex, coed with males and females on every other floor, or entirely coed? _____

- Is visitation permitted by members of the opposite sex? If so, where, how often, and under what circumstances? _____
_____

- What is the college's policy on refusing or changing roommates? _____
_____

- How late do students stay up? _____

- Do some dorms have reputations for being "party" dorms? Are others for more serious students? _____
_____

- Are some dorms for specific majors? If so, note the names of each one. _____
_____

- Describe the laundry facilities and their location. Ask students how much money it takes to wash and dry a load of laundry. (Sometimes dryers require more than one cycle.) _____
_____

- Is there a kitchen for student use? _____

- Is storage space outside of dorm rooms available for students to use during the school year?
_____

- Is there summer storage space for returning students? _____

Food

- Describe the eating facilities _____
_____
_____
_____

- What is your opinion of the food? Is there enough variety? _____
_____

- What do students say about the food? (Is it good only when visitors are present?) _____

  _____

- What provisions are made to deliver meals to ill students? _____

  _____

Campus Safety

- What is the crime rate on campus? What kinds of crimes have been reported in the past few years?_____

  _____

- What safety precautions are in place? _____

  _____

- Describe campus security. Is a night escort service available? _____

  _____

Student Vehicles

- Are freshmen allowed to have cars on campus? _____
- What fees are required? _____
- How far is freshman parking from the dormitories and classrooms? _____
- What extra fee, if any, is required? _____

College Administration

- Was the admissions office organized? _____
- Was it prepared for your prearranged visit? _____
- Did it schedule class visits for you or give you an accurate list of classes and times that you might visit? _____
- Did any thought go into its choice of student ambassador for you? Does your student ambassador have interests in common with yours? _____
- Did your student ambassador answer your questions satisfactorily? Were you given enough guidance and direction? Were you given too much? _____

  _____

Surrounding Area

- Is the campus in the country, the suburbs, or a city? _____
- What is the nearest city? How large is it? _____

- Where can you buy toiletries, clothes, and school supplies? _____

- Can you buy fresh fruit or other favorite foods nearby? Explain. _____

  _____

- What opportunities are available for recreation and cultural outings? _____

  _____

- Do you have friends or relatives nearby or within a reasonable driving distance? _____

  _____

- Do you think that you would feel at home here? Why or why not? _____

  _____

  _____

- Does this visit inspire any ideas for your admissions essay? If so, record them here. _____

  _____

  _____

  _____

  _____

  _____

Other Notes:

General College Facts

College, Location	Costs	Scholarships, Aid	Requirements	Comments

Use this form to list general information about colleges that your students consider. Copy extra forms as required.

College Class Evaluation Form

College _____ Course Title _____

Course (Comment on content, appeal, level of difficulty, future interest, etc.) _____

_____

_____

_____

_____

Professor (Comment about teaching style, response to student questions, and ability to explain clearly. Also indicate whether instructor is a professor or graduate student.) _____

_____

_____

_____

_____

_____

Size of class_____

Students (Comment on participation, enthusiasm, behavior, friendliness, etc.) _____

_____

_____

_____

_____

Notes (Use a notebook for extensive notes.) _____

_____

_____

_____

_____

_____

_____

_____

Chapter 8

Making the Grade

My experiences with homeschooling are all very positive, having served colleges and universities on both the east and west coasts. After ten years, I have come to believe that homeschoolers have more of a challenge and therefore almost always rise to that challenge and outperform their "traditional" peers in college-level experiences.

David Hawsey, Associate Vice President, Juniata College

Anecdotally, homeschoolers are strong elementary and secondary students, but the acid test of their academic preparation occurs when they are compared with traditional students at the college level.

The Survey

In preparation for writing this book, I surveyed admissions directors and deans of enrollment from colleges all over the country about their experiences with homeschoolers. Originally, it was curiosity that led me to contact colleges because I had read much about higher education's purported prejudice against homeschooled students. Although I knew that some homeschoolers had had trouble with colleges, we had not experienced any, so I wondered how widespread the problems were. As far as I could tell, no one had actually invited colleges to voice their opinions about homeschooled students, so I decided to do it myself. My primary goal in conducting such an extensive national survey was to build a bridge of accurate information between homeschoolers and colleges in order to make the admissions process easier and more congenial for both.

How I Chose Colleges to Survey

To obtain a good sampling of colleges, I contacted public, private, nondenominational, and denominationally affiliated colleges and universities from all fifty states and the District of Columbia. The majority of these were at least four-year institutions. I used the following criteria in choosing colleges:

1. I had to be able to reach the college through email. When online forms were provided without email addresses, I usually did not contact the colleges. In rare cases, I pasted the survey into comment boxes on the forms.
2. I contacted colleges that specifically expressed interest in homeschoolers through advertising if I could obtain their email addresses. I included institutions without full four-year degree programs in this category only; all other colleges were four-year institutions.

3. I contacted colleges listed in the Ecola Newsstand: College Locator website (http://www.ecola.com/college/) that met at least one of the following qualifications:

   a. Colleges were at least moderately selective based on ACT/SAT scores and the percentage of freshmen from the upper half of the high school class (as reported in *Peterson's Four-Year Colleges '97*).

   b. Colleges offered majors that appeared to be underrepresented among the more selective schools.

   c. Colleges were affiliated with denominations that appeared to be underrepresented among the more selective schools.

4. For state universities with several campuses, I chose campuses of various sizes within the system.

5. In states with numerous colleges, I selected a variety of schools based on selectivity and affiliation. In states with few, I included all but the least selective schools.

In all, I sent email surveys to 945 colleges. Nine of these colleges sent automatic responses geared to prospective students. From the remaining 936 colleges, I received responses from 263 colleges (28%) in forty-six states. The survey questioned admissions departments about their institutions' experience with and interest in homeschoolers, the documentation they need from homeschoolers, any extra requirements for homeschoolers, and scholarship availability. I worded questions so as to avoid the possibility of injecting bias into my interpretation of results.

Table 8A
Acceptance/Matriculation of Homeschoolers at 263 Colleges

Colleges that have accepted homeschoolers

Yes	238
No Response	11
None applied	9
Not sure	3
No	2

Colleges that have enrolled homeschoolers

Yes	217
No response	13
No	12
Not sure	12
None applied	9

Interest in Homeschoolers

Of the colleges that responded, 91 percent have accepted and 83 percent have enrolled homeschoolers. (See Table 8A.) Over 94 percent expressed interest in receiving applications from homeschoolers.

Experience with Homeschoolers

Homeschoolers have a reputation for being well-prepared and diligent students. To ascertain whether or not colleges agree with that assessment, I asked admissions leaders whether they had noticed any particular strengths or weaknesses in students from homeschooling backgrounds. These were open-ended questions, with no prompting from me, so all the characteristics named came directly from colleges. The particular strengths and weaknesses they noted are itemized in Tables 8B and 8C. The results indicate that homeschoolers have generally lived up to their good reputation.

One hundred eighty-five colleges answered the question about homeschooler strengths. (See Table 8B.) Of those responding to the question, 21 percent noticed no strengths particular to homeschoolers. For instance, Pat Lynch of the University of Oklahoma contends, "Strengths and weaknesses are as varied as non-homeschooled students and depend largely on the nature of the homeschool experience."

Other colleges have had different experiences, and 79 percent reported specific strengths (some more than one) in their home-educated students. The most common strength mentioned was academic

Table 8B

Homeschooler Strengths: Number of Colleges Reporting Each
263 Colleges, 185 responding to question

Academic

73 Academically strong students, extremely well prepared, capable, intelligent, etc.

39 No strengths particular to homeschoolers noticed

29 High or higher standardized test scores

27 English, communication, verbal skills; articulate; well-read; strong in literature, writing, reading comprehension

23 Motivated, committed, self-directed, stimulated, intense, show initiative

20 Independence in thinking, learning, working, studying, etc.

19 Self-discipline, including organization, time management, responsibility, work ethic, sense of purpose

17 Research and study skills, study habits

12 Love of learning; excitement, eagerness, curiosity, enthusiasm about learning

6 Creative, resourceful, insightful, flexible, flexible thinkers

5 Focused

4 Good, thorough background, strong educational background

3 Keep high GPA in college

3 More willing to participate in debates and discussions, use logical thinking, question philosophies, etc.

2 Completed interesting independent research projects, unique experiences

1 Have positive view of (college) teachers

1 Strong community involvement

1 Strong in science and math

1 Strong structured curriculum used

1 Have especially strong skills in area of interest: music, writing, art

1 It varies

Social Adjustment, Other Characteristics

20 Socially adjusted, well-rounded, fit in well, stable

9 Mature

9 Strength of moral character, faith, values, family relationships

7 Confident, secure

5 Smooth adjustment to college

2 Add interesting diversity

2 Campus leaders

2 Want to make a positive difference with their lives

2 Get involved on campus

1 Loyal

1 Politically aware

Colleges Not Responding to Question

59 N/A—no homeschool students, not enough students to generalize, or do not track student success

19 No response

© 1998 Jeanne Gowen Dennis

Table 8C

Homeschooler Weaknesses: Number of Colleges Reporting Each
263 Colleges, 180 responding to question

Academic

- 87 No noticeable weaknesses, in general, compared with traditional students
- 21 Laboratory sciences (mentioned weakness in, lack of, or need for inclusion), science
- 12 Foreign languages, especially speaking (1 mentioned only need for inclusion)
- 9 Math skills
- 4 Learning and study skills—taking notes, outlining, adapting to various teaching styles
- 3 Choosing curriculum; weak curriculum, incoherent curriculum
- 3 (Sometimes) strong grades coupled with weak test scores (grade inflation)
- 2 Fail to meet minimum entrance requirements
- 2 Learning curve in classroom is greater, adjustment to classroom environment
- 2 Low standardized test scores among nonadmitted students
- 1 Communication: speech, group discussions
- 1 Lack of involvement in the arts
- 1 Verbal (literature, writing)

Character / Social Adjustment

- 15 Social immaturity, adapting to college life
- 15 Interaction, relationships with peers (some said occasional, minor, or rare)
- 9 Lack of community involvement, extracurricular activities during high school, sports involvement (seven more recommended involvement in the community and with peers, and three recommended getting a well-rounded background)
- 6 Group cooperation, working in teams
- 4 Trouble dealing with inflexible schedules or set programs
- 3 Inflexible in accepting beliefs of others or unwilling to have assumptions challenged (some students)
- 2 Lack of experience in classroom settings
- 1 Not enough extracurricular involvement on campus
- 1 Homesickness
- 1 Quieter during campus visit
- 1 Tendency to get upset when criticized by teachers
- 1 Offended by language, morals, and lack of work ethic of peers

Admissions Process

- 11 Documentation and transcripts: nonprofessional presentation, insufficient documentation, defensiveness or noncooperation in supplying documentation
- 3 Tendency to delay standardized testing; miss scholarship, admissions timelines
- 1 Form opinions about colleges before visiting

Colleges Not Responding to Question

- 60 N/A—no homeschool students, not enough students to generalize, or do not track student success
- 23 No response

(40%). Other strengths that were frequently mentioned included high standardized test scores (16%), verbal skills (15%), motivation (12%), independence (11%), social adjustment (11%), self-discipline (10%), and study skills (9%). One of the most interesting observations made by colleges was that homeschool students demonstrate a love of learning (7%).

"In my view," says Robert G. Voss of Worcester Polytechnic Institute, "they have a love of learning that is far beyond that of the student coming out of the traditional high school. In other words, they've been allowed to fall in love with things, to fall in love with the idea of learning. Now this is, of course, only the group we see here, and we have pretty high quality students here."

Colleges were almost evenly divided on the question of weaknesses in homeschoolers. Of the 180 colleges that responded to the question, 52 percent noted weaknesses or expressed concerns, and 48 percent found no noticeable weaknesses in homeschoolers compared to traditional students. Twelve percent mentioned either the need for or the lack of laboratory sciences. (Refer to Table 8C.)

"The biggest problem we face is having sufficient information to judge whether the student has had the necessary course work required for admission," says Martha H. Moore of the University of Illinois at Urbana-Champaign. "It can be a challenge, especially in the laboratory sciences and foreign language areas."

The other most frequently named weaknesses included social immaturity (8%), peer interaction (8%), foreign languages (7%), documentation and transcripts (6%), math skills (5%), and extracurricular involvement (5%).

From the results, it is obvious that colleges have experienced homeschool students with both strong and weak social skills.

"I know the big argument against homeschoolers is usually that they socially may not be as functional as others because they're not exposed to other people. But I've not ever observed that. Quite the contrary...I think that they're...just as social as anybody else and socially aware," says Ray Hardee of Gardner-Webb University.

Jeff Palm of Hawaii Pacific says that this issue always comes up when people talk about homeschoolers. He says that others ask how homeschooled students can adjust socially when they have not been in a group atmosphere. Palm calls this "a misnomer, because there are so many things you can do outside of a high school now."

Others have noted, however, some weakness in the social area. For instance, Randy Comfort, Dean of Admissions at Greenville College, says, "Although it's a stigma, some homeschoolers come to college lacking the ability to interact socially with students of their own age."

Some colleges are concerned that homeschooled students might struggle more than traditional students with leaving home. However, Gary Ray of Lee University has observed that homeschool parents often have more trouble letting go than their students do.

Although colleges have had a variety of experiences with homeschoolers, it appears from the survey that the majority have been positive.

Proof of Graduation

The decision whether or not to earn a GED or a certified diploma is always of concern to homeschoolers planning for higher education. In the survey, I asked each college whether or not they required either of these for admission. Of the 263 respondents, nearly 54 percent did not require the GED or a certified diploma for admission, although 6 percent had this requirement for financial aid at the time of the survey, and 6 percent recommended or preferred that students obtain one of these documents. Almost one-third of the respondents required one of these documents for admission (about 32%), with an additional 6 percent requiring it under some circumstances. Nine percent of the colleges

Table 8D
College Requirements for Homeschoolers:
Certified Diploma and/or GED Requirements

1st Edition Survey: 263 Colleges

Is a certified diploma or a GED required for admission?

No	111
Yes	83
No, but required for financial aid	15
Sometimes, depending on situation	15
No, but preferred or recommended	15
No response	13
Other	7
No set policy	4

2nd Edition Survey: 121 Colleges
(All answered original survey.)

Is a certified diploma[1] required for admission?

No	81
Yes	22
Preferred	3
No response	1

Is a GED required for admission?

No	95
Yes	7
Yes if no diploma	2
Individual basis	1
Yes for financial aid	2
Either certified diploma or GED is required	11
Neither certified diploma nor GED required, but recommended	2
Certified diploma or GED required if no transcript	1

1. Some admissions officials seemed confused by the term "certified diploma." Some appear to have defined it as a diploma certified by the parents; others defined it as a diploma certified by an agency outside of the family, such as a school or government agency.

offered no response, had no set policy, or had other policies that did not fit into one of these categories. (See Table 8D.)

While preparing the second edition of *Homeschooling High School,* I surveyed the colleges listed in Appendix A again to find out if their requirements for a GED or certified diploma had changed. Of the 206 colleges contacted, 121 responded. Of these, 18.2 percent required a certified diploma, 2.5 percent preferred a certified diploma, and 5.8 percent required a GED. Those that required either one of these documents comprised approximately 9.1 percent of the respondents. Two-thirds (66.9 percent) of the colleges did not require a certified diploma, and 78.5 percent did not require a GED. Approximately 0.8 percent of the colleges required one of these documents if the student had no diploma, and another 1.7 percent of colleges required a GED for financial aid. (See Table 8D.)

Documentation Required

Colleges also vary in their requirements for transcripts and supporting documentation. Because their responses were so diverse, I can only approximate the percentages that fit general categories. (See Appendix A for details.) Based on the original survey, approximately 32 percent of colleges preferred a traditional transcript alone. Some of these would accept transcripts only from outside organizations. About 67 percent of colleges wanted to receive more information from homeschoolers in the form of course descriptions, portfolios, reading lists, and/or other materials. Another 1 percent of respondents had varying requirements that did not fit these categories. Most colleges required students to provide ACT and/or SAT I scores. Prospective students should check with individual colleges to see whether they prefer one of these tests over the other.

Of the 121 colleges that updated or reviewed their admissions information for Appendix A for the second edition, 7.4 percent preferred or required more information from homeschooled applicants than they required at the time of the first survey. Extra documentation may include a student portfolio, course descriptions, reading lists, or other information.

Scholarships

The availability of scholarships is always a primary concern for parents and students alike. Most colleges have merit scholarships, and many have scholarships for participation in sports, music, and other activities. At 50 percent of the colleges surveyed for the first edition, homeschool students were equally eligible with other students for merit and other scholarships. (See Table 8E.) An additional 29 percent considered homeschoolers equally but required a certified diploma or GED for admission. In the latter group, four institutions would allow only a certified diploma to qualify students for scholarships; a GED would disqualify them. Several colleges also reported having awarded their top merit scholarships to homeschoolers.

When I surveyed the colleges in Appendix A about scholarship eligibility for the second edition, 55.4 percent to 74.4 percent of colleges considered homeschoolers equally eligible with other applicants and 16.5 percent to 35.5 percent considered homeschoolers equally but had extra requirements for admission. Because some admissions officials seemed confused[1] about my definition of "certified diploma," I have given a range of numbers for these results.

When comparing these responses with those of the same colleges for the first edition of this book, it appears that a slightly higher percentage of admissions offices are requiring a certified diploma than before. However, since the definition of "certified diploma" was confusing to some, this may be only a perceived increase and not a genuine one. A slightly lower percentage of these colleges are requiring a GED for homeschooler admission than was the case before.

Summary of Survey Results

Most colleges seek applicants with strong academic backgrounds who are active in their schools, churches, or communities. They want to enroll students who will be an asset to their campuses. As a result, some colleges are seeking well-rounded students while others prefer students with one or two areas of strength that will help round out the student body.

It is obvious from both surveys that most colleges are in favor of having homeschoolers enroll in their institutions and are finding home high school graduates to be strong students who are desirable additions to their academic communities. The admissions officials who corresponded with me for the second edition continued to report overwhelmingly positive experiences with homeschool graduates. In fact, many endeavor to find new ways to market their colleges to homeschooled students. However, not all colleges have had good experiences with the home-educated students who have applied. Some students have not prepared adequately for college, and certain parents have not kept good records.

My study's verification of homeschoolers' general readiness for college adds credence to Brian Ray's findings reported in *Strengths of Their Own: Homeschoolers Across America,* which describes the success of elementary- and secondary-level homeschoolers through self-reported standardized test scores.

Some homeschooling opponents have criticized Ray's study because Ray is a homeschool advocate and because the homeschoolers involved participated in the survey voluntarily. I believe that

Table 8E
Scholarship Eligibility for Homeschoolers

1st Edition Survey: 263 Colleges

Considered on an equal basis with other applicants	132
Considered equally, but extra requirements for admission	75
No response	20
Considered equally, but have harder time competing or ineligible for certain scholarships	19
Need-based aid only (eligible)	6
Homeschool scholarship[1]	7
No set policy	5
Probably not able to compete	2
Consult specific departments	1
Scholarships for state residents only	1
No scholarships	1
Not sure	1

2nd Edition Survey: 121 Colleges

Considered on an equal basis with other applicants[2]	67–90
Considered equally, but extra requirements for admission[2]	20–43
Considered equally, but have harder time competing	3
Ineligible for certain scholarships	3
N/A no tuition or no scholarships	3
No set policy	1
No response	1
Need-based aid only (eligible)	11
Homeschool scholarship	6

1. This number is included in the 132 colleges that considered homeschoolers on an equal basis with other applicants.
2. Because some admissions officials seemed confused by the term "certified diploma," I have included a range of numbers here.

the arguments of the critics are, for the most part, unfounded. First of all, in virtually all surveys, those who participate do so voluntarily. Second, many (if not most) surveys are conducted or financed by people who have some idea of what they hope the outcomes to be. Often those involved have a vested interest in the results. Although quibblers claim that voluntary participation necessarily eliminated low scores, Ray's data show that even some homeschoolers with extremely low test scores participated in the study. Critics also claim that Ray's association with homeschooling biased his interpretation of the results. However, this seems to be a case of the pot calling the kettle black. As most educated people know, statistics can be manipulated to say almost anything. Researchers often slant their questions and/or their interpretation of results to suit their own purposes.

So if you decide to homeschool through high school, proceed with confidence that colleges are interested in those homeschool graduates who have worked diligently to receive a high-quality education. If you do your job well and your students apply themselves, most doors to higher education appear to be wide open for you.

What This Means for You

Some of the homeschooler strengths colleges mentioned seem to be the result of the homeschooling process; others are the result of good training and hard work. Use these survey results as a planning tool. If your students desire traditional college degree programs, then make sure that they are ready to learn in a college setting and that you are ready to document their education to the school's satisfaction. However, do not be tempted to tailor your high school program just to suit colleges if it is at the expense of your students' individual needs and interests. Capitalize on the advantages inherent in the homeschooling process. Do not settle for second best to mimic traditional, institutionalized education. Provide the best education you can for your students, and they will most likely rise to any challenge.

Mistakes to Avoid

From the survey, I was able to identify ten major mistakes homeschoolers tend to make when preparing for and applying to college.

1. Quitting While You're Ahead

According to Ray's study, 89 percent of homeschoolers intend to continue homeschooling through high school. However, parents often feel inadequate when they think about teaching secondary students. Many give up and send their children to school because they doubt their ability to prepare their students for college. However, the facts do not support these fears.

David Christ, director of Admissions at Bob Jones University, cited a study done on the campus comparing homeschooled college graduates with those from public schools and Christian schools.[2] The study evaluated student success and campus leadership in academic, cognitive, spiritual, affective-social, and psychomotor areas.

"Homeschoolers ranked first in forty-two of the sixty-three indicators evaluated. They are obviously doing well on our campus," Christ says.

The psychomotor group was the only area where homeschoolers failed to outrank their public school and Christian school peers by a significant margin. This group included athletics and other physically oriented activities.

It is true that some homeschooling parents choose traditional high school for their children because they feel it is the best decision for them. However, many parents send their teens to school because the thought of planning and teaching high school subjects seems overwhelming, especially if they have younger children to teach. Some of them have homeschooled for many years and simply feel burnt out. If this describes you, I hope that you will reconsider your decision and that the information in this book will encourage you to finish the good work you have begun.

Michael Farris believes that sending a homeschooled student to high school is "a reversal" and "really shortsighted." He continues, "First of all, they're going to be going backwards academically…[and] the moral preparation that you give them in the last few semesters is so important."

Homeschool mom Debbie Musselman says, "I *loved* high school homeschooling because I got to interact with [my children] intellectually on things that I would never have interacted with them on as just a mom when they came home at the end of a school day. We dealt with some moral issues. We dealt with social issues—just all kinds of things as a result of the reading and the interacting over the reading. So, if people can stick it out through high school, I think it's really worth it."

2. Confined to a Closed System

Homeschool students often lack classroom experience and extracurricular involvement, making the transition to college more difficult than it needs to be.

"The experience we have had with homeschooled students is that they are well motivated and generally more enthusiastic, but they lack the experience of classroom settings and campus atmosphere, which can be a culture shock," says Kristopher T. Loretz, admissions counselor at Albertus Magnus College.

As I mentioned earlier, it is important to provide opportunities for your students to learn in a variety of settings and to ensure that they have opportunities to cooperate with other students on group projects.

Geoffrey Gould, Director of Undergraduate Admissions at Binghamton University (SUNY), says, "I would recommend that, where possible, high school-aged students blend their home schooling with a course or two at a local high school or community college, perhaps during the summer. This will ease them into the constraints of life in the conventional classroom, which they will need if planning to go to college. Of course, distance learning over the Internet is another option, but at some point, the social experience of the classroom or the workplace must be confronted."

Gould goes on to say, "Adjustment without loss of one's particular values is both a challenge and an opportunity. If homeschooling becomes a completely either-or experience, there may be risks for persons wanting to have a mainstream career. Among homeschoolers I have met, there is a degree of seriousness of purpose I find impressive. I suspect these individuals will do well in any setting, but it may be easier on their adjustment to reach out in some of the ways I have described as they near completion of high-school level studies."

Gould also suggested using email for study groups as well as for "semiacademic" and "semisocial" exchanges with fellow homeschoolers. He recommends this as a strategy to "enhance the interactivity of learning," which will help students cooperate with their peers in college.

Homeschoolers also should participate in their communities in meaningful ways. Extracurricular activities, jobs, and volunteer work all strengthen students' college applications. Marc Williar of Flagler College encourages students to involve themselves in activities that demonstrate a willingness to give of themselves for others. For those students interested in military service academies, extracurricular activities are essential. The U.S. Air Force Academy's website states that although many students qualify academically for admission, "many records are not strong enough to compete due to a significant weakness in the area of extracurriculars," which they use to "predict leadership potential."

3. Missing the Minimum

In their effort to provide a stimulating curriculum, some homeschoolers fail to complete the traditional high school courses required by most colleges. Make sure that you know what courses will be required at the colleges where your students will apply. Make a special effort to provide strong courses in laboratory sciences, foreign languages, and higher-level math.

Homeschoolers learn by doing, by seeking out, by having to prove they know all that traditionalists know, and then some! What college that says it values these things in its brochures would dare deny a student of this caliber? Privately, few can afford to, or want to. But need-blind admissions is fast eroding into a system of assessing a family's ability to pay for private education, and where most systems for financial needs analysis and awarding of financial aid are based on the old system of GPA/SAT etc., homeschoolers must learn how to educate colleges and then translate their own achievements into admission and merit scholarships. To this end, colleges must also take responsibility to learn all we can, or miss out on a fast-growing, legitimate way of learning and demonstrating college-level success.

David Hawsey, Associate Vice
President, Juniata College

Don Vos of Concordia University Nebraska says, "Contact local or choice colleges early on...even as early as the freshman or sophomore year to talk about requirements, as they vary from school to school."

You also need to make sure that your students are working at the correct grade level. Kerry Durgin of Hood College remembers one instance where a homeschooler was not. "I interviewed a homeschool student [while working] at another college, a very pleasant girl, very nice. She certainly was proud of what she had accomplished, and should have been. She said she wanted to get into English, and we were talking about the kinds of reading she had done and it was only at the ninth-grade level.... I was trying to understand if she had been the one that chose those things to read or if the family had been helping her...where the hole was, and could she make that three-year leap and suddenly read a senior-level novel and be able to work with it."

I asked Dr. Richard Cornelius, an English professor of almost forty years, for his high school literature recommendations. You will find his list in Appendix D. Compare this list to the literature your students are reading. To verify that students are working at or above grade level in other subjects, compare their work with the assignments in traditional high school textbooks.

Suellen Ofe describes some homeschool applicants who were not admitted to Huntingdon as having "a very narrow focus in their high school curriculum," especially in high school reading material. "Some of these were home-schooled strictly for religious segregation; the works they were allowed to read and their academic curriculum did not show a broad-based representation. These students also tended to have a more difficult time accepting ways of thinking that contradicted their own beliefs."

4. Playing Guessing Games

A common mistake homeschoolers make is not communicating early enough and often enough with college admissions departments. Instead of asking what colleges want from them, some homeschoolers guess or assume. If you guess incorrectly, it can be a frustrating waste of time for both you and the admissions staff. Also, do not make colleges play guessing games with you. Make it easy for them to accept your students by answering their questions and responding promptly to any reasonable request for information.

I asked Tim Utter of Concordia University-St. Paul what homeschoolers can do to increase their chances of acceptance. He answered, "We would love for them to simply inquire—they never really do!"

Durgin agrees. "They need to stop by and talk to us. I would say that for any of our students, to tell you the truth. Just come in and talk. We're not going to put them under a hot light and fire questions at them. We want to get a sense of whether or not they would fit in here. Nine times out of ten I think they will...."

5. Enrolling Sight Unseen

As I mentioned earlier, colleges strongly recommend that prospective students pay them a visit during high school. Homeschoolers are not alone in their failure to visit colleges before deciding to enroll. This is a common problem. Many high schoolers apply only to the college closest to their home without investigating it to see whether or not they would be happy there. Others form utopian ideas about distant colleges and visit them for the first time at freshman orientation. By then it is too late to select a different school. I believe that a good percentage of the large numbers of college dropouts and transfers can be attributed to this lack of investigation. I cannot stress it enough. Visit!

6. Displaying Defensiveness

Perhaps because of past rejection and prejudice, some homeschoolers have an "us" and "them" attitude towards admissions directors. Don't assume that college personnel are prejudiced against homeschoolers. If they are, you have an opportunity to help them understand homeschooling better. The homeschooling pioneers who came before you have already done much of the work. If colleges really have no interest in homeschooled applicants, spend your money elsewhere.

The majority of colleges that responded to my survey are enthusiastic about having homeschool students apply. All of these colleges would welcome students who qualify for admission. However, one college, because of its strict admissions policy, does not actively recruit homeschoolers, although homeschoolers are enrolled on that campus. So approach colleges with a friendly, confident, and professional attitude.

According to Michael Farris, colleges are "on a diversity kick, and [homeschoolers] add to their diversity in an interesting way." He theorizes that "a lot of the more traditional, elite schools like having homeschoolers around because [they're] kind of off the beaten path."

If your student is not accepted to a college, do not automatically assume that it is because you homeschooled. Colleges are looking for students who will adjust well to their particular campuses, so rejections should not necessarily be taken personally.

Also, be reasonable in your dealings with colleges. Some homeschool applicants and their parents have demonstrated uncooperative attitudes toward admissions personnel, refusing even reasonable requests. Unless your students are truly being treated unfairly, you should never act stubbornly or militantly toward colleges.

"We have some wonderful homeschooled students currently enrolled on our campus," says one director of admissions. "We have, however, had students who balk at having to provide ANY academic/transcript type of information as a part of the application process. I don't think any college would be comfortable admitting students without appropriate information that can speak to their potential for success."

Keep in mind that one of your jobs as guidance counselors is to provide colleges with information about your students and their education. You will fare better with a pleasant, cooperative attitude. As the old adage goes, "You catch more flies with honey."

7. A Day Late and a Dollar Short

Punctuality is one area where homeschoolers can definitely use some improvement. As those of us who have homeschooled know, we have a reputation among ourselves for being habitually late.

During the college application process, many homeschoolers miss deadlines, and when they are in college, some expect to get away with turning in assignments after they are due. It takes practice for punctuality to become a habit. Give your students some deadlines and require them to complete their work on time. During the junior and senior years, see to it that your students know the deadlines for test registration, college applications, and scholarship applications. Also, make sure they are aware of the final dates for notifying colleges of their acceptance or refusal of any scholarships and offers of admission. Make them responsible for meeting the deadlines, though. Do not nag them or do it for them. Recently, a homeschooler I know missed all the application deadlines and had to wait to enter college.

An anonymous respondent from a major state university mentioned the importance of being early with college applications. "Course descriptions and knowing what text was used are always helpful. Many times we have to request this information, which slows the admission process down.... Apply early in the cycle so that we can resolve any problems that might arise."

> *To enhance their chances of acceptance, homeschoolers should participate in organized athletics, charitable organizations, youth groups outside the church, employment, and anything that will help them learn social and leadership skills. These students in particular need to demonstrate a breadth of experiences outside the academic realm to be competitive.*
>
> Paul Hartzog, Associate Director of Admissions, Rockford College

8. Hiding Your Light

Many homeschoolers are afraid to use their assets to their advantage. "I believe a homeschooled applicant to any institution should view his or her background as a strength and not feel in any way deficient because of it. It is hoped that this will help other institutions that are not as accepting of homeschoolers to become more friendly to them," says Eric Synstelien of the University of Dallas.

David Hawsey, Associate Vice President of Juniata College, recommends that students "'market' themselves to colleges in a way that reflects who they are, not just what they learned."

Some published articles have suggested not drawing attention to the fact that you homeschooled. In most cases in most states, I disagree. For one thing, you will not be able to hide the fact unless you have purposely hidden it. Besides, colleges are beginning to court homeschoolers. It is better to be honest right up front. Do not hide what could be a decided advantage.

If a college is not homeschooler friendly, go elsewhere unless it is absolutely the best place for your student. In that case, you should consider using an umbrella school (preferably accredited) whose diploma the college will accept. For example, according to Beth Vellalos, a homeschooling mom, the state of Hawaii does not recognize any part of a high school education received at home. Should students decide to return to public high school later, they would then have to begin in the ninth grade. Therefore, if you live in Hawaii, it is recommended that you carefully consider the option of homeschooling in high school as a four-year commitment. Students who intend to apply to Hawaii public colleges should thoroughly research the requirements for admission.

9. Handwritten Horrors

As a home educator, you are a legitimate teacher, so you should deal with colleges in a professional manner. Admissions officers have to review many applications in a limited time, so it is important to make a good first impression. Besides, reviewing applications is a tedious job. Make the process as pleasant for them as possible, but do not be tempted to try to get their attention with gimmicks. Your students' applications will have to stand on their own merits.

It is shocking, but some homeschoolers fail to present a professional image when they deal with colleges. Lydia Knopf of Biola University reported that several applicants submitted handwritten transcripts signed by their parents. "It is difficult for our admissions office to discern the validity and reputability of this type of transcript. The student very well may have received an excellent education, but the one important document for college admittance does not adequately reflect this when it is handwritten."

It is common courtesy in the business world to send clear, concise, computer-generated or typed correspondence. Colleges are businesses, too, and they deserve to be treated with common respect. Your transcript is also a reflection of you and the education you have provided. If your training has been excellent, make your correspondence and your transcript reflect it.

The following anonymous comment demonstrates a horrifying lack of professionalism, provoking justifiable doubts:

We do accept transcripts from parents IF they look official and are signed and dated. We have received some transcripts that looked more like a grade sheet than an official transcript. Here's an example...We received one "transcript" from a homeschooler that was evidently just thrown together by a parent. I called the parent with a question about the kind of math course mentioned on the transcript. Her reply was, "Oh, well, we really didn't spend much time in that course. And by the way, I forgot to put French II on the transcript. I taught her that, too." It's that kind of thing that scares me!

I would encourage parents to produce accurate, official-looking documents for their students. I have even had some parents tell me that they don't keep transcripts at all. Parents need to be aware of the problems that they may be causing for their students by not keeping accurate records. Our home-schooled students seem to do very well.... It's the admission process that often proves to be a problem, because we want to adhere to the same requirements for all of our applicants. I really do understand why parents want to homeschool, and I do want to help the students come here. It's just important that the parents understand that we want to be compassionate with them while sticking to our standards.

Home school students should take care to complete our entrance requirements.... The lab science and the foreign language study usually pose the most difficulty. To fulfill our requirements, some home-school applicants take course work at their local high school and/or enroll in local college courses. We accept one semester of college work as equivalent to a year of high school study.

Susan Wertheimer, Assistant Director of Admissions, University of Vermont

Cases like these are the exception rather than the rule. (See chapter 10 to learn about transcript preparation.)

10. Arrogant Attitudes

Regrettably, homeschooling excellence can breed homeschooler arrogance. Michael Farris has had what he calls "overwhelmingly positive" feedback from colleges about homeschoolers. "Just like anything, it's not a hundred percent...but the percentages are much in favor of homeschooling." He contends that homeschoolers' abilities in reading, language arts, and communication are generally significantly higher than those of their public school counterparts. "In math and science they do better, but the degree of disparity isn't as great," he says.

Farris sees initiative and a willingness to "think outside the box" as homeschoolers' greatest strengths. However, he considers arrogance the greatest weakness of homeschoolers. "I see that a lot.... Because homeschoolers have had to defend themselves from prosecution, we're always bent on telling people how wonderful homeschooling is and how great our kids are. Yeah, our kids are really good, but they're arrogant…much of the time."

Farris suggests giving to the community to overcome homeschool arrogance. "We ought to do more service projects, where we get out and help the poor and go into the city center and teach reading—other kinds of activities that give a much more humble approach to life."

Actually, when the homeschooling movement really began picking up momentum, I was worried about both academic and social adjustment. I have been proved wrong; our homeschooled students thrive both in and out of the classroom. The values, the work ethic, and the independence of the students seem to be very solid. I believe that increased opportunity to travel and the opportunity to become involved in extracurricular activities with a local school supplement what generally appears to be solid academic preparation.

Marc G. Williar, Director of Admissions, Flagler College

Pride and arrogance should not be products of homeschooling. Christian homeschoolers, especially, should understand that we have no reason to boast. "For we are God's workmanship, created in Christ Jesus to do good works, *which God prepared in advance for us to do*" (Ephesians 2:10, emphasis mine). God even prepared homeschooling in advance. Instead of expressing pride or arrogance, homeschool parents should feel humility and joy that God has provided such important work for them. Students need to realize that they are privileged to receive a home education. According to Cara Transtrom, homeschool graduate and former admissions counselor, "Homeschoolers have been given much, so much will be required of them" (See Luke 12:48b). Encourage your students to use their reported strengths of maturity, self-discipline, motivation, and enthusiasm to help others. Then maybe their weaknesses will become strengths as well.

The Need for Accountability

Although homeschooling embodies the independent spirit, homeschoolers still have a responsibility to others for the quality of the job they do.

Accountable to Colleges

We are obviously accountable to the colleges our children attend. Katherine Hallas of Marlboro College expressed concern that homeschooled students "may have the freedom to shy away from areas or fields that they are not interested in…." She wonders what prevents students from skimming on important areas of study such as math. "If students don't like an area of study—are they doing the bare minimum? Who is pushing them?" Although she realizes that this can also be a problem among students in traditional schools, she has a valid point.

Who is pushing your students? Are you holding them accountable for academic assignments and projects? Do you allow "skimming over" important areas simply because they have a distaste for the subject?

Hallas continues, "I am sure most homeschool programs are designed very well to make sure a student is getting a well-rounded education. However, how can we in admissions know or identify the ones who aren't?"

Other admissions directors share Hallas's concerns. Some colleges feel they need concrete evidence that students will succeed at their institutions, and so they impose stricter admissions standards on homeschoolers. Admissions staffs are accountable to their colleges, and they cannot continually admit students who are unable to thrive at their institutions.

"We all worry about the professor who calls in gentle puzzlement or vehement outrage about the clearly incompetent student who has landed in his/her midst," says Jonathan P. Reider, Senior

Associate Director of Admission at Stanford University. "It happens here, I know, so it must happen elsewhere too. I use the term 'risk averse' to describe this behavior on our part, as if we were an insurance company evaluating a race car driver for life insurance. Why should we take a risk? The homeschooler has to realize that—at this point, unfortunately, any home-schooler is at least a modest risk in any admission officer's eyes, and they have to counter that assumption ahead of time. Those who do will be more successful." (Stanford University admitted only 12 percent of its applicants in 2003.)

Apparently, most college admissions policies regarding homeschool-ers are based either on the college's perception of homeschooling or on past experiences. If colleges have misconceptions, it is up to home-schoolers to correct them. Prejudice is usually the result of ignorance. As colleges learn more about homeschooling, there will be greater accept-ance of it as a viable form of education, and as more homeschoolers suc-ceed on college campuses, more colleges will recruit them.

> *We do our best to review each applicant on an individual basis realizing each student has unique qualities to con-tribute to our community. It is important that they are not shy in addressing their strengths and how they feel they can be successful on our campus.*
>
> Michelle Whittingham, Associate Director, Office of Admissions, Eastern Washington University

Accountable to Other Homeschoolers

If the level of excellence is not upheld by all homeschoolers, the entire homeschooling community will reap the consequences. All need to ensure that colleges' future encounters with homeschoolers are rewarding ones. For this to happen, there must be a consensus. Everyone must agree that to call oneself a homeschooler is to commit oneself to excellence, thoroughness, and accountability.

Excellence and homeschooling should be synonymous, and they often are. However, a small number of those who school at home are irresponsible and have given some college personnel the wrong impression about home education. I suppose there will always be some who homeschool without the commitment to excellence shared by most. Just make certain that you are not among them. Then do everything you can to give col-leges and potential employers an accurate impression of your students' home education.

> *Most homeschoolers want their children to have a good education. Why would you subject yourself to such a rig-orous schedule if you didn't? I want my children to have a better education than I did.*
>
> Risa Killingsworth, homeschooling mom

Accountable to Society

Teaching your children affects more than just your immediate fami-lies. It affects our entire society, one would hope, for the better. Like par-enting, it is an awesome responsibility. People who have a vested interest in your homeschooling success include your children and grandchildren, their future college friends, spouses, employers, and employees, and even, to some extent, your communities and our country. All home-schoolers need to commit themselves to providing the best education possible for the sake of their children and everyone with whom they will interact in the future. Obviously, education in this sense includes training in morality and character as well as in academic and practical subjects.

If you are Christian, you probably realize that your children are gifts from the Lord, given for a short time. At the very least, you are accountable to God for your homeschooling efforts. You are stewards of these precious treasures until they are grown and ready to fulfill God's individual plans as adults. So give homeschooling your best effort, depending on God to do the rest.

Accountability is easier when you keep good records. In the next chapter, you will find out what records you should keep, with some suggested formats.

Let another praise you, and not your own mouth; someone else, and not your own lips.

Proverbs 27:2

---

1. Although 40 of the colleges require a certified diploma or GED for admission, 23 of those colleges circled the response that said, "Homeschoolers considered on an equal basis with other applicants" instead of the one reading "Homeschoolers considered equally for scholarships, but for admission they have to fulfill extra requirements, such as certified diploma, GED, or other test (such as SAT II)." Evidently some consider a diploma "certified" by the parents as a certified diploma, whereas others use this term for diplomas verified or awarded by a government agency, a school, or another entity outside of the family. My definition is the latter. I took the responses at face value, so the number of colleges requiring a certified diploma for admission (according to my definition) may be deceptively high.
2. R. S. Galloway and J. P. Sutton, "College Success of Students from Three High School Settings: Christian School, Home School, and Public School." National Christian Home Educators Leadership Conference, October 10, 1997.

Chapter 9

Vital Statistics

Keep good records of curriculum outlines, textbooks, and other resources. Provide as much objective information as possible regarding the student's academic achievement.

Diane M. Weber, Senior Associate Director
of Admission, Miami University, Ohio

During high school, you need to keep track of what your students study and how well they progress academically. You should also record their extracurricular activities, awards, and accomplishments. Colleges may also request medical records, especially immunization records. Keeping accurate and up-to-date records as your children progress will make your job easier later when you have to document their education for colleges and employers. I have included several forms at the end of this chapter to help you get started. Feel free to make copies and use them at your discretion. Do not feel obligated to use anything that you can do without. For example, I never used time sheets. I knew approximately how much time each subject took and awarded credits accordingly. We always exceeded the required number of hours. My friend Karen Dunlap, on the other hand, kept detailed records of the time her children spent on each subject.

[Homeschoolers are] often self-motivated, [achieve] higher test scores, and in general are better students. One weakness is that they aren't always in sync with the "calendar" for applying to college and seeking financial aid. Another issue is that they don't all keep adequate (or orderly) records of their studies.

Matt Osborne, Vice President,
Enrollment Services, Judson
College, Illinois

Records You Should Keep

The following record-keeping forms are included in this book. Use extra copies of these forms as required:

1. **Time Sheet**—For keeping track of how time is spent each day. You may also use this form to list daily activities without recording the time spent on them.

2. **Course Time Sheet (Time Sheet modified by you for individual courses)**—If you fill in the name of a course on this form, you may use it to record time spent only on activities for that course. Use this either on a daily basis or in conjunction with time sheets used to record daily work. In the latter case, you would use general time sheets for daily records and then transfer information for individual courses onto course time sheets at the end of each week or month. Again, you may record course activities without indicating duration.

3. **Reading/Media Lists**—List books, movies, videos, periodicals, and other media used for educational purposes. Indicate which course you used the media for. This will make it easier when and if you write course descriptions. If it is more convenient, use separate pages for courses requiring extensive reading or media. You might want to include leisure reading on the lists. If you do, indicate "leisure" in the "Course" column.

4. **Assignment Sheets**—Record what you expect students to complete in a given amount of time. If your students plan their own time, they can use these forms to report their plans to you. That way, you can hold them accountable and help them plan a balanced schedule that is neither overambitious nor lackadaisical.

5. **Progress Report**—For recording grades and comments for each subject. When we used outside teachers, I had them complete these forms along with student recommendation forms.

6. **Grade Report**—In case you or your students like more traditional report cards.

7. **Student Recommendation**—Recommendations are an extremely important part of the college admission process. Most colleges ask for recommendations from guidance counselors or teachers. Home-educated students are at a disadvantage here because their teachers and counselors are usually their parents. To circumvent this problem, ask every adult who teaches or works with your student to complete one of these forms soon after his or her contact with the student. Do not wait until the junior or senior year. Provide a self-addressed, stamped envelope with each form to make it easy for the person to return it to you. Enclose copies of several completed forms with your transcripts and college applications.

8. **Extracurricular Activities**—To record student activities outside of class time. Be sure to record the amount of time spent because this can make a difference to colleges and/or scholarship providers. Also indicate any awards and other recognition your students receive.

Forms for Summarizing Records

The preceding forms can all be used on an ongoing basis, and the information on them can be summarized for colleges and employers on the following forms:

9. **Course Work Form**—Fill out one for each course that your students complete. You may either send copies of these forms directly to those colleges that ask for as much information as possible or condense the information for inclusion on Subject Area Course Description forms for those colleges that prefer brief descriptions. Fill out Course Description forms for every course as soon as your students complete them. Then you will have the information handy when you write transcripts or answer admissions questions later. (For suggestions on naming courses, see next page.)

10. **Subject Area Course Description Forms**—For each subject area, list the courses completed and a brief description of what was studied. See "Writing Course Descriptions" later in this chapter for more details.

11. **Student Data Form**—This form should accompany your transcript. Use it to summarize student activities and accomplishments and to list test scores and biographical information for colleges and employers.

12. **School Data Form**—Fill out one of these forms for each school where your student took classes during high school. There is space to list teachers and their credentials, if you wish. You may use this form for your own records or for sending to colleges.

13. **Photos (no form)**—Another option is to take photographs of your students during their labs and other activities. These can be a nice addition to admissions packages and can be used to make a high school memory book later.

From Records to Transcripts

Keeping sufficient documentation in an orderly fashion will save you time when you write transcripts. (See chapter 10 for detailed instructions.) Even if your students will receive official transcripts from other programs, such as umbrella or correspondence schools, you still should consider writing your own transcript. Invariably, you will do more in your homeschool than other programs require, so only you can give an accurate picture of the education you provide. Writing your own transcripts will allow you to describe your entire curriculum and enumerate your students' extracurricular activities, work experience, travel, and so on. These details will help colleges see your students more clearly than a typical school or correspondence transcript ever could.

Even if your students do not intend to pursue higher education, having accurate and up-to-date transcripts is important. First, transcripts will help to document for employers and other interested parties what your students have accomplished during the high school years. They will also provide source material for writing resumes.

Naming Courses

Naming courses is easy. Any curriculum catalog lists the names of typical high school subjects, such as World History, Biology, Algebra II. However, these general titles may not fit your self-designed courses. For each course you teach, select a title that accurately describes, in as few words as possible, what your children have studied.

William J. Katip of Robert Morris College says, "I think it is best if you make your transcript look as much like a traditional transcript as possible. Try to use names for courses that pretty much [follow] the traditional names. It's fine to use your own system for 'extra' courses, but it works best if you use traditional names for science, math, English, etc."

Although homeschoolers tend to be innovative in their studies, most colleges seem to prefer that students take traditional courses. Realize that if you blaze your own trail, some colleges will lack confidence in your students' ability to succeed in a traditional program, and they may rely heavily on standardized tests for verification that your students can handle college work. Make sure that your students are able to describe what they studied and explain why they chose particular topics and learning methods.

If you use Alpha Omega Lifepac type of curriculum or Wisdom Booklets from the Advanced Training Institute, make sure that you do not simply list the booklets your students completed. This would be meaningless to colleges. Instead, give the courses traditional names and describe the booklets' contents in your course descriptions.

Hypothetical Course Titles

Drugs, Immunity, and Disease
Adult/Infant/Child First Aid/CPR
Food and Nutrition
Introduction to Engineering
Roofing Methods and Materials
Small Business Management
Geometric Art
Origins Science
Writing for Publication
Children's Book Illustration
American Sign Language
Economics: Two Schools of Thought
History of Mathematics
College Vocabulary
Intermediate Computer Programming
Native American History and Culture
Medieval & Renaissance Architecture
History of Polyphonic Music
Pastel Portraiture
Automobile Maintenance
Politics and the Individual
Communism: Theory and Reality
Capitalism: Theory and Reality
Piano Pedagogy

Learning Categories

Classify your courses into learning categories. This will help you determine whether or not you have met college requirements. It also will help colleges evaluate your students' applications quickly. General categories and courses that fit into them include the following:

Language Arts (LA)

This category includes all courses about language, literature, and communication. Examples include Grammar, Composition, American Literature, English Literature, World Literature (Classic Literature in translation and Foreign Literature in translation), Rhetoric, Speech, Debate, Creative Writing, Poetry.

Mathematics (M)

All areas of mathematics fall into this category: General Math, Consumer Math, Algebra I, Algebra II, Geometry, Trigonometry, Calculus, Probability, Statistics, etc. A course entitled History of Mathematics belongs in this category only if it also involves the application of mathematical formulas and principles. If the course is a study only of the lives of famous mathematicians, it belongs under social studies.

Science (S)

All areas of science and engineering belong in this category. The following courses would be included here: Physical Science, Geology, Mineralogy, Astronomy, Physics, Astrophysics, Engineering Physics, Biology, Botany, Horticulture, Plant Physiology, Plant Pathology, Zoology, Entomology, Ethology, Chemistry.

Social Studies (SS)

This is a catchall category for anything relating to people and how they live and interact. It includes courses in history, cultures, geography, government, civics, philosophy, worldviews, comparative religions, psychology, child development, family living, parenting, sociology, interpersonal communications. Economics is usually grouped with high school social studies but may be included under business. Colleges might allow some other business courses to fulfill social studies requirements. Check with their admissions departments to be sure.

Foreign Languages (FL)

Include all languages except English in this category (unless English is your second language). Examples include Spanish, French, German, Russian, Chinese, Japanese, and other modern languages, as well as classical languages like Latin, Greek, and Biblical Hebrew. Signing for the deaf falls into this category, too, although some colleges will not allow sign language to fulfill foreign language requirements.

The Arts (A)

This category covers Art, Art Appreciation, Art History, Painting, Color Theory, Sculpture, Drawing, Commercial Art, Graphic Design, Woodcarving, craft courses, and Interior Decorating (or list this with Life Skills). Also include Music, Music Theory, Music Appreciation, Music History, training in a musical instrument, Voice, Choir, Band, Orchestra, Drama, Musical Theatre, Acting, Mime, Juggling, Dance, Stage Movement, Liturgical Dance, and similar courses.

Business (B)

This category includes Accounting, Marketing, Consumer Behavior, Advertising, Small Business Management, Computer Programming, other computer courses, Keyboarding, Typing, sometimes Economics.

Life Skills

This category is for anything that helps prepare students in a practical way for their adult lives. Some examples are Home Economics; Clothing; Sewing; Tailoring; Carpentry; Electricity; Gardening; courses about building, repairing, or maintaining homes or vehicles; Auto Mechanics; Plumbing; Cooking and Baking; Speed Reading.

Health/PE (PE)

Include here calisthenics, aerobics, swimming, gymnastics, tennis, archery, track, cross-country, football, basketball, martial arts, soccer, Food and Nutrition, Immunity and Disease, sex education, First Aid/CPR, etc.

Other

This category is the place for Bible courses that do not incorporate philosophy or history as a principle component and whatever else does not fit into another learning category. You may list Bible or Religion as a separate category if you wish. Realize that colleges may not grant credit for Bible/Religion courses and your students will need to take these in addition to the minimum number required for college admission.

Defining Type of Credit

As you probably realize, it makes no sense to give the same type of credit for playing basketball as you give for learning calculus. A high GPA will not fool colleges if cooking, physical education, and painting are averaged with academic courses. If you differentiate between academic and other courses on your transcript, it will save colleges the trouble of doing it for you and give you more credibility.

Academic courses require substantial amounts of reading and writing. They might have a lecture component or utilize videotapes or audiotapes. These courses require the student to do more than just hands-on work. For example, for a food and nutrition course to be classified as academic, the student should not just plan and cook meals. If the student studies the nutritional values of foods, various theories of food combining, the effects of nutrition on health and disease, procedures for food safety, and so on, and then applies this information to meal planning and preparation, it would be an academic course.

Nonacademic courses are primarily hands-on. Examples include painting without studies in value, composition, perspective, and color theory; piano lessons without music theory; carpentry without extensive study of methods and materials.

Another category of courses is noncredit. Although these courses are worth mentioning, they do not require sufficient study or activity to warrant high school credit. You will have to use your own judgement here. I did not give credit for driver education, but I did give non-academic credit for Homeschool Choir.

Advanced Placement (AP) courses are rigorous courses that use college textbooks to prepare students for AP examinations. (Refer to chapter 6.) Advanced courses can also be called honors courses. AP and honors courses often receive more weight in the GPA than other high school subjects do. (See discussion of determining grade weights later in this chapter.) Usually, these courses receive one

I do have trouble accepting the accreditation that is often on transcripts [because of] a few unusual cases where cooking classes were on the same level as biology and chemistry... usually the standardized score or GED is a better indication of the student's academic potential for university work.

Angé Peterson, Director of Admission & Retention, Pittsburg State University more quality point than a regular high school course. Whereas a regular one-credit course would receive 4 points for an A, 3 points for a B, 2 points for a C, and so on, honors courses would receive 5, 4, and 3 points, respectively. Some people award extra credits for these courses as well. It is your choice whether or not to assign honors or AP designations to any of your students' courses. If you do, be prepared to back up extra credit and higher quality points with documentation.

Writing Course Descriptions

Although detailed course descriptions are not usually part of a traditional school's transcripts, homeschoolers should have this information available in case colleges request it. For each course description include the following:

1. Course title
2. Grade, credit type, amount of credit
3. High school year in which course was completed (9, 10, 11, or 12)
4. Description of what the student studied, learned, or accomplished in the course
5. Description of lab activities, if applicable
6. List of resources used (textbooks, videos, books, etc.)
7. Any outside seminars or workshops that were part of the course
8. (Optional) name of teacher, especially if not the parent
9. (Optional) teacher credentials, especially if impressive

To make writing course descriptions easier, fill out a course work form for each class as your student completes it. Then when you are ready to write course descriptions for the transcript, all your information will be compiled. See the sample language arts course descriptions sheet for an example of how to write your own course descriptions. Include labs with science courses. If your student began foreign language courses before grade 9, you may want to indicate when the earlier years of language study were completed. In the sample transcript (chapter 10), Latin II is an example of a course sequence that began before high school.

Assigning Grades

If you use a traditional curriculum, you are probably familiar with giving tests and calculating grades based on test scores. However, if you have developed your own program, you might not know how to assign grades. (If you do not plan to assign grades, refer to the discussion about keeping records in chapter 6.)

The Lord abhors dishonest scales, but accurate weights are his delight.

Proverbs 11:1

First, you need to determine how you will evaluate your students' work. Will you use tests, papers, oral reports, or other measures? Next, decide what percentage of the final grade each test, quiz, paper, or other assignment will contribute to the final grade. You should determine these percentages *before beginning a course*. Do not change the percentages unless you discover during the course that a paper, project, or other assignment requires more work and contributes more to the curriculum than you had originally planned. It is unethical to change a percentage simply to raise a student's final grade in the course.

Figuring Grades by Averaging

If all forms of evaluation receive equal weight, such as when there are nine tests and one final exam, each contributing 10 percent to the grade, simply average the grades to obtain the final grade. (Add the grades and divide by the number of grades.)

Often you will not want to give equal weight to all forms of student evaluation. Here is an example for a biology class where tests, papers, etc., have different values based on the amount of work required and their contribution to the whole course. If this hypothetical biology course required extensive lab work, the lab work percentage could be raised accordingly.

Quizzes	4 @ 5% each	20%
Tests	2 @ 10% each	20%
Final exam		20%
Term paper		20%
Lab work		20%

Suppose a student taking this biology class received the following grades:

Quiz 1	100	Test 1	87	Term paper	95
Quiz 2	78	Test 2	84	Lab work	90
Quiz 3	89			Final exam	93
Quiz 4	94				

You could calculate the final grade thus:

1. Find the average of the quizzes.

Quiz 1	100
Quiz 2	78
Quiz 3	89
Quiz 4	94

$$361 \div 4 = 90.25$$

2. Find the average of the tests.

Test 1	87
Test 2	84

$$171 \div 2 = 85.5$$

3. Since these scores (90.25 and 85.5) each make up 20% of the final grade, you can average them with the other three components that are also worth 20% each:

Quizzes	90.25	20%	
Tests	85.50	20%	$453.75 \div 5 = 90.75$
Term paper	95.00	20%	Round the decimal to a whole
Lab work	90.00	20%	number. (Round up if 0.5 or above;
Final exam	93.00	20%	round down if below 0.5.)
	453.75	100%	

This student's final grade is 91.

4. To determine a letter grade, refer to the grading scale you have decided to use. (See the Grading Scales section and the Grading Scales charts later in this chapter.)

To determine how a student is doing at any time during the course, multiply each grade by the percentage the grade is worth. Then add the answers for each grade together and divide by the total percentage available to date. (Changing the percentages to decimal form makes this easier.) For example, if the student has completed two quizzes and one test, he or she has earned 20% of the final grade, 5% for each quiz and 10% for the test:

Quiz 1:   100 x 0.05 = 5.0
Quiz 2:   78 x 0.05 = 3.9
Test 1:   87 x 0.10 = 8.7
                         17.6 ÷ 0.20 = 88%

So 88% is the student's grade to date.

Using a Scoring System to Figure Grades

Another easy way to keep track of grades is to use a scoring system where each quiz, test, etc., can earn scores up to the percentage the item represents in the final grade. Here is how the scoring system would work for the preceding example.

Evaluation	Percent of Final Grade	Possible Score	Grade/100 x Possible Score	Total Score
Quiz 1	5	5	100/100 x 5 =	5.00
Quiz 2	5	5	78/100 x 5 =	3.90
Quiz 3	5	5	89/100 x 5 =	4.45
Quiz 4	5	5	94/100 x 5 =	4.70
Test 1	10	10	87/100 x 10 =	8.70
Test 2	10	10	84/100 x 10 =	8.40
Term Paper	20	20	95/100 x 20 =	19.00
Lab Work	20	20	90/100 x 20 =	18.00
Final Exam	20	20	93/100 x 20 =	18.60
Final Grade	100	100		90.75 or 91%

After you have the number grade, go to the grading scale you are using to find the final letter grade for the course. To figure out how a student is doing at any time during the course, divide the total score to date by the possible score to date and multiply by 100. In other words, if the student has taken quizzes numbers 1 and 2 and test number 1, the total score he or she could possibly have earned is 20. The scores earned for these three instruments equal 17.60. Divide 17.60 by 20.00 to get 0.88. Multiply this by 100. The student's grade to date is 88%.

Using a College Type of Point System

Instead of using grades based on percentages, some college professors prefer using a point system for grading. At the beginning of a term, the students receive a syllabus that lists what they are required to do in the class and the points they can earn for each item. Students really like this system because it gives them more control over their grades. They know how many points they need to get an A in the class, and they have a choice to do the extra work required to earn that grade. The syllabus usually lists reading, papers, and other work that students can do for extra credit if their test grades are not high enough to earn the final grades they want.

You may want to try this system in your school. The following is a sample of how the point system might work for an English literature class. Note that 150 possible extra credit points are already built in.

The best comment that I received was from a father whose daughter had a 4.0 GPA. He said, "We stay with the subject until she masters it!" That is just one of the benefits of home schooling.

Rodney Miller, Dean of Records/ Registrar, Covenant College

English Literature Grade 12

Requirements	Possible Points
Daily reading, listening assignments	75
Reading and narrating back two assigned novels	200
Three tests	300
Two 3-page papers with sources (various topics to be discussed in class)	200
One 5-page explication on *Hamlet*	200
Viewing and writing a critique of 5-hour video of *Pride and Prejudice*	75
Act out one scene of the play of your choice	25
Attend a live Shakespeare performance	50
Convert one page of a work written in Old or Middle English into modern English	25

Evaluation

A	975–1000+	C	825–849
A-	950–974	C-	800–824
B+	925–949	D+	775–799
B	900–924	D	750–774
B-	875–899	D-	725–749
C+	850–874	F	000–724

This system would be especially good to use for courses that require hands-on or creative work, such as shop or clothing construction. Students who are having trouble with their grades can earn extra credit by making other projects while getting extra practice at the same time.

Assigning Grades Without Testing

Many homeschool teachers evaluate their students' work in other ways besides testing. Let us take an example of a hypothetical U.S. history class where the teacher required the student to do extensive reading and research into primary source documents. The student was required to summarize the readings orally to the teacher and to provide reports and evaluations of his research in the form of speeches and essays. The teacher evaluated the student's work according to the following formula:

40%	Completed reading assignments (oral reports to teacher)	
40%	Research reports (written)	
	Understanding of concepts	50%
	Analysis and interpretation	30%

	Presentation and style	10%
	Grammar, punctuation, etc.	10%
20%	Speeches	
	Content	60%
	Presentation	40%
100%		

Suppose this student earned the following grades:

Reading assignments (40%)
        95, 91, 89, 100, 98, 88, 94, 99, 95, 100. Average **94.9**

Research Reports (40%)
        Report 1:   Concepts   96 x 0.50 =   48.0
                         Anal./Interpr. 91 x 0.30 =   27.3
                         Pres./Style   88 x 0.10 =   8.8
                         Gram./Punc.   100 x 0.10 =   10.0
                                                           94.1
        Report 2:   Concepts   93 x 0.50 =   46.5
                         Anal./Interpr. 98 x 0.30 =   29.4
                         Pres./Style   92 x 0.10 =   9.2
                         Gram./Punc.   97 x 0.10 =   9.7
                                                           94.8

Find the average of the two scores: 94.1 + 94.8 / 2 = **94.45**

Speeches (20%)
        Speech 1:   Content   95 x 0.60 =   57.0
                         Presentation   92 x 0.40 =   36.8
                                                           93.8

        Speech 2:   Content   98 x 0.60 =   58.8
                         Presentation   95 x 0.40 =   38.0
                                                           96.8

Average the two scores: 93.8 + 96.8 / 2 = **95.3**

Final Grade

Reading assignments   94.9 x 0.40 = 37.96
Research reports   94.45 x 0.40 = 37.78
Speeches   95.3 x 0.20 = 19.06
                                    94.8%, or 95%

Using the scoring system with this example, the grade would be figured according to the chart on the next page.

Evaluation	Percent of Final Grade	Possible Score	Grade/100 x Possible Score	Total Score
Reading 1	4	4	95/100 x 4 =	3.80
Reading 2	4	4	91/100 x 4 =	3.64
Reading 3	4	4	89/100 x 4 =	3.56
Reading 4	4	4	100/100 x 4 =	4.00
Reading 5	4	4	98/100 x 4 =	3.92
Reading 6	4	4	88/100 x 4 =	3.52
Reading 7	4	4	94/100 x 4 =	3.76
Reading 8	4	4	99/100 x 4 =	3.96
Reading 9	4	4	95/100 x 4 =	3.80
Reading 10	4	4	100/100 x 4 =	4.00
Total Reading	40	40		37.96
Report 1: Concepts	10	10	96/100 x 10 =	9.60
Report 1: Anal./Interpr.	6	6	91/100 x 6 =	5.46
Report 1: Presentation/Style	2	2	88/100 x 2 =	1.76
Report 1: Grammar/Punc.	2	2	100/100 x 2 =	2.00
Total Report 1	20	20		18.82
Report 2: Concepts	10	10	93/100 x 10 =	9.30
Report 2: Anal./Interpr.	6	6	98/100 x 6 =	5.88
Report 2: Presentation/Style	2	2	92/100 x 2 =	1.84
Report 2: Presentation	2	2	97/100 x 2 =	1.94
Total Report 2	20	20		18.96
Speech 1: Content	6	6	95/100 x 6 =	5.70
Speech 1: Presentation	4	4	92/100 x 4 =	3.68
Total Speech 1	10	10		9.38
Speech 2: Content	6	6	98/100 x 6 =	5.88
Speech 2: Presentation	4	4	95/100 x 4 =	3.80
Total Speech 2	10	10		9.68
Total Reading	40	40		37.96
Total Report 1	20	20		18.82
Total Report 2	20	20		18.96
Total Speech 1	10	10		9.38
Total Speech 2	10	10		9.68
Final Grade	100	100		94.8 or 95%

Grading Scales

Teachers award letter grades according to various grading scales. I have included three sample grading scales for both regular and AP/Honors courses. You may use any grading scale you wish, as long as you define it on the transcript, but you might want to use the scale your local public or Christian school is using, especially if there is a possibility that your child will transfer there. If you want to assign pass/fail grades for noncredit courses, indicate P or F on the transcript. Pass/fail grades carry no weight. (The weight helps you determine the student's GPA. See chapter 10.)

You may enter either letter grades or number grades on your transcript. If your student takes courses from other schools, your transcript might have a combination of letter and number grades, depending on how you and the other schools record grades. Whether you use letters or numbers, the weight will remain the same.

Awarding Credits

Usually one high school credit is equal to one year of study. You may award credits in any of the following ways:

1. Credits may be awarded according to the number of student/teacher contact hours, or Carnegie units. Carnegie units may be 120 to 180 hours, so if you award credits this way, you need to specify the number of hours you have used to award credit. Another option is to award one Carnegie unit for each year-long high school course completed. Use whatever definition you prefer, but be sure to define your terms.
2. Mastery of the material is another way to grant credit. In this method, you grant credit when the student knows the course material thoroughly. Alternatively, you may grant credit for a predetermined level of mastery and grade accordingly. (For instance, 80% mastery might earn credit with a grade of C.)
3. A third method is using a combination of Carnegie units and mastery of material.
4. Another method is to grant credit for reaching a predetermined level of proficiency, such as with a student contract. This method is especially useful for skill-oriented classes such as carpentry or sewing.

Summary for Awarding Credits

1 credit	1 year of study	120–180 Carnegie units	Mastery/proficiency
1/2 credit	1 semester of study	60–90 Carnegie units	Mastery/proficiency
1/4 credit	1/2 semester of study	30–45 Carnegie units	Mastery/proficiency

(Note: On the sample transcript in chapter 10, the twelfth-grade philosophy class was awarded two credits. The material covered in this course would be equivalent to two one-year courses.)

Dividing Course Work Into Four Years

Like many other homeschoolers, we kept school in session year-round, with periodic breaks throughout the year. Therefore, Christine took some courses that began in spring and ended in fall or winter. Her art appreciation course was split into two nonconsecutive semesters. (In that case we called the courses Art Appreciation I and Art Appreciation II, each worth one-half credit.)

If you teach school during "school months" and take summers off, list the courses under the years in which they were studied. If you teach year-round, you might want to include a statement explaining your schedule in your cover letter to colleges or on your transcript. We used the statement, "School was in session year-round. Therefore, some courses overlapped traditional school years."

You will need to divide the courses into four groups for ninth, tenth, eleventh, and twelfth grades so that the numbers of credits for each year will be similar. Record the actual completion date for each course on the transcript. By dividing the courses, you are simply assigning the credits to particular grades in high school to make the transcript easier to evaluate.

Composing a Narrative Evaluation

If you have not assigned grades and you feel that a traditional transcript format would misrepresent your student's homeschool education, you may write a narrative evaluation. If you choose this method, it would be a good idea to have your student write a summary of his or her education as well. Submit both your evaluation and your student's summary to colleges with application materials.

Michael Farris describes how he evaluated his daughter's high schooling for college admissions. "I wrote a five or six page essay about what Christy had done in high school and gave my evaluation.... I told them I thought she was about an A-minus student judged on an absolute scale and an A student probably judged on the way schools go these days. She had SAT scores in the low 1200s, and so because I think my essay of her high school performance and her SAT scores matched up, they said fine. And she was given an academic scholarship to begin with and she's graduating with a 3.9 grade point average."

Applying to Highly Selective Colleges

Applying to Ivy League and other highly selective colleges is much more involved than applying to other schools. Since these colleges attract the nation's best students, they can afford to be extremely particular about those they admit.

To increase their chances of acceptance, Jonathan Reider of Stanford University recommends that homeschool students get involved in community institutions such as church, scouts, volunteer work, or whatever can amplify their extracurricular profiles. "Show us that you are a social being as well as an intellectual one," he says. "You will have to live here in a community of peers. How will you handle that?" He also recommends involvement in a "normal" academic situation like a community college course so that you can submit letters of recommendation from academic teachers outside the family.

Some of our brightest home schoolers have been admitted on the basis of portfolio assessment and ACT/SAT scores.

Dennis Hendrickson, Associate Director of Admissions, University of Northern Iowa

Reider adds, "Parents may indeed be able to be objective, but the admission office needs to be convinced. It also shows that you can adapt to a regular academic calendar and structure. Above all, tell us how you like to think and about what. What drives you to learn? Are you a 'thinker'? (Insert picture of Rodin's statue here.) Prove it to us. (No, we don't want a portfolio of all your work. Just tell us.)"

Reider also encourages students to include information about their homeschools by answering a series of questions in their applications. "How did this come about? Why did you choose homeschooling? What did you gain from it? What were the costs to you? What was your schedule on a typical day? Where did you go for resources outside the home? What did you like best? Least? How were you evaluated? Was your mother a tough/easy grader?"

Stanford prefers not to receive traditional transcripts from parents. According to Reider, grades and credits are almost meaningless, since there is little or no comparative context. Reider feels that attempts to create a normal-looking high school transcript serve little purpose. Instead he wants to know what students have learned and what they can do. The only transcript data he wants are course titles and content with dates of completion and test scores (SATs, ACTs, and APs).

Reider has noticed that, ironically, less selective schools are more particular about course requirements and GEDs than Stanford and other highly selective schools are. Perhaps the reason is that by nature of their selectivity, tougher schools weed out poorly prepared students.

Even highly selective colleges vary in the type of documentation they prefer from homeschoolers. Amherst College offers the following guidelines:

1. A complete description of high school course work and texts used should be submitted by the homeschool teacher; the courses should conform to or exceed the standards of the student's state and, of course, Amherst's own recommended high school curriculum.
2. The homeschool teacher should provide a detailed written recommendation of the student covering academic and personal areas.
3. Outside recommendations should come from people who have known the applicant in contexts other than academics.
4. Standardized tests including ACT or SAT I and three SAT II tests.
5. The student should include some samples of writing done in the course of his or her schooling, perhaps a short piece and a longer research paper.
6. Grades or other evaluations should be included.
7. Any additional documentation is helpful.

Massachusetts Institute of Technology (MIT) expressed interest in receiving traditional transcript information from parents with course descriptions and names of textbooks and other resources.

Check with admissions departments of particular colleges for their preferences in documentation for homeschooled applicants.

Guidance counselor Donna Poole says that the application process for those applying to the most selective colleges is intense. She said that essay topics are more integrative and reflective than are those for other schools. Some of the colleges that she has dealt with have required not a transcript but a hand-printed copy by the guidance counselor of every semester grade the student made, with the school's grading scale included. She says that these colleges ask a lot more of everyone involved.

Poole offers the following recommendation to students who wish to apply to highly selective schools. "Keep a resume. We do this for all of our kids…. Begin at least in ninth grade to record honors and awards, community service, extracurricular involvement, and part-time jobs. You need *everything* recorded. Keep a running log…of every time you serve in the soup kitchen. Ivy League schools are looking for service, leadership, and grades."

Now that you know how to keep good records of your high school training, it is time to put them all together into a professional application package. Chapter 10 will walk you through the process step-by-step.

Each one should test his own actions. Then he can take pride in himself,
without comparing himself to somebody else, for each one should carry his own load.

Galatians 6:4-5

Time Sheet

Name _____ **Grade** _____ **Course** (optional) _____

Date	Activity	Time Spent	Total to Date

Date	Activity	Time Spent	Total to Date

Reading List—Books

Name _____ **Grade** _____ **Course** (optional) _____

Book Title	Author	Topic/Course	Date

Book Title	Author	Topic/Course	Date

Reading List—Periodicals/Journals

Name _____ **Grade** _____ **Course** (optional) _____

Periodical (Issue #)	Article Title	Topic/Course	Date

Periodical (Issue #)	Article Title	Topic/Course	Date

Videos and Other Media

Name _____ **Grade** _____ **Course** (optional) _____

Title	Topic/Course	Type*	Date

* **V:** Video or movie, **N:** Radio or television news, **TV:** Television program, **Th:** live theatre, **O:** other

Assignments

Name _____ **Grade** _____ **Course** (optional) _____

Assignment/Course	Assigned	Due	Completed

Assignment/Course	Assigned	Due	Completed

Progress Report

Student: _____ School Name: _____

Grade/Year in High School: _____

Course Title: _____ Instructor: _____

Grades Earned: 1st Semester _____ 2nd Semester _____ Final _____

Comments: _____
_____
_____
_____
_____
_____
_____
_____

Signature: _____ Date _____

Progress Report

Student: _____ School Name: _____

Grade/Year in High School: _____

Course Title: _____ Instructor: _____

Grades Earned: 1st Semester _____ 2nd Semester _____ Final _____

Comments: _____
_____
_____
_____
_____
_____
_____

Signature: _____ Date _____

Grade Report

Student: _____ School Name: _____

Grade/Year in High School: _____

Course Title	Quarters:	1st Semester 1	2	2nd Semester 3	4	Final

Days Absent:

Attitude:

Timeliness:

Neatness:

Comments:

Grading Scale:

Signature of Teacher_____ Date _____

Student Recommendation

Student: _____

Date of Birth: _____ **Class of (year)** _____

The following information will be included in the student's high school file and will be submitted with college applications.

How long have you known the student and in what capacity? _____
_____
_____
_____
_____

Please comment on the student's personality and character. _____
_____
_____
_____
_____
_____
_____
_____

If your contact was as an instructor, please comment on the student's academic ability, cooperation, and class participation. If you were not an instructor, please comment on the student's abilities and cooperation in whatever activities were involved. _____
_____
_____
_____
_____
_____
_____
_____
_____
_____
_____

Would you be willing for colleges to contact you about the student? Yes _____ No _____

Name _____ Phone _____

Address _____

Signature_____ Date _____

Extracurricular Activities

Name _____ **Grade** _____

Date	Activity	Time Spent	Total to Date

Date	Activity	Time Spent	Total to Date

Coursework

Title of Course: _____

Course Description: _____

Learning Category _____
Number of credits _____ *Check one:* academic _____ non-academic _____ AP _____ non-credit _____
Calendar year(s) taken _____ year in high school _____
First semester: Season/year _____ Grade earned _____
Second semester: Season/year _____ Grade earned _____
Did course overlap traditional school years? _____ If so, which grades? _____
Completion date _____ Final grade for course _____
Was the course split (taken over two or more non-consecutive semesters)? _____
Teacher _____

Textbooks and other resources used _____
_____
_____
_____
_____
_____
_____
_____
_____

Field trips, projects, term papers, speeches, lab work, etc. (Include resources used.) _____
_____
_____
_____
_____
_____
_____
_____
_____
_____
_____
_____
_____

Experts consulted (if any) _____
_____
_____
_____

Comments _____
_____
_____

Language Arts Course Descriptions

Course Title: **Date Completed:**

Description:

Texts and Resources Used:

Course Title: **Date Completed:**

Description:

Texts and Resources Used:

Course Title: **Date Completed:**

Description:

Texts and Resources Used:

Course Title: **Date Completed:**

Description:

Texts and Resources Used:

Mathematics Course Descriptions

Course Title: **Date Completed:**

Description:

Texts and Resources Used:

Course Title: **Date Completed:**

Description:

Texts and Resources Used:

Course Title: **Date Completed:**

Description:

Texts and Resources Used:

Course Title: **Date Completed:**

Description:

Texts and Resources Used:

Social Studies Course Descriptions

Course Title: **Date Completed:**

Description:

Texts and Resources Used:

Course Title: **Date Completed:**

Description:

Texts and Resources Used:

Course Title: **Date Completed:**

Description:

Texts and Resources Used:

Course Title: **Date Completed:**

Description:

Texts and Resources Used:

Science Course Descriptions

Course Title: **Date Completed:**

Description:

Texts and Resources Used:

Course Title: **Date Completed:**

Description:

Texts and Resources Used:

Course Title: **Date Completed:**

Description:

Texts and Resources Used:

Course Title: **Date Completed:**

Description:

Texts and Resources Used:

Arts Course Descriptions

Course Title: **Date Completed:**

Description:

Texts and Resources Used:

Course Title: **Date Completed:**

Description:

Texts and Resources Used:

Course Title: **Date Completed:**

Description:

Texts and Resources Used:

Course Title: **Date Completed:**

Description:

Texts and Resources Used:

Business Course Descriptions

Course Title: **Date Completed:**

Description:

Texts and Resources Used:

Course Title: **Date Completed:**

Description:

Texts and Resources Used:

Course Title: **Date Completed:**

Description:

Texts and Resources Used:

Course Title: **Date Completed:**

Description:

Texts and Resources Used:

Foreign Language Course Descriptions

Course Title: **Date Completed:**

Description:

Texts and Resources Used:

Course Title: **Date Completed:**

Description:

Texts and Resources Used:

Course Title: **Date Completed:**

Description:

Texts and Resources Used:

Course Title: **Date Completed:**

Description:

Texts and Resources Used:

Life Skills Course Descriptions

Course Title: **Date Completed:**

Description:

Texts and Resources Used:

Course Title: **Date Completed:**

Description:

Texts and Resources Used:

Course Title: **Date Completed:**

Description:

Texts and Resources Used:

Course Title: **Date Completed:**

Description:

Texts and Resources Used:

Physical Education, Health, Other Course Descriptions

Course Title: **Date Completed:**

Description:

Texts and Resources Used:

Course Title: **Date Completed:**

Description:

Texts and Resources Used:

Course Title: **Date Completed:**

Description:

Texts and Resources Used:

Course Title: **Date Completed:**

Description:

Texts and Resources Used:

Language Arts Course Descriptions (Sample)

Course Title: Grammar and Composition   **Date Completed:** 5/20XX

Description: Grammar: parts of speech, phrases, clauses, usage, mechanics, spelling, vocabulary, diagramming, syntax; Composition: sentence patterns, paragraphs, outlines, letters, poetry, drama, stories, nonfiction, poetry, communication skills, the origin of language, semantics.

Texts and Resources Used: Alpha Omega Lifepacs, *Glencoe English 9, The Write Source*

Course Title: American Literature   **Date Completed:** 5/20XX

Description: American novels, short stories, essays, poems, plays, biographies; literary terms and devices; Authors included: Alcott, Bradford, Hawthorne, Franklin, Irving, Twain, Crane, J. F. Cooper, Patton, Voigt, Steinbeck, Mansfield, Thoreau, Yolen, Bradbury, Keller, Longfellow, Frost, Lowell, Millay, Eliot, Holmes, Poe, Cummings, Emerson, Sandburg, Van Dyke, Hemingway, Thurber, Whitman, others.

Texts and Resources Used: Literature anthologies from A Beka and others, classes in short stories, Hemingway, and poetry; *American Poetry and Prose,* Houghton Mifflin; *Poems That Live Forever,* Doubleday; entire works.

Course Title: Writing for Publication   **Date Completed:** 5/20XX

Description: Composition, including descriptive, persuasive, editorial, essay, non-fiction, fiction, letters, etc. Reviewed parts of speech, sentence structure, phrases, clauses, levels of English usage, agreement, verb tenses, correct use of pronouns and modifiers, clear sentences, effective paragraphs; marketing.

Texts and Resources Used: 30-hour professional writers conference: Beginner's symposium, workshops in general writing, fiction, historical fiction, alternative markets, and private consultations with editor/authors; *Warriner's English Grammar and Composition: Complete Course; English Handbook,* BJU Press; writer's magazines and books.

Course Title: British Literature   **Date Completed:** 5/20XX

Description: Short stories, poetry, drama, essays, longer works; Authors included: Shakespeare, Pope, Donne, Foxe, Dickens, Eliot, Wren, Sayers, Doyle, Hurnard, Stevenson, Milton, Shaw, R. Browning, MacDonald, Byron, Noyes, Tennyson, E. Browning, Yeats, Keats, Chaucer, Shelley, Coleridge, Jonson, Austen, Defoe, Swift, Wells, Christie, others.

Texts and Resources Used: Literature anthologies; entire works (including three Shakespeare plays and two others on video); Shakespeare class; poetry class; *Poems That Live Forever,* Doubleday

School Data*

Name of School _____

Address of School _____

_____

Type of School _____ (Home, correspondence, private, public, community college, etc.)

Phone _____ Fax _____ E-mail _____

Accreditation (if applicable) _____

Dates of Student's Enrollment _____

Full-time _____ Part-time (# hours or # courses) _____

Contact Person/Title _____

Credits and Grading (Fill in or check all that apply.)

Credits based on Carnegie units: 1 credit = 120_____ 140 _____ 160 _____ 180 _____ hrs.

Credits determined by: completion of course material _____ mastery of material _____

Credits determined by other means (explain) _____

_____

Grading scale: A = _____ to _____   B = _____ to _____   C = _____ to _____

D = _____ to _____   F = _____ to _____

Grading based on other factors (explain) _____

_____

Pass/fail grades only _____ No grades given (explain) _____

_____

High School Faculty^

Name	Qualifications/Experience	Course taught

* (Fill out one form for each school where your student took classes.)

^ (Optional, for your records, or for colleges) Include anyone who taught your child in an academic, workshop, or lab setting. For private, public, and correspondence schools, use this space to list courses or to note other pertinent information.

Student Data

Name _____

Nickname (if any) _____ Social Security # _____

Graduation Date _____ Class Rank (if applicable) _____ out of _____

Test Scores

ACT: Date _____ Comp. _____ Eng. _____ Math _____ Reading _____ Sci. Reas. _____
ACT: Date _____ Comp. _____ Eng. _____ Math _____ Reading _____ Sci. Reas. _____
SAT: Date _____ Verbal _____ Math _____
SAT: Date _____ Verbal _____ Math _____
PLAN: Date _____ Eng. _____ Math _____ Reading _____ Sci. Reas. _____
PSAT: Date _____ Verbal _____ Math _____ Writing _____
SAT II, other tests _____

_____

Activities and Accomplishments

Activity	Awards, other recognition	Dates involved

Work Experience

Title	Responsibilities	Type^	Dates involved

^ Use codes as follows: P = paid work; V = volunteer work; A = apprenticeship; B = barter

Travel

Destination	Dates

Grading Chart for Scoring System

Student: _____ **Semester/Year** _____

Course Title: _____

Form of Evaluation	Percent of Final Grade	Possible Score	Grade/100 x Possible Score	Total Score

Form of Evaluation	Percent of Final Grade	Possible Score	Grade/100 x Possible Score	Total Score

Grading Scales

Quality Points (Weight) - Scale 1					
Letter Grade	Numeric Grade	1 Credit	0.75 Credit	0.5 Credit	0.25 Credit
A A+	90-100	4.00	3.00	2.00	1.00
B B+	80-89	3.00	2.25	1.50	0.75
C C+	70-79	2.00	1.50	1.00	0.50
D D+	60-69	1.00	0.75	0.50	0.25
F	Below 60	0.00	0.00	0.00	0.00

Quality Points (Weight) - Scale 2					
Letter Grade	Numeric Grade	1 Credit	0.75 Credit	0.5 Credit	0.25 Credit
A A+	93-100	4.00	3.00	2.00	1.00
B B+	86-93	3.00	2.25	1.50	0.75
C C+	77-85	2.00	1.50	1.00	0.50
D D+	70-76	1.00	0.75	0.50	0.25
F	Below 70	0.00	0.00	0.00	0.00

Quality Points (Weight) - Scale 3					
Letter Grade	Numeric Grade	1 Credit	0.75 Credit	0.5 Credit	0.25 Credit
A+	93-100	4.00	3.00	2.00	1.00
A	93-100	4.00	3.00	2.00	1.00
A-	90-92	3.67	2.75	1.84	0.92
B+	87-89	3.33	2.50	1.67	0.83
B	83-86	3.00	2.25	1.50	0.75
B-	80-82	2.67	2.00	1.34	0.67
C+	77-79	2.33	1.75	1.17	0.58
C	73-76	2.00	1.50	1.00	0.50
C-	70-72	1.67	1.25	0.84	0.42
D+	67-69	1.33	1.00	0.67	0.33
D	63-66	1.00	0.75	0.50	0.25
D-	60-62	0.67	0.50	0.34	0.17
F	Below 60	0.00	0.00	0.00	0.00

To figure GPA for the year: 1. Add total credits. 2. Assign weight (quality points.) 3. Find sum of quality points. 4. Divide sum of quality point by total credits.

To figure cumulative GPA (for multiple years): 1. Find total number of credits for all years involved. 2. Find sum of quality points for all years involved. 3. Divide sum of all quality points by total credits.

Honors/AP Grading Scales

Quality Points (Weight) - Scale 1

Letter Grade	Numeric Grade	1 Credit	0.75 Credit	0.5 Credit	0.25 Credit
A A+	90-100	5.00	3.75	2.50	1.25
B B+	80-89	4.00	3.00	2.00	1.00
C C+	70-79	3.00	2.25	1.50	0.75
D D+	60-69	2.00	1.50	1.00	0.50
F	Below 60	0.00	0.00	0.00	0.00

Quality Points (Weight) - Scale 2

Letter Grade	Numeric Grade	1 Credit	0.75 Credit	0.5 Credit	0.25 Credit
A A+	93-100	5.00	3.75	2.50	1.25
B B+	86-93	4.00	3.00	2.00	1.00
C C+	77-85	3.00	2.25	1.50	0.75
D D+	70-76	2.00	1.50	1.00	0.50
F	Below 70	0.00	0.00	0.00	0.00

Quality Points (Weight) - Scale 3

Letter Grade	Numeric Grade	1 Credit	0.75 Credit	0.5 Credit	0.25 Credit
A+	93-100	5.00	3.75	2.50	1.00
A	93-100	5.00	3.75	2.50	1.00
A-	90-92	4.67	3.50	2.34	1.17
B+	87-89	4.33	3.25	2.17	1.08
B	83-86	4.00	3.00	2.00	1.00
B-	80-82	3.67	2.75	1.84	0.92
C+	77-79	3.33	2.50	1.67	0.83
C	73-76	3.00	2.25	1.50	0.75
C-	70-72	2.67	2.00	1.34	0.67
D+	67-69	2.33	1.75	1.17	0.58
D	63-66	2.00	1.50	1.00	0.50
D-	60-62	1.67	1.25	0.84	0.42
F	Below 60	0.00	0.00	0.00	0.00

To figure GPA for the year: 1. Add total credits. 2. Assign weight (quality points.) 3. Find sum of quality points. 4. Divide sum of quality point by total credits.

To figure cumulative GPA (for multiple years): 1. Find total number of credits for all years involved. 2. Find sum of quality points for all years involved. 3. Divide sum of all quality points by total credits.

Chapter 10

Professional Packaging

It is helpful when a transcript is well organized and looks like a "traditional" transcript on a four-point scale.... Presentation is very important.

Randy Comfort, Dean of Admissions, Greenville College

The college application process is long, involved, and potentially expensive, so it pays to do it well. Meeting deadlines, following directions carefully, and imparting a professional look to your transcript and application materials will influence colleges in your students' favor, as long as their high school preparation has also been good.

Professionalism

Your entire interaction with colleges should be on a professional level, which will foster an attitude of mutual respect. Keep in mind that you are a professional teacher, even if your only salary is the happiness and success of your children. (What better payment could there be?) When you correspond with a college, your letter should be typed or printed on a letter-quality printer. Check for correct grammar, punctuation, and spelling. Make sure your letter or package is clearly and neatly labeled and that you have affixed the correct amount of postage. The transcript, in particular, should be flawless, just like a job résumé. Presumably you have given your child an excellent education, and your transcript should reflect that excellence.

Transcripts

The homeschool transcript is the most important document that you as parents will supply to colleges (unless you write a narrative evaluation instead). Transcripts are not as difficult to make as they look. Just follow the instructions below, and you will have a professional-looking transcript in no time.

I have provided transcript forms for your use. However, you may prefer to design your own transcript. If you do, according to Gary Ray of Lee University, the following elements must be present:

Some homeschoolers seem shocked when we mention a need for a transcript. I have even been told by parents that there is no transcript and they can't believe that [the college] is requiring one. If a signed, official transcript and ACT/SAT arrives with an application and application fee, any student is considered for admission.

Anonymous

(This college accepts official-looking transcripts prepared, signed, and dated by parents.)

1. Student name
2. Homeschool name, address, and phone number
3. Course titles
4. Courses listed chronologically by year
5. Grades, either numeric or letter
6. Grading scale used
7. Grade point average
8. Evidence that student has met minimum requirements, such as four years of English
9. Projected graduation date or graduation date
10. Parent signature

Ray said that he would also like to see consistency with state requirements and a one-page overview describing the school and the curriculum used. (The grading scale may be included on this page.)

Colleges vary slightly on what they would like to see. According to Lydia Knopf, Biola University relies heavily on the traditional look to a transcript, with the following features:

1. Professional, typed
2. Course titles
3. Semester grades and cumulative grades
4. Semester and cumulative credits
5. Dual credits from college that count for high school (perhaps with an asterisk designation)
6. PSAT/SAT scores, ACT scores
7. State proficiency exam (if applicable)
8. Dated and signed, sent in a sealed envelope

Realize that even if you include test scores on the transcript, you still must arrange for testing services to send official results directly to colleges.

In addition to wanting the official transcript, some colleges will request information about the curriculum you used and/or course descriptions. Always include biographical information about your students with transcripts. Colleges will want to know about students' extracurricular activities, awards, accomplishments, hobbies, travel, and so on. In just a few pages of information, you need to help admissions people understand who your students are and where they fit academically.

Using Transcript Forms in This Book

There are two types of transcripts in this book (simple and comprehensive). The simple one is for colleges that want transcripts with only essential details. It is also useful for proving academic eligibility for car insurance good-student discounts. (Never call the documentation you send to insurance companies a "progress report." Call it a transcript.) First I will explain how to write the simple transcript. Then I will give step-by-step instructions for the comprehensive transcript.

Simple Transcript

I have filled out a sample transcript at the end of this chapter, with the title "High School Transcript Sample." Look at this form as you read these instructions.

Top Section of Transcript

This is the information section that colleges need for identifying and contacting your students and you.

1. Fill in your student's name, address, phone number, gender, birth date, and graduation date or projected graduation date.
2. Enter the name of your school. (Several colleges mentioned that you should have a school name.)
3. List yourself as the person to contact.

Middle Section of Transcript

This is where you will record information about the courses that your student has completed. I suggest that you record one year at a time.

1. Under "Grade/Year," list the grade in the far-left column. Type the year or years in the next column. You need to list the grade and year(s) only once for each grade level.
2. Under "Course Title," list the courses your student has completed for each grade level. You may separate the sections for each grade with lines, if you wish.
3. Fill in grades and credits for each semester. Usually students complete half of a one-credit course in one semester and a full one-credit course in two semesters. The final grade is the average of the two semester grades. (Refer to chapter 9 for instructions on assigning grades.)
4. Add the credits from both semesters in each course to yield the final credit (usually half a credit for a half-year course and one credit for a full-year course).
5. Fill in credits in the "Yearly/Cumulative Totals: Credits/GPA" column.
    a. Add the number of credits in the Final Grade/Credits ("Final Gr./Cr.") column for each grade and place that number next to "Credits" in the right-hand column.
    b. Add this number to the cumulative credits in the section above and place your answer next to "Cum. Credits." (For ninth grade, simply enter the number of credits your student completed that year.)
6. To calculate grade point averages (GPAs), you need to find the quality points earned for each subject. (Refer to chapter 9.) If you wish, make a copy of the partially completed transcript and use it as a worksheet.
    a. Take out the grading scale you have chosen to use. Find the row with your student's final grade for each course. Go across the row to the column with the amount of credit you are awarding for the course. The weight or number of quality points earned is where the row and column intersect.
    b. Pencil in the weight next to the number of credits for each course.
    c. Add the quality points for each grade separately and pencil in the totals.
    d. To find the GPA for a single year's courses, divide the total quality points for that year by the total credits for that year.
    e. To figure the GPA for multiple years, first add the total quality points for those years together. Then find the sum of credits for those years. Divide the total number of quality points by the total number of credits to find the cumulative GPA. (If this sounds confusing, follow the step-by-step instructions for the comprehensive transcript and then fill out the simple transcript.)
7. To calculate the academic GPA for each year, subtract the number of non-academic credits from total credits, which will give you the total of academic credits. Then subtract the number of non-academic quality points from the total number of quality points, yielding the academic quality points. Finally, divide the academic quality points by the academic credits. The answer is the academic GPA. For cumulative academic GPAs, do the same as above but add the total number of academic quality points and credits for all the years involved. Then divide quality points by credits to get the cumulative academic GPA to date.

Bottom Section of Transcript

1. Use the space at the bottom of the form to define your method of grading and awarding credits and to list student interests and activities.
2. Sign and date each copy that you send out. Do not sign and date your original. Some homeschoolers have their transcripts notarized. You may do that too if you wish.

Comprehensive Transcript

The second transcript allows room for more details. If you follow these instructions step-by-step, you should have no trouble completing the transcript like a professional. It is a two-page transcript that may be copied on both sides of a sheet of quality paper or cover stock.

Filling Out Draft Transcript

A document as complex as a transcript leaves much room for error. Therefore I recommend that you complete the draft transcript form before filling out the final transcript. Refer to the Comprehensive High School Transcript (Sample) and the coded transcript as you follow the instructions below. (Please note that codes are printed on the coded transcript only.)

The easiest way to complete a transcript is to fill in each corresponding section as your student finishes a semester. At the end of the first semester, complete sections A, B, and C in the sector for the corresponding year. After the second semester, fill in sections D, E, F, G, H, J, and T. After each school year, make sure that you have completed sections A through J and T for that year. If you got a late start and need to record grades for more than one year, work on one year at a time.

Some forget to indicate a cumulative GPA. Many more forget to include the fact that the student graduated and the date of completion of requirements. Both indication of graduation and the date are required for us to use the transcript for official processing, particularly federal financial aid qualification.

David Ormsbee, Dean of Enrollment, Cedarville University

School and Student Information (Section AA)

1. Enter student's full name, gender, birth date, and social security number.
   Note: Although a social security number is optional, most colleges and universities use this number for student identification. It is also required if you apply for financial aid.
2. Enter your student's graduation date or projected graduation date.
3. Enter the name of the person colleges should contact if they have questions. This is usually the homeschool teacher.
4. Enter your school name and your address, phone number, fax number, and/or email address if applicable.

Course Titles—Column A

Column A is the section where you will record course titles for all four years. Section A1 is for grade 9 courses, section A2 for grade 10 courses, section A3 for grade 11 courses, and section A4 for grade 12 courses.

Ninth-Grade Courses

1. Enter the course titles for the subjects your student studied during ninth grade in column A1. The order of courses is up to you. However, you should be consistent for all four years. For example, if you list language arts courses, then math, then science, and so on, use the same order for each year. You might want to list nonacademic and noncredit courses last. Courses

taken outside of the home or by correspondence should be indicated with a symbol of your choice. Define the symbol in section BB.

2. Place a caret (^) or another symbol beside titles of nonacademic courses. Define the symbol in section BB. (See sample transcript.)
3. For noncredit courses type "noncredit" after the course title.
4. If any course is continued into the next grade, mark an asterisk or another symbol beside it. Place a note defining the symbol in section BB. On the sample transcript, I used "Overlapped traditional school years" to indicate courses that were taken over consecutive school years. For example, this would include a course taken during second-semester freshman year through first-semester sophomore year. On the sample transcript, French I is an example of this.
5. If the course included extensive laboratory work, indicate this by typing "(lab course)" or "(with lab)" beside the course title.
6. If the class was taught at the beginning college level to prepare student for AP (Advanced Placement) exams, type "(AP)" after the course title.

Tenth-Grade Courses

1. Enter course titles in column A2.
2. Follow the instructions for ninth-grade courses, above.

Eleventh-Grade Courses

1. Enter course titles on page 2, column A3.
2. Follow the instructions for ninth-grade courses, above.

Twelfth-Grade Courses

1. Enter course titles on page 2, column A4.
2. Follow the instructions for ninth-grade courses, above.

First Semester—Columns B and C

Ninth-Grade Courses

1. For the courses you have listed in A1, enter the first-semester grades in B1.
2. Enter the semester credits awarded for those classes in C1. For noncredit courses enter "0.00" in column C. (See sample transcript, Grade 10 Driver Education.)
3. If a course was taken only during the second semester, leave spaces B and C blank. (See sample transcript, Grade 9 Geology.)

Tenth-Grade Courses

1. For courses in A2, enter first-semester grades in column B2.
2. Enter first-semester credits in column C2.

Eleventh-Grade Courses

1. For courses in A3, enter first-semester grades in column B3.
2. Enter first-semester credits in column C3.

Twelfth-Grade Courses

1. For courses in A4, enter first-semester grades in column B4.
2. Enter first-semester credits in column C4.

Second Semester—Columns D and E

Ninth-Grade Courses

1. For the courses you have listed in A1, enter the second-semester grades in D1.
2. Enter the semester credit awarded for those classes in E1.
3. If a course was taken only during the first semester, leave spaces D and E blank. (See sample transcript, Grade 9 Astronomy.)

Tenth-Grade Courses

1. For courses in A2, enter second-semester grades in column D2.
2. Enter second-semester credits in column E2.

Eleventh-Grade Courses

1. For courses in A3, enter second-semester grades in column D3.
2. Enter second-semester credits in column E3.

Twelfth-Grade Courses

1. For courses in A4, enter second-semester grades in column D4.
2. Enter second-semester credits in column E4.

Date Complete—Column F

Ninth-Grade Courses

1. In F1 enter the month and year in which each course listed in A1 was completed.
2. If a course was not completed during the year, leave the corresponding space blank. (See sample transcript, Grade 9 French I.)

Tenth-Grade Courses

For courses in A2, enter the completion dates in column F2.

Eleventh-Grade Courses

For courses in A3, enter the completion dates in column F3.

Twelfth-Grade Courses

For courses in A4, enter the completion dates in column F4. *Skip column J for now and go to columns G and H.*

Final Grade/Credits—Columns G and H

Ninth-Grade Courses

1. In G1 enter the final grade for each course listed in A1.
2. In H1 enter the total amount of credit earned for each course.
3. If the course has not been completed, leave column G blank but enter the number of credits earned in column H. (See sample transcript, Grade 9 French I.)
4. Place a caret (^) or another symbol you have chosen beside the credit number for any nonacademic courses.
5. Place an asterisk (*) or another symbol you have chosen beside the credit number for a course that overlapped traditional school years.

Tenth-Grade Courses

1. In G2 enter the final grade for each course listed in A2.
2. In H2 enter the total amount of credit earned for each course.
3. Follow the instructions for ninth-grade courses, above.

Eleventh-Grade Courses

1. In G3 enter the final grade for each course listed in A3.
2. In H3 enter the total amount of credit earned for each course.
3. Follow the instructions for ninth-grade courses, above.

Twelfth-Grade Courses

1. In G4 enter the final grade for each course listed in A4.
2. In H4 enter the total amount of credit earned for each course.
3. Follow the instructions for ninth-grade courses, above.

Weight (Quality Points) - Column J

This column is for recording the quality points earned for each course. Quality points are used to determine grade point averages. Take out the grading scales chart and set it in front of you. You should have chosen a grading scale already. (Refer to chapter 9.) I used grading Scale 2 for the comprehensive sample transcript. You may choose to award more quality points for AP and honors courses. If you do, use the honors grading scale for those courses only.

Ninth-Grade Courses

1. For the courses listed in A1, locate the final grades (from column G1) on the grading scale you chose. Then find the total amount of credit (from column H1) for each of those courses on the scale. The weight for each course is the number where the grade and the credit intersect. For example, on the sample transcript, the weight for grade 11 U.S. Government is found on quality points scale 2 by going across the grade B/B+ line until it intersects the 0.5 credit column. The student earned 1.5 quality points for that course.
2. For those courses that were not completed during the year, use the amount of credit listed in column H and the grade recorded in column B or D to determine the number of quality points earned to date. (See sample transcript, Grade 9 French I.)
3. Insert the number of quality points earned for each course into column J1.
4. Repeat these steps for the remaining courses.

Tenth-Grade Courses

Following the instructions for ninth-grade courses, find the quality points earned for each course listed in A2 and enter the numbers in J2.

Eleventh-Grade Courses

Following the instructions for ninth-grade courses, find the quality points earned for each course listed in A3 and enter the numbers in J3.

Twelfth-Grade Courses

Following the instructions for ninth-grade courses, find the quality points earned for each course listed in A4 and enter the numbers in J4.

Credits and Grading (Section BB)

The first page of the transcript has space in section BB for you to define your grading system. Here are some sample ways to do it:

1. Carnegie units (1 unit=120 hours) and mastery; A 94–100; B 86–93; C 77–85; D 70–76; F below 70.
2. Carnegie units (1=180 hours); A 90–100; B 80–89; C 70–79; D 60–69, F 0–59.
3. Mastery: A^+, A 93–100; A^- 90–92; B^+ 87–89; B 83–86; B^- 80–82; C^+ 77–79; C 73–76, C^- 70–72; D^+ 67–69; D 63–66; D^- 60–62; F Below 60
4. Mastery: A = complete mastery; B = 85% mastery; C = 75% mastery; D = 65% mastery; F = less than 65% mastery of material.

If there is not enough room in the box for all the information, type, "See Credits and Grading, page ___," and then record this information on the page you have indicated. Also, you might want to include a grading scale chart showing the weight you assigned to each grade on one of the supplemental pages of the transcript.

Totals for the Year: Sections T1-T7

Follow the steps below. Then use the summary of steps at the end of this section to verify your answers.

Grade 9—Section T1 (See summary of steps below.)

1. Add the numbers in column H1. (This gives you **total credits** for the year.) Enter the sum here _____.
2. Enter this sum beside **Credits** in section T1.
3. Add the numbers in J1. (This is the **total number of quality points** earned for the year.) Enter the sum here _____.
4. Divide the sum you entered in step 3 by the number you entered in step 1. This yields the **GPA** for the year. If the student passed every course with at least a D, your answer will be between 1.00 and 4.00. If the student earned all A's and B's, the answer will be between 3.00 and 4.00. (The only exception to this is when students have taken honors courses and have been awarded extra quality points for them. In that case, the result may be higher than 4.00.) Enter your answer here _____.
5. Enter the number you found in step 4 beside **GPA for year** in section T1.
6. Next add the number of **nonacademic credits** listed in H1. Enter the sum here _____.
7. Now subtract your answer to step 6 from the number you entered in step 1. This will give you the number of **academic credits**. Enter your answer here _____.
8. Enter the answer to step 7 beside **Academic Credits** in section T1.
9. In column J1, find the total number of **quality points awarded for nonacademic courses**. Record that number here _____.
10. Subtract the answer you found in step 9 from the answer you found in step 3. (This is the total number of **quality points earned for academic courses** for the year.) Enter your answer here _____.
11. Divide your answer to step 10 by your answer to step 7. Again, the result should fall between 1.00 and 4.00 if the student passed all courses (or possibly higher with honors courses). Your answer is the **academic GPA** for the year. Enter the number here _____.

12. Enter the answer to step 11 beside **Acad. GPA for year** in section T1.
13. Be sure to check all your numbers twice. You may use the summary section below to check your figures.

Summary for Filling Out Section T1
    1a. Find the **total credits** for the year. _____
    2a. Find the **total quality points** for the year. _____
    3a. Divide total quality points by total credits to find the **GPA** for the year. _____
    4a. Find the total **academic credits** for the year. _____
    5a. Find the total **quality points for academic courses** for the year. _____
    6a. Divide total academic quality points by total academic credits to find the student's **academic GPA** for the year _____

Grade 10—Section T2 (See summary of steps below.)

14. Add the numbers in column H2. (This gives you **total credits** for the year.) Enter the sum here _____.
15. Enter the sum in step 14 beside **Credits** in section T2.
16. Add the numbers in J2. (This is the **total number of quality points** earned for the year.) Enter the sum here _____.
17. Divide the sum you entered in step 16 by the number you entered in step 14. This yields the **GPA** for the year. If the student passed every course with at least a D, your answer will be between 1.00 and 4.00. If the student earned all A's and B's, the answer will be between 3.00 and 4.00. (See note about honors courses above.) Enter your answer here _____.
18. Enter the number you found in step 17 beside **GPA for year** in section T2.
19. Next, add the numbers of **nonacademic credits** listed in H2. Enter the sum here _____.
20. Now subtract your answer to step 19 from the number you entered in step 14. This will give you the number of **academic credits**. Enter your answer here _____.
21. Enter the answer to step 20 beside **Academic Credits** in section T2.
22. In J2, find the total number of **quality points awarded for nonacademic courses**. Record that number here _____.
23. Subtract the answer you found in step 22 from the answer you found in step 16. (This yields the total number of **quality points earned for academic courses** for the year.) Enter your answer here _____.
24. Divide your answer to step 23 by your answer to step 20. Again, your answer should fall between 1.00 and 4.00 if the student passed all courses. Your answer is the **academic GPA** for the year. Enter the number here _____.
25. Enter the answer to step 24 beside **Acad. GPA for year** in section T2.
26. Be sure to check all your numbers twice. (Use the summary section below.)

Summary for Filling Out Section T2
    7a. Find the **total credits** for the year. _____
    8a. Find the **total quality points** for the year. _____
    9a. Divide total quality points by total credits to find the **GPA** for the year. _____
    10a. Find the total **academic credits** for the year. _____
    11a. Find the total **quality points for academic courses** for the year. _____
    12a. Divide total academic quality points by total academic credits to find the student's **academic GPA** for the year. _____

Cumulative Data for Grades 9 and 10—Section T3 (See summary of steps below.)

27. Add the total credits in step 1 to the total credits in step 14. (This number is the **cumulative total of credits**.) Enter your answer here _____.

28. Record the answer to step 27 beside **Cumulative Credits** in T3.

29. Add the total quality points in step 3 to the total quality points in step 16. (This is the total of **quality points earned in grades 9–10**.) Enter your answer here _____.

30. Divide the answer to step 29 by the answer to step 27 to find the **cumulative GPA** for grades 9–10. Enter your answer here _____.

31. Record the answer to step 30 beside **Cumulative GPA** in T3.

32. Add the total credits in steps 7 and 20. (This will give you **cumulative academic credits**.) Enter your answer here _____.

33. Record the answer to step 32 beside **Cum. Acad. Credits** in T3.

34. Add the total quality points from steps 10 and 23. This gives you the **cumulative academic quality points**. Enter your answer here _____.

35. Divide the answer to step 34 by the answer to step 32 to find the **cumulative academic GPA**. Enter your answer here _____.

36. Record the answer to step 35 beside **Cum. Acad. GPA** in T3.

Summary for Filling Out Section T3

13a. Find **cumulative credits** by adding the answers to 1a and 7a. _____

14a. Find **cumulative quality points** by adding 2a and 8a. _____

15a. Divide 14a by 13a to find **cumulative GPA**. _____

16a. Find **cumulative academic credits** by adding 4a and 10a. _____

17a. Find **cumulative academic quality points** by adding 5a and 11a. _____

18a. Divide 17a by 16a to find **cumulative academic GPA**. _____

Grade 11—Section T4 (See summary of steps below.)

37. Add the numbers in column H3. (This gives you **total credits** for the year.) Enter the sum here _____.

38. Enter the sum in step 37 beside **Credits** in section T4.

39. Add the numbers in J3. (This is the **total number of quality points** earned for the year.) Enter the sum here _____.

40. Divide the sum you entered in step 39 by the number you entered in step 37. This yields the **GPA** for the year. If the student passed every course with at least a D, your answer will be between 1.00 and 4.00. If the student earned all A's and B's, the answer will be between 3.00 and 4.00. (See note on honors courses, above.) Enter your answer here _____.

41. Enter the number you found in step 40 beside **GPA for year** in section T4.

42. Next, add the numbers of **nonacademic credits** listed in H3. Enter the sum here _____.

43. Now subtract your answer to step 42 from the number you entered in step 37. This will give you the number of **academic credits**. Enter your answer here _____.

44. Enter the answer to step 43 beside **Academic Credits** in section T4.

45. In J3, find the total number of **quality points awarded for nonacademic courses**. Record that number here _____.

46. Subtract the answer you found in step 45 from the answer you found in step 39. (This yields the total number of **quality points earned for academic courses** for the year.) Enter your answer here _____.

47. Divide your answer to step 46 by your answer to step 43. Again, your answer should fall between 1.00 and 4.00 if the student passed all courses. Your answer is the **academic GPA** for the year. Enter the number here _____.
48. Enter the answer to step 47 beside **Acad. GPA for year** in section T4.
49. Be sure to check all your numbers twice. (Use the summary section below.)

Summary for Filling Out Section T4

19a. Find the **total credits** for the year. _____
20a. Find the **total quality points** for the year. _____
21a. Divide total quality points by total credits to find the **GPA** for the year. _____
22a. Find the total **academic credits** for the year. _____
23a. Find the total **quality points for academic courses** for the year. _____
24a. Divide total academic quality points by total academic credits to find the student's **academic GPA** for the year. _____

Cumulative Data for Grades 9 to 11—Section T5 (See summary of steps below.)

50. Add the total credits in step 27 to the total credits in step 37. (This number is the **cumulative total of credits**.) Enter your answer here _____.
51. Record the answer to step 50 beside **Cumulative Credits** in T5.
52. Add the total quality points in step 29 to the total quality points in step 39. (This is the total of **quality points earned in grades 9–11**.) Enter your answer here _____.
53. Divide the answer to step 52 by the answer to step 50 to find the **cumulative GPA** for grades 9–11. Enter your answer here _____.
54. Record the answer to step 53 beside **Cumulative GPA** in T5.
55. Add the total credits in steps 32 and 43. (This will give you **cumulative academic credits**.) Enter your answer here _____.
56. Record the answer to step 55 beside **Cum. Acad. Credits** in T5.
57. Add the total quality points from steps 34 and 46. This gives you the **cumulative academic quality points**. Enter your answer here _____.
58. Divide the answer to step 57 by the answer to step 55 to find the **cumulative academic GPA.**
59. Record the answer to step 58 beside **Cum. Acad. GPA** in section T5.

Summary for Filling Out Section T5

25a. Find **cumulative credits** by adding the answers to 13a and 19a. _____
26a. Find **cumulative quality points** by adding 14a and 20a. _____
27a. Divide 26a by 25a to find **cumulative GPA.** _____
28a. Find **cumulative academic credits** by adding 16a and 22a. _____
29a. Find **cumulative academic quality points** by adding 17a and 23a. _____
30a. Divide 29a by 28a to find **cumulative academic GPA.** _____

Grade 12—Section T6 (See summary of steps below.)

60. Add the numbers in column H4. (This gives you **total credits** for the year.) Enter the sum here _____.
61. Enter the sum in step 60 beside **Credits** in section T6.
62. Add the numbers in J4. (This is the **total number of quality points** earned for the year.) Enter the sum here _____.

63. Divide the sum you entered in step 62 by the number you entered in step 60. This yields the **GPA** for the year. If the student passed every course with at least a D, your answer will be between 1.00 and 4.00. If the student earned all A's and B's, the answer will be between 3.00 and 4.00. (See note above concerning honors courses.) Enter your answer here _____.

64. Enter the number you found in step 63 beside **GPA for year** in section T6.

65. Next, add the numbers of **nonacademic credits** listed in H4. Enter the sum here _____.

66. Now subtract your answer to step 65 from the number you entered in step 60. This will give you the number of **academic credits**. Enter your answer here _____.

67. Enter the answer to step 66 beside **Academic Credits** in section T6.

68. In J4 find the total number of **quality points awarded for nonacademic courses**. Record that number here _____.

69. Subtract the answer you found in step 68 from the answer you found in step 62. (This yields the total number of **quality points earned for academic courses** for the year.) Enter your answer here _____.

70. Divide your answer to step 69 by your answer to step 66. Again, your answer should fall between 1.00 and 4.00 if the student passed all courses. Your answer is the **academic GPA** for the year. Enter the number here _____.

71. Enter the answer to step 70 beside **Acad. GPA for year** in section T6.

72. Be sure to check all your numbers twice. (Use the summary section below.)

Summary for Filling Out Section T6

    31a. Find the **total credits** for the year. _____

    32a. Find the **total quality points** for the year. _____

    33a. Divide total quality points by total credits to find the **GPA** for the year. _____

    34a. Find the total **academic credits** for the year. _____

    35a. Find the total **quality points for academic courses** for the year. _____

    36a. Divide total academic quality points by total academic credits to find the student's **academic GPA** for the year. _____

Cumulative Date for Grades 9 to 12—Section T7 (See summary of steps below.)

73. Add the total credits in step 50 to the total credits in step 60. (This number is the **cumulative total of credits**.) Enter your answer here _____.

74. Record the answer to step 73 beside **Cumulative Credits** in T7.

75. Add the total quality points in step 52 to the total quality points in step 62. (This is the total of **quality points earned in grades 9–12**.) Enter your answer here _____.

76. Divide the answer to step 75 by the answer to step 73 to find the **cumulative GPA** for grades 9–12. Enter your answer here _____.

77. Record the answer to step 76 beside **Cumulative GPA** in T7.

78. Add the total credits in steps 55 and 66. (This will give you **cumulative academic credits**.) Enter your answer here _____.

79. Record the answer to step 78 beside **Cum. Acad. Credits** in T7.

80. Add the total quality points from steps 57 and 69. This gives you the **cumulative academic quality points**. Enter your answer here _____.

81. Divide the answer to step 80 by the answer to step 78 to find the **cumulative academic GPA**.

82. Record the answer to step 81 beside **Cum. Acad. GPA** in T7.

Summary for Filling Out Section T7

37a. Find **cumulative credits** by adding the answers to 25a and 31a. _____

38a. Find **cumulative quality points** by adding 26a and 32a. _____

39a. Divide 38a by 37a to find **cumulative GPA.** _____

40a. Find **cumulative academic credits** by adding 28a and 34a. _____

41a. Find **cumulative academic quality points** by adding 29a and 35a. _____

42a. Divide 41a by 40a to find **cumulative academic GPA.** _____

Student Data: Section CC

At the top of page two of the comprehensive transcript (section CC), type in your student's name, the school name, and a list of activities, awards, travel, and anything else that may be of interest to colleges.

Subject Area Totals—Section S1-S2

Section S1-S2 is at the bottom of page 2 of the comprehensive transcript. This is where you will summarize the types of courses your student has taken. Colleges will use this information to assess whether or not your student has fulfilled their minimum subject-area requirements. When you plan your high school curriculum, you should relegate every course to a learning category. This will assist you in trying to meet minimum course requirements. (Refer to "Learning Categories" in chapter 9.)

For each subject area, add the number of credits taken in grades 9–12. To keep yourself from getting confused, list the courses with their credits on a separate piece of paper according to category. Then add the credits together. To be sure you have not missed a course, add the total number of credits in all subject areas and compare that number with the total credits your student has completed.

1. On line S1, enter the totals for each subject area. Record them here, if you wish.
   Language Arts _____ Math ____ Science ____ Social Studies ____
   Foreign Language _____ The Arts ____ Business ____ Life Skills ____
   Health/PE ____ Other ____

2. Find the numbers of nonacademic credits for each subject area. Enter them here, if you wish.
   Language Arts _____ Math ____ Science ____ Social Studies ____
   Foreign Language _____ The Arts ____ Business ____ Life Skills ____
   Health/PE ____ Other ____

3. Subtract non-academic credits (step 2) from totals credits (step 1) in each area to find academic credits.
   Language Arts _____ Math ____ Science ____ Social Studies ____
   Foreign Language_____ The Arts ____ Business ____ Life Skills ____
   Health/PE ____ Other ____

4. Enter totals found in step 3 onto line S2 of the transcript.
   Skip section DD for now. DO NOT sign the transcript.

Final Checking

Put the draft transcript away for a day or two. Then check it for

1. Mathematical errors.
2. Misspellings.

3. Consistency in order of courses.

4. Agreement between subject area totals and total credits (sections S1-S2 and sections T1-T7).

5. Omissions. Compare the list of courses with your other school records.

Filling Out the Final Transcript

Complete the final high school transcript only after you have completed the draft transcript and have **checked it at least twice. Accuracy is essential.** After you have done that, you are ready to copy the draft transcript onto the official high school transcript form. Be sure to continually check the final transcript for transcription errors as you fill it out.

1. Transfer all the information from the draft transcript onto the final transcript, continually watching for transcription errors. Again, do not sign or date the original.

2. Check the final document carefully.

3. Make copier copies of the transcript, using good-quality paper, cover, or card stock and a good copier.

4. Fill out the affirmation section (DD) before sending copies to colleges.

Affirmation: Section DD

Section DD is at the bottom of page 2. Fill out this section *only on copies*. By signing and dating the transcript, you are attesting to its accuracy.

1. Sign your name. If you prefer, both parents may sign.

2. (Optional) Give your title as teacher, principal, vice principal, or facilitator of your homeschool. If you wish, you may have a notary witness your signature.

3. Record the date of your signature.

Supporting Documentation

Material you should include with your transcripts depends on what individual colleges want. Some prefer only a standard transcript with test scores. Others require course descriptions, lists of curriculum, samples of student work, and other documentation. Refer to chapter 9 for information about keeping records that will back up your transcripts.

If colleges are open to receiving more information, you should capitalize on your students' unique or unusual experiences by including with your transcript well-documented information about their activities . We included a list of Christine's published writing and pictures from her three summer tours performing with the Young Continentals. Also, supply a list of awards and other recognition of your students' achievements.

College Applications, Essays, and Interviews

Parents have a limited role when it comes to college applications, essays, and interviews. It should go without saying, but students should fill out their own college applications, write their own essays, and answer their own interviewers. Your students may ask your advice, but the work should be their own. Your main job is to make sure that they read and follow all directions carefully and send in a neat and attractive application package. You also may use the college application checklist at the end of this chapter to help your students make sure they do not forget any important steps in the application process.

College Applications

Before anything else, students should check application deadlines for all the colleges where they plan to apply. There may be different deadlines for institutional scholarship applications, so students should note them as well. Buy a calendar that can be devoted exclusively to the college application process. On it you and your students can keep track of deadlines, test dates, and so on. Record when you mail applications and when responses or requests for additional information come in. A calendar also would be useful when you are researching colleges to record phone conversations with admissions offices. Enter the name of the college, the phone number, and the name of the person you spoke with. If there is enough room, note the important points of the conversation. Also enter dates for college visit weekends, upcoming campus events, etc.

Many colleges send applications with their brochures and catalogs, but in other cases, your students will have to request application forms. There is a standard application that more and more colleges are using. Application over the Internet is also becoming popular. If you have access to the Internet, check college websites for information about applying.

> *I want to encourage home-schoolers. We're finding that they're very well prepared for the "real world," and we feel they're just as strong contenders for acceptance spots and scholarships as any other students—and in some cases, they've proven to be even more qualified.*
>
> Ray Hardee,
> Gardner-Webb University

Colleges often include recommendation forms for teachers or counselors to complete. Others ask for the names and contact information for people who can attest to the student's academic ability and character. Most homeschoolers do not have outside guidance counselors, and they may not have outside teachers. If this is the case with your student, call the colleges and ask whether they will accept recommendations from other adults who know the student. Be ready with suggestions, such as youth directors or coaches. Students should ask these people whether they would be willing to act as references. If they are, then provide the forms for their recommendations along with stamped envelopes addressed to the colleges. Although you may include your assessment of your student's accomplishments, colleges want to hear from outside parties as well. Barbara Strickler, Vice President for Enrollment at the University of Tampa, says, "Parents should not write recommendations for their own students. Seek outside validation of character and ability."

Completing Application Forms

Filling out application forms can be time consuming, but encourage students to expend the effort to do it well. Some colleges will ask students to handwrite their application. If the college does not specify how it wants the application completed, it should be typed. Before your student enters anything on the form, make a couple of copies of it. Then have the student fill out a draft copy. Both you and your student should go over the form for mistakes and omissions. Then complete another draft, incorporating your corrections. If you have time, let it sit a few days. Then recheck it before the student completes the official application form. Check the final application for typographical errors and correct them before sending in the application package.

Essays

Many colleges request that students write one or more essays as part of the application process. I have included some sample essays in Appendix E.

Poole says, "I think parents should proofread the applications for college and for scholarships. I look at every single college application that a senior does at our school. I send it back to the drawing board if it's incomplete or sloppy." She says that you should watch especially for typographical errors that they might miss, such as "county" for "country."

Students must write their own college entrance and scholarship essays without help from you or anyone else. However, parents should review essays. Rather than make suggestions, which might border on helping them too much, ask questions that will make students think about how they might refine their writing. For example, if students make promises to readers and do not deliver, point to the section and ask them if they think they told readers what they promised to tell them. On unclear passages, ask whether they think that what they wrote would come across clearly to someone who does not know them and have them verbalize what they meant to say. Other comments you may make include "Can you organize this better?" and "Can you clarify this point?" Ask really generic questions to force students to see their own errors.

Essays are at the heart of our application process and give students the opportunity to present themselves in the best possible light.

Admissions Staff,
St. John's College, Maryland

You might also have them write a summary of what they wanted to say. Then have them check to see whether they followed through. They should go through the essay several times, checking for only one type of error each time, such as those in clarity, punctuation, spelling, grammar, extraneous words, strong verbs, continuity, transitions, consistency in tone and style, consideration of their audience.

For many years, schools have taught students to write five-paragraph essays, with a topic paragraph, three supporting argument paragraphs, and a concluding or summary paragraph. However, colleges are no longer interested in formulated five-paragraph essays, according to Carla Williams, a writing consultant who teaches both homeschool and public school students. Colleges want to see more creativity in the admissions essays they receive from prospective students. Williams suggests that students strengthen their writing with catchy leads, strong verbs and nouns, and smooth transitions.

It's pretty important that homeschool students interview at the college. [There is] this perception that maybe they don't get along as well with their peers, and it may not be true. It certainly isn't true in individual cases, and I'd like to know. I'd like to meet the homeschooled student.

Robert G. Voss, Worcester
Polytechnic Institute

Interviews

Some colleges require prospective students to have interviews with admissions staff either on or off campus before final admissions decisions are made. Students should be on time, dress nicely (office dress), be respectful, and be themselves. Although parents may sometimes be present during interviews, this is one time that adults should not speak unless spoken to. Do not be tempted to answer for your children or expand on what they have said unless asked. Admissions counselors want to get to know your students. Do not give counselors a bad impression by eclipsing your children during interviews. Your work is to prepare your students beforehand by telling them what to expect.

Follow this recommendation from Robert J. Massa, Dean of Enrollment at Johns Hopkins University:

I'd say at any highly selective college, homeschooled students should establish a contact within the admissions office and have an interview where they review their coursework and what they have accomplished in school and in the community...and to explain their objectives for this next stage of their education. I would add, as much as we want to hear from parents as well, that the students be the ones to arrange the interview and explain their accomplishments, goals, and objectives—not the parent/teacher.

During interviews counselors will most often ask why students chose to homeschool, what curriculum they used, and what outside activities they participated in. They might want to know what students like to do in their spare time, why they applied to that college, and why they think the college is right for them. They might even ask why the college should accept them. Students need to familiarize themselves with catalogs and have some questions ready before the interview. That way, they can show intelligent interest and not waste counselors' time asking for information that they should already have. Interviews are good opportunities for students to find out more about the colleges as well. The more students know about a college, the better chance they will have of finding that "perfect fit."

Above all, help your students keep a positive outlook about interviews, so that they will not feel overly nervous. They will most likely do fine. Bruce Campbell of Houghton College says that because homeschoolers are adult oriented and self-confident, they seem to shine in interview settings.

Submitting Transcripts with Applications

When your student has completed college applications and essays and you have completed the transcript, work together with him or her to put together an attractive package. Your package should include the following:

The hardest part of the review is understanding the quality of the actual curriculum a student may follow. Standardized tests, writing samples, and personal interviews have helped to give us a better understanding of the overall academic preparation.

Christopher Lydon, Dean of
Enrollment Management,
Providence College

1. College application completed by student.
2. College essay written by student.
3. Anything else the college specifically requests.
4. A check or money order for the application fee.
5. A letter from the homeschool teacher or principal telling how long the student was taught at home, the names of other schools attended, and any other pertinent information.
6. A copy of your student's high school transcript completed and signed by parent/teacher. (Be sure to include a graduation date or projected graduation date.)
7. Additional information, such as student information, school information, course descriptions (if college requests them), standardized test scores (if not included on the transcript).
8. A close-up photograph of the student. (One admissions counselor said that it is hard to say no when the applicant's face is staring at him.)
9. Copies of recommendation forms completed by other adults familiar with the student's character, abilities, and accomplishments.
10. (Optional) Color-copied pictures of student in action—dissecting, volunteering, speaking, performing, building, working, playing sports, etc.
11. Copies of transcripts from any other schools attended. I recommend that you include these, if available, even though colleges will want official transcripts sent to them directly by the schools. (Ask the schools to send official transcripts and inform the college that the schools will be sending them.) While the admissions office is waiting for the other transcripts to arrive, it will have your student's complete package available for review.
12. Portfolio of sample work (optional—check with the college for preferences).

If your student submits an application over the Internet, you will need to send the transcript and supporting materials separately, just as a traditional high school would.

Although some colleges may say that they want as much information as possible from home-schoolers, homeschool applications take extra time for admissions committees to evaluate. Make their job as easy for them as possible by editing your documentation until it is both well organized and concise.

Packaging

We packaged our transcript in an attractive folder with two inside pockets. In the left pocket I placed a letter from me to the admissions office and the complete transcript with course descriptions, etc. On the right were the college application, essay, copies of recommendations, and a few pages of color-copied photos. This particular folder had slots for a business card on the inside left pocket. We inserted a close-up photo here. (We had to increase the size of the slits to fit the photo.) On the outside we put an attractive label that read, College Application for (Our Daughter's Name) Submitted to (College's Name.) We slid the folder into a neatly labeled (typed) envelope and sent it via priority mail. One admissions office commented to our daughter on the quality of her application package in comparison with others they receive.

However you decide to package your student's transcript and application, make sure that everything is neat, organized, and attractive. Then when admissions directors are sorting through piles of applications, your student's will stand out from the rest.

Acceptance, Then What?

After students have applied and been accepted to colleges, they will have to decide which offer of admission they will accept. Then they will need to notify colleges, usually by April 1, whether or not they plan to enroll. Once students have decided to accept an offer of admission, they should immediately notify the college and submit all their housing, insurance, and other forms on time, and preferably not at the last minute. Housing slots fill up fast, especially in large public universities.

If your students are offered scholarships, they may have to sign forms accepting the scholarships before they decide whether or not to accept the colleges' offers of admission. Accepting a scholarship simply holds it; it is not a promise to attend the particular school unless the form specifically says so. Students should sign and return these forms promptly if there is any chance they will attend the colleges that sent them. Otherwise that scholarship money may be awarded to someone else.

Early Decision

Early decision, sometimes called early admission, is a program that students should use only for their top-choice college and only if they are certain to attend the college if they are accepted. When students apply for early decision, they are *obligated* to attend the college if they are accepted. In 2003 Stanford University changed their policy for early admission, eliminating compulsory enrollment for students in this program. Other colleges may change their policies as well. However, under no circumstances should your students apply to more than one school for early decision.

Do not confuse early acceptance with early decision or early admission. Early acceptance is for students who are younger than the normal age for college or who have not yet graduated from high school.

What If They Say No?

Depending on the competitiveness of colleges and student credentials, your children might not be accepted at all the schools to which they apply. That is why it is important to include at least one school where the student is certain to be accepted. It is difficult to cope with rejection, especially concerning something as important as college. Students need to realize that hundreds of other students receive rejections from colleges, too. Acceptance rates for the more competitive schools are sometimes extremely low. A rejection should not be taken personally. If every college turns down your students, maybe they aimed too high. Perhaps they should prove themselves at a community college and then apply again the next year.

Conclusion

Homeschooling is one of the most wonderful gifts you can offer your teenagers, and it is one of the best ways to keep family relationships healthy. I hope that what I have written here will encourage you that you *can* do it. Even when you feel overwhelmed, keep in mind that there are many of us who have gone before you, and our children are succeeding. Often they succeed in spite of our inadequacies.

When homeschoolers graduate, it is a bittersweet time for parents. Another friend and I grieved for a whole year before our children left home, knowing how lonely we would be for these wonderful young adults who were our almost constant companions. Leaving Christine in Tennessee was one of the hardest things I ever had to do, but the adjustment was not as bad as I had anticipated. My friend had the same experience. Knowing that our children were where God wanted them to be made all the difference.

Education is absolutely critical. It's one of the biggest gifts we can give our children. Its purpose is to broaden their view of the world and help them see that they can make a difference.... It's the idea that each of us can change the world.... It just takes one person.

Debbie Musselman,
veteran homeschool teacher

Graduation for homeschool parents is the conclusion of one of the most rewarding activities of our lives, but it is just as fulfilling to watch these students go out into the world as better persons because of their homeschool experiences.

If homeschooling through high school is right for your students, do not let anyone or anything stop you from doing it. Commit yourselves to doing the best job you can, and then persevere all the way to graduation and college admission. You will be glad you did.

Let us not become weary in doing good, for at the proper
time we will reap a harvest if we do not give up.

Galatians 6:9

College Application Checklist
Timing

8th-10th grades
- Find out requirements of several potential college choices.
- Tailor your curriculum to meet requirements.
- Have people who teach or work with students fill out recommendation forms.
- Begin a file for storing records, recommendations, and college information.

10th grade
- Take PSAT and/or PLAN test (optional).
- Do more research on possible colleges; attend college fairs.
- Reevaluate your curriculum to make sure you are meeting your goals and colleges' requirements.
- Begin researching private scholarships.
- Have people who teach or work with students fill out recommendation forms.
- Keep your files and records updated.

11th grade
- Form relationships with admissions representatives no later than 11th grade.
- Take PSAT National Merit Qualifying Test in fall.
- Begin researching scholarships if you have not done so.
- Attend college fairs.
- Narrow down college choices.
- Plan college visits for winter, spring, and/or early fall of 12th grade.
- Take ACT and/or SAT in spring of 11th grade.
- Make college visits.
- Send thank-you notes to colleges and hosts.
- Evaluate colleges based on visits.
- Have people who teach or work with students fill out recommendation forms.
- Keep files and records updated.

12th grade
- Retake ACT and/or SAT in early fall.
- Make final college visits.
- Send thank-you notes after visits.
- Evaluate colleges based on visits.
- Decide where to apply no later than early fall.
- Stay in contact with college admissions representatives.
- Have people who teach or work with students fill out recommendation forms.
- Compile records and write transcript and supporting documentation.
- Apply for scholarships, leaving ample time for meeting requirements, such as writing essays.
- Submit federal financial aid forms (FAFSA) as soon after January 1 as possible. (You need proof of your family income for the previous year.)
- Find out each college's application and scholarship deadlines from its materials. Do not miss a deadline. Deadlines are inflexible.
- Apply early for admission. This will give you the best chance for institutional scholarships. Also, early application will assure you of dormitory space, should it be limited.

Process

- Call or write colleges for information.
- Read materials carefully.
- Call with detailed questions.
- Take college entrance exams. (Decide whether or not to have scores sent automatically.)
- Evaluate colleges using comparison charts.
- Choose your top three or four schools.
- Visit your top three or four choices.
    (Evaluate schools according to guidelines in chapter 7 using the college search evaluation form.)
- Apply to colleges:
    Fill out applications.
    Write essays.
    Revise essays.
    Have someone read essays.
    Revise again, and as many times as necessary.
    Give recommendation forms to people with addressed, stamped envelopes.
    Prepare portfolio.
    Search for scholarship money.
    Apply for scholarships and financial aid.

Parents

- Prepare transcript and cover letter and/or request official transcripts from other schools.
- Aid in decision-making process.

What to Send

- Letter from homeschool parent(s)
- Transcript
- Application
- Essays
- Portfolio, if requested
- Information about extracurricular activities, travel, published work, volunteer and paid work experience
- Reading list, if requested or if unusually impressive
- Recommendations from others, unless they will be sending them
- Pictures (optional)
- (See Appendix A for homeschool requirements from many colleges that participated in the survey.)

High School Transcript

Name: **Gender:**   **Birth Date:**

Address:

School Name: **Graduation date:**

Phone: **Person to Contact:**

Grade/Year Course Title	1st Sem. Grade/Credit	2nd Sem. Grade/Credit	Final Grade/Credit	Yearly/Cumulative Totals Gen./Academic Credits/GPA

Credits & Grading: **Activities:**

Signed: _____   **Date:** _____

High School Transcript (Sample)

Name: Homeschool Student   **Gender:** M   **Birth Date:** M/D/Y
Address: Street Address
        Hometown, State ZIP
School Name: Anyname Academy   **Graduation date:** M/D/Y
Phone: 000-000-0000   **Person to Contact:** Mom or Dad

Grade/Year	Course Title	1st Sem. Grade/Credit		2nd Sem. Grade/Credit		Final Grade/Credit		Yearly/Cumulative Totals Gen./Academic Credits/GPA
9 05–06	Intro. Biblical History	B	0.50	A	0.50	A	1.0	Credits: 7.0
	English Composition	A	0.50	A	0.50	A	1.0	Acad. Credits: 6.0
	Geography	B	0.50	B	0.50	B	1.0	
	Astronomy	B	0.50		---	B	0.5	
	Geology (with lab)		---	A	0.50	A	0.5	GPA: 3.29
	Algebra I	C	0.50	B	0.50	C	1.0	Acad. GPA: 3.42
	Latin II	B	0.50	A	0.50	A	1.0	
	Art: Sculpting/Painting	D	0.50	B	0.50	C	0.5	Cum. Credits: 7.0/6.0
	Physical Education	B	0.25	B	0.25	B	0.5	Cum. GPA: 3.29/3.42
10 06–07	Bible: Poetic Books	A	0.50	A	0.50	A	1.0	Credits: 7.0
	World Literature	B	0.50	A	0.50	A	1.0	Acad. Credits: 6.5
	World History	A	0.50	A	0.50	A	1.0	
	Biology (with lab)	B	0.50	A	0.50	B	1.0	GPA: 3.79
	Geometry	A	0.50	A	0.50	A	1.0	Acad. GPA: 3.77
	Latin III	A	0.50	A	0.50	A	1.0	
	Music Appreciation	B	0.25	B	0.25	B	0.5	Cum. Credits: 14.0/12.5
	Physical Education	A	0.25	A	0.25	A	0.5	Cum. GPA: 3.54/3.60
11 07–08	Bible: Gospels	A	0.50	A	0.50	A	1.0	Credits: 6.5
	American Literature	B	0.50	B	0.50	B	1.0	Acad. Credits: 6.0
	U.S. History/Govt.	A	0.50	A	0.50	A	1.0	
	Chemistry (with lab)	A	0.50	B	0.50	B	1.0	GPA: 3.54
	Algebra II	C	0.50	A	0.50	B	1.0	Acad. GPA: 3.5
	Latin IV	A	0.50	A	0.50	A	1.0	Cum. Credits: 20.5/18.5
	Physical Education	A	0.25	A	0.25	A	0.5	Cum. GPA: 3.54/3.57
12 08–09	Bible: Acts-Revelation	A	0.50	A	0.50	A	1.0	Credits: 6.5
	English Literature	A	0.50	A	0.50	A	1.0	Acad. Credits: 5
	AP European History	B	0.50	B	0.50	B	1.0	
	Trigonometry	C	0.50	B	0.50	B	1.0	GPA: 4.0
	AP Latin	B	0.50	A	0.50	A	1.0	Acad. GPA: 4.0
	Keyboarding/Wd. Proc.	A	0.50	A	0.50	A	1.0	Cum. Credits: 27/23.5
	Physical Education	A	0.25	A	0.25	A	0.5	Cum. GPA: 3.65/3.66

Credits & Grading: A 90–100; B 80–89; C 70–79; D 60–69; F below 60; Weight for one-credit (120 hr.) courses: A= 4; B=3, C=2, D=1, F=0: AP Courses: A=5, B=4, C=3

Activities: Basketball, Soccer, State Historical Society Volunteer, Publish local homeschool newsletter

Signed: _____   **Date:** _____

Comprehensive High School Transcript (Coded)

Student: AA

Date of Birth:

Graduation Date:

Gender:

Phone:

Contact:

School:

Address:

SS #

Grade 9 Course Titles	First Semester Grade/Credit	Second Semester Grade/Credit	Date Complete	Weight 4.0 scale	Final Grade/Credits~	Grade 9 Summary
A1	B1	D1	F1	J1	H1	Credits: T1
	C1	E1			G1	GPA for year:
						Academic Credits:
						Academic GPA:

Grade 10 Course Titles	First Semester Grade/Credit	Second Semester Grade/Credit	Date Complete	Weight 4.0 scale	Final Grade/Credits~	Grade 10 Summary
A2	B2	D2	F2	J2	H2	Credits: T2
	C2	E2			G2	GPA for year:
						Academic Credits:
						Acad. GPA for year:
						Cumulative Credits: T3
						Cumulative GPA:
						Cum. Acad. Credits:
						Cum. Acad. GPA:

Test

Scores:

~Credits and Grading:

BB

Student: CC

School:

Activities/Awards:

Grade 11

Course Titles	First Semester Grade/Credit		Second Semester Grade/Credit		Date Complete	Weight 4.0 scale	Final Grade/Credits~		Grade 11 Summary
A3	B3	C3	D3	E3	F3	J3	G3	H3	

Grade 11 Summary:
Credits: T4
GPA for year:

Academic Credits:
Acad. GPA for year:

Cumulative Credits: T5
Cumulative GPA:

Cum. Acad. Credits:
Cum. Acad. GPA:

Grade 12

Course Titles	First Semester Grade/Credit		Second Semester Grade/Credit		Date Complete	Weight 4.0 scale	Final Grade/Credits~		Grade 12 Summary
A4	B4	C4	D4	E4	F4	J4	G4	H4	

Grade 12 Summary:
Credits: T6
GPA for year:

Academic Credits:
Acad. GPA for year:

Cumulative Credits: T7
Cumulative GPA:

Cum. Acad. Credits:
Cum. Acad. GPA:

Subject Area Totals 9-12:	Lang. Arts	Math	Science	Social Studies	Foreign Languages	The Arts	Business	Life Skills	Health/PE	Other
Number of credits earned:	S1									
Academic credits earned:	S2									

Comprehensive High School Transcript (Sample)

Student: Homeschool Student	**Gender:** F	**SS # 000-00-0000**	**School:** Home School High School
Date of Birth: 4/26/84	**Phone:** 000-000-0000		**Address:** Home Street Address
Graduation Date: May 16, 2001	**Contact:** Parents' Names		Home City, State, Zip

Grade 9

Course Titles	First Semester Grade	First Semester Credit	Second Semester Grade	Second Semester Credit	Date Complete	Weight 4.0 scale	Final Grade	Final Credits~	Grade 9 Summary
Introduction to Biblical History	B+	0.50	A	0.50	Dec-97	4.0	A	1.0	Credits: 8.0
English Composition	A	0.50	A+	0.50	Apr-98	4.0	A	1.0	GPA for year: 3.19
World History—Creation to 1500 A.D.	87	0.50	88	0.50	Jun-98	3.0	B	1.0	
Astronomy	86	0.50			Nov-97	1.5	B	0.5	Academic Credits: 6.5
Geology (lab course)			97	0.50	Jun-98	2.0	A+	0.5	Acad. GPA for year: 3.31
Algebra I	C	0.50	B	0.50	Jun-98	2.0	C+	1.0	
Latin II	B	0.50	B	0.50	May-98	3.0	B	1.0	
French I*			A	0.50		2.0		0.5*	
Art-sculpting^	D	0.50			Dec-97	0.5	D	0.5^	
Carpentry^	A	0.25	A	0.25	Jul-98	2.0	A	0.5^	
Physical Education^	B	0.25	B	0.25	May-98	1.5	B	0.5^	

Grade 10

Course Titles	First Semester Grade	First Semester Credit	Second Semester Grade	Second Semester Credit	Date Complete	Weight 4.0 scale	Final Grade	Final Credits~	Grade 10 Summary
Bible—Poetic and Prophetic Books	A	0.50	A	0.50	Apr-99	4.0	A	1.0	Credits: 7
World Literature	B+	0.50	A	0.50	May-99	4.0	A	1.0	GPA:for year: 3.57
World History—1500 to the Present	B	0.50	B+	0.50	May-99	3.0	B	1.0	
Oceanography	C	0.50			Feb-99	1.0	C	0.5	Academic Credits: 6.5
Biology (lab course)*			B	0.50		1.5		0.5*	Acad. GPA for year: 3.54
Geometry	A	0.50	A	0.50	Jun-99	4.0	A	1.0	Cumulative Credits: 15.0
French I, cont.	A	0.50			Nov-98	2.0	A	0.5*	Cumulative GPA: 3.37
French II*			A	0.50		2.0		0.5*	Cum. Acad. Credits: 13
Music Appreciation	B	0.25	B	0.25	Jun-99	1.5	B	0.5	Cum. Acad. GPA: 3.42
Physical Education^	A	0.25	A	0.25	May-99	2.0	A	0.5^	
Driver Education (non-credit)			Pass	0.00	Jul-99	0.0	P	0.0	

Test

Scores: Place test scores sticker here, or copy test scores here.

~Credits and Grading:
Carnegie Units (1 Unit = 120 hrs.); A 94-100; B 86-93; C 77-85; D 70-76; F Below 70

^Non-academic course *Overlapped traditional school years

Student: Home School Student **School:** Home School High School

Activities/Awards: Tennis 9-12; Choir 9-12; Volunteer at nursing home 9-12; City softball team 9-11; Part-time receptionist for dentist 11-12; Traveled in 35 States; Town Youth Volunteer of the Year, 2000; Summer Mission trips to Mexico, 9, 11

Grade 11 Course Titles	First Semester Grade/Credit		Second Semester Grade/Credit		Date Complete	Weight 4.0 scale	Final Grade/Credits~		Grade 11 Summary
New Testament	A	0.50	A	0.50	Apr-00	4.0	A	1.00	Credits: 6.75
American Literature	B	0.50	B+	0.50	May-00	3.0	B	1.00	GPA for year: 3.41
U.S. History	C	0.50	C+	0.50	May-00	2.0	C+	1.00	
U.S. Government			B+	0.50	May-00	1.5	B+	0.50	Academic Credits: 6.0
Biology, cont. (lab course)	A	0.50			Oct-99	1.5	B+	0.50*	Acad. GPA for year: 3.33
Entomology (lab course)			A+	0.50	Jun-00	2.0	A+	0.50	
Algebra II	B+	0.50	A	0.50	May-00	4.0	A	1.00	Cumulative Credits: 21.75
French II, cont.	A	0.50			Dec-99	2.0	A	0.50*	Cumulative GPA: 3.38
Physical Education^	A	0.25	A	0.25	May-00	2.0	A	0.50^	Cum. Acad. Credits: 19
Adult/Infant/Child CPR^			A	0.25	Jul-00	1.0	A	0.25^	Cum. Acad. GPA: 3.39

Grade 12 Course Titles	First Semester Grade/Credit		Second Semester Grade/Credit		Date Complete	Weight 4.0 scale	Final Grade/Credits~		Grade 12 Summary
English Literature	A	0.50	A	0.50	May-01	4	A	1.0	Credits: 7.5
Philosophy—Worldviews/Religions	A	1.00	A	1.00	May-01	8	A	2.0	GPA for year: 3.73
Geography/World Cultures	B+	0.50	A	0.50	May-01	4	A	1.0	
Economics	A	0.50			May-01	2	A	0.5	Academic Credits: 7.0
Marriage and Family Living			A	0.50	May-01	2	A	0.5	Acad. GPA for year: 3.71
Chemistry	B+	0.50	B+	0.50	May-01	3	B	1.0	Cumulative Credits: 29.25
Trigonometry/Calculus	C+	0.50	B+	0.50	May-01	3	B	1.0	Cumulative GPA: 3.47
Physical Education^	A	0.25	A	0.25	May-01	2	A	0.5^	Cum. Acad. Credits: 26
									Cum. Acad. GPA: 3.48

Subject Area Totals 9-12:	Lang. Arts	Math	Science	Social Studies	Foreign Languages	The Arts	Business	Life Skills	Health/PE	Other
Number of credits earned:	4.0	4.0	4.0	6.5	Latin 1.0 French 2.0	1.0	0.5	1.0	2.25	3.0
Academic credits earned:	4.0	4.0	4.0	6.5	3.0	0.5	0.5	0.5	0.00	3.0

High School Transcript (Draft)

Student: Gender: School:

Date of Birth: Phone: Address:

Graduation Date: Contact:

SS #

Grade 9

Course Titles	First Semester Grade/Credit	Second Semester Grade/Credit	Date Complete	Weight 4.0 scale	Final Grade/Credits~	Grade 9 Summary
						Credits:
						GPA for year:
						Academic Credits:
						Acad. GPA for year:

Grade 10

Course Titles	First Semester Grade/Credit	Second Semester Grade/Credit	Date Complete	Weight 4.0 scale	Final Grade/Credits~	Grade 10 Summary
						Credits:
						GPA: for year:
						Academic Credits:
						Acad. GPA for year:
						Cumulative Credits:
						Cumulative GPA:
						Cum. Acad. Credits:
						Cum. Acad. GPA:

Test Scores:

~Credits and Grading:

Student: **School:**

Activities/Awards:

Grade 11

Course Titles	First Semester Grade/Credit	Second Semester Grade/Credit	Date Complete	Weight 4.0 scale	Final Grade/Credits~	Grade 11 Summary
						Credits:
						GPA for year:
						Academic Credits:
						Acad. GPA for year:
						Cumulative Credits:
						Cumulative GPA:
						Cum. Acad. Credits:
						Cum. Acad. GPA:

Grade 12

Course Titles	First Semester Grade/Credit	Second Semester Grade/Credit	Date Complete	Weight 4.0 scale	Final Grade/Credits~	Grade 12 Summary
						Credits:
						GPA for year:
						Academic Credits:
						Acad. GPA for year:
						Cumulative Credits:
						Cumulative GPA:
						Cum. Acad. Credits:
						Cum. Acad. GPA:

Subject Area Totals 9-12:   Lang. Arts   Math   Science   Social Studies   Foreign Languages   The Arts   Business   Life Skills   Health/PE   Other

Number of credits earned:

Academic credits earned:

High School Transcript

Student:	Gender:	School:
Date of Birth:	Phone:	Address:
Graduation Date:	Contact:	

Grade 9

Course Titles	First Semester Grade/Credit	Second Semester Grade/Credit	Date Complete	Weight 4.0 scale	Final Grade/Credits~	Grade 9 Summary
						Credits:
						GPA for year:
						Academic Credits:
						Acad. GPA for year:

SS #

Grade 10

Course Titles	First Semester Grade/Credit	Second Semester Grade/Credit	Date Complete	Weight 4.0 scale	Final Grade/Credits~	Grade 10 Summary
						Credits:
						GPA:for year:
						Academic Credits:
						Acad. GPA for year:
						Cumulative Credits:
						Cumulative GPA:
						Cum. Acad. Credits:
						Cum. Acad. GPA:

Test
Scores:

~Credits and Grading:

Student: School:

Activities/Awards:

Grade 11

Course Titles	First Semester Grade/Credit	Second Semester Grade/Credit	Date Complete	Weight 4.0 scale	Final Grade/Credits~	Grade 11 Summary
						Credits:
						GPA for year:
						Academic Credits:
						Acad. GPA for year:
						Cumulative Credits:
						Cumulative GPA:
						Cum. Acad. Credits:
						Cum. Acad. GPA:

Grade 12

Course Titles	First Semester Grade/Credit	Second Semester Grade/Credit	Date Complete	Weight 4.0 scale	Final Grade/Credits~	Grade 12 Summary
						Credits:
						GPA for year:
						Academic Credits:
						Acad. GPA for year:
						Cumulative Credits:
						Cumulative GPA:
						Cum. Acad. Credits:
						Cum. Acad. GPA:

Subject Area Totals 9-12:   Lang. Arts   Math   Science   Social Studies   Foreign Languages   The Arts   Business   Life Skills   Health/PE   Other

Number of credits earned:

Academic credits earned:

Appendix A

College Homeschool Requirements

College Homeschool Requirements[1]

Name of College*	Traditional Transcript Only	Course Descriptions, Textbook Titles, etc., with Traditional Transcript	Other Information, Comments (Most require ACT or SAT even if not indicated.)	GED or Certified Diploma**	Tips; How to Increase Chance of Acceptance	Have Accepted/ Enrolled Home-Schoolers
Adams State College CO	✓	Might be useful in some situations.	ACT or SAT.	Not required		yes/yes
Albany College of Pharmacy, Union University NY		Anything that helps us to evaluate a home-schooler's education: course descriptions, text-books used, etc.	ACT or SAT. Program requires strong background in math & science, includ. chem. & precalculus.	Diploma or GED required		yes/yes
Albertus Magnus College CT	Traditional transcript helpful; keep separate from educational profile.	Any & all information like that; separate high school profile.	Recommendation from counselor, tutor, or teacher (at least one from outside the family), 2.7 or higher GPA, SAT, essay or bio/resume.	Certified diploma required (certified by source outside the family) or GED in lieu of it.		yes/yes
Alverno College WI		Course descriptions, names of textbooks, & some sense of the outcomes of the courses. Prefer this detail to a traditional transcript unless program followed makes title, grades, credits meaningful.	We would be happy to see a portfolio (papers, projects, etc.) Due to the nontraditional nature of Alverno, happy to look at alternative ways of educating students.	Require ACT	Do well on required placement test: analytical reading, writing, math, algebra.	yes/yes
Amherst College MA		Complete description of high school work & texts used with grades or other evaluations; conform to or exceed your state & Amherst requirements; additional documentation helpful. No prescribed set of prerequisite courses required for admission.	Detailed recommendation from home teacher covering acad. & personal areas; outside recommendations from context other than academics. Evaluation is case by case. ACT or SAT 1 & 3 SAT IIs.	High school diploma not required for any candidate. Standardized tests required.	Student: include samples of writing assignments: short piece & research paper.	yes/yes
Azusa Pacific University CA	Transcript from homeschool org. or parents.		Meet basic requirements of a diploma program. Indicate lab work for science & involvement in outside group sports/activities.	Not required	Increase involvement in community, church activ. Get strong test scores.	yes/yes
Babson College MA		Traditional transcript with detailed course descriptions, names of textbooks, etc.	Recommendations, essay, application. SAT/ACT.	Either GED or state high school diploma equivalent from a board of education	Show leadership potential through work &/or community involvements. Strong math prep.	yes/yes

College						
Baptist Bible College MO	Request pkt. of info. for home-school students; includes transcript examples.			ASSET test or GED for federal aid		yes/yes
Barat College of DePaul University IL	✓	Depends how detailed the transcript is.	All applicants viewed equally. Type of school does not hinder acceptance. Primary element after graduation is a favorable pastor's recommendation.	✓		yes/yes
Barnard College NY		Course descriptions; any & all information pertaining to student's educational training.	How many times per week teacher met with student, how long course lasted (# weeks), & on what basis the grade was determined.	Not required	Get involved in community. Show leadership skills & ability to work in groups outside family.	Have received few applications; none admitted.
Bennington College VT		Transcript, if available, course descriptions, & reading lists. Be sure to document academic work.	Interview required of all applicants will be particularly important, as will essays & required writing samples.	May be required for federal financial aid	Bennington students compose & direct own curriculum w/ faculty guidance.	yes/yes
Berea College KY		✓		Not required	Good evaluations from teacher; good test record.	yes/yes
Berklee College of Music MA	Equiv. info if avail. We are used to working with non-traditional info.	Transcript when available. Especially want course descriptions. Also textbooks used for music history, theory, etc.	Describe typical day; how instruction is conducted, info. on how student will perform in a structured environment.	GED required only in states that don't offer homeschooling certificate	Try to participate in ensembles, group playing opportunities.	Accepted/ probably enrolled but not tracked.
Bethany College KS		Would appreciate any supporting materials that might accompany the homeschool transcript.	ACT &/or SAT.	Not req'd unless circumstances cause admiss. committee to look deeper		yes/yes
Bethel College IN		Traditional transcript; also course content, listing of texts & curriculum.	SAT or ACT.	Not required		yes/yes
Binghamton University (SUNY) NY		We'd like as much detail as possible, including course descriptions, but not detailed course syllabi.	SAT or ACT; record of any work done in conventional school setting. We are a pretty selective, competitive college.	Required unless transferring from another college or university	Sample old SAT/ACT/SAT II tests. Take 1-2 courses at community college or local high school.	Yes, but few have applied; don't track enrollment.

Name of College*	Traditional Transcript Only	Course Descriptions, Textbook Titles, etc, with Traditional Transcript	Other Info, Comments (Most require ACT or SAT even if not indicated.)	GED or Certified Diploma**	Tips; How to Increase Chance of Acceptance	Have Accepted/ Enrolled Homesch'lers
Biola University CA	Professional, reputable-looking transcript. Semester & cumulative grades & credits, dual h.s./college credit, dated, signed.	Course information should be organized & available to admissions staff if a concern arises. Concise portfolio might be helpful.	Applic. w/ transcript, SAT or ACT, two references, & interview.	GED or state proficiency if no transcript	Take college-prep. classes, dual-credit college courses; come for interview; score well on SAT.	yes/yes
Bloomfield College NJ		✓	Interviews might be helpful.	Certified diploma or GED		None have applied.
Bob Jones University SC		Traditional transcript plus any additional clarifying info. especially in areas where h.s. program has been unique or broader than would be expected.	Any information that describes or clarifies achievements & describes activities & experiences that broadened student's horizons.	Need date of graduation; certified diploma/GED not required	BJU has much experience with homeschoolers, so no extra hurdles.	yes/yes
Bowling Green State University OH		Traditional transcript with course descriptions.	Optional portfolio review; suggest waiting until traditional info. has been reviewed.	Case by case	Ability to handle college work—shown through grades, test scores, or portfolio.	yes/yes
Bradley University IL	Trad. transcript, particularly if it is part of a certified homesc. program.		Other information if it indicates how student compares to other students.	Not required	Affiliate w/ a program that has some standard measurement or form of assessment.	yes/yes
Brescia University KY		The more information given, the better we can analyze student for placement.	ACT or SAT & 2-page personal biography.	Recommended, not required	GED or diploma would be helpful. If not in sports, be involved socially w/ peers.	yes/yes
Bryan College TN	Typically prefer this; depends on individual student.	Case by case. Helpful to have descriptions, but not required. Will notify parents if more information is necessary.	ACT or SAT; require ACT as ability-to-benefit test for financial aid.	Not required	Take challenging classes; consider dual-enrolling some courses at a college or Christian school.	yes/yes. Offers homeschool scholarships.
Calvin College MI		Traditional transcript format. Course description, etc. helpful, but not always necessary. We request supporting information when clarification is needed.	Academic/educational recommendation; ACT or SAT.	Not required		yes/yes

230

School	Transcript	Course Descriptions	Tests	Diploma/GED	Advice	
Cameron University OK	Transcript; should indicate that the student has graduated.		ACT or SAT. Student's h.s. class must have graduated.	Not required		yes/yes
Campbell University NC		Traditional transcript w/ signature of school administrator. Additional information optional but helpful, especially reading material, math books.	Interview with admissions staff.	GED not required. Certified diploma required.	Perform well on stand. tests, good documentation; consider dual enrollment college classes.	yes/yes
Campbellsville University KY		Official transcript; list of curriculum used, texts used for each class; lab exper. w/ name & location of facilities used.	2.0 GPA; 19 ACT or 890 SAT; application; official transcripts for any college credits.	Certified diploma	Report types of extracurricular activities.	yes/yes
Carson-Newman College TN	✓		Would like to know if curriculum transcripts, etc. are approved by a state homeschooling association. If not, GED may be required for federal or state aid.** ACT (SAT may be accepted later.)	See left.	Score high on entrance exams; show participation in missions, volunteer work, or community service.	yes/yes
Catawba College NC		✓	Letters of recommendation, SAT scores.	✓	Work hard.	yes/yes
Cedarville University OH	Standard high school transcript. Need a cum. GPA, indication of graduation, & date requirements completed	Supplemental material helpful but not necessary.	Both indication of graduation & the date are required for us to use the transcript for official purposes, particularly federal financial aid qualification. Rely heavily on ACT/SAT scores.	Not required	Take good college-prep curriculum. Take ACT/SAT tests more than once. We consider highest composite score of all tests.	yes/yes — Designated one of Leadership Scholarships for homeschool applicants.
Central Missouri State University MO	Transcript required.	Course descriptions may be requested.	ACT or SAT required.	CD or GED may be requested	Present a complete profile of academic achievement.	yes/yes
Central Washington University WA		These things are a good beginning; also ask homeschoolers (students do the writing) to explain how they met [state] core req'd for admiss. (4 yrs. Eng., 3 math, 2 foreign language, 2 sci., 2 hist.)	CWU values a diverse student population…homeschoolers can do well here.	No, although a certified diploma is very useful	Match breadth & depth of experience & learning of trad. students.	yes/yes
Christopher Newport University VA		Description of courses & grades would be helpful. If affiliated with a public school, documentation of high school diploma is welcomed.	ACT or SAT.	No response		yes/yes
Citadel, The SC		These are essential. The State Commission on Higher Education has rigid minimum admissions standards. An offer of enrollment is not extended to anyone failing to meet these minimums.	The fullest set of information will make our review proceed judiciously. Review catalog; make sure courses satisfy requirements.	✓	Take the strongest & most academic courses possible.	yes/unknown

231

Name of College*	Traditional Transcript Only	Course Descriptions, Textbook Titles, etc., with Traditional Transcript	Other Info, Comments (Most require ACT or SAT even if not indicated.)	GED or Certified Diploma**	Tips; How to Increase Chance of Acceptance	Have Accepted/ Enrolled Homesch'lers
College of St. Benedict MN		This information is very helpful in our admission decisions & in our honors program invitation process.	Prepare a thorough application, submit a thoughtful & well-written essay, visit & meet with admissions counselor.	Not required	See left.	yes/yes
College of the Ozarks MO		Yes, if not under an accredited curriculum. Letter or percent grades. Do not accept "pass" grades.	ACT or SAT.	Not required	Begin application process one year before you wish to enroll.	yes/yes
College of the Southwest NM	We require a standard type of transcript from the homeschool teacher.	If the homeschool is accredited, the transcript will stand on its own. If the homeschool is unaccredited, the student will need a GED along with the transcript.	Homeschoolers are at no disadvantage when applying to College of the Southwest. Doing their best on ACT or SAT is important. Homeschoolers are most welcome.	GED required if not an accredited homeschool	The higher the GPA, ACT or SAT, & class rank, the better.	yes/yes
Colorado Christian University CO	✓		ACT or SAT scores; on-campus placement testing.	No	Personal interview is strongly encouraged.	yes/yes
Colorado School of Mines CO	✓	Generally assume a course covers the same general material from one school to another, homeschooling included, so detailed course descriptions marginally useful.	A statement or personal essay about homeschool experience would be helpful.	A diploma from a high school or GED	Score well on ACT/SAT.	yes/yes
Columbia College SC	✓		Name of independent homeschooler association if applicable.	Not required	Use an indep. homeschooler assoc. to certify courses/credits/ grading system.	yes/yes
Columbus College of Art and Design OH		✓	Portfolio of artwork; application; recommendation from a non-relative. Contact early in application process.	✓	Use an independent homeschooler assoc. to certify courses/credits/ grading system.	yes/unknown
Concordia University MN	Copy of your homeschool transcript		Application, ACT, two letters of recommendation.	No	Simply inquire about how you can improve your chances for admission.	yes/yes
Concordia University NE	✓		List of activities not required but usually helps. Contact colleges early about requirements.	Certified diploma	Keep transcript up-to-date; complete a core-area college course during last yr.	yes/yes

Concordia University OR	Require transcript with grades, date of graduation. Courses should fulfill reasonable curricula. (Parent-prepared okay.)		Required of all applicants: test scores, essay, rec. from non-relative who can vouch for academic ability, character, & personality.	No		yes/yes
Connecticut College CT	Traditional transcript.	Parameters of the particular program used. Info on how class pace is determined, how student is tested, if student does "group work," etc. Don't need syllabi, portfolios, or bibliographies unless we ask for them. Strongly recommend personal interview.	Evaluate based on level of course work & grades, extracurr. activities, writing, personal qualities/talents, standardized tests. ACT or SAT IIs required; SAT Is are optional for all applicants.	Yes, for federal guidelines related to ability-to-benefit (GED)	Take initiative in pursuing community activities. Take comm. college courses. Participate in volunteer orgs.	yes/yes
Cornell University NY		Request list of required application materials. Committee wants to understand depth & variety of experience.	Standardized test scores.	Not required		yes/yes
Cornerstone University MI	Traditional transcript.	Traditional transcript format. Curriculum list helpful, especially if it is out of the norm for home educators. Will request list of curriculum if concerns arise.	Complete a college-preparatory curriculum. Indicate graduation date on transcript. ACT or SAT scores must meet or exceed minimum standards.	Not required	Simply inquire about how you can improve your chances for admission.	yes/yes
Covenant College GA	Short, concise transcript with letter grades & course descriptions by year.	Separate portfolio with list of texts, reading list, etc. When outside tutors are used, list with text info.	Admissions application. College is becoming more selective because of limited space.	No, but if no cert. diploma, must pass ATB* test for federal financial aid	Make use of internships, dual enrollment, extracurricular activities.	yes/yes
Crossroads Bible College IN	Transcript from homeschool teacher	Helpful but not mandatory.	Will accept parent-prepared transcript. We are available to provide college courses for homeschoolers in their h.s. jr. & sr. years for college credit.	GED preferred but not required. ACT or SAT helpful.	Contact admissions at 800-822-3119 ext. 230.	yes/yes
Crown College MN	Sufficient if transcript is kept & submitted by an outside venue.	Yes, if transcript is combination of a variety of curriculum sources & if kept exclusively by the parent. Transcript must be signed by parent or primary educator indicating that all requirements for high school graduation in the state in which they reside have been met. Must include date of graduation.	Note if student has ever attended a traditional school. Acceptance based on Christian character, GPA, and ACT or SAT.	Not required	We rely heavily upon the ACT or SAT score.	yes/yes
Cumberland College KY		Traditional transcript with course descriptions, names of textbooks, etc.	Required of all applicants: application, test scores, essay, rec. from non-relative	Preferred		yes/yes
Denison University OH	✓		Evaluation methodology	Certified diploma	Interview on or off campus.	yes/yes

Name of College*	Traditional Transcript Only	Course Descriptions, Textbook Titles, etc., with Traditional Transcript	Other Info, Comments (Most require ACT or SAT even if not indicated.)	GED or Certified Diploma**	Tips; How to Increase Chance of Acceptance	Have Accepted/ Enrolled Homesch'lers
Dominican University IL	Traditional transcript may not be appropriate.	Appreciate course descriptions, but textbook names not nec. Require SAT or ACT; attach more importance to scores for homeschooled applicants than for others.	Would like name of official who oversees homeschooling in the state in which the homeschooler resides.	✓	More extensive essay to assess writing ability. Portfolio helpful.	yes/yes
Dordt College IA	Certified grades through public or private school or homeschool org.	If the family cannot provide certified grades, we request a complete description of their curriculum & the completion of the GED test.	ACT or SAT scores. We are seeking homeschoolers.	GED test if grades are not certified	Have an excellent academic record & ACT or SAT scores.	yes/yes
Eastern Illinois University IL		✓	Dates & times.	Varies per catalog copy	Full documentation.	yes/yes
Eastern Washington University WA		Traditional transcript information. Course descriptions & textbook information would be helpful. Contact financial aid & scholarship office so students are not overlooked.	SAT or ACT; personal statement that describes homeschooling experience & anything else they think we should know to make an informed admission decision. Will look at content & level of writing skills.	Can be helpful; not required	It is important that students are not shy in addressing their strengths & how they feel they can be successful on our campus.	yes/yes
Eastman School of Music NY		✓	ACT/SAT.	Not required but preferred	Practice. Musical accomplishments come first.	yes/yes
Eugene Bible College OR	✓		Classes, grades, graduation date, class rank (if appl.) SAT/ACT/CAT scores.	Not required but appreciated	Min. 2.5 GPA & good test scores	yes/yes
Faith Baptist Bible College IA	✓		Copies of any certification of state approval of homeschool program or paperwork required by student's home state.	Preferred if not working through a satellite institution.	GED or school through a satellite school that makes transcripts & dipl.	yes/yes
Faulkner University AL		Traditional transcript information. Course descriptions & names of textbooks & other resources would help tremendously.	Complete the required number of units of study; ACT; SAT.	Not required	Raise ACT/SAT scores; get in touch w/ an admiss. counselor early in sr. yr.	yes/yes
Fisk University TN		✓		Dipl., GED, or cert. transc. req'd		yes/yes
Flagler College FL		Want traditional transcript. Course descriptions, etc. can be helpful, but often not required. Would not hesitate to call for clarification.	Show evidence of completion of high school course with marks earned; graduation date. Strongly encourage on-campus interview. (Admit <25%-30%). Recommendation from nonparent.	Not required	Be early decision candidate; take solid course of study; be involved in high school, church, or community.	yes/yes

College	Transcript	Documentation	Testing / Admission	Diploma	Advice	Homeschoolers admitted / financial aid
Florida Institute of Technology FL	✓			Not required	The more documentation we have to predict success, the better.	yes/yes
Franciscan University OH	✓		Require parent-prepared notarized transcript with graduation date (date courses completed)	Not required	Complete a solid college-prep curriculum; must submit ACT or SAT scores	yes/yes
Friends University KS	✓		ACT or SAT.	Not required	Apply in timely manner for admiss. & scholarship info.	yes/yes
Gardner-Webb University NC	Preferred	We don't require course descriptions, but it's nice to have that information. Require transcript or portfolio showing all grades, extracurricular activities & out-of-classroom experiences.	Meet state requirements for graduation; SAT or ACT; essay of things student's been involved in.	Not required	Possible campus interview	yes/yes
Geneva College PA		Flexible; appreciate knowing as much as possible. Want to know that student has completed all courses necessary for graduation & that curriculum is college prep.	Test scores. By & large, home-schooled students don't have a problem getting accepted.	Not required	Use a solid college-prep. curriculum.	yes/yes
Georgetown College KY	✓	Not if all the traditional transcript information is made available to us.	Try as best as possible to duplicate the requirements for non-homeschooled students. Essay, ACT/SAT, & recommendations may be required.	Not required	Take college-prep. courses in sci., math, for. lang. Dual enrollment.	yes/yes
Georgia College and State University GA	✓		Admission based solely on SAT/ACT & eight SAT II tests. Prepare for SAT II subject exams & take exams while material is fresh.	Not required	For ANY student: broad-based acad. backgr.; assume leadership roles in school, church, community activ.	yes/yes
Goddard College VT		As much supporting documentation as possible.	Reading lists, samples of work, papers written, etc.	Cert. dipl. or GED; strongly recommend GED; nec. for fed. fin. aid		yes/yes
Golden Gate University CA		Traditional transcript. Course descriptions would be useful, but detailed information regarding textbooks is not necessary.	Enroll few students directly from high school.	✓		Not aware of any applications
Gonzaga University WA	High school transcript required.	Portfolio of student's work, including writing samples, a description of studies done in mathematics (w/examples when approp.), & examples of science projects. Also application essay, a list of activities & honors or a resume, & counselor/ dean's report, which can be filled out by a parent.	ACT &/or SAT; activities; community involvement; two letters of recommendation, one addressing academic accomplishments by someone other than a parent.	Certified diploma; GED only if no diploma available	Demonstrate through app. the thoroughness of homeschooling; score well on tests.	yes/yes

Name of College*	Traditional Transcript Only	Course Descriptions, Textbook Titles, etc., with Traditional Transcript	Other Info., Comments (Most require ACT or SAT even if not indicated.)	GED or Certified Diploma**	Tips; How to Increase Chance of Acceptance	Have Accepted/ Enrolled Homesch'lers
Grace College IN		Transcript, course titles, grades, credits, course descriptions, & names of textbooks.	ACT or SAT results.	Only if student wants fed. aid	Do well in courses & on SAT or ACT.	yes/yes
Grace University NE	Not in most cases	Not in most cases	ACT	Certified dipl, ACT of 20, or GED if ACT < 20	Meet academic criteria (ACT of 20 or above).	yes/yes. Offers homeschool scholarship
Grand Canyon University AZ		Yes, with grades.	SAT or ACT.	Not required		yes/yes
Greenville College IL	Well-organized transcript like traditional transcript; four-point scale.		High school reading list helpful.	Not required if good scores on ACT or SAT	Presentation important. Outside service projects, other activities.	yes/yes
Grove City College PA	Some form of a transcript is required.	Transcript plus course descriptions, grades, textbooks, other resources, additional documents that would set them apart from other applicants (for all applic.).	A portfolio of student's educational experience (optional); SAT or ACT required. On-campus interview highly recommended.	Not required if some form of transcript is available	Be well-rounded; do not be isolated; show how home-schooling has broadened experiences.	yes/yes
Gutenberg College OR	Transcript with course titles, grades, credits.	Brief course descriptions; textbook names helpful for math & science.	A brief statement by parent responsible for instruction as to how parent approached the task of educating his/her student. SAT required.	Diploma or GED required. Parent diploma okay.	Generally use documentation from those respons. for educ. in conj. w/ essays & test scores.	yes/yes
Hampden-Sydney College VA	✓	✓	Standardized test scores.	GED	Personal interview.	yes/yes
Hannibal-LaGrange College MO	✓	Not in most cases.	Generally if students are eligible for admission, we can meet academic weaknesses, if any, through remedial courses.	Not required		yes/yes
Harding University AR		As much documentation as possible, especially if info. is not in a traditional transcript format.		No, but GED may be nec. for fed. fin. aid	Prepare for personal interview to enhance chance for scholarship.	yes/yes
Hardin-Simmons University TX	✓	As much documentation as possible, especially if info. is not in a traditional transcript format.	SAT or ACT	Not required if full admission scores are met on ACT or SAT		yes/yes

College						
Hawaii Pacific University HI	Traditional transcript (parent's okay). Rely on test scores more.	Descriptions in special cases only; e.g. Hawaiian Ecology class & trying to get into Marine Biology program.	Personal essay with background info. (i.e., why homeschooled.) Rec's from outside family—employer, pastor, etc. SAT or ACT.	Certified diploma; GED not required	Pick up a college course at a comm. college or univ. or a high school course.	yes/yes
Heidelberg College OH	✓		Evidence of nonacad. studies, e.g. music lessons, community service, art classes.	Prefer certified diploma; not nec. with excell. acad. record & test scores to prove it	Certified diploma or GED if grades avg. or below.	yes/yes
High Point University NC	✓		National test scores.	Not for admission; for state/fed. aid		yes/yes
Hillsdale College MI		✓		Prefer certified diploma; GED required if no official transcript	High achiev. on stand. tests. Obtain quality leadership, work, & volunteer experience.	yes/yes
Hobe Sound Bible College FL	Official transcript from reputable homeschool org.		SAT or ACT. GED may disqualify stud. from some acad. scholarships. Homesch. scholarship avail.	GED required if no official transcript		yes/yes
Hood College MD	It helps.	What was studied, books read—novels, etc.—not everything, but good sampling.	Inform us if you worked with a school district	Not required	Come in & talk with admissions.	yes/yes
Hope International University CA	Official transcript from acceptable association, if available	Course descriptions would be helpful in some cases. In most cases, not necessary.	SAT or ACT	GED required if no official transcript	Keep grades up & get good SAT/ACT scores.	yes/yes
Houghton College NY		Transcript. Course descriptions should include text, publisher, edition, & focus if the course had a specific focus within a broad academic area. Can include specific assignments completed (e.g., 20-page paper on church history).	Also supplemental activities such as field trips, letters to editors. Reading list, writing sample.	No, but New Yorkers need GED or an ability-to-benefit test to receive aid.	Be well rounded; take course or two at community college or 4-year college. Interview at the college.	yes/yes
Huntingdon College AL		Present a comprehensive transcript/portfolio.	Standardized test scores.	Certified diploma	Score well on ACT or SAT; write an essay or provide at least one writing sample.	yes/yes
Illinois State University IL		Transcript—include class rank, GPA, & GPA scale. Course descriptions would be beneficial in evaluating transcripts for our required course specifics.	ACT score of 23 or greater or SAT score of 1050 or greater.	Require GED	Prepare for ACT/SAT.	yes/yes
Jamestown College ND		✓	Standardized tests (ACT, SAT, etc.) ACT≥18; SAT≥870	Not required but recommended	On-campus interview.	yes/yes

Name of College*	Traditional Transcript Only	Course Descriptions, Textbook Titles, etc., with Traditional Transcript	Other Info., Comments (Most require ACT or SAT even if not indicated.)	GED or Certified Diploma**	Tips; How to Increase Chance of Acceptance	Have Accepted/ Enrolled Homesch'lers
John Brown University AR		✓	SAT or ACT scores.	ACT for federal financial aid; Certified diploma	Visit campus; interview with admissions staff & faculty.	yes/yes
Johns Hopkins University MD		Traditional transcript with **SHORT** course descriptions on separate sheet. Descriptions with point of reference on texts (e.g., for physics we used Haliday & Resnick's *Introduction to Physics*, the text used for freshman physics at the Univ. of ___).	Standardized test scores. Take one, preferably two courses per senior year semester at comm. college. Letters of recommendation from c.c. teacher & someone in the community with whom student has worked.	Not required	Student (not parent) establish contact with admissions office to interview & discuss objectives.	yes/yes
Johnson State College VT		✓	SAT or ACT. Any description of how student homeschooled, range of activities, how achievement was tested, etc.	For federal financial aid	Certification of competencies via SAT or other achievement tests.	yes/yes
Judson College IL	Transcript with graduation date	Helpful to have course information with transcript. Reading lists for literature courses.	Complete ACT or SAT during spring of junior year. ACT or SAT required.	GED required if student cannot produce diploma or transcript	Pursue a well-rounded course of study; document outcomes. Score well on ACT or SAT.	yes/yes
Juniata College PA		Anything you can send to help us understand the skills acquired, knowledge attained, or attitude of personal & professional success—including helping others achieve the same.	Market yourself to colleges in a way that reflects who you are, not just what you have learned.	✓	Develop portfolio w/ cover letter; visit; personal interview.	yes/yes
Kalamazoo College MI	✓		Interview with admissions counselor. Questions typically relate to the homeschooling experience; why chosen, advantages, disadvantages.	✓	Homeschool through nat'l. program or association curriculum.	yes/yes
Kansas Wesleyan University KS		✓	Accept portfolios of work. ACT or SAT required.	Certified diploma	Encourage a campus visit.	yes/yes
Kent State University OH	✓	Experience working in teams or groups.	Prove high school diploma or equivalent	See left	Score well on ACT or SAT.	yes/yes
Lake Forest College IL		Transcripts, course descriptions, etc. Even a syllabus would be helpful. Require a graded paper with application, a few samples of writing, including a research paper.	Look for some connection to the outside world—service, sports, job. Must meet admission course requirements.	Not required	On- or off-campus interview. Take ACT/SAT more than once; take some subject tests (SAT II).	yes/yes

238

College		What Information Is Helpful	Requirements	Diploma / GED	VISIT! / Comments	
Lebanon Valley College PA		More information than a transcript is needed. Course descriptions would be helpful.	Require certified diploma along the lines of PA Homeschoolers Assoc. diploma or GED for PA state grant assistance.	See left		yes/yes
Lee University TN	Traditional transcript (chronological) with school name, address, phone; GPA, grad. date.	Look for consistency with state requirements. Overview page describing school, grading scale, curriculum used.	Fulfill basic course requirements. ACT or SAT scores. Be involved in group activities with peers.	Not required	Collaborate with others on courses; professional presentation of transcript.	yes/yes
Lewis & Clark College OR		Course descriptions, etc., as well as how the student was evaluated. Tests & reading lists are helpful.	Instruction schedule, duration; educational & experiential background of teacher. Graded portfolio of work.	GED may be required for fed. financial aid	Comm. college courses; do well on SAT I or ACT.	yes/yes
Liberty University VA		Transcript with grades, credits, test scores, etc. & course descriptions, names of textbooks, resources used, etc.	Official transcript is one that arrives in a sealed envelope, original copy w/ approp. signatures, with raised seal from a recognized high school, college, or approved state agency; not photocopied.	All applicants without diploma (& transcript) from a recognized high school need a GED	Acceptance likely with min. scores on SAT I & SAT II writing or ACT; 2.0 min. GPA.	yes/yes
Louisiana College LA		Transcript, course descriptions, textbook titles, writing sample. Test scores or GED.	Must meet ACT/SAT requirements for admiss. 20 ACT/930 SAT or GED 50% ea. section	See left.	Score min. req. on ACT/SAT. Provide organized portfolio.	yes/yes
Lynchburg College VA		Official transcripts with grades, cumulative grade point average; course descriptions & bibliographies of course work.	SAT or ACT	Prefer official transcript or certified diploma. GED if none.	Strongly encourage campus visit & interview.	yes/yes
Marlboro College VT	Transcript with other information.	The more information the better, including list of books read, projects completed, & areas of study. Enjoy reading a statement/essay: why student chose homeschooling, what he/she liked or disliked about it, views of educ. in general.	Description of other activities.	For financial aid only	Strong writing skills.	yes/yes
Marquette University WI		Transcript, course descriptions, & textbooks used are very helpful.	Welcomes applications from homeschool students	Not required		yes/yes
Mars Hill College NC	✓		Recommendations for college success.	✓	Essay reflecting learning experiences & decision for choosing homeschooling.	yes/yes
Massachusetts Institute of Technology MA		✓	Be distinct in our applicant pool through activities & interests in community, achievements, & accomplishments.	Not required	Show evidence of academic excellence. (Also see left.)	yes/yes

Name of College*	Traditional Transcript Only	Course Descriptions, Textbook Titles, etc., with Traditional Transcript	Other Info, Comments (Most require ACT or SAT even if not indicated.)	GED or Certified Diploma**	Tips; How to Increase Chance of Acceptance	Have Accepted/ Enrolled Homesch'lers
McDaniel College MD		We are looking for indications that candidates have the background to be successful in a rigorous academic environment. The more course descriptions, texts, & resources cited, the easier it makes this process.	SAT or ACT test scores.	Not required; possibly for fed. financial aid		yes/yes
McKendree College IL	Prefer traditional transcript.	Course descriptions would be very helpful. List resources but not textbook names. Detailed portfolio if not completing diploma with an organization.	ACT or SAT. Letters of recommendation.	For financial aid only	Demonstrate that student can succeed. ACT or SAT scores important. Writing sample essential.	yes/yes
Mesa State College CO		✓	Portfolio. ACT or SAT required.	Not required	Visit with admissions counselors early.	yes/yes
Messiah College PA	Transcript with grades		SAT or ACT	Not required	Academically rigorous transcript with competitive SAT or ACT scores.	yes/yes
Miami University OH		These are required for consideration. Keep good records of curriculum outlines, textbooks, resources.	Provide as much objective info. as poss. regarding student's academic achievement.	Not required	See left.	yes/yes
Michigan State University MI	Traditional transcript required.	On transcript include complete course listing & statement addressing high school completion/ date of graduation. Course descriptions & additional curricular information is encouraged.	ACT or SAT. In the case of multiple attempts, best composite score considered.	Not required	Maximized academic preparation	yes/yes
Midland Lutheran College NE	✓		ACT or SAT	Required	Do well on ACT.	yes/yes
Mississippi College MS		We accept either. (Traditional transcript only or with course descriptions, etc.)	Visit campus before making college choice.	Not required	Score well on ACT or SAT. Demonstrate you're a good match for MC.	yes/yes
Mississippi University for Women MS	Official homeschool transcript showing completion of college prep curriculum	If no official transcript, submit portfolio showing work completed, course descriptions, & performance levels.	ACT or SAT required	Not required; add'l. univ. testing may be required	Specific documentation, strong test scores.	yes/yes
Montana State University-Billings MT	Traditional transcript; checked for college-prep. requirements.	ACT COMPASS test (min. 21 math, 60 reading, 31 Eng.), or may use the national ACT exam (min. 14 Eng, 15 math) instead of GED or h.s. diploma.	Willingness to sit for ACT or ACT COMPASS test (all 3 parts) if no accredited diploma or GED. Used for financial aid & placement.	Not required	See left.	yes/yes

School	Official transcript & ACT or SAT			If no transcript, GED & ACT or SAT required	See left.	yes/yes
Moody Bible Institute IL	Official transcript & ACT or SAT	Yes, we need course descriptions if it is not a standard curriculum.	Academic subjects should be seriously taken into consideration.	If no transcript, GED & ACT or SAT required	See left.	yes/yes
Mount Vernon Nazarene University OH		Official transcript preferred if avail. Descriptions of courses helpful for advising & placement purposes. Pursue college-preparatory curriculum.	ACT; official transcript from any public h.s. attended. If learning disabled, copy of official test & diag. Begin search process early.	Not required	Good references, essay, campus visit, ACT score 18 or above.	yes/yes
North Park University IL		Yes. Anything that adds credibility to academic preparation is good.		Not required at present	High test score & full college-prep background.	yes/yes
Northern Illinois University IL		Everything would be helpful. When in doubt we tend to rely on ACT/SAT test scores for the admission decision.	Anything that would help us make the most informed decision.	Only if I cannot make a decision with what is submitted. GED not required.	Provide complete information.	yes/yes
Northern Michigan University MI	From agency or school district; if from parent, notarized with statement attesting to its accuracy.	Not unless the student is planning to seek departmental advanced standing. Check www.nmu.edu/prospect for homeschool link.	Also require a final transcript showing proof of high school graduation, date of high school graduation or completion. ACT or SAT.	GED if family cannot provide a transcript	Solid preparation in the academic core. Prepare for ACT/SAT.	yes/yes
Northwestern College MN		More is better.	Work to improve preparation in math & science.	No, according to state law		yes/yes
Northwestern College IA	✓		Recommendation from someone who can address student's academic, social, & spiritual strengths & maturity level.	Not required		yes/yes
Northwestern Oklahoma State University OK		✓	We have few homeschooled students because of our size, but they are very well received.	Not required	Include ACT or SAT scores	yes/yes
Oglethorpe University GA		We request a full portfolio detailing all high school work, incl. courses, textbooks, assignments, writing examples, extracurr. activ., etc. At least two rec. from those with direct knowledge of acad. perf., extracurr. activ., character, & /or maturity.	Evidence must show appropriate completion of courses in English, social studies, mathematics, science. Personal interview with senior admissions officer.	Not required	Request homeschool admission brochure & portfolio guidelines.	yes/yes
Ohio Dominican College OH	Transcript with clear titles of classes.		Standardized test scores if available—helps for scholarships.	Not required	Have an official transcript prepared; standardized test scores.	yes/yes
Ohio Wesleyan University OH		We would like to see these. The more information we have, the better decision we can make.	Clear description of all courses taken; how knowledge learned was evaluated.	For financial aid; diploma or GED is ability-to-benefit test.	Work hard & tell us as much as poss. about self & educ. background.	yes/yes

Name of College*	Traditional Transcript Only	Course Descriptions, Textbook Titles, etc., with Traditional Transcript	Other Info, Comments (Most require ACT or SAT even if not indicated.)	GED or Certified Diploma**	Tips; How to Increase Chance of Acceptance	Have Accepted/ Enrolled Homesch'lers
Oklahoma Wesleyan University OK	Typed official transcript signed by parent w/ graduation date.	Course descriptions, textbook titles, etc., if a transcript cannot be produced.	ACT or SAT.	Not required	Send more info. & come to visit our campus.	yes/yes
Oral Roberts University OK	✓		SAT or ACT scores. ORU offers Home School College Program, whereby h.s. homeschoolers earn college credit by correspondence.	GED if not graduated	Score well on SAT/ACT. Present a full transcript.	yes/yes Offers home-school scholarship.
Ottawa University KS		We would appreciate receiving course descriptions & names of textbooks. Report a grade point average.	Take ACT/SAT in timely fashion, in the end of junior year or October of senior year.	Not required, but GED nec. for fed. fin. aid	Good college-prep program. Partic. in activities.	yes/yes
Palm Beach Atlantic University FL	This is sufficient if receiving an accredited diploma.	If not receiving a high school diploma through one of the accrediting agencies, send course descriptions, reading lists, papers completed.	Make sure to remain balanced with course work. Take the SAT/ACT seriously.	Not required	Take the most challenging courses available.	yes/yes
Patrick Henry College VA		Requires official transcripts from all institutional schools & umbrella schools; parent-prepared transcripts are fine for all homeschool courses. Transcript must include course name, credit, time, & grade received.	ACT or SAT.	Not required	Be certain high school course requirements have been met & application is carefully prepared.	yes!/yes!
Pensacola Christian College FL	✓	Helpful but not necessary.	Time frames of study & definite graduation date. Have a home-school scholarship.	Not required	Keep records.	yes/yes
Philadelphia Biblical University PA		Traditional transcript with a list of courses, descriptions, & grades. Also some indication that the student graduated, if possible.	ACT or SAT.	Indiv. basis. COMPASS test rec. as ATB* for fed. fin. aid, PBU awards	Apply as early as possible. Visit our campus & be interviewed by an admiss. counselor.	yes/yes
Pittsburg State University KS	Require a transcript but will compare it with standardized test scores.		21 ACT or SAT	GED if ACT score not acceptable	Courses comparable to precollege curric. designated by state of Kansas.	yes/yes
Providence College RI		✓	Writing samples, personal interview.	For federal financial aid	Provide details about content of courses; SAT II tests; AP exams.	yes/yes

College	Note	Transcript Requirements	Additional Requirements	Preferred	Advice	Interview/Visit
Queens University of Charlotte NC		Traditional transcript with course descriptions, textbooks used, reading lists, etc.	Sample of writing—the more extensive, the better. Involvement in church, music lessons, community, etc. ACT or SAT scores.	Preferred	Strong SAT or ACT, good recommendations, dual-enrollment college classes.	yes/yes
Robert Morris College PA	Traditional type of transcript using trad. course titles.	Recommendation from another adult besides parents who could speak to the academic ability &/or work habits of the student.	Work with other homeschoolers on projects; combined classes; music, sports; interact with peers. SAT/ACT.	No response	Study hard. Get good grades or prepare good portfolio.	yes/yes
Rockford College IL		We would like to see course descriptions & a brief accreditation statement along with the transcript.	ACT/SAT scores.	✓	Activities that help student learn social & leadership skills.	yes/yes
Rocky Mountain College MT		Transcript, course descriptions, etc. Organized, varied, & demanding curriculum.	Essays & letters of rec. Perform well on ACT/SAT. Extracurricular experiences. Standardized test or other ability-to-benefit test (GED) needed for scholarships/federal assistance.	GED is not required	Looking for what student will contribute to college community.	yes/yes
Sacred Heart University CT		Transcript, course descriptions, textbooks, etc. Info. about involvement in activities in school or community.	Require standardized test scores & letters of recommendation.	Preferred but not required	Interview with an admissions counselor.	yes/yes
Saint Anselm NH	Prefer traditional information.	If program has been created by the family, need more comprehensive listing of material covered & work required in each subject.	SAT or ACT; description of program student is enrolled in.	Not required		yes/yes
Saint John's College MD		The more thorough the description of the homeschool curriculum, the better.	St. John's offers a very unusual & demanding curriculum. Review catalogue carefully before applying. SAT/ACT.	Not required	Essays are at the heart of our application process.	yes/yes
Saint John's College NM		Traditional transcript with course descriptions, etc. We prefer students to be as descriptive as possible about what they studied. Include bibliography.	Our application is highly self-selecting, so we try our best to give as much information as possible to applicants so they can make the best decisions for themselves. SAT or ACT.	For financial aid	Read our catalog because our program is so unique. Visit campus. Sit in on classes.	yes/yes
Saint John's University MN	See College of St. Benedict.					
Saint Mary's College IN		Helpful to have descriptions of courses, names of textbooks, & syllabus. Our admissions committee reviews each applicant's file thoroughly.		✓	Meet with an admissions counselor.	yes/yes

Name of College*	Traditional Transcript Only	Course Descriptions, Textbook Titles, etc, with Traditional Transcript	Other Info, Comments (Most require ACT or SAT even if not indicated.)	GED or Certified Diploma**	Tips; How to Increase Chance of Acceptance	Have Accepted/ Enrolled Homesch'lers
Saint Vincent College PA		Traditional transcript with texts, course descriptions, etc. The more information that is submitted to the Admission Committee, the more informed the decision.		✓	Strong courses, good grades, good College Board scores.	yes/yes
Shimer College IL	Transcript or equivalent.	Descriptions for any courses that are NOT clearly of standard content (e.g., algebra, English literature).	PSAT, SAT, ACT, or equivalent recommended. Be prepared to read & discuss works that challenge your assumptions & make you think for yourself. Accepts & welcomes early entrants.	Diploma, GED, or ability-to-benefit test is required for those who have not completed high school.	Send required materials promptly. Campus visit & interview; enthusiasm for Shimer approach to education.	yes/yes Offers home-school & non-traditional schooling scholarship.
Simpson College CA	✓		SAT/ACT.	Only if student doesn't place above 50th percentile on SAT/ACT	Do well on SAT or ACT.	yes/yes
South Dakota School of Mines & Technology SD		Submit transcript if available. Course descriptions would be helpful, but not textbooks or other resources.	Take homeschooling seriously. Understand the time involved. Admission requires ACT w/ min. composite score of 18, subtest min. of 17. Homeschoolers treated equally for admission & scholarship consideration.	Not required for admission. GED or equivalent required for financial aid.	On scholarship apps, note you homeschooled to explain lack of class rank.	yes/yes
South Dakota State University SD		Submit transcript if available. Course descriptions would be helpful, but not textbooks or other resources. Homeschoolers are not discriminated against in any way, including competing for scholarships.	For admission, require ACT with minimum composite score of 18 & minimum subtest scores of 18 Eng., 20 math, 17 reading, 17 reasoning.	Not required for admission	On scholarship apps. indicate that you homeschooled to explain lack of class rank.	yes/yes
Southampton College NY		Traditional transcript with course descriptions.	Outside recommendations, perhaps from local school administrator or other mentor. HSers encouraged to apply. Offers Friends World Prog.—contract learning envir. studying abroad.	Official proof of graduation from high school; cert. dipl. or GED	Visit for an interview.	yes/yes
Southern California College CA		Traditional transcript with course descriptions.	Usually need diploma from accredited high school (not GED) for academic scholarships; SAT or ACT.	✓		yes/yes

University		Transcript / Documentation	Testing	Diploma	Keys to Success	
Southern Nazarene University OK		Need traditional transcript. Course descriptions, etc. helpful.	ACT or SAT.	Not required	Prepare well for ACT or SAT. Group activities.	yes/yes
Southern Utah University UT		Traditional transcript with courses taught & grades received. Texts & resources not necessary.	ACT/SAT scores.	Accredited diploma or GED w/ min.scores: composite 50; sectional 45	Put some concentration in areas tested by the ACT.	yes/unknown
Southern Wesleyan University SC		Transcript with course descriptions, etc. Will accept parent-prepared transcript as long as we have some documentation from the home-school assn. that they are using (course work req'd, standards parents held to, etc.)	GPA on 4.0 scale; class rank; SAT or ACT scores. Take PSAT in fall of junior year for National Merit competition.	Prefer certified diploma	Become involved in church & community.	yes/yes
Southwest Baptist University MO	✓	Transcript with course identification & GPA. Parent prepared transcripts are acceptable. Acceptance, course placement, & scholarships will be determined based on ACT/SAT & GPA (4.0 scale).	ACT/SAT.	Certified transcript or GED	Prepare well for ACT/SAT.	yes/yes
Southwestern College AZ		Transcript from outside organization	On transcripts: subjects, grades, GPA, date of graduation, ACT/SAT scores.	✓		yes/yes
Southwestern University TX	✓	✓	ACT or SAT	Certified diploma	Score in the top 50% of our SAT distribution.	yes/yes
Stanford University CA		Course titles & content; dates of completion; SAT, ACT, AP scores. Do not require traditional transcript. What has student learned? What can he/she do?	Student: write about reasons for, experiences in homeschool & how evaluated. Tell how you like to think & about what. What drives you to learn?	Not required	Community involvement, dual enrollment, rec. from acad. teacher.	yes/yes
Syracuse University NY		Transcript, course titles & descriptions, textbook names, other curricular info, test scores, recommendations from teacher(s) & someone in community, personal statements from applicant. Any info. that would enable us to make knowledgeable, thoughtful admissions decisions.	Encourages personal interviews for all applicants—offered on campus & in offices in NYC, Wash. DC, & over 30 other locations. Prefer ACT if applicant intends to apply for financial aid under ATB option.	All applicants must provide a GED or certified diploma signed by participating school district	Perform well in challenging curric. Partic. in comm. service, other volunteer activ. Be involved outside classroom.	yes/no
Tabor College KS	✓	Not necessary unless some form or method that doesn't compute to a standard GPA format. Prefer not to receive portfolio-style transcript.	ACT (or SAT). Was student involved in athletics, music, debate, church?	Not required	Persistence; exposure to different teaching styles.	yes/yes

Name of College*	Traditional Transcript Only	Course Descriptions, Textbook Titles, etc, with Traditional Transcript	Other Info, Comments (Most require ACT or SAT even if not indicated.)	GED or Certified Diploma**	Tips; How to Increase Chance of Acceptance	Have Accepted/ Enrolled Homesch'lers
Taylor University-Fort Wayne IN	Traditional transcript required	Beneficial for admission, scholarship, & placement decisions but not required.	ACT or SAT	Not required	Enroll in dual-credit opportunity at Taylor or other univ.	yes/yes
Texas Tech University TX	✓		Grad. from accred. h.s., min. age, SAT/ACT 1080/24. Grad. of non-accredited high school on probation unless 29 ACT or 1270 SAT	Get accredited diploma; with GED have to wait one year to enroll		yes/yes
Thomas More College KY		The more information provided, the better.		Not required	Work closely with admissions staff.	yes/yes
Truman State University MO		Course information, grades, class rank if avail, cocurricular activities, ACT or SAT, admission essay. Students are encouraged to apply by the early admission deadline of November 15.	4 English, 3 math, 3 social studies/history, 3 natural science, 1 fine arts, 2 same foreign language.	Recommend certified diploma	Display acad. & co-curricular achievement consistent with student body.	yes/yes
Tusculum College TN	Required.	Beneficial but not required.	ACT or SAT.	Certified diploma required		yes/yes
Union University TN	✓	Require core subjects: English (4), math (3), natural sciences (3), social studies (3), foreign languages/art (2), & electives (7).	Activities, field trips, student's reading list beneficial for scholarship decisions.	No	Apply. We feel homeschoolers fit in well.	yes/yes
United States Air Force Academy CO (Some quoted from website.)		Transcript with course title, length, date of completion, grade, grading scale, GPA, curric./course descriptions, text/materials used, etc.	Certified diploma not required. Will accept GED. Place more weight on SAT/ACT in those cases.	See left	Extracurricular activities important to predict leadership.	yes/yes
United States Coast Guard Academy CT		Transcript with course descriptions along with other resources. Need proof that homeschool program is certified.	PSAT, SAT, ACT. Look at transcript, test scores, extracurricular activ., employment, letters of rec., leadership skills, etc.	Must be a high school graduate; will accept GED	We encourage anyone to apply & compete.	yes/yes
United States Military Academy NY		The more information, the better. Have to be in some sort of program that will give us a ranking (how he/she compares to other students in the same program, based on testing & grades).	SAT or ACT. Evaluation: acad. achievement 60%, leadership potential 30%, physical aptitude 10%. Partic. in athletics, extra-curr. activ. through school district, church, scouts, community, etc., (to demonstrate lead. potential).	Preferred	Make files, objectively, look as similar to other files as possible.	yes/yes
University of Arizona AZ		Transcript, etc. Also any information that explains what we see on the transcript.	Information about student's special talents & academic potential not indicated on transcript or in tests. Standardized tests.		Complete college-prep curriculum: 16 units in math, Eng. lab sci, soc, sci, foreign lang, fine arts	yes/yes

School	Accredited curriculum provider — require transcript	Eclectic/independent approach — course descriptions	Also helpful	GED requirement	Admissions view	Admit
University of Dallas TX	If accred. curr. provider such as Kolbe or Seton—require transcript from institution.	If homeschooled student has taken a more eclectic or independent approach, we require course descriptions & textbooks used.	Also helpful is to explain any experiential learning.	In ltd. # of cases (<10%), require GED because of insufficient documentation	View background as strength; don't feel deficient because of it.	yes/yes
University of Evansville IN	✓	Like well-rounded students, academically prepared for college coursework	Evaluated as individuals for potential success at UE.	Not required	Visit campus & interview.	yes/yes
University of Florida FL	Preferred.		Provide SAT II results in disciplines of Eng., math level 2, science, social sci., for. lang.	Not required	See left	yes/yes
University of Illinois at Urbana-Champaign IL		Traditional transcript, course descriptions, textbook list, some idea of the amount of writing & laboratory time required of student. The more we know about curric., the better.	GED may be waived if some courses at community college or more trad. evaluation. Decision based on strength of ACT/SAT scores, type of homeschool experience, personal statement.	Sometimes (see left). Office of admiss. & dean of particular college of univ. review each applic.; requirements vary	Augment home-school experience with courses at community college or local high school, especially lab sciences	yes/yes
University of New Hampshire NH		Check with admissions department for details.	We are interested in homeschool applicants.	No response		yes/yes
University of New Haven CT		Some documentation of course work, with some narrative from student's teacher(s).	SAT or ACT; personal statement from applicant.	GED	Personal interview on campus.	No response
University of Northern Iowa IA	✓	If no traditional transcript, we will require some form of portfolio assessment.	Extracurricular activities. We may request an interview.	Not required	Do well on ACT or SAT; meet course requirements.	yes/yes
University of Oklahoma-Norman OK	✓	We require a record of coursework completed & verification of graduation.	Students must meet performance requirements by ACT or SAT scores.	✓	Do well on ACT or SAT.	yes/yes
University of Pittsburgh PA	This is the most crucial info. Present in straightforward manner.	Additional information welcomed; may or may not make significant impact on decision except in borderline or scholarship decisions. Portfolios helpful but do not substitute for eval. by state-cert. educ. specialist.	If we can't get a certified transcript, we need an end-of-the-year report done by a state-certified education specialist. Very interested in homeschoolers.	Certified diploma	Completion of demanding course load, strong standardized test scores.	yes/yes
University of Saint Francis IN		✓	Homeschoolers are not disadvantaged in admission process.	Recommend certified diploma	Provide requested information.	yes/no
University of Tampa FL	Preferred	The more information, the better. Recommendations helpful. Description of curriculum.	SAT or ACT. Personal statement from applicant.	No; sometimes req'd by state & other fin. aid programs	Perform well on standardized college entrance tests.	yes/yes
University of Vermont VT		Trad. academic information very imp. & time-saving. Open to reviewing supplemental info. Course descriptions, etc., helpful when determining whether entrance requirements have been met.	We also like to see official copies of any homeschool-related documentation submitted to the home state's education department.	✓	Complete entrance requirements; essay, ACT, or SAT.	yes/yes

Name of College*	Traditional Transcript Only	Course Descriptions, Textbook Titles, etc., with Traditional Transcript	Other Info, Comments (Most require ACT or SAT even if not indicated.)	GED or Certified Diploma**	Tips; How to Increase Chance of Acceptance	Have Accepted/ Enrolled Homesch'lers
University of Wisconsin-Green Bay WI		✓	Would like to know whether the family utilized a national or standard homeschool curr. program from an assoc. or simply designed its own.	Not required; will use own evaluations to verify skills	Demonstrate preparedness for college.	yes/yes
University of Wisconsin-Superior WI		✓	How long student has been homeschooled. Anything that would indicate social skills/development.	Certified diploma, some have GED	ACT/SAT & personal interview.	yes/yes
Ursinus College PA		✓	Extra writing samples describing experiences.	✓	Visit. Interview. Also see left.	yes/yes
Washington and Jefferson College PA		✓	Recommendations.	✓	Do well on standardized tests; involvement in community.	yes/yes
Washington State University WA		We will review candidates' credentials individually. Must provide an academic portfolio to document completion of academic core requirements.	SAT or ACT required. Additional info., including a portfolio, interview or GED may be required at a later point in appl. process.		Each homeschool application considered on an individual basis.	yes/yes
Washington University in St. Louis MO		We will review each applicant individually & don't require a standard transcript or forms.	Standardized test scores may be given a little more weight. Have admitted homeschoolers for more than a decade.	Not required		yes/yes
Wayne State University MI		✓	"Credentials" of instructors.	No policy established.	Take AP, ACT, SAT, CLEP, etc.	no/no
West Virginia Wesleyan College WV		✓	Writing sample, SAT or ACT results. May require interview with admissions staff member.	Certified diploma		yes/no
Western Baptist College OR	Certified transcript not required but preferred. (Traditional format.)		SAT or ACT.	Not required; CD or GED for fed. financial aid.		yes/yes
Western Michigan University MI		Homeschool transcript: semester grades 9-11 with subject names; name of curric. program if they followed specific one; final transcript after 12th grade, noting graduation.	Admissions application, grades based on a 4-point scale, expected graduation date. WMU has homeschool student organization.	Not required with transcript	Contact early. Will do everything poss. to assist homeschoolers in process.	yes/yes

	✓	Activities & leadership involvements.	✓	Score well on SAT/ACT.	
Westmont College CA					yes/yes
Whitman College WA	Most definitely. The more information, the better. It quells any fear that may result regarding curriculum.	Present curriculum clearly to reassure admissions officer that applicant has capacity to succeed on our campus.	Not required	See left.	yes/yes
Willamette University OR	Portfolio to include samples of work, comprehensive list of books read, & list of any activities in which applicant participated outside the home.	SAT I or ACT required. Two letters of recommendation required (1 parent/teacher & 1 non-family). Interview strongly recommended.	Not required	Participation in activities outside the home. Strong test scores (1200+).	yes/yes
William Jewell College MO	Transcript required. Additional information would be helpful, including information about activities that augment the educational experience.	ACT or SAT, essay, at least 2 letters of rec. from individuals familiar with student's academic work or character. Be involved in the community.	Not required	Most challenging courses poss.; extracurric. activ., campus interview, solid essay.	yes/yes
William Woods University MO	Yes. In light of the special circumstances, we appreciate any supporting documentation.	SAT or ACT, two acad. refs. If parent only teacher, letter describing student's acad. background & at least one ref. from nonfam. member commenting on academic ability & promise.	Certified diploma. GED only if transcript not available.	Credentials of instructors; narrative documentation about academic circumstances.	yes/yes
Worcester Polytechnic Institute MA	Accept transcripts from homeschool teachers. Include course descriptions, etc. Be sure to have 4 years of math through pre-calculus & 2 lab sciences (physics, biology, chemistry).	We put a lot of weight on the test scores for homeschool students.	Not required	Interview at the college required.	yes/yes

[1]Please note: The information in this table was correct at the time of the survey or was updated by the college for the second edition. Since policies can change, prospective students should check with individual colleges for their requirements at the time of application. Several colleges asked not to be included in this table. Please contact them directly for their homeschool requirements.

*Inclusion of a college or university in this survey does not constitute an endorsement of its educational program or philosophy.

**For information about federal financial aid and ability-to-benefit, refer to Chapter 6.

Resources for the Home High School

Inclusion of companies and products in this list does not constitute an endorsement of the organizations, institutions, publications, products, or services represented. This list is not meant to cover all worthy resources or suppliers. Ideas presented do not necessarily represent the opinions of the author or publisher. *Please note: Because of the volatile nature of online communications, websites and email addresses may change. Also, because many of these companies are family owned, addresses, phone, and fax numbers may change, as well.* Telephone and fax numbers beginning with the prefixes 800, 866, 877, and 888 should be toll-free. Semicolons and periods at the end of email addresses and websites on this list are for editorial purposes only and are not part of the email addresses or URLs.

Contents:

General Curriculum

A Beka Book Inc., PO Box 19100, Pensacola, FL 32523-9100; 877-223-5226, 850-478-8933; International 850-478-8933; website: www.abeka.com. All subject areas.

Affordable Christian Textbooks & Supplies, 549 North Route 83, Grayslake, IL 60030; 800-889-2287; fax: 847-546-8078; email: mpACTS@aol.com; website: www.actstextbooks.com.

Alpha Omega Publications, 300 North McKemy Avenue, Chandler, AZ 85226-2618, 800-622-3070, 602-438-2717; website: www.home-schooling.com. All subject areas. Also *Switched-On Schoolhouse:* Alpha Omega CD-ROM curriculum based on LIFEPAC Gold. Answers in Genesis Creation elective.

AMC Technology, The Soft Side of Education, Box 2094, Carlsbad, CA 92018-2094, 800-490-2792; Fax: 760-720-1010; email: andre@amcweb.net; website: amcweb.net; Educational CD-ROMs—reference, literature, science, math, art history, etc., K-12.

Annenberg CPB Projects, 901 E Street NW, Washington, DC 20004, 202-879-9600, 800-LEARNER; email: info@learner.org; website: www.learner.org. Videos, DVDs for foreign languages (*French in Action, Destinos, Fokus Deutsch*), other high school and college subjects; teacher resources. Online training broadcasts for teachers on Annenberg/CPB Channel: www.learner.org/channel/channel.html.

Atco School Supply, Inc., 425 E. Sixth St. #105, Corona, CA 92878-1707, 909-272-2926, 888-246-ATCO (orders); fax: 909-272-3457, website: www.atco1.com. Catalog with full product descriptions; all subjects, all grades.

The Back Pack, PO Box 125, Ernul, NC 28527, 252-244-0728; website: www.thebackpack.com, email: backpack@thebackpack.com. New and used textbooks and supplemental materials.

Bluestocking Press (See under Social Studies).

Bob Jones University Press, Greenville, SC 29614-0062, 800-845-5731; fax: 800-525-8398; email: bjupinfo@bjup.com; website: www.bjup.com. All subjects, all grades. (See also BJ Testing and Evaluation Service under Resources for Home Guidance Counseling.)

Builder Books, Inc., P.O. Box 5789, Lynnwood, WA 98046, 425-778-4526, 800-260-5461 (orders only). Discount books, some high school curriculum.

Cerebellum Corporation, 2890 Emma Lee Street, Falls Church, VA 22042, 800-238-9669, email: info@cerebellum.com; website: www.cerebellum.com. Videotapes: math, business, science, economics, sociology, others.

Christian Book Distributors, P.O. Box 7000, Peabody, MA 01961-7000, 978-977-5000 or 800-2474784 (orders), 978-977-5050 or 800-788-1221 (customer service), fax: 978-977-5010; website: christianbook.com. Discounted books and curriculum.

Christian Liberty Press, 502 W. Euclid Avenue, Arlington Heights, IL 60004, 800-832-2741 (catalogs), 847-259-4444 (customer service); email: custserv@christianlibertypress.com; website: www.christianlibertypress.com. Curriculum, etc.

Christian Light Publications, P.O. Box 1212, Harrisonburg, VA 22801-0768, 540-434-0768, fax 540-433-8896; email: office@clp.org; website: www.anabaptists.org/clp. Curriculum only or full service.

Cornerstone Curriculum Project, 2006 Flat Creek Place, Richardson, TX 75080, 972-235-5149; website: www.CornerstoneCurriculum.com. Specializing in Biblical worldview training. *Worldviews of the Western World:* incorporates philosophy, art, music, government, economics, science, math, and literature. Also separate art and music courses.

Covenant Home Curriculum, N63 W23421 Main Street, Sussex, WI 53089, 800-578-2421 or 262-246-4760; fax: 262-246-7066; email: educate@covenanthome.com; website: www.covenanthome.com. Eclectic classical curriculum.

Critical Thinking Books & Software, P.O. Box 448, Pacific Grove, CA 93950-0448, 800-458-4849, 831-393-3288; fax: 831-393-3277; email: ct@criticalthinking.com; website: www.criticalthinking.com. Books and software to promote critical thinking in major subject areas.

Debra Bell's Home School Resource Center, P.O. Box 67, Palmyra, PA 17078. , 717-838-5273, 800-937-6311 (orders only); fax: 717-832-7733; email: hsrc@debrabell.com. Resources and curriculum with reviews.

Educators Publishing Service, Inc., 31 Smith Place, Cambridge, MA 02138-1089, 800-435-7728 or 617-547-6706; fax: 888-440-2665 or 617-547-0412; email: epsbooks@epsbooks.com; website: www.epsbooks.com. Language arts, college entrance reviews, math, tests and measures, learning differences.

Elijah Company, 1053 Eldridge Loop, Crossville, TN 38571, 888-235-4524, fax: 931-456-6284; email: elijahco@elijahco.com; website: www.elijahco.com. Catalog of books and materials, information, and book reviews.

For Such a Time as This Ministries, James P. Stobaugh, 510 Swank Road, Hollsapple, PA 15935,814-479-7719; email: JPSTOBAUGH@aol.com; website: www.forsuchatimeasthis.com. American, British, and World Literature critical thinking courses, history unit studies, The Mindtrap Game II, *SAT Preparation Course for the Christian Student,* other resources.

FUN Books, Dept. W, 1688 Belhaven Woods Court, Pasadena, CA 21122-3727, 410-360-7330, 888-FUN-7020 or 888-386-7020; email: FUN@FUN-Books.com; website: www.funbook.com. Books for unschooling.

God's World Books Educational Catalog, P.O. Box 2003, Asheville, NC 28802-8203, 800-951-2665 (orders); 888-492-2307 (customer service); fax: 800-537-0447; service@gwbc.com (customer service), hisdeas@gwbc.com (ideas); website: www.gwbc.com.

High School Hub, a "noncommercial learning portal to high-quality free online educational resources for high school students": http://highschoolhub.org/hub/hub.cfm; Links to sites with help and information for all high school subjects. It looks wonderful.

Home Life, Inc., P.O. Box 11990, Fenton, MO 63026-1190, 800-346-6322 or 636-529-0137; email: svc@home-school.com; website: www.home-school.com. Mary Pride's books, other resources; links to general curriculum sites.

The Home School, 15 Wellman Ave., North Chelmsford, MA 01863, 800-788-1221, 978-251-6012; website: www.Thehomeschool.com. Catalog of books and curriculum; subscription service for telephone help.

Homeschooling Headquarters.com, 28 Public Square, Medina, OH 44256, 866-725-2662 or 330-725-2665; email: sales@homeschoolingheadquarters.com; website: homeschoolingheadquarters.com. Curriculum.

Homework Spot (high school section); website: http://homeworkspot.com/high. Links to information and websites on every subject; reference materials, tips, etc.

In His Steps, 1618 Kendolph, Denton, TX 76205, 940-566-6123, 800-583-1336 (orders only); fax: 940-383-0443; email: Info@InHisSteps.com; website: www.inhissteps.com. Books and curriculum.

Instructional Media Services, P.O. Box 711, Merton, WI 53056, (262) 369-9200, Fax 262-538-1491; email: imsinfo@imseducates.com; website: www.imseducates.com. Educational multimedia that may be rented for home use.

JoyceHerzog.com, 578 Randall Rd., Ballston Spa, NY 12020, 800-745-8212; email: office@joyceherzog.com; website: www.joyceherzog.com. Learning products & services.

k-12®, K12 Inc., 8000 Westpark Dr., Suite 500, McLean, VA 22102, 1-888-YOUR K12 (968-7512). Curriculum directed by William J. Bennett. A "comprehensive, standards-based curriculum" using "traditional materials and innovative technology." Includes necessary materials not easily found at home. Computer and Internet access needed. Eventually will include high school grades.

Landmark's Freedom Baptist Curriculum, 2222 East Hinson Avenue, Haines City, FL 33844-4902, 800-700-LFBC; fax: 941-422-0188; email: LFBC@juno.com; website: http://www.landmarkbaptistchurch.org/lfbc/. Curriculum for all grades, all subjects.

Learning Streams, 1550 Oak Industrial Lane, Suite F, Cumming, GA 30041, 800-401-9931 or 678-679-1127, fax: 678-679-1132; website: www.learningstreams.com. Homeschool curriculum, software and educational games.

Lifetime Books & Gifts, 3900 Chalet Suzanne Drive, Lake Wales, FL 33859-6681, 863-676-6311, 800-377-0390 (orders only); fax: 863-676-2732; email: info@lifetimebooksandgifts.com; website: www.lifetimebooksandgifts.com. *The Always Incomplete Resource Guide:* curriculum, information, good books for children and adults, music, games, toys, out-of-print book search, book reviews.

Robinson Self-Teaching Curriculum, Robinson Curriculum, 3321 Sesame Drive, Howell, MI 48843, 517-546-8780; fax: 517-546-8730; email: support@robinsoncurriculum.com; website: www.robinsoncurriculum.com. Complete course of study (except math) for grades 1–12 and Original Source Library on CD-ROM, some print books.

Shekinah Curriculum Cellar, Home Educator's Warehouse, 1815 Whittington Road, Kilgore, TX 75662, 903-643-2760; fax: 903-643-2796; email: customerservice@shekinahcc.com; website: www.shekinahcc.com. All subjects, all grades.

Sing 'n Learn, 2626 Club Meadow Drive, Garland, TX 75043-1102, 800-460-1973, 972-278-1973 (Dallas area); website: www.singnlearn.com. Songs to help with memorization for chemistry, life science, social studies, other subjects.

Sonlight Curriculum, International Homeschoolers Curriculum, 8042 South Grant Way, Littleton, CO 80122-2705, 303-730-6292; fax: 303-795-8668; email: main@sonlight.com; website: www.sonlight-curriculum.com. Literature-based, unit study-type curriculum.

The Sycamore Tree, 2179 Meyer Place, Costa Mesa, CA 92627, 714-668-1343 (information); 800-779-6750 (orders); fax: 714-668-1344; email: info@sycamoretree.com; website: www.sycamoretree.com. Curriculum, complete program for K-12.

The Teaching Company, 4151 Lafayette Center Dr., Suite 100, Chantilly, VA 20151-1232, 800-TEACH-12; fax: 703-378-3819; email: custserv@teachco.com; website: www.teachco.com. Video high school courses taught by "top" teachers.

Timberdoodle Company, E 1510 Spencer Lake Road, Shelton, WA 98584, 360-426-0672; fax: 800-478-0672; email: mailbag@timberdoodle.com; website: www.timberdoodle.com. Many unusual and hard-to-find items, e.g., Fischertechnik kits.

Veritas Press, 1250 Belle Meade Drive, Lancaster, PA 17601, 800-922-5082, 717-519-1974; fax: 717-519-1978; email: Info@VeritasPress.com; website: www.VeritasPress.com. "A full-service curriculum provider with a classical specialization." Offers free consulting service to help parents select materials.

The Weaver Curriculum, Scripture-based unit study program for K–12; available from Alpha Omega. (See above).

Language Arts and Foreign Languages

1100 Words You Need to Know, by Murray Bromberg and Melvin Gordon, Barron's Educational Series.

Annenberg CPB Projects (See under General Curriculum.)

Berean Bookshelf, 17 Peacock Lane, Tijeras, NM 87059, 505-281-1854, 866-281-1854 (orders), info@bereanbookshelf.com, website: www.bereanbookshelf.com. Specializes in classic literature.

Bolchazy-Carducci Publishers, Inc., 1000 Brown Street, Unit 101, Wauconda, IL 60084-3120, 800-392-6453 or 847-526-4344; fax: 847-526-2867; email: info@bolchazy.com; website: www.arteslatinae.com. Latin and Greek curriculum and books.

Bradrick Family Enterprises, 25 Geissler Rd., Montesano, WA 98563, 360-249-2472. *Understanding Writing* curriculum.

Concordia Language Villages, Concordia College MN, 901 8th St. S., Moorhead, MN 56562, 800-222-4750, 218-299-4544; email: info@ConcordiaLanguageVillages.org; website: http://www.cord.edu/dept/clv. "World language and culture education program for ages 7-18," basically a foreign language camp.

Electric Library ("Search *millions* of articles fast"), www.newsdirectory.com; online research and links to newspapers, magazines, TV, government sites.

The Elements of Style, by William Strunk Jr. and E. B. White.

Essentials of English Grammar: A Practical Guide to the Mastery of English, by L. Sue Baugh.

The Gift of Reading, 423 Maplewood, San Antonio, TX 78216. Orders: Trudy Palmer, PO Box 460514, San Antonio, TX 78246-0514, 210-828-5179. Reading, vocabulary, writing, learning difficulties.

GraceWorks Ministries Press, 8400 N 44th Street E, Valley Center, KS 67147, 800-639-5635; email: mail@hisgraceworks.com; website: www.hisgraceworks.com. *Signs for His Glory!* sign language courses; *His Chosen Bride;* planners.

The Grammar Key®, P.O. Box 33230, Tulsa, OK 74153, 800-480-0539. Streamlined grammar course.

Guide for Writing Research Papers Based on MLA Documentation, website: http://webster.commnet.edu/mla/index.shtml.

How to Write Term Papers and Reports, by L. Sue Baugh.

Institute for Excellence in Writing, P.O. Box 6065, Atascadero, CA 93423, 800-856-5815; fax: 603-925-5123; email: info@writing-edu.com; website: www.writing-edu.com.

Language Camps for Youngsters (some for teens studying foreign languages): http://www.swopnet.com/geo_rodeowriter_2000/lang_camps.html.

Language Links: http://polyglot.lss.wisc.edu/lss/lang/langlink.html. For teachers and students of most foreign languages.

A Manual for Writers of Term Papers, Theses, and Dissertations, by Kate L. Turabian, University of Chicago Press.

Meyers Institute for Communication and Leadership, P.O. Box 7, Dayton, TN 37321, 423-570-1000; fax: 423-570-1001; email: info@myersinstitute.com; website: www.myersinstitute.com. *Secrets of Great Communicators* speech course; online leadership course; worldview training.

On Writing Well: The Classic Guide to Writing Nonfiction, by William Knowlton Zinsser.

Paradigm Online Writing Assistant: http://www.powa.org. "An interactive, menu-driven, online writer's guide and handbook" that looks wonderful.

Pen and Page Academic Services: http://www.penandpage.com. Shakespeare reading journals for *Macbeth* and *Hamlet;* grammar lessons and quizzes

Playpen to Podium: Giving Your Child the Communication Advantage in Every Area of Life, by Jeffrey L. Myers.

Power-Glide Foreign Language Courses, 1682 West 820 North, Provo, UT 84601, 800-596-0910; fax: 801-343-3912; email: support@power-glide.com; website: www.power-glide.com. Foreign language courses with strong audio content.

Purdue University's Online Writing Lab (OWL): http://owl.english.purdue.edu.

Reading Between the Lines: A Christian Guide to Literature, by Gene Edward Veith, Crossway Books. Available from Good News Publishers at http://www.gnpcb.org.

TextWord Press, Inc., 222 44th St., Brooklyn, NY 11232, 718-765-8940; fax: 718-680-1875; email: info@textword.com; website: www.textword.com. "High school [literature] textbooks of distinction that promote academic excellence and preserve traditional family values."

Toastmasters International—Youth Leadership Program. Sponsored by local Toastmasters clubs. For information, write Toastmasters International, PO Box 9052, Mission Viejo, CA

92690, or phone 949-858-8255; email: edu@toastmasters.org; website: www.toastmasters.org. Complete directory of Toastmasters clubs on website.

Total Language Plus, P.O. Box 12622, Olympia, WA 98508, 360-754-3660, Fax: 360-754-3505; email: customer@totallanguageplus.com. Language arts curriculum from a Christian perspective; "focused on teaching thinking and communication skills using literature as a base."

Using Sources, from Hamilton College, NY; website: http://www.hamilton.edu/academics/resource/wc/usingsources.html. Guidelines for using sources correctly in writing.

Math and Science

A+ Projects in Biology, A+ Projects in Chemistry, A+ Projects in Astronomy, A+ Projects in Earth Science, A+ Projects in Physics by Janice VanCleave.

Advanced Learning Associates, 32 Godfrey Lane, Milford, MA 01757, 508-478-5648; email: bunt@world.std.com; website: http://world.std.com/~bunt/edu.html. Complete kits of secondary science lab materials, links to educational websites.

American Chemical Society, www.acs.org. Information about Chemistry Olympiad.

American Mathematical Society, Mathematics on the Web: http://www.ams.org/mathweb/mi-mathbytopic.html#fractals. Links to various math sites.

Apologia Educational Ministries, 1106 Meridian Plaza, Suite 220, Anderson, IN 46016, 888-524-4724; fax: 765-608-3290; website: http://www.apologia.com. Science curriculum by a former university professor designed especially for homeschoolers.

At Home Science, Inc., 412 13th Street, Glenwood Springs, CO 81601, 970-947-0050, 866-206-0773; fax: 208-575-0270; e-mail: info@AtHomeScience.com; website: http://www.chem-kits.com/index.html. "Specializing in science kits and laboratory supplies for college and high school distance-learning courses in the natural sciences."

Awesome Experiments in Light and Sound and *Simple Optical Illusion Experiments,* by Michael DiSpezio.

The Biology Place, www.biology.com. "Online resources of the leading biology programs for high school and college."

Blue Spruce Biological Supply, Inc., 701 Park Street, Castle Rock, CO 80109, 800-825-8522, 303-688-3396 (metro Denver); fax: 303-688-3428; email: sales@bluebio.com; website: http://bluebio.com. Preserved and live specimens, prepared slides, lab equipment, etc. Just about anything you could want for biological sciences.

Bluestocking Press (See under General Curriculum), Math.

Bob Jones University Press; dissection kit. (See contact information under Curriculum Suppliers.)

Carolina Biological Supply Company, 800-227-1150 (product information), 800-334-5551 (customer service); email: carolina@carolina.com; website: www3.carolina.com. Check homeschool resources page: http://www3.carolina.com/homeschool/default.asp. Includes supplies and information for Biology, Earth Science, Chemistry, Physics, Environmental Science; AP® science; lab materials lists for various sciences.

Castle Heights Press, Inc., 2578 Alexander Farms Drive, Marietta, GA 30064; phone or fax: 770-218-7998; email: julicher@aol.com; website: www.flash.net/~wx3o/chp. Kits for science labs at home; science curriculum.

The Catalyst, Chemistry Resources for the Secondary Teacher on the Web, http://www.thecatalyst.org. Includes links to high school chemistry sites with tutorials and other helpful information. Demos at www.thecatalyst.org/m05demos.html.

Chalk Dust Company, 11 Sterling Court, Sugar Land, TX 77479, 800-588-7564, 281-265-2495; fax: 281-265-3197; email: sales@chalkdust.com; website: www.chalkdust.com. Math videotapes; textbooks; solutions guides.

The Chemistry Place, www.chemplace.com. Interactive tutorials; quizzes; web resources for high school and college chemistry.

Chemistry Resources (links chemistry units to annotated websites): http://www.dist214.k12.il.us/users/asanders/chemhome2.html.

The ChemTeam: http://dbhs.wvusd.k12.ca.us/ChemTeamIndex.html. A tutorial for high school chemistry.

Conceptual Physics: http://www.phschool.com/science/cpsurf/index.html.

Cornell Math and Science Gateway: www.tc.cornell.edu/Edu/MathSciGateway. Provides links to resources in mathematics and science for educators and students in grades 9–12.

Curriculum Links for Science Teachers: http://pluggers.esu8.k12.ne.us/~esu8web/curriculum/science.html.

Discovering Electricity, by Neil Ardley.

Eclectic Homeschool Online Science Experiments: http://eho.org/scienceexperiments.htm.

Electric Library (See under Language Arts.)

Exploratorium, Museum of Science, Art, and Human Perception, 3601 Lyon Street, San Francisco, CA 94123-1099, 415-561-7337; website: www.exploratorium.edu. Science information, hands-on activities, etc.

Fisher Science Education, 4500 Turnberry, Hanover Park, IL 60133; 800-955-1177; fax: 800-955-0740; email: info@fisheredu.com; website: www.fisheredu.com. Educational division of Fisher Scientific serving K-12.

Friendly Chemistry: A Guide to Learning Basic Chemistry, by Joey and Lisa Hajda. High-school-level chemistry course, complete with manipulatives and games to aid student understanding. Available from Hideaway Ventures, RR 2 Box 96A, Berwyn, NE 68819, 800-774-3447; email: orders@friendlychemistry.com; website: www.friendlychemistry.com.

General Chemistry interactive CD-ROM: http://www.brookscole.com/chemistry_d.

General Chemistry Online: http://antoine.frostburg.edu/chem/senese/101/index.shtml. Great information for teachers and students.

High School Hub: biology: http://highschoolhub.org/hub/biology.cfm; chemistry: http://highschoolhub.org/hub/chemistry.cfm; earth science: http://highschoolhub.org/hub/science.cfm; physics: http://highschoolhub.org/hub/physics.cfm.

HMChem: http://hmchemdemo.clt.binghamton.edu. "Web-based resource site for General Chemistry." Source for electronic chemistry curriculum from Houghton-Mifflin with simulations from Binghamton University.

Home Training Tools, 3008 Harrow Drive, Billings, MT 59102, 800-860-6272 or 406-628-6614; fax: 406-628-6454; email: customerservice@hometrainingrools.com; website: www.hometrainingtools.com. Chemicals, microscopes, preserved specimens, other science lab equipment and supplies; kits geared to specific curricula.

Institute for Math Mania, P.O. Box 910, Montpelier, VT 05601, 800-NUMERAL; email: pigonmath@aol.com; website: http://members.aol.com/mathmania. Offers a free catalogue for Math Maniacs.

Key Curriculum Press, 1150 65th Street, Emeryville, CA 94608, 800-995-MATH (US and Canada), 510-595-7000 (local and international); fax: 800-541-2442; 510-595-7040 (local and international); website: www.keypress.com; email: info@keypress.com or orders@keypress.com. Math books and software, including *Discovering Geometry* (our favorite math book).

Lab Science: The How, Why, What, Who, 'n' Where Book, by Barbara Shelton. Available from homeschooloasis.com.

The Lyman Library, Museum of Science Boston, 617-589-0170; email: library@mos.org; website: www.mos.org/learn_more/lyman.html. Members and homeschoolers in New England may borrow books, videos, and CD-ROMs by mail. Anyone with reference questions about science or technology may contact the staff by email or phone for assistance.

Mad About Physics: Braintwisters, Paradoxes, and Curiosities, by Christopher P. Jargodzki and Franklin Potter.

Math for Morons Like Us: http://library.thinkquest.org/20991/home.html.

MathXpert Systems, 2211 Lawson Lane, Santa Clara, CA 95054, 800-361-1001, Fax: 408-567-0659; website: www.mathxpert.com. Mathematics software to help students learn high school algebra through college calculus.

MJWood Resources. "Quality educational resources for high school science teachers." Website: www.mjwoodresources.ca. Free monthly science demos, other resources.

The Mole Hole: A Resource for High School Chemistry Teachers: www.chemmybear.com.

Moody Science Videos, Moody Video, 820 North La Salle Boulevard, Chicago, IL 60610, 312-329-4352, 800-842-1223; website: www.moodyvideo.org. Creation-based science videos.

National Directory, physics equipment suppliers: http://www.nationaldirectory.com/Reference/Education. (Also search from home page for other sciences.)

Old Fashioned Products, Inc., "Muggins! Math," 4860 Burnt Mtn. Rd., Ellijay, GA 30540, 800-962-8849; fax: 706-635-7611; email: muggings@ellijay.com; website: www.mugginsmath.com. Fun, challenging math/critical thinking games.

The Physics Classroom: http://www.glenbrook.k12.il.us/gbssci/phys/Class/BBoard.html. A high school physics tutorial.

Professor B Enterprises, Inc., P.O. Box 2079, Duluth, GA 30096, 800-VIP-MATH, 770-814-8888; email: info@profb.com; website: www.profb.com. Professor B Math Program.

Preparing for General Physics: Math Skill Drills and Other Useful Help, by Arnold D. Pickar.

Relevant (High School) Chemistry on the Web: www.chemistrycoach.com/high.htm. Lists many informative sites.

Sargent-Welch (part of science education division of VWR International), 800-932-5000, 800-727-4368 (orders); orders fax: 800-676-2540; email: sarwel@sargentwelch.com; website: www.sargentwelch.com. "Full-line, all-discipline, supplier of science education lab equipment and apparatus."

Saxon Publishers, Inc., 2600 John Saxon Boulevard, Norman, OK 73071, 800-284-7019; 405-329-7071; fax: 405-360-4205; email: info@saxonpublishers.com; website: www.saxonpub.com. Saxon math, physics.

Schaum's Easy Outlines: College Physics by Fredrick J. Bueche and Eugene Hecht.

Science Labs-in-a-Box, Inc., P.O. Box 1657, Kyle, TX 78640, 800-453-1708; fax: 512-268-2766; email: Info@ScienceLabs.com; website: www.sciencelabs.com. Complete kits of science lab materials and supplies for grades 1-12, beginning electronics kits.

Science Projects, 13440 T. I. Boulevard, Suite 6, Dallas, TX 75243, 972-470-0395, 972-669-2577; website: www.scienceprojects.net. Comprehensive catalog of equipment, books, specimens, chemicals, and lab supplies for virtually every field of science.

Science Teachers' Resource Center: http://chem.lapeer.org. Labs, demonstrations, and ideas for teaching high school science.

S.O.S. Math: http://www.sosmath.com. Free source of math review material; has links to math sites on the WWW.

StudyWorks! Online: The Physics Classroom: http://www.physicsclassroom.com. A high school physics tutorial.

Timberdoodle. Fischertechnik building kits. (See General Curriculum.)

Tobin's Lab, Inc., 15055 Glen Verdant Dr. or P.O. Box 725, Culpepper, VA 22701, 540-937-7173; email: info@tobinslab.com; website: www.tobinslab.com. "Hands-on science materials for families, ages 3 through adult."

TOPScience, TOPS Learning Systems, Inc., 10970 S. Mulino Road, Canby, OR 97013, 888-773-9755 (orders only), 503-263-2040 (customer service); fax: 503-266-5200; email: topsideas@yahoo.com; website: http://topscience.org. Hands-on science resources; free online instructions for mini-labs.

U. S. Geological Survey, USGS National Center, 12201 Sunrise Valley Drive, Reston, VA 20192; 888-ASK-USGS, 703-648-4000, website: www.usgs.gov/tracks/teachers.html. Interesting website with science and mapping information for all ages and educational information and activities for K–12.

Social Studies, Art, Music, Bible, and Miscellaneous Resources

American Bible Society, 1865 Broadway, New York, NY 10023-7505, 212-408-1200; website: www.americanbible.org or www.bibles.com. Bibles in many languages.

Artistic Pursuits, Inc., email: alltheanswers@artisticpursuits.com; website: www.artisticpursuits.com. *Artistic Pursuits: The Elements of Art and Composition, Senior High Book 1 (Drawing)* and *Book 2 (Color).* "A comprehensive art program designed to involve the student in the creative process while developing observational skills."

Bluestocking Press, P.O. Box 2030, Shingle Springs, CA 95682-2030; orders: 800-959-8586; orders or customer service: 530-621-1123; fax: 530-642-9222; email: uncleric@jps.net; website: www.BluestockingPress.com. Specializing in American history; also publisher of the Uncle Eric books (connecting economics, government, history, law, etc.), Knowledge Products audio history, mathematics. A geography text is projected to release by 2004.

Diana Waring—History Alive!, P.O. Box 378, Spearfish, SD 57783; fax/phone: 605-642-7583; email: diana@dianawaring.com; website: www.dianawaring.com. World history in Christian perspective; also homeschooling column online at Best of the Christian Web www.botcw.com.

Electric Library (See under Language Arts.)

Gordon School of Art, P.O. Box 28208, Green Bay, WI 54324-0208, 800-210-1220 or 920-437-2190, email: gordon@netnet.com; website: www.newmasters.com. *New Masters Program,* a rigorous system of formal art training.

Help! My Teenager Wants to Drive! by Charles Taylor. Driving curriculum, available from The Elijah Company. This can be found at many different online bookstores.

How Great Thou Art Publications, Box 48, McFarlan, NC 28102, 800-982-3729; fax: 704-851-3111; email: sales@howgreatthouart.com; website: www.howgreatthouart.com. Art curriculum, teacher's manuals, videos, supplies.

Liberty Fund, Inc., 8335 Allison Pointe Trail, Suite 300, Indianapolis, IN 46250-1684, 317-842-0880; fax: 317-577-9067; email: books@libertyfund.org; website: www.libertyfund.org. Books about America's founding and the Constitution, American and European history, law, and ecomonics. Many books contain primary sources.

National Directory: http://www.nationaldirectory.com/Reference/Education. Links to educational websites.

National Driver Training Institute, 4432 Austin Bluffs Pkwy., Colorado Springs, CO 80918, 800-942-2050; website: www.usdrivertraining.com. Parent-taught driver education program. Certified Graduated Driver License Program. "Creating safe drivers for life."

National Gallery of Art, Department of Education Resources, National Gallery of Art, 2000B South Club Drive, Landover, MD 20785, 202-737-4215; email: EdResources@nga.gov; website: http://www.nga.gov/education/ep-main.htm. Art slide programs, multimedia programs, videos, CD-ROMs, etc., available for free loan.

New Creation Music Center, 11475 Foxhaven Drive, Chesterland, OH 44026, 800-337-4798, 216-729-8288; website: www.newcreationmusic.com. Musical instruments for sale or rent; music software.

Training Our Daughters to Be Keepers at Home, by Mrs. Craig (Ann) Ward, Smiling Heart Press. Available from Lifetime Books & Gifts (see under Curriculum and Homeschool Suppliers). Seven-year home economics course for girls 11-18. Contains much practical information, such as bookkeeping, growing food, sewing.

WallBuilders, Inc., P.O. Box 397, Aledo, TX 76008-0397, 817-441-6044 (inquiries); 800-873-2845 (orders); email: wbcustomerservice@wallbuilders.com; website: www.wallbuilders.com. An organization "dedicated to the restoration of the moral and religious foundation on which America was built." Educational resources for history and current events. Source for David Barton's excellent tapes and videos on America's Christian heritage.

YWAM Publishing, P.O. Box 55787, Seattle, WA 98155, 800-922-2143 (Visa and Mastercard orders only); fax: 425-775-2383; email: information@ywampublishing.com; website: www.ywampublishing.com. Missions, American history, general homeschooling, character issues, and this book! Some publications in Spanish.

Extracurricular Opportunities

A.C.T.I.O.N. Ministry (Active Christian Training In One Name), P.O. Box 1761, Ventura, CA 93002, 805-653-0782, or P.O. Box 682531, Franklin, TN 37068, 615-395-9844; voicemail/pager: 888-542-9186; email: aim@actionministry.org; website: www.actionministry.org. Conduct ministry road-school tours for homeschoolers 12-18, featuring biblical training in music, mime, drama, movement, sign language, and public speaking. A.C.T.I.O.N. Impact Ministry teams in various states.

The Continentals, Continental Ministries, P.O. Box 6972, Ventura, CA 93006-6972, 805-289-3450; fax: 805-289-1527; email: singers@continentalsingers.org. Talent Department 800-481-7464; email: talent@continentalsingers.org. Touring ministry opportunities for singers, instrumentalists, and technicians for ages 12 and up; Performing Arts School.

International Family Missions, P.O. Box 309, Lafayette, CO 80026-0309, 303-665-7635; fax 303-661-0732; Email: ifm@internationalfamilymissions.org; website: http://www.norrisfamily.com/ifm.

YWAM Nashville, P.O. Box 78219, Nashville, TN 37207-9818, 615-696-3096; email: YWAMinfo@YWAMnashville.org; website: www.ywamnashville.org. Short-term outreaches; mission training.

Teaching and Home Guidance Counseling

10 Real SATs, published by The College Board.

Academy Curriculum Exchange: www.ofcn.org/cyber.serv/academy. A variety of lesson plans contributed by teachers in schools.

ACT Registration, P.O. Box 168, 2201 N. Dodge Street, Iowa City, Iowa 52243-0168, 319-337-1270; website: www.act.org. Helpful information, ACT tests, and other services.

AP Examination preparation: http://store.collegeboard.com. Purchase books, software, videos, and CD-ROMs that contain study helps and released AP tests. Look in the Parent Products and Education Professional Products sections.

Barron's Educational Series: www.barronseduc.com/main.htm. Test preparation books.

Bear's Guide to Earning Degrees by Distance Learning, by John and Mariah Bear.

BJ Testing and Evaluation Service, BJ Home Education Services, Customer Services, 1700 Wade Hampton Blvd., Greenville, SC 29614-0062, 800-845-5731; fax 800-525-8398; email: testing@bju.com.

CampusLifeCollegeGuide.com. Features some Christian colleges; some articles.

The Campus Life Guide to Christian Colleges and Universities, edited by Mark Moring.

Canon Press, P.O. Box 8729, Moscow, ID 83843-8729, 800-488-2034; fax: 208-882-1568; email: canorder@moscow.com; website: www.canonpress.org. Books on education, faith, and other subjects, such as *Brightest Heaven of Invention: A Christian Guide to Six Shakespeare Plays.*

Challenges for the College Bound: Advice and Encouragement from a College President, by Jay L. Kesler.

Choosing the Right College 2004: The Whole Truth about America's 100 Top Schools, edited by Jeremy Beer. Check for latest edition. Intercollegiate Studies Institute, 3901 Centerville Road, P.O. Box 4431, Wilmington, Delaware 19807; phone: 302-652-4600; website: www.isi.org.

ChristianColleges.com: www.christiancolleges.com. Links to Christian college websites.

Christian Connector: www.christianconnector.com. Search for Christian colleges online.

CLEP (College Level Examination Program), P.O. Box 6600, Princeton, NJ 08541-6600, 800-257-9558; fax: 609-771-7088; email: clep@info.collegboard.org; website: www.collegeboard.com//clep/index.html.

The College Application Essay, by Sarah Myers McGinty, College Entrance Examination Board (The College Board). Takes students step-by-step through the process.

College Board Headquarters, 45 Columbus Ave., NY, NY 10023-6992, 212-713-8000; College Board Online: www.collegeboard.com. SATI, SATII, PSAT.

College Student's Guide to Merit and Other No-Need Funding, by Gail Ann Schlachter and R. David Weber.

Colleges That Change Lives: 40 Schools You Should Know About Even If You're Not a Straight-A Student, by Loren Pope.

Colleges That Encourage Character Development: A Resource for Parents, Students, and Educators (The Templeton Guide), by John Templeton Foundation.

College Internet Connection, Private and Home School Friendly Colleges and Universities: http://rsts.net/colleges. (Not a comprehensive list.)

CollegNet: www.collegnet.com. Online college search.

CollegeXpress: www.collegexpress.com. College search, scholarship search, loan search.

Crown Financial Ministries, P.O. Box 100, Gainesville, GA 30503-0100, 800-722-1976; 770-534-1000; website: www.cfcministry.org. *Career Direct Guidance System,* print or CD-ROM version; *Youth Exploration Survey;* teen/college finance information.

Discover Your Best Possible Future: A Step-by-Step Guide to Choosing a College, a Major, a Career, by Diane Eble and Richard Hagstrom, Campus Life Books/Zondervan. Out of print but worth the search.

The Dying of the Light: The Disengagement of Colleges and Universities from Their Christian Churches, by James Tunstead Burtchaell, Wm. B. Eerdmans.

Ecola College Locator: http://www.ecola.com/college/search.

FAFSA on the Web, U.S. Department of Education: www.fafsa.ed.gov. Free application for federal student aid.

Faith at State: A Handbook for Christians at Secular Universities, by Rick Kennedy.

FastWeb: www.fastweb.com. Free scholarship and college search service on the Internet.

Federal Student Aid Homepage, 800-4-FED-AID; website: www.ed.gov/offices/OSFAP/Students. *The Student Guide,* free and published annually, gives detailed information about federal financial aid programs.

FinAid! The SmartStudent Guide to Financial Aid, website: www.finaid.org. Information on scholarships, loans, savings, and military aid. Newsletter.

Finding God at Harvard, edited by Kelly Monroe. Testimonies of faith surviving in a secular academic environment.

GED: CALEC (Center for Adult Learning and Educational Credentials), One Dupont Circle NW, Suite 250, Washington DC, 20036, 202-939-9475; website: www.gedtest.org.

Getting In: Inside the College Admissions Process, by Bill Paul. Insightful, especially if students are interested in the most selective schools.

Getting Into the ACT: Official Guide to the ACT Assessment.

Getting Smarter: Simple Strategies to Get Better Grades, by Lawrence Greene and Leigh Jones-Bamman.

Greenes' Guides to Educational Planning: Making It into a Top College: 10 Steps to Gaining Admission to Selective Colleges and Universities, by Howard Greene and Matthew Greene.

Hobson's CollegeView: www.collegeview.com. College search, including virtual campus tours and online applications.

How to Prepare for College (VGM How to Series), by Marjorie Eberts and Margaret Gisler.

How to Study: A Practical Guide from a Christian Perspective and *Writing a Research Paper,* by Edward J. Shewan. Available from lifetimebooksandgifts.com

Inside American Education: the Decline, the Deception, the Dogmas, by Thomas Sowell.

Milligan's (graduation supplies), 109 St. Joseph Avenue, Breton, Alabama 36426, 1-800-544-4696 (orders), 251-867-5895 (customer service); website: http://www.milligans.com. Caps and gowns, custom diplomas, awards, etc. Sells to homeschoolers.

NewsDirectory College Locator: http://newsdirectory.tucows.com/college.

Options for the High School Graduate and *An Instruction Booklet for the Parents of College Bound Students,* by Linda O'Brien. Available from Woodburn Press, P.O. Box 153, Dayton, OH 45419.

Peterson's Guides: www.petersons.com. College search, test preparation, financial aid. Also various printed guides for four-year colleges, Christian colleges, etc.

The Portable College Adviser: A Guide for High School Students, by Wendy H. Robbins.

The Princeton Review: Cracking the SAT and other test preparation guides. Updated yearly. Website: www.princetonreview.com.

SAT examination preparation: http://store.collegeboard.com. Purchase books, software, and videos that contain study helps and released tests. Look in the Parent Products and Education Professional Products sections.

Scholarship information: FAFSA on the Web, FinAid, SRN Express, college financial aid offices, high school counselors' offices, newspapers, magazines, scholarship books, local service organizations, companies, banks, and other sites listed in this section.

SRN Express (Scholarship Resource Network Express): www.srnexpress.com. Search engine and database of private scholarships, fellowships, grants, educational loan programs, non-need based aid, etc.

Summit Ministries Guide to Choosing a College by Dr. Ronald H. Nash and J. F. Baldwin. For a copy, contact Summit Ministries, P.O. Box 207, Manitou Springs, CO 80829, 719-685-9103, fax: 719-685-9330; email: info@summit.org.

Thompson Peterson's: www.peterson's.com/ugchannel. College search, financial aid, test preparation, etc.

U.S. Department of Education, Office of Postsecondary Education, U.S. Department of Education, 1990 K St., NW, Washington, DC 20006, 800-USA-LEARN; website: www.ed.gov/offices/OPE. Resources for those planning for postsecondary education.

U.S. News and World Report (partly fee-based): www.usnews.com/usnews/edu/college/cohome.htm. "America's Best Colleges" (print or Premier Online editions).

What Color Is Your Parachute? A Practical Manual for Job Hunters and Career Changers, by Richard Nelson Bolles, Ten Speed Press. Updated annually.

Learning Differences

ADD and the College Student: A Guide for High School and College Students with Attention Deficit Disorder, edited by Patricia O. Quinn, M.D..

Adolescents and ADD: Gaining the Advantage, by Patricia O. Quinn, M.D. Talks about treatment with drugs, information about improving study skills, student experiences. Good bibliography.

Autism information links: http://www.weirdkids.com/autism/aboutautism.htm.

College and Career Success for Students with Learning Disabilities, by Roslyn Dolber.

Coping with a Learning Disability, by Lawrence Clayton and Jaydene Morrison, the Rosen Publishing Group.

Essential Learning Institute, 334- 2nd Street, Catasauqua, PA 18032-2501, 800-285-9089, 610-264-8355; email: eli@polyweb.net; website: http://ldhope.com/index.htm. Homeschool learning disabilities package.

The Gifted Kids' Survival Guide: A Teen Handbook, by Judy Galbraith and Jim Delisle. (I don't agree with everything here, but it gives insights into personalities and problems.)

A Guide for Caring Teachers and Parents: THE IMPOSSIBLE CHILD In School–At Home, by Doris J. Rapp with Dorothy L. Bamberg, Practical Allergy Research Foundation.

Homeschool Central Special Needs Links: http://homeschoolcentral.com/special.htm.

"Homeschooling Your Special Needs Child," Suite University Course: www.suite101.com/course.cfm/17312/overview/8209.

How To Reach and Teach Children and Teens with Dyslexia: A Parent and Teacher Guide to Helping Students of All Ages Academically, Socially, and Emotionally, by Cynthia M. Stowe.

Gifted Development Center: http://www.gifteddevelopment.com. Resources for homeschooling gifted students.

Is This Your Child's World? How You Can Fix the Schools and Homes That Are Making Your Children Sick, by Doris J. Rapp.

Johns Hopkins University Center for Talented Youth, Distance Education, Johns Hopkins University, 3400 N Charles Street, Baltimore, MD 21218; email: ctyinfo@jhu.edu; website: http://cty.jhu.edu/cde/index.html. Distance courses for eligible youth in math, science, and writing.

JoyceHerzog.com. (See under General Curriculum.)

The K&W Guide to Colleges: For Students With Learning Disabilities or Attention Deficit Disorder, by Marybeth Kravets and Imy F. Wax.

Learning Disabilities A to Z: A Parent's Complete Guide to Learning Disabilities from Preschool to Adulthood, by Corinne Smith and Lisa Strick.

The Magic Feather: The Truth About "Special Education," by Lori Granger and Bill Granger, E.P. Dutton. Written by parents whose son was misdiagnosed as retarded and uneducable even though he could read above his grade level.

NATHHAN—National Challenged Homeschoolers Associated Network, P.O. Box 39, Porthill, ID 83853, 208-267-6246; email: nathanews@aol.com; website: http://nathhan.com. Articles, lending library, family directory, membership. Christian.

National Academy for Child Development, P.O. Box 380, Huntsville, UT 84317, 801-621-8606; fax: 801-621-8389; email: nacdinfo@nacd.org; website: www.nacd.org. "International organization of parents and professionals dedicated to helping children and adults reach their full potential through the use of innovative techniques and research."

National Association for Gifted Children, 1707 L Street, N.W, Washington, DC 20036, 202-785-4268; fax 202-785-4248; email: nagc@nagc.org; website: www.nagc.org.

Overcoming Dyslexia: A New and Complete Science-Based Program for Overcoming Reading Problems at Any Level, by Sally Shaywitz.

Parents' Complete Special Education Guide: Tips, Techniques, and Materials for Helping Your Child Succeed in School and Life, by Roger Pierangelo and Robert Jacoby, Center for Applied Research in Education.

Peterson's Colleges with Programs for Students with Learning Disabilities or Attention Deficit Disorders.

Power Learning Network: www.powerlearningnetwork.com. Uses computer technology to assist students, grades 4 and up, who have difficulty learning in traditional ways.

Succeeding with LD: 20 True Stories About Real People with LD, by Jill Lauren.

Teaching Adolescents With Learning Disabilities: Strategies and Methods, by Donald D. Deshler, Edwin S. Willis, and B. Keith Lenz, Love Publishing Company.

Unlocking Potential: College and Other Choices for People with LD and AD/HD, by Juliana M. Taymans and Lynda L. West.

Recommended by Kyle Hughes, Learning Disabilities Specialist:

Books About Students with Learning Differences

Greg Louganis: Diving for Gold, by Joyce Milton, Random House.

Reach for the Moon: What Once Was White, by Samantha Abeel. A collection of poems and short stories by a thirteen-year-old girl with learning disablities.

Books to Build Self-Esteem

Positive Self-Talk for Children: Teaching Self-Esteem Through Affirmations, by Douglas Bloch, Bantam Books.

Stick Up for Yourself! Every Kid's Guide to Personal Power and Positive Self-Esteem, by Gershen Kaufman and Lev Raphael, Free Spirit Publishing.

Understanding Learning Differences and Strategies for School Success

Keeping a Head in School: A Student's Book About Learning Abilities and Learning Disabilities, by Mel Levine, Educator's Publishing Service. (Hughes strongly recommends this as "one of best books available." Explains nature of learning disabilities in lay terms.)

The School Survival Guide for Kids with LD (Learning Differences), by Rhonda Cummings and Gary Fisher, Free Spirit Publishing.

The Survival Guide for Teenagers with LD (Learning Differences), by Rhonda Cummings and Gary Fisher, Free Spirit Publishing.

Understanding Learning Disabilities: How Difficult Can This Be? (video), Richard D. Lavoie, PBS Video. (Hughes recommends this highly for parents, teachers, and siblings. May be available for checkout from local school district—contact director of special education.)

When Your Child Has LD, by Rhonda Cummings and Gary Fisher.

Communication and Parenting

How to Talk So Kids Will Listen and Listen So Kids Will Talk, by Adele Faber and Elaine Mazlish, Avon Books.

Related Topics

Perfectionism: What's Bad About Being Too Good? by Miriam Adderholdt-Elliott, Free Spirit Publishing.

Procrastination: Why You Do It, What to Do About It, by Jane B. Burka and Lenora M. Yuen, Addison-Wesley.

To Be Gifted and Learning Disabled, by Susan M. Baum, Steve V. Owen, and John Dixon, Creative Learning Press.

Curriculum Guide

Understanding LD, by Susan McMurchie, Free Spirit Publishing.

Self-Advocacy

Developing Self-Advocacy Skills: A Program for Students K–12, by Kyle Hughes. Includes student and teacher assessment tools, parent resources, and student-generated IEP (individual educational plan). Order from Kyle Hughes, 7256 S. Xanthia Street, Englewood, CO 80112 ($17.50 + $2.75 s&h).

Character Development

Dr. S. M. Davis, Park Meadows Baptist Church, 800 Memorial Park Road, Lincoln, IL 62656, 217-732-6900; website: http://www.drsmdavis.com/content/about.html. *Changing the Heart of a Rebel* and other materials.

Doorposts, 5905 SW Lookingglass Drive, Gaston, OR 97119, 503-357-4749; fax: 503-357-4909; email: questions@doorposts.net; website: www.doorposts.net. Bible-based character training products.

The Holy Bible.

How a Man Prepares His Daughters for Life (Lifeskills for Men), by Michael Farris.

How a Man Prepares His Sons for Life (Lifeskills for Men), by Michael O'Donnell.

Raising the Mondern-Day Knight, by Robert Lewis and Stu Weber.

Worldview Training

Cornerstone Curriculum Project, 2006 Flat Creek, Richardson, TX 75080, 972-235-5149; website: www.cornerstonecurriculum.com. *Starting Points: Where Our Thinking Begins,* a worldview primer, and *Worldviews of the Western World.*

Meyers Institute for Communication and Leadership (see under Language Arts).

Nehemiah Institute, Inc., 3575 Harrodsburg Rd., Suite 150, Lexington, KY 40513, 800-948-3101; fax: 605-229-4090; email: info@nehemiahinstitute.com; website: http://www.nehemiahinstitute.com. PEERS testing, "an objective means for measuring the understanding of how biblical principles apply to all areas of life." Also **Developing a Biblical Worldview** study course.

Summit Ministries, P.O. Box 207, Manitou Springs, CO 80829, 719-685-9103; fax: 719-685-9330; email: info@summit.org; website: www.summit.org. *Understanding the Times,* Summit Conferences.

Summit Ministries at Bryan College, P.O. Box 7000, Dayton, TN 37321, 423-775-2041; email: summit@bryan.edu; website: http://www.bryan.edu/worldview/summit/index.html.

Worldview Academy, P.O. Box 310106, New Braunfels, TX 78131, 830-620-5203; fax: 830-643-0217; email: registrar@worldview.org; website: www.worldview.org.

Courtship versus Dating

Choosing God's Best, by Dr. Don Raunikar, Multnomah.

The Courtship Connection, P.O. Box 424, Temperance, MI 48182, 734-847-5210; email: kmorris895@aol.com; website: www.courtshipconnection.com. Materials on courtship, character training, and parental guidance.

Dating with Integrity: Honoring Christ in Your Relationships with the Opposite Sex, by John Holzmann.

Her Hand in Marriage, by Douglas Wilson.

His Chosen Bride: Applying Proverbs 31 as a Single Young Woman, by Jennifer J. Lamp.

I Kissed Dating Goodbye, by Joshua Harris.

Lady in Waiting, by Debby Jones and Jackie Kendall. Book, devotional journal, and study guide.

Of Knights and Fair Maidens, by Jeff and Danielle Myers.

R Generation, 26897 Matthews Road, Parma, ID 83660, 800-942-0177; fax: 208-722-5189;

website: www.ericandleslie.com. Source for books, music, and videos by authors, speakers, and musicians Eric and Leslie Ludy. (*When God Writes Your Love Story, When Dreams Come True,* and *His Perfect Faithfulness.*)

Homeschooling Information, Organizations, and Websites

About.com Homeschooling: http://homeschooling.miningco.com.

Adventist Home Educator: http://www.adventisthomeducator.org.

Alliance for Parental Involvement in Education, P.O. Box 59, East Chatham, NY 12060-0059, 518-392-6900; email: allpie@taconic.net; website: www.croton.com/allpie. "Nonprofit organization which assists and encourages parental involvement in education, wherever that education takes place." Resources, workshops, lending library, etc.

Association of Canadian Home-Based Education (ACHBE), email: homeschool-ca-admin@flora.org or homeschool-ca-org-owner@flora.org; website: www.flora.org/homeschool-ca/achbe. Includes contact information by province/territory.

The Basic Steps to Successful Homeschooling, by Vicki A. Brady.

The Big Book of Home Learning, Volume 3: Junior High to College, by Mary Pride.

Books4Homeschool: www.books4homeschool.com. Curriculum recommendations and links to "most popular" homeschool sites.

Cafi Cohen's books: *Homeschooler's College Admissions Handbook, Homeschooling the Teen Years,* and *What About College.* Website: http://homeschoolteenscollege.net.

Canadian Home Based Learning Resource Page: www.flora.org/homeschool-ca.

Catholic Homeschool Network of America (CHSNA), Catherine Moran, President, P.O. Box 6343, River Forest, IL 60305-6343; fax: 330-652-3380; email: moran@netdotcom.com; website: www.geocities.com/Heartland/8579/chsna.html.

Catholic Homeschool Links: http://homeschoolcentral.com/catholic.htm.

Charlotte Mason High School Study Guide, by Lynn Hocraffer; http://homepage.bushnell.net/~peanuts/.html/CMhighschool.html. Complete breakdown of the schedule, subjects, and basic methods Charlotte Mason used; links to other sites.

Christ-centered Homeschool Webring: www.webring.org/cgi-bin/webring?ring=christ_hs_ring;list.

Christian Home Educators Curriculum Manual: Junior/Senior High, by Cathy Duffy, Grove Publishing.

Christian Homeschool Fellowship on the Web: www.chfweb.com. Homeschooling High Schoolers Forum, links, bookstore, etc.

Christian Unschooling, by Teri J. Brown and Elissa Wahl, Champion Press LTD; website: www.championpress.com/Level4Books/Unschooling.htm.

Classical Education and the Home School, by Douglas Wilson, Wes Callihan, and Douglas Jones.

Designing Your Own Classical Curriculum: A Guide to Catholic Home Education, by Laura Berquist, Ignatius Press; website: http://www.ignatius.com/books/dyo-p.htm.

Eclectic Homeschool Online: www.eho.org. Articles, reviews, support, message boards, email newsletter, lists of national homeschool organizations, and much more.

Family Education Network®, website: http://familyeducation.com. General site that has a home-schooling section.

Favorite Resources for Catholic Homeschoolers: website: www.love2learn.net.

Finding Homeschool Support on the Internet: www.geocities.com/Athens/8259.

Government Nannies: The Cradle-to-Grave Agenda of Goals 2000 and Outcome Based Education, by Cathy Duffy.

Grove Publishing: http://grovepublishing.com. Cathy Duffy's website featuring reviews, book, links, and news flashes.

The High School Handbook: Junior and Senior High School at Home (6th ed.), by Mary Schofield, Christian Home Educators Press, P.O. Box 2009, Norwalk, CA 90651-2009, 800-564-CHEA; website: http://www.cheaofca.org/products.htm.

Holt Associates, P.O. Box 89, Wakefield, MA 01880-5011, email: Info@HoltGWS.com.

Home Education Network, Inc., *Homeschooling USA!* Radio Broadcast, P.O. Box 37, Quinter, KS 67752, phone and fax: 785-673-4244. Homeschooling information and archived programs can be heard at www.homeschoolingusa.com. Vicki A. Brady, author of *The Basic Steps to Successful Homeschooling* and *Quiet Moments for Homeschool Moms and Dads,* also reviews homeschool products and programs. To have a product or program reviewed, email a request to vicki@homeschoolingusa.com.

Home School Internet Resource Center, 334 2nd Street, Catasauqua, PA 18032-2501, 800-863-1474; email: email: hsschool@rsts.net; website: http://rsts.net. *Homeschool Times* newspaper, online tutoring, list of homeschool-friendly colleges and universities, Curriculum Recycler, Homeschool Mall, educational links, distance learning, etc.

Home School Legal Defense Association, P.O. Box 3000, Purcellville, VA 20134-9000, 540-338-5600; website: www.hslda.org. Legal representation for members. News, articles, legal updates, and information about homeschooling all over the world.

Home Schooling on a Shoestring: A Jam-Packed Guide, by Melissa L. Morgan and Judith Waite Allee.

Home Schooling on the Threshold: A Survey of Research at the Dawn of the New Millennium, by Brian D. Ray, NHERI Publications.

Home Schooling the High Schooler, by Diana McAllister and Candice Oneschak.

HomeEducator.com: www.HomeEducator.com. "The place for educational entrepreneurs," from the publishers of *Home Educator's Family Times.*

Homeschool Central: http://homeschoolcentral.com. Website packed with information, lists, and links.

Homeschool Discussion List: http:/groups.yahoo.com/group/hshs.

Homeschool Oasis, website of Dave and Barb Shelton: www.homeschooloasis.com.

Homeschool World: www.home-school.com. Sponsored by *Practical Homeschooling* magazine. Packed full of information, articles, resources, links, store.

The Homeschool Zone: www.homeschoolzone.com.

Homeschool.com. Articles, information, links, books, and online courses; exists to "provide resources, information and support to all homeschooling families."

Homeschooler's Curriculum Swap: http://theswap.com.

Homeschooler's Guide to Portfolios and Transcripts, by Loretta Heuer, Peterson's.

Homeschooler's High School Journal, Fergnus Services. Available from http://www.pahomeschoolers.com/journal.html.

Homeschooling All the Way Through High School, by Renee Mason.

Homeschooling Children with Special Needs website: http://www.banggai.org/rcglasser/needs.html. Links to several helpful sites.

Homeschooling for Excellence by David and Micki Colfax.

Homeschooling Handbook, The: From Preschool to High School by Mary Griffith, http://www.marygriffith.com/work2.htm.

Home Education Magazine Homeschooling Information and Homeschool Resource Pages, website: www.home-ed-magazine.com.

Homeschooling Kids with Disabilities website: http://members.tripod.com/~Maaja/index.htm. (Has lots of pop-up ads.)

Hothouse Transplants: Moving from Homeschool to the "Real World," by Matthew Duffy, available from Grove Publishing.

The How and Why of Home Schooling, by Ray E. Ballmann, Crossway Books; www.homeschoolingheadquarters.com.

Jon's Homeschool Resource Page: www.midnightbeach.com/hs/Welcome.html.

Kaleidoscapes: www.kaleidoscapes.com.

LDS/Mormon Homeschooling: http://www.gomilpitas.com/homeschooling/religion/mormon.htm.

Muslim Homeschool Network and Resource: http://www.muslimhomeschool.com.

NATHHAN—National Challenged Homeschoolers Associated Network, Box 39 Porthill, ID 83853; 208-267-6246; email: nathanews@aol.com; website: http://www.nathhan.com. articles, lending library, discussion board, family directory, membership. "Christian families homeschooling special needs children."

National Center for Home Education, One Patrick Henry Circle, Purcellville, VA 20132, 540-338-7600; fax: 540-338-8606; email: nche@hslda.org.

National Christian Forensics and Communications Association (NCFCA), 2441-Q Old Fort Pkwy. #394, Murfreesboro, TN 37128-4162; 615-896-8598; fax: 615-494-5857; email: Office@NCFCA.org; website: www.ncfca.org. Home school debate tournament in cooperation with HSLDA, recommended speech and debate resources, contact information for regional NCFCA directors.

National Home Education Network (NHEN), P.O. Box 1652, Hobe Sound, FL 33475-1652; fax 413-581-1463; website: www.nhen.org. Homeschooling information, help, support, networking for homeschoolers from all backgrounds and beliefs.

National Home Education Research Institute (NHERI), PO Box 13939, Salem, OR 97309, 503-364-1490; fax: 503-364-2827; email: mail@nheri.org; website: www.nheri.org.

National Home School Debate Tournament: see National Christian Forensics and Communications Association in this section.

Repairing the Ruins: The Classical and Christian Challenge to Education, edited by Douglas Wilson, Canon Press.

Resources for Unschooling: http://www.inspirit.com.au/unschooling/resources/varioushs-inglinks.html.

The Right to Home School: A Guide to the Law on Parents' Rights in Education, by Christopher J. Klicka.

Senior High: A Home-Designed Form+U+La, by Barbara Shelton.

Strengths of Their Own: Home Schoolers Across America, Academic Achievement, Family Characteristics, and Longitudinal Traits, by Brian D. Ray, NHERI Publications.

Trivium Pursuit, Harvey and Laurie Bluedom, PMB 168, 429 Lake Park Blvd., Muscatine, IA 52761, 309-537-3641, website: www.triviumpursuit.com. "Applying Classical Christian Education to Homeschooling; Grammar, Logic and Rhetoric—Knowledge, Understanding and Wisdom."

The Ultimate Guide to Homeschooling, by Debra Bell. Available from Debra Bell's Home School Resource Center, www.hsrc.com.

Weirdkids.com: www.weirdkids.com. Links to educational publishers and other websites of possible interest to home educators.

Correspondence, Umbrella, Satellite Programs, Online courses, Satellite TV Courses, etc.

A Beka Correspondence School and Video instruction, A Beka Book, Inc., P.O. Box 18000, Pensacola, FL 32523-9100, 877-223-5226, fax: 800-874-3590; email: Information@ABeka.com. Website: www.abeka.com. International contact information: 850-478-8933 (phone); 850-478-8558 (fax); international@abeka.com (email). Affiliate of Pensacola Christian College.

Academy of Home Education, Bob Jones University, 1700 Wade Hampton Blvd. Greenville, SC 29614-0062, 877-252-4348; fax: 864-271-8187; email: ahe@bju.com; website: www.bju.edu/ministries/acad_home_ed or www.ahe.bjup.com. Curriculum and support services through correspondence.

Accelerated Christian Education (ACE School of Tomorrow), P.O. Box 299000, Lewisville, TX 75029-9000, 800-925-7777 (orders), 972-315-1776; fax: 972-315-2862; email: info@ACEministries.com or HomeSchooling@ACEministries.com; website: www.schooloftomorrow.com. Curriculum and support services through correspondence.

Advanced Training Institute International, Box One, Oak Brook, IL 60522-3001, 630-323-2842; fax: 630-323-6746; email: info@ati.iblp.org; website: http://ati.iblp.org/ati/index.php. Biblically-centered home-based education program.

American School, 2200 East 170th Street, Lansing, IL 60438, 800-531-9268 or 708-418-2800; website: http://www.americanschoolofcorr.com. Curriculum and support services through correspondence.

BJUP HomeSat, 1700 Wade Hampton Blvd., Greenville, SC 29614, 800-739-8199; fax: 888-525-8398; email: hsatinfo@bju.edu, website: www.bjup.com/services/bjhomesat. Elementary and secondary distance-learning materials from BJU Press via satellite.

Bridgestone Academy, 300 North McKemy Ave., Chandler, AZ 85226-2618, 800-682-7396; website: www.home-schooling.com. Alpha Omega LIFEPAC Curriculum and support services through correspondence.

Bridgeway Academy (The Home School Academy), 334 2nd Street, Catasauqua, PA 18032, 800-863-1474, fax: 610-266-7817; email: office@homeschoolacademy.com; website: http://homeschoolacademy.com. Accredited online school.

Cambridge Academy, 3855 SE Lake Weir Ave., Ocala, FL 34480, 800-252-3777; email: info@cambridgeacademy.com; website: cambridgeacademy.com. Curriculum and support services through correspondence.

Christa McAuliffe Academy, 2520 West Washington Avenue, Yakima, WA 98903, 509-575-4989; fax: 509-575-4976; email: cma@cmacademy.org; website: www.cmacademy.org. Internet high school.

Christian Liberty Academy School System, 502 W. Euclid Avenue, Arlington Heights, IL 60004, 800-348-0899 or 847-259-4444; email: custserv@homeschools.org; website: www.homeschools.org. Curriculum and support services through correspondence.

Christian Light Education, PO Box 1212-J, Harrisonburg, VA 22803-1212, 540-434-0768; fax: 540-433-8896; email: office@clp.org; website: www.clp.org. Curriculum only or full service, grades 1-12; Mennonite.

Clonlara School, 1289 Jewett Street, Ann Arbor, MI 48104, 734-769-4511; fax: 734-769-9629; email: info@clonlara.org; website: www.clonlara.org. Correspondence high school with a contact teacher for each family.

Compuhigh, Clonlara School Compuhigh, 515 Wilson Ave., Morgantown, WV 26501, 866-859-0777; email: stan@compuhigh.com or marianne@compuhigh.com; website: http://compuhigh.com. Online high school.

Cool School (from Cyber Oregon Online), 905 4th Ave. SE, Albany, OR 97321-3199, 541-812-2623; fax: 541-926-6047; email: admin@coolschool.k12.or.us; website: www.coolschool.k12.or.us. Distance education from Oregon Public Education Network.

Eagle Christian High School, 2526 Sunset Lane, Missoula, MT 59804, 888-EAGLE4U; fax: 406-549-5047; email: principal@eaglechristian.org; website: www.eaglechristian.org. Internet high school.

Escondido Tutorial Service, 2634 Bernardo Avenue, Escondido, CA, 92029, 760-746-0980; email: gbt@gbt.org; website: www.gbt.org. Online Christian classical education.

Home Study International, 12501 Old Columbia Pike, Silver Spring, MD 20904-6600, 800-782-4769 or 301-680-6570; fax 301-680-5157. Accredited distance education for preschool through college.

K-12® Virtual Academy, K12 Inc., 8000 Westpark Dr., Suite 500, McLean, VA 22102, 888-968-7512 (Virtual Academy), 1-888-YOUR K12 (968-7512). Virtual public and private schools using curriculum directed by William J. Bennett. Available in some states. More states to be added. Eventually will include high school grades.

Keystone National High School, School House Station, 420 West 5th St., Bloomsburg, PA 17815-1564, 800-255-4937 or 570-784-5220; fax: 570-784-2129; email: info@keystonehighschool.com; website: www.keystonehighschool.com. Online or traditional correspondence high school.

Kolbe Academy, 2501 Oak Street, Napa, CA, 94559, 707-255-6499; fax: 707-255-1581; email: homeinfo@kolbe.org; website: www.kolbe.org. Accredited Catholic classical education by correspondence.

Lincoln Christian Academy, 800 Memorial Park Road, Lincoln, IL 62656, 217-732-6901; fax: 217-732-6907; website: www.cwd.com/lca. Correspondence school using ACE School of Tomorrow curriculum.

List of satellite schools: www.chec.org/Resources/Satellite.

Oak Meadow School, P.O. Box 740, Putney, VT 05346, 802-387-2021; fax: 802-387-5108; email: info@oakmeadow.com; website: www.oakmeadow.com. Correspondence school for pre-school through high school.

Our Lady of the Rosary School, The Homeschool for Roman Catholics, 116 1/2 North Third Street, Bardstown, KY 40004-1542, 502-348-1338; fax: 502-348-1943; email: admission@bellsouth.net; website: www.olrs.com.

Pennsylvania Homeschoolers, RR 2 Box 117, Kittanning, PA 16201; 724-783-6512; fax: 724-783-6512; email: richmans@pahomeschoolers.com; website: www.pahomeschoolers.com. AP Courses Online, test preparation classes.

Royal Academy, Home Education and Family Services, Royal Academy, Inc., P.O. Box 1056, Gray, Maine 04039, 207-657-2800; fax: 207-657-2404; email: royala@securespeed.net; website: www.homeeducator.com/HEFS/royalacademy.htm. Custom-designed curriculum.

Seton Home Study School, 1350 Progress Drive, Front Royal, VA 22630, 540-636-9990; email: info@setonhome.org; website: www.setonhome.org/new.htm. Catholic homeschooling for K-12.

Summit Christian Academy, DFW Corporate Park 2100 North Highway 360, Suite 503, Grand Prairie, TX 75050, 800-362-9180; email: sca100@aol.com; website:www.scahomeschool.com. Correspondence school using a variety of materials.

Switched-On Schoolhouse, Alpha Omega Publications. Five core subject CD-ROM series using Alpha Omega Curriculum for grades 3-12; website:www.switched-onschoolhouse.com.

Sycamore Tree Center for Home Education, 2179 Meyer Place, Costa Mesa, CA 92627, 714-668-1343; 800-779-6750 (orders); fax: 714-668-1344; email: info@sycamoretree.com; website: www.sycamoretree.com. Accredited, complete homeschool program for K-12.

Texas Tech University Outreach and Extended Studies, Box 42191, Lubbock, TX 79409-2191, 800-692-6877 or 806-742-7288; fax 806-742-7288; email: distlearn@ttu.edu; website: www.dce.ttu.edu. Accredited distance education for K-12 and beyond.

University of Arizona Extended University, Independent Study through Correspondence, The University of Arizona, Extended University, P.O. Box 210158, Tucson, AZ 85721-0158, 520-626-4222 or 800-772-7480; fax: : 520-621-3269; E-mail: dykstral@email.arizona.edu; website: http://www.eu.arizona.edu/corresp.

University of Nebraska–Lincoln Independent Study High School, P.O. Box 839400, Lincoln, NE 68583-9400, 402-472-2175; fax: 402-472-1901; email: unlishs2@unl.edu; website: http://NebraskaHS.unl.edu. High school courses and diploma program by correspondence. Two diploma tracks, general education and college preparatory. Online course management system, Way Cool, allows students to submit assignments, check grades, and access online courses on the Internet.

University of Oklahoma Independent Learning High School, OUILHS, 1600 Jenkins, Room 101, Norman, OK 73072-6507, 800-942-5702, 405-325-1921; fax: 405-325-7687; email: ouihs@ou.edu; website: http://ouihs.ou.edu. Accredited high school diploma through distance learning.

West River Academy, 779 Jasmine Court, Grand Junction, CO 81506, email: wracademy@aol.com; website: www.geocities.com/wracademy. An umbrella school for unschoolers, including high school diploma program.

Westbridge Academy, 1610 West Highland Avenue, #228, Chicago, IL 60660-1206, 773-743-3312. "A college preparatory school for academically advanced homeschoolers."

Periodicals

Creation Magazine, Answers in Genesis, P.O. Box 6330, Florence, KY 41022, 859-727-2222, 800-778-3390 (customer service); 800-350-3232 (information); AIG website: www.answersingenesis.org/home.asp. Also available internationally.

Eclectic Homeschool Online Magazine, P.O. Box 50188, Sparks, NV 89435-0188, 775-626-0554; email: eclectic@echo.org; website: www.eho.org.

Home Education Magazine, P.O. Box 1083, Tonasket, WA 98855-1083, 800-236-3278, 509-486-1351; fax: 509-486-2753; email: HEM@home-ed-magazine.com; website: www.home-ed-magazine.com.

Home Educator's Family Times, P.O. Box 708, Gray, Maine 04039-0708, 207-657-2800, 207-657-6889; fax: 207-657-2404; email: famtimes@homeeducator.com; website: www.HomeEducator.com/FamilyTimes.

Home School Digest, Wisdom's Gate, P.O. Box 374, Covert, MI 49043, email: subs@homeschooldigest.com; website: www.homeschooldigest.com/index.htm. Family discipleship, Christian character, and Biblical worldview.

HomeSchool Channel on Crosswalk.Com, website: www.crosswalk.com/family/home_school. Articles, e-newsletters, Internet broadcasts from Terri Camp.

Homeschool Times e-zine: http://www.homeschooltimes.com.

The Homeschool Zone, email: help@homeschoolzone.com; website: www.homeschoolzone.com. Many free online newsletters and services.

Homeschooling Today, P.O. Box 436, Barker, TX 77413, 281-492-6050; email: subscriptions@homeschooltoday.com; website: www.homeschooltoday.com. Pull-out art lesson/reproduction, living literature, etc.

Jewish Home Educator's Network, J.H.E.N. c/o Lisa Hodge Kander, 2122 Houser, Holly, MI 48442; website: http://snj.com/jhen. Quarterly newsletter.

The Link **Homeschool Newspaper,** 587 N. Ventu Park Road, Ste. F-911, Newbury Park, CA 91320, 888-470-4513; fax: 805-493-9216; email: svc@home-school.com; email: mary.thelink@verizon.net; website: www.homeschoolnewslink.com. Online and printed versions available.

Practical Homeschooling, Home Life, Inc., P.O. Box 1190, Fenton, MO 63026-1190. Customer Service: 800-346-6322 or 636-529-0137; email: svc@home-school.com; website: www.home-school.com catalog/pages/phs.php3.

The Teaching Home, Box 20219, Portland, OR 97294-0219, 503-253-9633; fax: 503-253-7345; email: customerservice@TeachingHome.com; website: www.TeachingHome.com.

World Magazine, God's World Publications, P.O. Box 20002, Asheville, NC 28802, 828-232-5260; fax: 828-253-1556. Weekly news magazine from a Christian perspective.

The World & I, 3600 New York Avenue, NE, Washington DC 20002, 800-822-2822; fax: 202-832-5780. Monthly magazine about current issues, historical research, science and technology, cultural and geographical studies, philosophy, religion, the arts.

Colleges of Special Interest to Homeschoolers

Gutenberg College, 1883 University Street, Eugene, OR 97403; 541-683-5141; fax: 541-683-6997; email: office@gutenberg.edu. "A classical 'Great Books' college that teaches from a biblical worldview using quality literature and thought." The majority of students were homeschooled and most of the staff homeschool their own children. Terry Stollar, Director of Admissions, says, "Homeschooling families are used to thinking outside the educational box and understand what real education entails—a good fit."

Patrick Henry College, One Patrick Henry Circle, Purcellville, VA 20132, 540-338-1776; fax: 540-338-8707; email: admissions@phc.edu; website: www.phc.edu. Four-year, Christian liberal arts college offering "a unique combination of classical learning and apprenticeship-based education." Mission: "to train Christian men and women who will lead our nation and shape our culture with timeless biblical values and fidelity to the spirit of the American founding." Degrees offered: B.A. in Classical Liberal Arts (Track in Education); B.A. in Government (Tracks in Intelligence and Foreign Policy, Journalism, and Public Policy); B.A. in History; B.A. in Literature (Tracks in Creative and Professional Writing and Literature—Graduate School Preparation). Faculty: 13 full-time, 12 hold Ph.D.'s, 1 with A.B.D. Merit and need-based aid available (91% of students receive financial aid). Freshman 2002 class: 1300 Average SAT or 20 Average ACT. Student Life: Intercollegiate Soccer, Intramural Athletics, Drama Troupe, Chorale, Ensemble, National Championship Intercollegiate Debate and Moot Court Teams.

Whitefield College, P.O. Box 6321, Lakeland, FL 33807, (863) 683-7899; email: info@whitefieldcollege.org; website: http://www.whitefieldcollege.org. Distance Learning, College at Home Degree Program. Training in vocations of Christian service. A.A., B.A. in Christian Studies, Philosophy, Counselling, and Education.

Just for Students

Students, this section is for you. It will help you learn some of the most important skills that college-bound students need to succeed: time management, reading, writing, public speaking, and interviewing.

Time Management

Time management skills will be invaluable to you in college. Here are some tips that might help you:

- Get into the habit of going to bed and rising early.
- Plan periodic study breaks instead of trying to lump all of your study time together.
- Studying from textbooks:
  - When you study from a textbook, learn to skim. Save careful reading for literature and those subjects where every word counts.
  - First do an overview of the chapter. Read the headings and subheadings and the first and last sentences of each paragraph.
  - Place marks where you have questions or where something is unclear and highlight important points.
  - Jot your questions in the margins or in a notebook.
  - Read the questions (if any) at the end of the chapter. Try to answer them.
  - Go back over the chapter to answer any questions you still have and to clarify points that were unclear. You might not have to reread the chapter at all.
  - When you go back to review the chapter later, skim your notes, answer your questions and the textbook questions, and reread anything that you think you need to review.
  - If your teacher has emphasized anything in class (or at the breakfast table), pay particular attention to those points.
  - Learn to answer questions in essay form with careful forethought.
- Do your least favorite subjects first. If you procrastinate or dawdle over the work, your whole day will be longer. Force yourself to be enthusiastic about finishing each subject.

- If necessary, promise yourself a break, a snack, or a walk in the fresh air when you finish. You will feel better when it is done, and you will be able to dive into subjects you enjoy without that other work hanging over your head.
- Long-term projects:
  - Start right away. The trick to getting large projects done on time is to work on them immediately and steadily. Time has a way of sliding by when you leave big projects to the last few days.
  - Define the tasks you have to complete by dividing the project into smaller increments.
  - Assign yourself dates when each part must be completed. Then go back and change those dates to a day or two earlier.
  - Do more than you think you need to each day.
  - Schedule some days for your work (especially writing) just to sit. Then you can come back to it with a fresh eye, and you will be more likely to catch mistakes and to recognize passages that are confusing or disorganized.
  - With the extra time you have saved, make last-minute changes and revisions.

Reading and Writing

Reading and writing will be your most frequent academic activities in college. For some courses, you may have to read fifty or more pages per night. Multiply that by five or six courses, add papers and other assignments, and you can see how important it is that you learn to read and write quickly and well.

Reading

When you expose yourself to the best literature, some of the knack for writing will rub off. Read as much as you can, and keep challenging yourself to read at increasingly higher levels. When you do not understand something, use the dictionary, an encyclopedia, or another reference. If necessary, ask someone more knowledgeable to explain a confusing passage to you.

Challenge yourself to read above your reading level, learning new vocabulary words as you go. It is important to comprehend what you are reading, but sometimes you should read straight through a chapter even when you do not understand it all. Then you can go back and figure out the difficult parts afterwards. That way you will be able to enjoy the flow of the writing. Also, take time to savor creatively written passages, as you would a good meal. Pay special attention to phrases that make you feel, smell, hear, and see, just as if you were in the story yourself. Include plenty of the classics, along with books in your areas of special interest.

Homeschool graduate Christina Musselman can attest to the importance of extensive reading for college preparation. She says that the most common complaint she heard from her college classmates was that they "never had to do this much reading in high school." Read as much as possible during high school so that you *will be* ready.

Writing

Expose yourself to a variety of authors so that you will experience different writing styles. This varied exposure will help you to grow as a writer and will prevent you from unwittingly copying someone else's style.

Write every chance you get, and work to increase your writing vocabulary. Choose a new word for the day or week and use it often. You might enjoy keeping a journal. No one else ever has to read it, and it does not have to be a diary. Make it a place where you record your thoughts, feelings, and observations. By writing on a regular basis, you learn to express in words what you think and feel. Eventually some of these thoughts and memories may provide interesting anecdotes for your more formal writing.

Keep a list of words or phrases that you especially like. If you copy quotes or unique ideas from someone else's material (including information you find online), make sure that you write down the references. You might want to find them again. Keeping good records will also keep you from accidentally plagiarizing other writers.

Make sure that you understand the importance of citing your sources. Study carefully the sections on avoiding plagiarism and documenting your sources in a good writing handbook. (Also see resources under Language Arts in Appendix B.) Plagiarism is an offense that is so serious in academia that it can result in a student's expulsion from college. To avoid plagiarizing, practice rephrasing passages in your own words with your own sentence order, structure, and style. Paraphrasing is an essential skill to learn in preparation for the many research papers you will have to write in college. Even when you paraphrase, be sure to give credit in your paper to the original sources. Anything copied verbatim must be in quotes with the reference cited.

The First Steps in the Writing Process

When you write for an assignment, there are two ways you might consider doing it, depending on your personality or prior training. Some people like to organize their thoughts in outline form. Then they write from that. Others prefer to get everything down while the creative juices are flowing and then organize it. Some use a combination of these two methods.

There are plenty of books that explain how to write by beginning with an outline, so I will not explain that here. If you have trouble writing from outlines, perhaps my suggestions will help you.

When you sit down to write, think about your topic. What do you want to say about it? What are your feelings about it? Jot down your thoughts. When something really hits you, just keep writing. Do not stop to organize it or to correct grammar or spelling. Just keep writing until you have no more to say. Get it all out as fast as you can. If you know that you want to quote something in your text, just make a quick note of it as you write. Do not stop to insert it. (Read it, though, if it will keep your thoughts flowing.)

When you have finished this stage, go back and reread what you have written. If more thoughts come to you, write some more. When you have written all you have to say, go back and analyze it. Ask yourself these questions:

- What is my topic?
- What is my main theme?
- What have I promised the reader? Have I delivered on that promise?
- Have I supported my arguments with concrete evidence or good quotes?

As you analyze it, begin to write an outline from what you have written. Then analyze the outline, asking yourself the same questions as before. Next, check your outline and your writing for organization. Does the order in which you wrote your thoughts make sense? It probably does not, so reorganize the outline until the thoughts in it seem to flow. Then reorganize the writing accordingly. Finally, check for errors in spelling, punctuation, and grammar.

Hobbling Along

No, you are not finished yet. You are not even close. This is only your first draft. At this point, consider taking a break unless you are really enjoying the process.

Professional writers know that writing is about 1 percent inspiration and 99 percent perspiration. If you want to learn to write, you have to be willing to revise, revise, and revise again. Try to look at it as a game or a challenge to make every possible improvement you can in your writing.

When you have taken a break and gotten away from your writing for a while, come back and read it. You will be amazed at the errors you will find. There will be passages where you will ask, "What did I mean by that?" So write what you meant. If you are using a word processor, save your second draft as a new file, just in case you want to change something back after you have revised the rest. Then recheck your writing for the following:

- Spelling errors
- Grammatical errors
- Punctuation errors
- Extraneous words (words that really, really, truly are not necessary for understanding).
- Check your verbs:
  - Are they strong, vivid words? (This is good.)
  - Do you have a lot of "to be" verb forms? (This is bad.)
  - Do you use "there is" or "there are" a lot? (This is also bad.)
- Check your nouns:
  - Are they descriptive? ("sycamore" not just "tree")
  - Do they tell exactly what you want your readers to imagine? ("rivulet" or "puddle" instead of "water")
  - Get rid of unnecessary adjectives and adverbs. Let your verbs and nouns carry most of the weight.

Now You Have It!

When you think you have made your writing the best it can be, lay it aside for a day or two. Do not even think about it. Then go back and revise it again. At this point, your writing might be finished. If you have doubts, lay it aside again and come back to it. Then ask one or two people to read it. Ask them to point out passages that need clarification. Ask if they think you have covered the topic adequately. Then change your work based on your reviewers' comments *if you agree with them.* Keep in mind that you are the writer. Put your writing aside again, at least for an hour or so. Then reread it once again. If you are satisfied, your piece is ready to turn in.

Never be satisfied with your first draft. Take time to revise as many times as necessary and you will learn how to write well. If you would like to read some college admissions and scholarship essays written by high school students, turn to Appendix E.

Public Speaking: Not as Scary as It Seems

The key to successful public speaking is preparation. Know your subject well and have an outline of what you intend to say.

Writing the Speech

Some people like to write out their speeches, and then they memorize them word for word—or even worse—they read to their audience. To avoid this temptation, organize your thoughts on notecards so that you can rearrange them as you revise your speech.

Revision is just as important in speech preparation as it is in writing. Let your speech rest for a few days, and then revise again.

Practice

After you feel confident that your speech is ready, practice it with note cards. If you will have a time limit, time yourself and adjust your speech accordingly. Practice in front of a mirror or with family or friends. Try looking at your audience (imaginary or real) as much as possible. Do not be tempted to bury your face in the cards. Speech is a means of communicating, and good communication requires eye contact.

Ask your practice listeners to give you ideas for improvement. Should you clarify some points? Give more examples? How was your posture? Your delivery? Did you teeter back and forth from one leg to the other? Did you repeat some other motion or sound that could annoy and distract your audience? (Pay special attention to "um," "and," "uh," "like," "you know," etc.)

The Delivery

If you are nervous before speaking, try alternately tensing and relaxing your leg muscles a few times or think of something humorous. When you take the podium, try to concentrate on your audience instead of on yourself. Keep in mind that you are speaking for their benefit, so care about them first. Learn to laugh at yourself, and then your mistakes will not feel devastating.

To minimize nervousness, some people recommend concentrating on a point at the back of the room when delivering a speech. I find a wall too impersonal; I would much rather find some friendly faces in the audience. After all, you are talking to them, not the wall. Sometimes a smile from a listener will help calm your jitters. Looking at the audience will also help you determine whether you are getting your message across. If your listeners are not involved in what you are saying, that is your cue to change gears a little. You should be able to do it, as long as you have prepared and know your subject well. Finish with a smile, and walk away from the podium with good posture and your head up. Speaking is really a lot of fun, once you get the hang of it. So give it your best.

The College Interview

Many colleges require prospective students to interview with admissions officers. Interviews usually have a twofold purpose: so that you can get to know the college, and they can get to know you. More than anything, colleges want students who attend their schools to be happy enough to stay until they graduate. Use the interview to find out everything that you need to know to make a wise decision. However, do not waste time asking for information that you should have gleaned from the college's printed materials. Do your homework before the interview so that you can ask intelligent questions.

Approach the admissions interview as you would a job interview. Dress professionally, which means office attire or "Sunday dress." Make sure that you look neat and smell clean. Be early, but do not enter the office until a few minutes before your scheduled time. You do not want them to feel pressured because you arrived too soon. By the same token, they should not have to wait for you.

At the interview, be yourself. Do not be afraid to admit your strengths, and even your weaknesses, if asked. As long as you speak humbly and respectfully, admissions officers will not think you are conceited when you relate your strengths. Do not overdo it on the weaknesses, or they will think you have no self-confidence. Your interviewers will want to know what you can offer their college community. They may ask why you want to attend that school, why it is the best place for you, and why the school should accept you.

If a parent attends the interview with you, it is essential that he or she let you do the talking. Do not put the parent in the uncomfortable position of having to answer for you. Admissions officers want to hear from students, not their parents. Homeschoolers have to be especially careful about this. Some people have the notion that homeschooled students are too dependent on their parents. Show them that you are mature enough to stand on your own. Most of all, be polite and smile once in a while. Friendliness makes everyone more comfortable.

You Can Do It!

Now you may approach the whole admissions process with confidence. Investigate colleges well, and weigh your decision carefully. If you have studied hard as a homeschooler and scored well on standardized tests, you are one of the best prospects for an admissions slot at most colleges. So go to it!

Apply your heart to instruction and your ears to words of knowledge.

Proverbs 23:12

Recommended Reading

It has always therefore been one of my main endeavours as a teacher to persuade the young that first-hand knowledge is not only more worth acquiring than second-hand knowledge but is usually much easier and more delightful to acquire.

C. S. Lewis from *God in the Dock*, "On the Reading of Old Books" [1]

This appendix contains reading lists for high school students. The first section contains recommendations from Dr. Richard Cornelius, who taught English at the college level for almost forty years. The second set of lists comes from Debbie Musselman, a veteran homeschool mom who used a literature approach for teaching most high school subjects. I have added a few additional favorites of my own and others at the end. You can find descriptions of many of these books in various homeschool catalogs. You might also want to consult a series of books called *Books for You: A Booklist for Senior High Students*. These books primarily list modern books, but a few classics are included in each edition. Various editions contain different lists of books.

No one would recommend that your students attempt to read all of the books listed here. I have included these lists so that you will have some idea of the kind of literature and the level of reading expected of high school students. You and your students will need to decide which books are best for your situation. Great literature deals with the human condition, a condition that includes sinfulness, hopelessness, cruelty, and condemnation as well as goodness, hopefulness, kindness, and redemption. Much of the literature at this level has bad language or portrays sinful lifestyles. Although in most cases evil is punished and characters learn from their errors, it is up to you and your students to decide how much of this exposure you are willing to tolerate in the books you read. Christians and others who prefer not to expose their students to material with questionable content may want to start with Cornelius's list "Quality Novel-Length Fiction Generally Supportive of Moral Standards," which appears at the end of his general list.

According to Cornelius, appreciation of great literature means recognizing its importance and admiring the artistry and God-given abilities of its authors. To evaluate literature and see its worth, you do not have to like, love, or agree with it. A significant work may have done a lot of good or a lot of damage. Cornelius cautions parents and teachers to consider a student's readiness to handle material and maintain distance from its undesirable content. He acknowledges that education is a risk but ignorance is risky, too. He says that you need wisdom and carefulness to maintain a balance between freedom and discipline. He suggests that you use common sense and assign only what you know.

To help educators determine the relative value of studying particular literary works and other media, Cornelius developed a Media Merit and Morality Model. You may find it useful. For each work, assign a rating for each of the eight factors listed below. Worthwhile works would have high ratings in rows 1-5. Works with high ratings in rows 6-7 are those that demand more of the student and the teacher. According to Cornelius, even very intelligent students often need to mature several years before finding these books significantly meaningful. Works with high ratings in row 8 can have serious negative consequences. For example, it is one thing to read the biblical account of David's sins of adultery and murder, but it is quite another thing to see them portrayed in a Hollywood film or, even more serious, to act them out in a school play.

Dr. Richard Cornelius's Media Merit and Morality Model

Rating	A-5 Very High	B-4 High	C-3 Average	D-2 Low	F-1 Very Low
1. Esthetic Craftmanship					
2. Ethical Consistency					
3. Eternal Certainty					
4. Evangelical Conduct					
5. Effective Curriculum					
6. Educational Complexity					
7. Experience Classification					
8. Engagement Conditions					

1. Esthetic craftsmanship: artistry and technique of composition, characters, creativity, grammar, imagery, plot, point of view, style, symbolism, theme, thought, content, etc.
2. Ethical consistency: accuracy, appropriateness of procedure, honesty, integrity, validity
3. Eternal certainty: fidelity to the truth of biblical absolutes and verities or to enduring relative truths of the arts, human experience, philosophy, politics, and science
4. Evangelical conduct: in accord with biblical standards of morality and decorum. Ratings: 5—Moral context that is: clear and detailed or aptly absent; 4—clear, brief, or implied; 3—sketchy, noncommittal; 2—unclear, questionable; 1—immoral
5. Effective curriculum: relevance to the totality of educational aspects: course aims, student abilities, teacher expertise, etc.
6. Educational complexity: background required to understand literary techniques, historical setting, and other technical matters
7. Experience classification: level of maturity necessary to achieve suitable esthetic distance and adequately handle artistic, moral, and philosophical facets
8. Engagement conditions: degree of involvement and participation of mind, body, and senses (5—Performing; 4—Viewing & hearing; 3—Viewing; 2—Reading; 1—Hearing)

Selected Reading List

by Dr. Richard M. Cornelius, Professor Emeritus of English, Bryan College

This list was compiled over several years as a guide for use by high school and college students and the adult general public. Some of the books were added to the list through other people's recommendations. Because Dr. Cornelius has not personally read all the books included here, he urges those who use this list to exercise caution and discernment. Refer to the discussion about selecting appropriate literature for students. Dr. Cornelius especially recommends works in bold type for high schoolers. The entries are coded as follows:

(A)   American Literature

(B)   British Literature

(W)   World Literature

(C)   From Dr. Cornelius's "Concise List of Significant Works with Edifying/Educational/ Entertaining Value." This code applies to most of the works listed below, so the (C) designation is included only if the title also appears on the following list (S).

(S)   From Dr. Cornelius's list for English Seminar, a class for advanced-level college English majors.

(18)   Eighteenth Century and Before (S-coded books only)

(19)   Nineteenth Century (S-coded books only)

(20)   Twentieth Century (S-coded books only)

Drama

*Aeschylus (W): *Agamemnon, The Libation Bearers, The Furies, Prometheus Bound, The Persians.*

Anderson, Maxwell (A): *Elizabeth the Queen,* **Valley Forge.**

*Aristophanes (W): *The Clouds, The Frogs.*

Calderón de la Barca, Pedro (W): *Life Is a Dream.*

*Chekhov, Anton (W): *The Cherry Orchard.*

Connelly, Marc (A): *The Green Pastures.*

Corneille, Pierre (W): *The Cid.*

Dryden, John (B): *All for Love, The Conquest of Granada.*

*Eliot, T. S. (A): *Murder in the Cathedral, The Cocktail Party.*

*Euripides (W): *Hippolytus, The Trojan Women, Medea.*

***Everyman* (B).**

*Goethe, Johann Wolfgang von (W): *Faust.*

Goldsmith, Oliver (B): *She Stoops to Conquer.*

Howard, Sidney (A): *The Late Christopher Bean.*

*Ibsen, Henrik (W): *A Doll's House,* **An Enemy of the People,** *The Wild Duck.*

Jonson, Ben (B): *Every Man in His Humor, Volpone, The Silent Woman, The Alchemist.*

Kalidasa (W): *Shakuntala.*

Kaufman, George S., and Morrie Ryskind (A): *Of Thee I Sing.*

Marlowe, Christopher (B): *Doctor Faustus.*

*Milton, John (B): *Samson Agonistes.*

*Molière (Jean Baptiste Poquelin) (W): *The Would-Be Gentleman, Tartuffe, The Misanthrope, The Miser, The Imaginary Invalid.*

*O'Neill, Eugene (A): *The Emperor Jones, Ah, Wilderness!*

*Racine, Jean (W): *Phaedra, Esther, The Litigants.*

Rostand, Edmond (W): *Cyrano de Bergerac.*

Sayers, Dorothy (B): *The Zeal of Thy House, The Man Born to Be King, Second Shepherd's Play.*

*Shakespeare, William (B): **A Midsummer Night's Dream;** *Romeo and Juliet;* **The Merchant of Venice;** **As You Like It;** *Twelfth Night; Henry IV, Parts 1 & 2; Henry V;* **Julius Caesar;** *Hamlet; Othello; King Lear;* **Macbeth;** *Antony and Cleopatra; The Tempest.*

*Shaw, George Bernard (B): *Androcles and the Lion,* **Arms and the Man,** *Pygmalion, Saint Joan.*

---

* Indicates authors and literary works of greatest historical importance. [Author's note: This group of authors and literary works is important for their influence on literature and culture. If you want to avoid unwholesome language and situations, be careful to preview especially twentieth-century books on this list before you assign them.]

Sheridan, Richard Brinsley (B): *The Rivals, The School for Scandal.*

Sherwood, Robert (A): *Abe Lincoln in Illinois.*

*Sophocles (W): *Oedipus Rex, Oedipus at Colunus, Antigone, Electra.*

Vega, Lope de (W): *The Sheep Well.*

Wilde, Oscar (B): ***The Importance of Being Earnest.***

Wilder, Thornton (A): ***Our Town,*** *The Skin of Our Teeth.*

Willliams, Tennessee (A): *The Glass Menagerie.*

Fiction

Alcott, Louisa May (A): ***Little Women.***

**Arabian Nights, The.* (W)

Asturias, Migel Angel (W): *The President* (S, 20).

*Austen, Jane (B): *Pride and Prejudice* (C, S, 19), *Emma, Sense and Sensibility, Mansfield Park.*

*Baldwin, James (A): *Go Tell It on the Mountain* (S, 20).

Balzac, Honoré de (W): *Eugenie Grandet* (S, 19).

Barrie, James M. (B): *The Little Minister.*

*Bellow, Saul (A): *Herzog, Humbolt's Gift* (S, 20).

Blackmore, R. D. (B): *Lorna Doone.*

*Brontë, Charlotte (B): *Jane Eyre* (C, S, 19).

*Brontë, Emily (B): *Wuthering Heights* (C, S, 19).

Buck, Pearl S. (A): *The Good Earth* (C, S, 20).

*Camus, Albert (W): *The Stranger, The Plague* (S, 20).

Capote, Truman (A): *In Cold Blood* (S, 20).

Carroll, Lewis (Charles Lutwidge Dodgson) (B): ***Through the Looking Glass, Alice in Wonderland.***

Cather, Willa (A): *My Antonia, O Pioneers!*

*Cervantes, Miguel de (W): ***Don Quixote*** (C, S, 18).

Cheever, John (A): *The Wapshot Chronicle* (S, 20).

Chesterton, G. K. (B): *The Innocence of Father Brown.*

*Conrad, Joseph (B): *Lord Jim, The Heart of Darkness* (C, S, 20).

*Cooper, James F. (A): ***The Deerslayer*** (C, S, 19), ***The Last of the Mohicans*** (C, S, 19), ***The Pilot*** (C, S, 19), ***The Spy, The Pathfinder.***

*Crane, Stephen (A): ***The Red Badge of Courage*** (C, S, 19).

*Dante Alighieri (W): *The Divine Comedy.*

*Defoe, Daniel (B): ***Robinson Crusoe*** (C, S, 18).

*Dickens, Charles (B): *David Copperfield* (C, S, 19), *Oliver Twist, The Pickwick Papers,* ***Great Expectations*** (C, S, 19), ***A Tale of Two Cities*** (C, S, 19), *Nicholas Nickleby.*

Dos Passos, John (A): *U.S.A.* (trilogy) (S, 20).

*Dostoevsky, Feodor (also spelled Dostoievsky or Dostoyevsky, Fyodor) (W): *Crime and Punishment.* (C, S, 19), *The Brothers Karamazov* (S, 19).

Doyle, Sir Arthur Conan (B): *The White Company, A Study in Scarlet,* ***The Hound of the Baskervilles.***

Dreiser, Theodore (A): *An American Tragedy* (S, 20).

Dumas, Alexandre (W): ***The Count of Monte Cristo, The Three Musketeers*** (C, S, 19).

*Eliot, George (Mary Ann Evans) (B): *Adam Bede* (C, S, 19), *The Mill on the Floss, Silas Marner* (S, 19).

Farrell, James T. (A): *Studs Lonigan* (trilogy) (S, 20).

*Faulkner, William (A): ***The Bear,*** *As I Lay Dying* (S, 20), *The Sound and the Fury* (S, 20), *Absalom, Absalom* (S, 20).

*Fielding, Henry (B): *Joseph Andrews* (C, S, 18), *Tom Jones* (S, 18).

*Fitzgerald, F. Scott (A): *The Great Gatsby* (S, 20).

*Flaubert, Gustave (W): *Madame Bovary* (S, 19).

Forster, E. M. (B): *A Passage to India* (S, 20).

Fuentes, Carlos (W): *The Death of Artemio Cruz* (S, 20).

Goethe, Johann Wolfgang von (W): *The Sorrows of Young Werther* (S, 18).

Golding, William (B): *Lord of the Flies* (S, 20).

Goldsmith, Oliver (B): *The Vicar of Wakefield.*

Greene, Graham (B): *The Heart of the Matter, The Power and the Glory* (C, S, 20).

*Hardy, Thomas (B): *The Mayor of Casterbridge* (C, S, 19), *The Return of the Native,* **Tess of the D'Urbervilles* (C, S, 19).

*Hawthorne, Nathaniel (A): ***The Scarlet Letter, The House of the Seven Gables*** (C, S, 19).

Heller, Joseph (A): *Catch-22* (S, 20).

*Hemingway, Ernest (A): ***The Old Man and the Sea*** (C, S, 20), *For Whom the Bell Tolls* (S, 20), **A Farewell to Arms* (S, 20), *The Sun Also Rises* (S, 20).

Hesse, Hermann (W): *Siddhartha, Steppenwolf* (S, 20).

*Homer (W): *The Iliad, The Odyssey.*

Howells, William Dean (A): *The Rise of Silas Lapham* (C, S, 19).

Hudson, W. H. (B): *Green Mansions.*

*Hugo, Victor (W): ***The Hunchback of Notre Dame*** (C, S, 19), ***Les Miserables*** (C, S, 19), *Toilers of the Sea.*

*Huxley, Aldous (B): *Brave New World* (S, 20).

Irving, Washington (A): ***The Sketch Book, Knickerbocker's History of New York.***

*James, Henry (A): *The Ambassadors* (C, S, 19), *Daisy Miller,* **The Portrait of a Lady* (C, S, 19).

Johnson, Samuel (B): *Rasselas.*

*Joyce, James (B): *Portrait of the Artist as a Young Man.*

*Kafka, Franz (W): *The Trial, The Castle* (S, 20).

Kipling, Rudyard (B): *Captains Courageous,* **Kim** (C, S, 20), *The Jungle Books.*

Lawrence, D. H. (B): Selected short stories (20). Lawrence can be very moral and very immoral. Selection is the key.

Lewis, C. S. (B): **Out of the Silent Planet**, *Perelandra, That Hideous Strength,* **The Screwtape Letters** (C, S, 20), **The Chronicles of Narnia** (series) (C, S, 20), *The Pilgrim's Regress.*

*Lewis, Sinclair (A): *Babbit, Main Street* (C, S, 20).

London, Jack (A): **The Call of the Wild** (C, S, 20), **The Sea Wolf.**

Mailer, Norman (A): *The Naked and the Dead* (S, 20).

*Malamud, Bernard (A): *The Fixer, The Natural* (S, 20).

*Mann, Thomas (W): *The Magic Mountain, Buddenbrooks* (S, 20).

Márquez, Gabriel García (W): *100 Years of Solitude* (S, 20).

Marshall, Catherine (A): *A Man Called Peter.*

Maugham, W. Somerset (B): *Of Human Bondage* (S, 20).

*Melville, Herman (A): *Billy Budd, Moby Dick.*

Morrison, Toni (A): *Beloved* (S, 20).

Nordhoff, Charles, and James Norman Hall (A): *Mutiny on the Bounty.*

Orwell, George (B): **Animal Farm** (C, S, 20), *1984* (S, 20).

Parkman, Francis (A): *The Oregon Trail.*

Pasternak, Boris (W): *Dr. Zhivago* (S, 20).

Paton, Alan (W): **Cry, the Beloved Country** (C, S, 20).

Percy, Walker (A): *The Moviegoer* (S, 20).

*Poe, Edgar Allan (A): *Tales of the Grotesque and Arabesque.*

*Proust, Marcel (W): *The Remembrance of Things Past* (S, 20).

Rawlings, Marjorie Kinnan (A): **The Yearling**.

Reade, Charles (B): *The Cloister and the Hearth.*

Richardson, Samuel (B): *Pamela* (S, 18).

Rizk, Salom (A): *Syrian Yankee.*

Rölvaag, Ole (A): *Giants in the Earth.*

Roth, Philip (A): *Portnoy's Complaint* (S, 20).

*Salinger, J. D. (A): *Catcher in the Rye, Rabbit Is Rich, Rabbit at Rest* (S, 20).

Saroyan, William (A): *The Human Comedy.*

Schoor, Gene (A): *The Jim Thorpe Story.*

*Scott, Sir Walter (B): *The Heart of Midlothian* (C, S, 19), **Ivanhoe** (C, S, 19), *Kenilworth, Waverley* (C, S, 19), *Old Morality.*

Sienkiewicz, Henryk (W): **Quo Vadis**.

*Singer, Isaac Bashevis (A): *In My Father's Court* (S, 20).

*Solzhenitzyn, Alexander (Also spelled Aleksandr Solzhenitsyn) (W): *One Day in the Life of Ivan Denisovich* (C, S, 20), *"We Never Make Mistakes."*

*Steinbeck, John (A): **The Red Pony**, *The Grapes of Wrath* (S, 20).

Stendhal, Henri (Marie-Henri Beyle) (W): *The Red and the Black* (S, 19).

Sterne, Laurence (B): *Tristram Shandy* (S, 18).

Stevenson, Robert Louis (B): **Treasure Island** (C, S, 19), **Kidnapped, Dr. Jekyll and Mr. Hyde** (C, S, 19).

Stowe, Harriet B. (A): **Uncle Tom's Cabin**. (C, S, 19).

*Swift, Jonathan (B): **Gulliver's Travels** (4 parts) (C, S, 18), *A Tale of a Tub.*

Ten Boom, Corrie (W): *The Hiding Place.*

*Thackeray, William M. (B): *Vanity Fair* (S, 19).

Tolkien, J. R. R. (B): **The Hobbit, The Lord of the Rings** (trilogy) (C, S, 20).

*Tolstoy, Leo (W): *War and Peace* (C, S, 19), *Master and Man, The Death of Ivan Ilyitch, Anna Karenina* (S, 19).

Turgenev, Ivan (W): *Fathers and Sons* (S, 19).

*Twain, Mark (Samuel Langhorne Clemens) (A): **The Adventures of Huckleberry Finn** (C, S, 19), **A Connecticut Yankee in King Arthur's Court, Life on the Mississippi.**

Verne, Jules (W): **Around the World in Eighty Days, 20,000 Leagues Under the Sea** (C, S, 19).

*Virgil (W): *The Aeneid.*

*Voltaire (François Marie Arouet) (W): *Candide* (C, S, 18).

Wallace, Irving (A): *The Chapman Report* (S, 20).

Wallace, Lew (A): **Ben Hur**.

Warren, Robert Penn (A): *All the King's Men* (S, 20).

Waugh, Evelyn (B): *Brideshead Revisited* (S, 20).

Wells, H. G. (B): *The War of the Worlds* (S, 20).

*Wharton, Edith (A): *Ethan Frome* (C, S, 20).

Wilder, Thornton (A): *The Bridge of San Luis Rey* (C, S, 20).

Wolfe, Thomas (A): *You Can't Go Home Again* (S, 20).

*Woolf, Virginia (B): *Mrs. Dalloway, To the Lighthouse* (S, 20).

Wouk, Herman (A): *The Caine Mutiny* (S, 20).

*Wright, Richard (A): *Native Son* (S, 20).

Zola, Émile (W): *The Trap, Nana, La Terre* (S, 19).

Miscellaneous

*Addison, Joseph, and Richard Steele (B): *The Spectator*.

Andrew, Brother: *God's Smuggler*.

*Aristotle (W): Poetics, *Nicomachean Ethics*.

*Augustine (W): *The Confessions*.

*Bacon, Sir Francis (B): **Essays**.

Bayly, Joseph: *The Gospel Blimp*.

Boswell, James (B): *Life of Samuel Johnson*.

Bryan, William Jennings (A): *Man, The Prince of Peace*.

*Bulfinch, Thomas (W): **Mythology** (or Edith Hamilton's version).

*Bunyan, John (B): **Pilgrim's Progress** (C,S, 18), The Holy War, *Grace Abounding to the Chief of Sinners, The Life and Death of Mr. Badman*.

Burgess, Alan (A): *The Small Woman*.

Curie, Eve (W): *Madame Curie*.

*Edwards, Jonathan (A): *Personal Narrative*.

*Emerson, Ralph Waldo (A): *The American Scholar, Nature, Self-Reliance*.

*Erasmus, Desiderius (W): *The Praise of Folly*.

Franklin, Benjamin (A): **The Autobiography**.

Gilbreth, Frank, and Ernestine Gilbreth Carey (A): *Cheaper by the Dozen, Bells on Their Toes*.

Hamilton, Edith (W): **Mythology** (or Thomas Bulfinch's version).

Heyerdahl, Thor (W): *Kon-Tiki*.

*Johnson, Samuel (B): *Lives of the English Poets*.

Lamb, Charles (B): **Essays of Elia**.

Lockhart, J. G. (B): *Life of Scott*.

Malory, Sir Thomas (B): *Morte D'Arthur*.

Montesquieu (W): *The Persian Letters*.

More, Sir Thomas (B): *Utopia*.

Ortega y Gasset, José (W): *The Revolt of the Masses*.

Parkman, Francis (A): **The Oregon Trail**.

Pascal, Blaise (W): **Thoughts** *(Pensées)*.

*Plato (W): *The Apology, Republic*.

Plutarch (W): *Lives of the Noble Greeks and Romans*.

Song of Roland, The (W).

Southey, Robert (B): *Life of Nelson*.

*Thoreau, Henry David (A): *Walden*.

Washington, Booker T. (A): **Up From Slavery**.

Zylstra, Henry (A): *Testament of Vision*.

Poets and Poems

Arnold, Matthew (B).

Auden, W. H. (B).

Benét, Stephen Vincent (A).

Beowulf (B).

*Blake, William (B).

Bradstreet, Anne (A).

Brooks, Gwendolyn (A).

Browning, Elizabeth Barrett (B).

*Browning, Robert (B).

Bryant, William Cullen (A).

Burns, Robert (B).

Byron, George Gordon, Lord (B).

Carroll, Lewis (B).

*Chaucer, Geoffrey (B): *The Nun's Priest's Tale, The Pardoner's Tale, The Franklin's Tale, The Knight's Tale, The Wife of Bath's Tale, The Clerk's Tale* (from *The Canterbury Tales*).

Coleridge, Samuel T (B).

Cowper, William (B).

Crashaw, Richard (B).

*Cummings, E. E. (A).

*Dante Alighieri (W).

Davidson, Donald (A).

de la Fontaine, Jean (W): *Fables*.

*Dickinson, Emily (A).

*Donne, John (B): Selections.

Dryden, John (B).

*Eliot, T. S. (A).

Emerson, Ralph Waldo (A).

Freneau, Phillip (A).

*Frost, Robert (A).

Gilbert, William S. (B).

*Goethe, Johann Wolfgang von (W).

Gray, Thomas (B).

Heine, Heinrich (W).

Herbert, George (B).

Herrick, Robert (B).

Holmes, Oliver Wendell (A).

*Homer (W).

*Hopkins, Gerard Manley (B).

Horace (W).

Housman, A. E. (B).

Hugo, Victor (W).

Johnson, Ben (B).

*Keats, John (B).

Kipling, Rudyard (B).

Lanier, Sidney (A).

Lear, Edward (B).

Lindsay, Vachel (A).

*Longfellow, Henry Wadsworth (A).

Lowell, James Russell (A).

Lowell, Robert (A).

MacLeish, Archibald (A).

Martial (W).

Masefield, John (B).

Merwin, W. S. (A).

Millay, Edna St. Vincent (A).

Miller, Joaquin (Cincinnatus Hiner) (A).

*Milton, John (B): *Paradise Lost, Paradise Regained*, short poems.

Moore, Marianne (A).

Ovid: *Metamorphoses* (W).

Pasternak, Boris (W).

*Pearl Poet (B): *The Pearl, Sir Gawain and the Green Knight*.

Petrarca, Francesco (W).

Pindar (W).

*Poe, Edgar Allan (A).

*Pope, Alexander (B).

Pound, Ezra (A).

Pushkin, Alexander (W).

Ransom, John Crowe (A).

Robinson, Edwin Arlington (A).

Rosetti, Christina (B).

*Sandburg, Carl (A).

Santayana, George (A).

*Scott, Sir Walter (B).

*Shakespeare, William (B).

*Shelley, Percy B. (B).

Sidney, Sir Phillip (B).

*Spenser, Edmund (B): *The Faerie Queene*, etc.

Stevenson, Robert L. (B).

Tate, Allen (A).

Taylor, Edward (A).

Teasdale, Sara (A).

*Tennyson, Alfred, Lord (B).

Thomas, Dylan (B).

Thompson, Francis (B).

Traherne, Thomas (B).

Tu Fu (W).

Vaughan, Henry (B).

*Virgil (W).

*Whitman, Walt (A): Selections.

Whittier, John Greenleaf (A).

*Wordsworth, William (B): Selections.

*Yeats, William B. (B).

Quality Novel-Length Fiction Generally Supportive of Moral Standards

American Literature

Cooper: *The Deerslayer, The Last of the Mohicans.*

Hawthorne: *The Scarlet Letter, The House of the Seven Gables.*

Twain: *Huckleberry Finn.*

Wallace: *Ben Hur.*

British Literature

Brönte, Charlotte: *Jane Eyre.*

Bunyan: *Pilgrim's Progress.*

Carroll: *Alice in Wonderland.*

Chesterton: *Father Brown, The Man Who Was Thursday.*

Defoe: *Robinson Crusoe.*

Dickens: *David Copperfield, Great Expectations.*

Lewis: *Out of the Silent Planet, Perelandra, That Hideous Strength.*

Scott: *The Heart of Midlothian.*

Swift: *A Tale of a Tub, Gulliver's Travels.*

Tolkien: *The Hobbit, Lord of the Rings* (trilogy).

World Literature

Cervantes: *Don Quixote.*

Dostoievsky: *Crime and Punishment.*

Homer: *The Iliad, The Odyssey.*

Hugo: *Les Miserables.*

Paton: *Cry, the Beloved Country.*

Solzhenitzyn, Alexander: *One Day in the Life of Ivan Denisovich, We Never Make Mistakes.*

Virgil: *The Aeneid.*

Debbie Musselman's High School Curriculum

Debbie cautions that the right curriculum for students differs. She chose some of the books on this list to meet specific needs in her daughters' lives. Use this as a sample of what a literature-based approach to home high schooling looks like.

Note: 1 = student 1; 2 = student 2

The following curriculum list © 1998 Debbie Musselman. Used by permission.

Science: Anatomy

Brand/Yancey: *In His Image; Fearfully and Wonderfully Made* – 1

Columbus University College of Physicians and Surgeons Home Medical Guide -1

Human Neurophysiology -1

Kapit/Elson: *Anatomy Coloring Book* – 1

National Geographic: *Curious Naturalist* – 1, 2

Sections of *Gray's Anatomy* – 1

Sunderland: *Darwin's Enigma* – 1

Science: Biology

Eyewitness Books: *Dictionary of Plants* – 1, 2

Eyewitness Books: *Dictionary of Animals* – 1, 2

Griffin: *Biology Coloring Book* – 1, 2

Milliken: *Milliken Plants* – 1, 2

Van Cleave: *A+ Projects in Biology* – 1, 2

Science: Chemistry

Cardulla: (videotapes): *Chemistry* – 2

Math

Key Curriculum Press: *Discovering Geometry* – 1

Key Curriculum Press: *Keys to Algebra* – 1

Lial, Hornsby, Schneider: *Trigonometry* – 2 (HarperCollins)

Manipulative Interludes for Algebra – 1

Miller/Salzman/Hestwood: *Basic College Mathematics* – 1 (HarperCollins)

Miller/Salzman/Hestwood: *Intermediate Algebra* – 2 (HarperCollins)

Saxon: *Algebra 1* – 1, 2

Stenmark/Thompson/Cossey: *Family Math* – 1

Wahl: *Mathematical Mystery Tour* – 1

Writing/Grammar/Vocabulary/ Handwriting

Continental Press: *Report Writing: Formula for Success* – 1

Getty/Dubay: *Italic Handwriting Book G* – 2

Hopper/Gale/Foote/Griffith: *Essentials of English* – 2

Lipman/Joyner: *How to Write Clearly* – 1

Lundquist: *English from the Roots Up* – 1, 2

Rico: *Writing the Natural Way* – 1, 2

Strunk/White: *Elements of Style* – 1, 2

Write Source: *The Write Source* – 1

Write Source: *The Mechanics of Writing* – 1, 2

Writing Strands – 1

Zinsser: *On Writing Well* – 1, 2

Zinsser: *Writing to Learn* – 1, 2

Art Appreciation

Muhlberger: *The Bible in Art* – 1

Smith: Chapters on artists of each period of history from Page Smith's history books – *1*

Music Appreciation

Beethoven Lives Upstairs – 1

Foreign Languages

AMR Educational Systems: *Spanish I* – 1, 2

Georgetown University Press: *Modern Russian I* – 1

Sign Language (weekly classes at local performing arts center) – 2

Sex Education

Lush, Jean: *Emotional Phases of a Woman's Life* – 1

Nilsson: *A Child Is Born* – 1

Weekly Reader: *Aids: What Teens Need to Know* – 1

Psychology

Coon: *Introduction to Psychology* – 2

Deaf Culture and Educational Philosophy

Greenberg: *In This Sign* – 2

Gannon: *Deaf Heritage* – 2

Macaulay: *For the Children's Sake* – *2*
Postman: *Amusing Ourselves to Death* – *2*
Trelease: *The Read-Aloud Handbook* – *2*

Geography

Blank maps of North, Central, and South America – *1*
Davis: *Why Greenland Is an Island, Australia Is Not, and Japan Is Up for Grabs* – *1, 2*
Geo-Safari – *1, 2*
Map work – *2*
National Geographic: *Our 50 States* – *1*
National Geographic: *Our World* – *1, 2*

Government and Economics

Audiotapes: *The Federalist Papers* – *1*
Bailey: *British Parliamentary Democracy* – *2*
Bastiat: *The Law* – *1, 2*
Collier/Collier: *Decision in Philadelphia* – *1*
Freidman/Friedman: *Free to Choose* – *1*
Greenhaven Press: *American Government: Opposing Viewpoints* – *1*
Hackett: *It's Your Choice* – *1, 2*
Hazlitt: *Economics in One Lesson* – *1*
Locke: "Second Treatise on Civil Government" – *1*
Maybury: *Ancient Rome and How It Affects You Today* – *1, 2*
Maybury: *Are You Liberal, Conservative, or Confused?* – *1, 2*
Maybury: *Money Mystery* – *2*
Maybury: *What Would Thomas Jefferson Think About This?* – *1*
Maybury: *Whatever Happened to Justice?* – *1, 2*
Maybury: *Whatever Happened to Penny Candy?* – *2*
Mayhew: "When Is Resistance a Duty?" – *1*
Rappard: *Collective Security in the Swiss Experience, 1291–1948* – *2*
Thoreau: "Civil Disobedience" – *1, 2*
Usborne: *Politics and Government* – *1*

American History

("A" after the student code number(s) indicates a book read aloud.)

General Introduction and Review

Blos: *A Gathering of Days* (Colonial America) – *1, 2*
Cooper: *Last of the Mohicans* – *1*
National Geographic: *The Story of America* – *1, 2*

The Civil War

Angle: *A Pictorial History of the Civil War Years* – *1*
Beatty: *Wait for Me, Watch for Me, Eula Bee* – *1, 2 (A)*
Claflin: *Sojourner Truth* – *1*
Crane: *Red Badge of Courage* – *1*
Douglass: *A Narrative of the Life of Frederick Douglass* – *1, 2 (A)*
Dubowski: *Robert E. Lee* – *1*
Fox: *Slave Dancer* – *1, 2 (A)*
Freedman: *Lincoln: A Photobiography* – *1*
Fritz: *Brady* – *1*
Fritz: *Stonewall* – *1*
Hunt: *Across Five Aprils* – *1, (2-A)*
Keith: *Rifles for Watie* – *1, 2 (A)*
Movie: *Gettysburg* – *2*
PBS series: *The Civil War* – *1, 2*
Smith: *Trial by Fire* – *1*
Steele: *Perilous Road* – *1*
Sterling: *Freedom Train* – *1*
Stevenson: *American History in Verse* – *1*
Watkins: *Co. Aytch* – *1, 2*

The Old West

Beatty: *Wait for Me, Watch for Me, Eula Bee* – *1, 2*
Bird: *A Lady's Life in the Rocky Mountains* – *1, 2*
Brink: *Caddie Woodlawn* – *1*
Oppel, comp.: *Tales of the West* – *1 (A)*
Stewart: *Letters of a Woman Homesteader* – *1*

1900 – 1920s

Keller: *The Story of My Life* – *1, 2 (A)*
Knight: *Lassie Come Home* (written during this time period) – *1*
London: *White Fang* – *1, 2*
Nixon: *Land of Hope* (Immigrants) – *1*
Skurzynski: *Good-Bye Billy Radish* (World War I) – *1*

1920 – 1930s

Aylward: *The Little Woman* – *1, 2*
Freedman: *Franklin D. Roosevelt* – *1*
Fritz: *Homesick* – *1*
Hunt: *No Promises in the Wind* – *1*
Lee: *To Kill a Mockingbird* – *1, 2*
Meigs: *Invincible Louisa* – *1, 2*
Smith: *Redeeming the Time* – *1*

World War II

Coerr: *Sadako and the Thousand Paper Cranes* – 1, 2 (A)

David: *A Child's War* – 1

deJong: *House of Sixty Fathers* – 1

Fry: *Assignment Rescue* – 1

Potok: *The Chosen* – 1, (2-A)

Ten Boom: *The Hiding Place* – 1

Walsh: *Fireweed* – 1

Post-World War II to the Present

Coe: *Young Man in Viet Nam* – 1

Griffin: *Black Like Me* – 1

Karnow: *Vietnam, a History* – 1

Rennert: *Civil Rights Leaders* – 1

Wouk: *The Caine Mutiny* – 1

Other Reading for History and Literature

"An Agreement of the Free People of England" – 2

Backrach: *Tell Them We Remember* – 1, 2

Beowulf – 2

Carson: *Gifted Hands* – 2

Carson: *Under the Sea Wind* – 2

Chaucer: *Canterbury Tales* – 1, 2

Collier/Collier: *Bloody Country* – 2

Collier/Collier: *Decision in Philadelphia* – 2

Commager/Morris: *The Spirit of Seventy-Six* – 1, 2

Cromwell: *God's Englishmen* – 1, 2

de Angeli: *A Door in the Wall* – 1, 2

"Declaration of Independence" – 2

"Declaration of the Stamp Act Congress" – 2

Defoe: *Robinson Crusoe* – 1

Dickens: *A Tale of Two Cities* – 1, 2

Dumas: *The Three Musketeers* – 1, 2

Eliot: *Silas Marner* – 1, 2

Foster: *The World of William Penn* – 1, 2

Freedman: *Immigrant Kids* – 2

Freedman: *Indian Chiefs* – 1, 2

Haugaard: *Hakon of Rogen's Saga* – 2

Hawthorne: *The Scarlet Letter* – 2

Houston: *Farewell to Manzanar* – 2

Hugo: *Hunchback of Notre Dame* – 1, 2

Hunt: *Up a Road Slowly* – 2

Jefferson: *Life and Selected Writings of Thomas Jefferson* – 1, 2

Johnston: *Joel: Boy from Galilee* – 1, 2

Kipling: *Kim* – 1, 2

L'Amour: *Last of the Breed* – 2

Lewis: *Out of the Silent Planet* – 1

Macaulay: *City* – 1, 2

Macaulay: *Pyramid* – 2

MacDonald: *Curate's Awakening* – 2

Marrin: *Hitler* – 1, 2

Marrin: *Mao Tse Tung* – 1, 2

Marrin: *Napoleon* – 1, 2

Marrin: *Stalin* – 1, 2

Martin: *Yankee Doodle Boy* – 2

"Mayflower Compact" – 2

McCullough: *Mornings on Horseback* – 2

McGraw: *Mara: Daughter of the Nile* – 2

McGraw: *The Striped Ships* – 1, 2

Melville: *Typee* – 1, 2

Miller: *Florence Nightingale* – 1, 2

Nicholson: *Chii-La-Pe and the White Buffalo* – 2

Oates: *Woman of Valor* – 1, 2

O'Dell: *Sing Down the Moon* – 1, 2

O'Dell: *The King's Fifth* – 1, 2

Paton: *Cry the Beloved Country* – 1, 2

Paulsen: *Clabbered Dirt, Sweet Grass* – 1, (2-A)

PBS production: *Franklin Roosevelt* – 2

Plato: *The Republic* – 1

Porter: *Scottish Chiefs* – 1, 2

Roberts: *Northwest Passage* – 1, 2

Scott: *Ivanhoe* – 1, 2

Scott: *Rob Roy* – 1

Sears: *WWII* – 1, 2

Shellabarger: *The King's Cavalier* – 1, 2

Speare: *Calico Captive* – 2

Speare: *The Witch of Blackbird Pond* – 2

St. Augustine: *Confessions of Augustine* – 1

Steinbeck: *The Red Pony* – 1, 2

Sutcliff: *Blood Feud* – 1, 2

Sutcliff: *Eagle of the Ninth* – 1, 2

Sutcliff: *The Silver Branch* – 1, 2

Taylor: *The First World War* – 1, 2

Thoreau: *Walden* – 1, 2

Tolstoy: *Sebastopol Sketches* – 1, 2

Twain: *The Prince and the Pauper* – 2

"U.S. Constitution and Amendments" – 2

Utley: *Indian, Soldier, and Settler* – 1, 2

Willard: *The Lark and the Laurel* – 2

Wilson/Moses: *Indian Lives* – 1

Winks, Brinton, Christopher, Wolff: *History of Civilization* – 1, 2

Wouk: *Caine Mutiny* – 2

Wyss: *Swiss Family Robinson* – 2

Zollinger: *Chapultapec* – 1, 2

Read-Aloud List

(Books were read in this order. Years 1–4 both students; years 5–6 student 2 only.)

Year 1

Peck: *A Day No Pigs Would Die*

Douglass: *A Narrative on the Life of Frederick Douglass*

Fox: *The Slave Dancer*

Keith: *Rifles for Watie*

Beatty: *Wait for Me, Watch for Me, Eula Bee* (AH)

Lohaus/White, Ed.: *A Colorado Christmas Anthology*

Oppel, comp.: *Tales of the West*

Henry, O.: *Short Stories*

Magorian: *Good Night, Mr. Tom*

Nixon, Joan L.: *Land of Hope*

Keller: *The Story of My Life*

Sutcliffe: *The Silver Branch*

Year 2

Twain: *Complete and Humorous Sketches of Mark Twain*

Skinner/Kimbrough: *Our Hearts Were Young and Gay*

Ten Boom: *The Hiding Place*

Coerr: *Sadako and the Thousand Paper Cranes*

Dickens: *A Christmas Carol*

Sheldon: *In His Steps*

Griffin: *Black Like Me*

McDowell, Hostetler: *Don't Check Your Brains at the Door*

Hawthorne: *Wonder Book*

McCullough: *Brave Companions*

Twain: *Roughing It*

Shelley: *Christian Theology in Plain Language*

Year 3

Colum: *Children's Homer*

Thucydides: *History* (selections)

Walsh: *Children of the Fox*

The Meditations of Marcus Aurelius

MacMullen: *Constantine*

Virgil: *The Aeneid*

Sutcliff: *The Shining Company*

Unknown: *The Arabian Nights*

Denny/Filmer-Sankey: *The Bayeux Tapestry*

Macaulay: *Cathedral*

Macaulay: *Castle*

Dante: *The Inferno, Purgatorio, Paradisio*

Kelly: *Trumpeter of Krakow*

Machiavelli: *The Prince*

Stevenson: *The Black Arrow*

Bunyan: *Pilgrim's Progress*

Morison: *Great Explorers*

Moody: *The Home Ranch*

Year 4

Maybury: *Uncle Eric Talks About Security*

Harris: *Saga of the Pilgrims*

Tranter: *Rob Roy MacGregor*

Collier/Collier: *My Brother Sam Is Dead*

Orczy: *Scarlet Pimpernel*

Roberts: *Captain Caution*

Austen: *Pride and Prejudice*

Engels/Marx: *Communist Manifesto*

Wallace: *Soul of the Lion*

Washington: *Up From Slavery*

Remarque: *All Quiet on the Western Front*

Tudor: *Tasha Tudor*

Camus: *The Plague*

Hemmingway: *The Old Man and the Sea*

Bradbury: *Farenheit 451*

Year 5

Fritz: *The Double Life of Pocahontas*

Petry: *Tituba of Salem Village*

Longfellow: *Hiawatha*

Languuth: *Patriots*

Spencer: *Indian Captivity of O. M. Spencer*

Hunt: *Across Five Aprils*

MacLachlan: *Sarah, Plain and Tall*

Wister: *The Virginian: A Horseman of the Plains*

Lewis: *The Lion, the Witch, and the Wardrobe*

Lewis: *Prince Caspian*

Lewis: *Voyage of the Dawn Treader*

Lewis: *The Horse and His Boy*

Lewis: *The Magician's Nephew*

Lewis: *The Last Battle*

Year 6

Grey: *West of the Pecos*

Cather: *Death Comes for the Archbishop*

L'Engle: *A Wrinkle in Time*

L'Engle: *A Wind in the Door*

L'Engle: *A Swiftly Tilting Planet*

McKinley: *The Hero and the Crown*

Potok: *The Chosen*

L'Engle: *Circle of Quiet*

Lewis: *The Great Divorce*

Marshall: *Christy*

Paulsen: *Clabbered Dirt, Sweet Grass*

MacDonald: *The Lost Princess*

White, E. B.: *One Man's Meat*

Tolkien: *The Hobbit*

From Homeschool Graduate and Associate Admissions Director Rachelle Reitz

Bastiat, Frederick: *The Law*

Bennett, William J.: *The Book of Virtues*

Boorstin, Daniel: *The Discoverers: A History of Man's Search to Know His World and Himself, The Creators: A History of Heroes of the Imagination, The Americans: The Democratic Experience,* and others

Classics

Some of Our Favorites Not Already Mentioned

The Holy Bible

Alcott, Louisa May: *Little Men, An Old-Fashioned Girl*

Barton, David: Tapes on America's Christian Heritage (available from Wallbuilders)

Breese, Dave: *Seven Men Who Rule the World From the Grave*

Doyle, Sir Arthur Conan: other Sherlock Holmes stories

Hilton, James (B): *Goodbye, Mr. Chips*

Knowledge Products audiotapes (available from Bluestocking Press)

Lewis, Beverly: *The Shunning, The Confession, The Reckoning*

Lewis, C. S.: *Mere Christianity*

Longfellow, Henry Wadsworth: *The Courtship of Miles Standish, Evangeline*

Macaulay, Susan Schaeffer: *How to Be Your Own Selfish Pig*

Paine, Thomas: "Common Sense"

Richardson, Don: *Peace Child* (exercise caution—graphic descriptions of cannibalism)

Ryken, Leland: *The Liberated Imagination, Realms of Gold, Words of Delight*

Schaeffer, Edith: *The Hidden Art of Homemaking*

Schaeffer, Francis: *How Should We Then Live?*

Thoene, Bodie and Brock: *Zion Covenant* and Zion Chronicles series

Twain, Mark: *The Adventures of Tom Sawyer*

Veith, Gene Edward: *Reading Between the Lines: A Christian Guide to Literature; State of the Arts; Postmodern Times*

Voigt, Cynthia: *Homecoming; Dicey's Song* (great stories with some objectionable language; deal with tough issues—parental abandonment, mental illness, bitterness, forgiveness, redemption)

Wiggins, Kate Douglas: *Mother Carey's Chickens*

Wodehouse, P. G.: Jeeves books, other books

Other Recommendations

The Eagle Forum website has an Ultimate Reading List. Check it out at http://www.eagleforum.org/educate/1997/june97/list.html.

Lynn Hocraffer's Charlotte Mason-type high school booklist:
http://homepage.bushnell.net/~peanuts/.html/HSbooklist.html

All Scripture is God-breathed and is useful for teaching, rebuking, correcting and training in righteousness, so that the man of God may be thoroughly equipped for every good work.

2 Timothy 3:16–17

1. C. S. Lewis, 1970, *God in the Dock*. Copyright © 1970 by C. S. Lewis Pte Ltd. As quoted in *The Quotable Lewis* by Martindale and Root published by Tyndale House, 1989. Curtis Brown, London.

Sample Essays

Essays are useful to admissions departments for getting to know students better and for judging their writing abilities. Essays should be flawlessly written and allow the unique personalities of their writers to shine through. Some colleges give applicants specific questions to answer; others may just ask you to tell them about yourself and why their college would be right for you. Often extra essays will be required for scholarship competitions, so I have included scholarship essays with the sample admissions essays below.

Christine (Dennis) St. Jacques, graduate of Bryan College
Presidential Scholarship Competition Essay

A Vision for Excellence

Since I was young, I have had a passion for theatre. However, I thought that I would have to become a nurse or a teacher in order to make a living and to make everyone else happy.

I concluded that nursing was not my ideal while I was still in elementary school. This decision was based on the rumor that nurses are required to dissect cadavers. Since I have always loved children, I held on to the idea of teaching, but my interests remained in the arts.

During high school, I began praying fervently for God's direction in my life. Eventually, I started teaching Sunday School, thinking it would give me a better idea of what a career as a teacher would involve. I found that I loved being with the children once a week, but I knew that I could not handle being a classroom teacher.

I continued praying and seeking the counsel of godly men and women in my life. Finally, I realized that the Lord has called me to work in the arts. My decision was confirmed by support from my parents and other adults I respect.

Now I am excited about my future. The Lord has given me a vision for a musical theatre group for homeschoolers. There is avid interest among homeschoolers in classes involving the arts.

Unfortunately, there are few instructors. My drama group would not only involve instruction, but also ministry. Our mission field would be mainly the elderly in nursing homes and children in hospitals. We would probably go into some churches, too.

Historically, Christians were the leaders in the arts. It is time we took them back for God's glory and the furtherance of His kingdom. My dream is to be a part of the restoration of excellence in the Christian arts today—to bring back the wholesome entertainment of the past, and to create new masterpieces that will show people the simple truth of God's unconditional love.

Studying communication arts with a concentration in dramatic arts will give me the background I need for this dream. The non-drama components of this major provide additional knowledge that can be useful in the many other aspects of theatrical production, including scriptwriting and technical work. In addition, a second major in history will provide a strong background for period drama, set designing, and costuming.

An education at a Christian college will challenge me and encourage me in my walk with Christ. Also, I feel that the support of like-minded sisters and brothers will serve to strengthen my commitment to the Lord and my commitment to excellence for His glory.

The arts have an influence on the mindset of people. In the book *How Should We Then Live?* Francis Schaeffer wrote, "A person's world view almost always shows through in his creative output...." Our society's world view is being illuminated through its creative endeavors, and people are accepting this view all too easily. Many of these creative works are superior in quality and in emotional appeal. They have excellence without godliness.

In the Christian world, it is often the opposite—we have godliness without excellence. Many secular shows have an emotional impact that Christian theatre frequently lacks. Because secular writers are willing to show people's struggles and hurts, a Broadway show like *Les Miserables* moves people. Christian theatre can be just as poignant, if only we can reach people's aching hearts. A drama can be stirring and still be free from immorality, profanity, and obscenity.

I am not saying that God cannot work through things with weaknesses. He can, and often does. Despite this, when we are serving God, we should be doing our best. The Bible says in Galatians 6:4, "Let everyone be sure he is doing his very best, for then he will have the personal satisfaction of work well done, and won't need to compare himself with someone else." It also says in 1 Corinthians 10:31, "Whatever you do, do all to the glory of God."

We are at a crucial time in history, a time when people seem to be falling further and further away from God. It is also a time when people's lives feel emptier than ever. You can see it in their eyes. There is a desperate need in every person that can only be filled with love—God's love.

The theatre arts have a power to influence people that nothing else has. I want to use theatre's effectiveness to reach people for God. I want to help show the world that excellence and godliness go hand in hand.

Christine (Dennis) St. Jacques, graduate of Bryan College Admissions Essay for Hillsdale College

Once upon a time, in the beautiful State of Colorado, there lived a little girl with pigtails. She loved doing anything creative: singing, dancing, acting, drawing, writing, and sculpting, not to mention inventing gourmet meals in her sandbox. This little girl loved being with her family and friends, and she enjoyed helping them, especially when helping involved picking strawberries. She was a smiling package of energy who dreamed of becoming everything she found inside and outside of her books.

As she grew, she continued to create. Gradually her dreams changed into visions, as did her pigtails into a French braid...

This little girl, with the strawberries staining her smile and pigtails framing her face, was I. Looking back over the years, I realize that I really have not changed that much. I still enjoy doing anything creative, being with loved ones, cooking gourmet meals (real ones), and eating strawberries.

My dreams are more realistic now, and my understanding of life is much clearer. My list of interests has become extensive. Along with the aforementioned, I have come to enjoy: traveling to foreign countries; learning about different cultures, their languages, and their histories; working with children; playing tennis; taking photographs; watching ice skating, old movies, and baseball with my family; and studying history and classic literature. I dislike anything immoral or hopeless.

I cannot tell you any more about myself without talking to you about my personal relationship with Jesus Christ. He has made me who I am today. As a Christian, I try in everything I do to honor and glorify God. I believe that Jesus set a life standard for us by His example. Therefore, I try to live my life according to His standards, rather than the world's. These standards are well presented in Colossians 3:12–14,17:

"Therefore, as God's chosen people, holy and dearly loved, clothe yourselves with compassion, kindness, humility, gentleness and patience. Bear with each other and forgive whatever grievances you may have against one another. Forgive as the Lord forgave you. And over all these virtues put on love, which binds them together in perfect unity.... And whatever you do, whether in word or deed, do all in the name of the Lord Jesus, giving thanks to the Father through Him."

My relationship with Jesus Christ impacts every area of my life. From my daily conversations, to my studies, to my hopes for the future.

The Lord has blessed me with many strengths: my creativity, a good memory, the stubbornness to be persistent, a love for people (especially children); and talents in the performing arts and related areas. I tend to be a perfectionist. My biggest weakness is probably that my perfectionism often causes me to procrastinate, because I worry that my work will not meet my own standards. I am also so ambitious that I try to accomplish too much. These two things, in turn, create problems with time management. Nevertheless, I am slowly learning to find a balance and use my weaknesses to my advantage.

In the future, I hope to become a godly woman who takes good care of her family and loves others the way Jesus did. More than anything, I desire to serve God and follow His will for my life.

In my opinion, a quality education is a significant part of preparation for life. Hillsdale's independent spirit and commitment to excellence, truth, and Western tradition impress me. I have great respect for our founding fathers and the principles on which our country was founded. My dream is to help revitalize, primarily in the arts, our Western Civilization's heritage of excellence based on sound principles and Judeo-Christian values. My impression is that Hillsdale strives to do the same in the area of higher education. For this reason, I believe that Hillsdale College could help me to achieve my goals for the future.

In addition, I favor the diversity of beliefs and cultures represented on campus. My faith is precious to me, yet I feel it is important to understand the views of others. A college whose professors, instead of indoctrinating their students, encourage them to discuss and analyze issues for themselves, is imperative for me.

Equally important are Hillsdale's high academic standards. My reason for going to college is not just for a degree; it is for an education—knowledge that will prepare me for life.

…The young woman stared through the window. She had watched the mailbox for weeks, praying the Lord would guide her to a college where her dreams could become reality. She gazed across the snow-painted lawn. Smiling at her icy replica of the Globe Theatre she thought, *'Tis a pity birds cannot perform Shakespeare. My theatre would be perfect for them!*

The sound of snow being compressed under wheels jerked the young woman from her daydream. She rushed out the door and slid to the mailbox. While thanking the mailman, she noticed a letter from Hillsdale College. She grasped it excitedly. Depositing the remaining mail on the Globe, she thought, *Okay Lord, this is it! Please, please, please!* She slowly opened the envelope…

TO BE CONTINUED

Ann (Freeman) Flanigan, graduate of Wheaton College
Admissions essay (one of four for Wheaton)

Describe a significant challenge or disappointment you have faced. How has this experience influenced you?

"Where did you say you go to school? What?!? What is that? School at your own house? Do you wake up late and do school in your pajamas? What about socialization?…"

For most of my early education I answered questions like these and many more. They pertain to a choice my family made for my education and an important influence in my life, home schooling. This one long-term experience has had a tremendous impact on my life. Its ramifications will affect me for the rest of my life. I consider it such a privilege to have had this experience. Home schooling has altered and molded my views and perspectives in significant ways.

I feel that I have been able to experience something that is relatively rare in our society. In my community, we are some of the pioneers in the field of home education. My parents first home schooled me when home education was relatively unknown. People wondered if it was legal. Although I home schooled my kindergarten year, I went back to public school until my fifth grade year. When we made the decision to return to home schooling, I was able to more fully understand that as a family, we were taking a non-traditional route to my education that wasn't universally well received.

For me, this is where the challenge began. For the first time in my life, I was singled out as one apart from the group, my circle of friends and peers. This was something that was very difficult for me. As I am one who feels comfortable fitting in with the crowd, this situation caused me to take a stand and be strong.

This was difficult for me to do at first. I found that many of my "friends" suddenly disappeared. I was forced to reach out to others, even if they weren't in my peer group, or my same age. When asked where I went to school, I had to be ready to explain what home schooling was and usually dealt with many other related questions.

I consider the many challenges I faced during my early education invaluable. A few of the rewards I have gained through this experience are: my strong relationship with Christ and my family, an education based on my interests and educational needs, and a desire and love to learn. Without interruption by a school bell, I have been able to concentrate on my studies and have truly enjoyed the learning process.

I believe that home schooling allowed me to learn many valuable lessons that will benefit me for the rest of my life as they have prepared me for what I will face later. An example of this is the fact that by necessity, I learned to stand and defend my convictions as I defended my alternative schooling process. I believe this is a valuable skill in our society and in the church body. It is so important to both know and be ready to defend Christianity. In this world, if we truly follow Christ, we can sometimes be viewed as non-traditional and be asked to stand and defend Him.

I am grateful to have had the opportunity of being educated by my parents who know and love me. I truly believe that the experience of home schooling has significantly benefited my life and that I will continue to reap the blessings of this undertaking.

Heidi Emerson
Admissions and Scholarship Essay

Fear: Motivation or Paralysis?

Once we crossed the border, I plastered my face against the van window, straining to read every billboard and shop sign in sight. My heart beat rapidly. Spanish! Spanish everywhere! I experienced the sudden urge to dive into a crowd of Mexicans and begin prattling off in the language of my soul. A growing sense of dread soon strangled my euphoria. My knowledge of Spanish came from the music I listened to and the books I read. Could I actually speak the language? Was I brave enough to try?

Fear can motivate or paralyze. In my case, it paralyzed. I spent four of my six days in Mexico speaking only when necessary. I was not willing to take any risks that might result in humiliation or rejection. My cowardice deeply disappointed me. This mission trip was a rare opportunity to learn about the people of Ensenada, Mexico, and I was wasting it.

A day before our trip ended, my fellow Americans and I were exiting a rural convenience store when a short, dark-skinned woman with a rack of beaded necklaces approached us. After purchasing several souvenirs at her booth, my group turned to leave. I hesitated, watching the woman wearily rearrange her goods. It occurred to me how vastly different our lives were. If she had the courage to face poverty, could I not at least find the nerve to show her that I cared? I spoke up, meekly complimenting the woman on her weavings.

She showed me various pieces, and a spark of life flickered in her dull eyes as she asked me where I was from. When I told her that I lived in the state of Colorado, in the United States, she turned her gaze to the north with a distant expression, as if aware of the vast distance between my home and hers. Then, looking down at her array of homemade jewelry, she selected a colorful woven bracelet and tied it around my wrist. I asked how much she wanted for it, but she shook her head. "It is free. Keep it until you can come back again." Her face softened in an earnest smile. I caught a glimpse of the warm, caring person concealed behind that grim mask of survival.

I walked away with tears, awestruck by such sudden and unexpected kindness. I had come to Mexico to give—to donate my time, my money, and my effort. When I finally learned to give a piece of myself, I received immeasurable compassion in the form of a simple bracelet. That woman saw how I was fighting my shyness and my fear of rejection, and she seemed to value the courage it took for me to stay and talk with her. Our conversation made me realize that I would have left Mexico with many regrets if I had not decided to confront my fears. Now, motivated by my experience in

Ensenada, I am learning to embrace intimidating situations in every area of my life and to exercise my love of Spanish by developing relationships with those who speak it.

Josh Hayes
Admissions Essay

To Paint a House

I do not like making phone calls. I never have liked calling people whom I did not know and asking them for information. A good leader does what he needs to do, whether it is something he likes doing or not, in order to get a job done. During the summer of 2001 I made thirty to forty phone calls to strangers, asking them to donate supplies to my Eagle project—cleaning and repainting the exterior of a two-story brick house that was over one hundred years old. The project was for an organization called Open Door Ministry, which works with the people of inner-city Denver. The reason that I called different organizations to get the materials donated was because I was the person in charge and responsible for planning the project and for leading others in carrying it out.

A few weeks after I had made the numerous phone calls getting money and materials donated to my project, I found myself standing in front of the huge brick house with fifteen people looking to me for instructions on how to scrape and clean the walls. I discovered on that day, as well as on the following weekends of painting the house, that being a leader is not easy. I also learned that if I scrape paint off of a wall above my head, I should probably wear safety goggles, unless I like the feeling of having paint chips in my eyes.

Good leadership is not just telling people what to do. Good leaders are willing to personally do the work and also manage the work through others. For example, a worker of mine came to me saying that he was having a hard time scraping the paint off the wall. I could have jumped in and started doing the work that he was supposed to be doing, but I didn't. I took the five-in-one tool from him, scraped part of the wall, and explained how to do it while I worked. I then gave the tool back to my worker and encouraged his progress before going on to see who else needed help, a break, a drink of water, or just someone to talk to. After four tiring days of working on that house, we finished the project. It was very satisfying to know that I had been the spearhead of something that would bless the lives of others and to know that I had learned so much about what being a leader looked and felt like.

New opportunities to lead and to follow frequently present themselves in my life. Whether I succeed or fail in these situations, I know that with each experience I am growing in character and in knowledge of how to be a good leader. This knowledge and ability to be a strong, effective leader will make me the most effective person that I can be.

Index of Forms and Tables

Index of Colleges

General Index

What Colleges Are Saying about Homeschoolers

Having worked with public schooled students in the past and now with homeschooled students here at Patrick Henry College, I can compare both groups from direct experience. Even if you control for factors such as standardized test scores or natural intelligence, without a doubt, homeschooled students in general are dramatically ahead of their public schooled peers. Homeschooled students tend to possess such qualities as self-discipline and intellectual curiosity that are rare among public school products and contribute significantly to their success in higher education and beyond.

Dr. Robert Stacey, Chairman of the Department of Government, Assistant Professor of Government, Patrick Henry College

We find homeschooled students are exceptionally motivated and capable!

Karen Everett, Director of Admissions, Montana State University-Billings

Our experiences with home schooled students have been excellent. Several faculty members encouraged us to enroll more.

Hildegarde Schmidt, Dean of Admissions and Financial Aid, Dominican University

Often, homeschooling engenders the same qualities that make for successful Marlboro students: self motivation, a passion for learning, and original thought. As such, homeschoolers have been among our strongest candidates for admissions.

Jennifer Blair, Associate Director of Admission, Marlboro College

We welcome home educated applicants! This growing population on our campus has performed outstandingly in our rigorous academic setting.

Mike Williams, Asst. VP for Admissions & Financial Aid, Harding University

Our experience has been great. As a rule, entering homeschool students have had slightly higher ACT/SAT scores. They have adjusted very well to our academics and campus life programs. They quickly rise to the top as campus leaders.

Margaret J. Weber, Director of Admissions, Franciscan University of Steubenville

I have always been impressed by the character and academic quality of the students I have met that have been homeschooled.

Anne Rebecca George, Associate Dean of Admission, Albertus Magnus College

Pittsburg State has had significant success with homeschoolers. They are good students with a strong academic work ethic.

Angé Peterson, Pittsburg State University

We find that those who are home schooled in many cases are better prepared for college.

Dr. R. Pepper Dill, Vice President of Enrollment Management, Greenville College

Our experience has been very positive. Homeschooled students have received our top scholarships and places in our Honors Program...[and] have been involved in student government, music, varsity sports— every area of campus life. Homeschooled grads have successfully entered medical school and grad programs, including those at the doctoral level.

Bruce Campbell, Houghton College

They have performed well in the classroom and made significant contributions to the campus community. Their adjustment to college life has been seamless.
Herbert V. Kerner, Jr., Dean, Admissions and Financial Aid, Campbell University

With part of our admission staff currently homeschooling their children, we welcome the opportunity to work with home schooled families.
Pete Kenow, Director of Admission, Concordia University, NE.

We actively recruit homeschoolers and provide scholarships to and in that effort. Currently eleven percent of our freshman class each year consists of homeschoolers. We have found homeschoolers were able to compete in all areas for academic and leadership scholarships.
Carroll W. Griffin, Assistant to the Provost for Enrollment Services and Director of Admissions, Union University

We appreciate receiving applications from home-schoolers as they add texture and diverse experiences to the applicant pool and our campus community.
Martha Merrill, Dean of Admission and Financial Aid, Connecticut College

Our faculty continues to comment on how well home schooled students "fit in." They are exceptionally well-prepared academically and typically are actively involved in the university community (i.e., music productions, community service projects).
Eileen T. Dills, Dean of Admissions and Student Financial Services, Queens College

We plan to expand our recruitment efforts in the area of home school students.
Karen L. Workentin, Dean of Student Enrollment Services, College of the Southwest

Homeschool students have been proven to be very well-prepared for college. We would enjoy having more at Kansas Wesleyan University.
Tina Thayer, Director of Admissions, Kansas Wesleyan University

We have an ever-increasing and vibrant homeschool population at Biola.
André Stephens, Director of Admissions, Biola University

We admit and enroll homeschoolers every year. They are a great addition to our community.
Nanette H. Tarbouni, Director of Admissions, Washington University in St. Louis

It is an honor to have them.
David B. Layton, Associate VP for Enrollment, Geneva College

Great experience. We love them.
Barbara Henry, Director of Admission, Oglethorpe University

Home-schooled students who succeed at Willamette are typically self-directed, creative, and service-minded. They actively engage in the campus community through community service projects, leadership positions, and our talent areas of debate, music, theatre, and athletics.
Robin C. Brown, Vice President for Enrollment, Willamette University